DANCE WRITINGS AND POETRY

DANCE WRITINGS *&* POETRY

EDWIN DENBY

EDITED BY ROBERT CORNFIELD

Yale University Press · New Haven and London

Published with assistance from the foundation
established in memory of Philip Hamilton McMillan
of the Class of 1894, Yale College.

Designed by Nancy Ovedovitz and set in Times Roman
type by Keystone Typesetting, Inc., Orwigsburg,
Pennsylvania. Printed in the United States of America.

Library of Congress Cataloging-in-Publication Data
Denby, Edwin, 1903–1983.
Dance writings and poetry / Edwin Denby; edited by
Robert Cornfield.
p.   cm.
Includes bibliographical references and index.
ISBN 0–300–07617–7 (cl),
      0–300–06985–5 (pbk. : alk. paper)
1. Dance — Reviews.   I. Cornfield, Robert.   II. Title.
GV1599.D393   1998
793.3 — dc21   98–2517

A catalogue record for this book is available from
the British Library.

The paper in this book meets the guidelines for
permanence and durability of the Committee on
Production Guidelines for Book Longevity of the
Council on Library Resources.

10   9   8   7   6   5   4   3   2   1

CONTENTS

DANCE WRITINGS

BIOGRAPHICAL NOTE

*E*dwin Orr Denby was born in Tientsin, China, on February 4, 1903, the third son of an American diplomat. His family left China in 1908 when his father was posted to Vienna, and at the outbreak of the First World War, the Denby family returned to the United States. After a few years in a Detroit private school, Edwin was sent to the Hotchkiss School in Connecticut, where he was voted in his senior year "the Biggest Grind" and where he received the Phi Beta Kappa trophy. At sixteen he began a brief and intermittent Harvard education, leaving in his sophomore year for a European sojourn. He returned the year after, and then decamped again at the beginning of his junior year for Austria. It was there that he began a serious study of movement at the Hellerau-Laxenburg School, a school originated by Emile Jacques-Dalcroze. After Denby completed the three-year program and received a diploma in gymnastics, he teamed with Claire Eckstein to form a dance troupe that performed in little theaters all over Germany.

In 1929 he spent a year at the State Theater of Darmstadt as a dancer, choreographer, and literary consultant. In the early thirties, Denby befriended Virgil Thomson, Aaron Copland, Alice B. Toklas (he later regretted that he had shied away from calling on Gertrude Stein), Lotte Lenya, and Kurt Weill, met Sigmund Freud and James Joyce, and saw Ballets 33 perform George Balanchine's productions of Weill and Bertolt Brecht's opera *The Seven Deadly Sins* and *Mozartiana* in Paris.

The triumph of Nazism drove him back to the United States in 1935, and he tried his hand at ranching and as a telephone repairman. He also co-adapted and performed as the back half of the horse in Orson Welles's 1936 Mercury Theater production of Eugène Labiche and Marc-Michel's *The Italian Straw Hat,* retitled *Horse Eats Hat.*

In 1936, at the urging of Aaron Copland, Minna Lederman invited Denby to contribute articles on dance to the bimonthly *Modern Music,* a journal for composers and serious musicians. His first piece was on librettos. It was a subject that had special meaning for him; in Germany some years earlier, he had written an adaptation of Franz von Suppé's operetta *Die neue Galathea,* and a year later, in 1937, he would provide Copland with the libretto for the one-act opera *The Second Hurricane.* Denby's next piece for *Modern Music* was on dance. In 1942 Virgil Thomson, then music critic for the *New York Herald Tribune,* suggested to his editors that Denby would make a good replacement for dance critics Walter Terry and Robert Lawrence, who had recently been drafted. Denby's stint concluded with Terry's return to civilian life.

The pieces written for *Modern Music* and the *Herald Tribune* were evidence that America had produced its finest dance critic to date. In 1949, B. H. Haggin edited and arranged a selection of Denby's dance writings for the volume *Looking at the Dance,* a book that became an immediate reference for imaginative dance writing. After the *Herald Tribune* post, Denby continued to write on dance for a number of journals, with regular contributions to *Dance Magazine* and Richard Buckle's British journal *Ballet.* In the early sixties, another volume of Denby's dance writings appeared, *Dancers, Buildings, and People in the Streets,* which contained two of Denby's best pieces: the great title essay, a ruminative piece intended as a lecture for Juilliard students but never delivered; and "Three Sides of *Agon,*" a study of the creation of a Balanchine masterpiece.

In addition to *The Second Hurricane,* Denby wrote other librettos for Copland that were never realized, including *The Sonntag Gang* and *Miltie Was a Hackie,* all of them attempts to capture the American character, by means of American speech and delineation of a national personality. In writing about ordinary Americans, Denby was explaining how it felt to be one. His poetic voice is "American" — characterized by succinct diction, tonal shifts, and almost brutally sharp imagery.

Denby was also a poet, a constant though scantily published one. Three slender volumes — *In Public, in Private* (1948), *Mediterranean Cities* (1956), and *Snoring in New York* (1974) — and a collection; *Selected Poetry* (1975), appeared during his lifetime. Since his death, his reputation as a poet has grown to match his standing as a dance critic. Ron Padgett has said of his poetry, "These are poems to live with, to read over a period of time. The reader should expect them at first to be elusive, eccentric, or awkward, with a high density of thought. By reflecting alternately on their tones and meanings, however, one gradually acquires a sense of their wholeness, and the particular craft behind that wholeness." The flat intermingled surfaces of de Kooning's paintings, the juxtapositions of cityscape and people in Rudolph Burckhardt's New York photographs and films, the cogency and surprise of Balanchine's inventions — all these find their semblance in Denby's writing.

In the late fifties he began to find writing increasingly difficult. The dance writing slowed, in part because Denby held no steady reviewing post, and perhaps also because of a rupture in his friendships with Lincoln Kirstein and Balanchine. His energies were engaged by his devotion to New York poets Frank O'Hara, James Schuyler, and John Ashbery, to the choreographer and dancer Paul Taylor, and to the painter Alex Katz. In these years, he was as constant an attendant of performances in the "downtown" scene as he was of the New York City Ballet.

Rudy Burckhardt, who had accompanied Denby when he returned to the United States in 1935, featured Denby in his films, notably *145 W. 21* (1936), in which Denby costarred with Aaron Copland, Paula Miller, and John Latouche; the 1970s' *Lurk* as a mad scientist, with Red Grooms as the scientist's creation; and *Money,* also in the 1970s, in which he played the richest man in the world. Concurrently, Denby participated in the theater works of Robert Wilson, in one piece intoning his own poetry and in another reading from the journals of Vaslav Nijinsky.

After some years of devastating illness and deteriorating memory, Denby died by his own hand in the summer of 1983. A friend realized later that Denby had spent the previous spring saying goodbye.

In 1986 a volume of Denby's dance writings appeared in conjunction with his collected poetry. The present volume is a selection from these two compilations. Although considerations of space have compelled me to leave out poems, essays, and reviews that others will consider essential, let this serve as an introduction and encouragement to those who are reading Denby for the first time to seek out other splendors by America's first dance critic of genius and one of its most elegant poets.

William Mackay generously supplied the bibliography. Ron Padgett selected the poetry and advised me on all aspects of this book. I am as grateful for his friendship as for his critical acumen. Yvonne and Rudolph Burckhardt's devotion to Edwin Denby and his work is the inspiring spirit of this book.

— Robert Cornfield

THE THIRTIES *AN ESSAY*

*P*at Pasloff asked me to write something for the show about New York painting in the thirties, how it seemed at the time. The part I knew, I saw as a neighbor. I met Willem de Kooning on the fire escape, because a black kitten lost in the rain cried at my fire door, and after the rain it turned out to be his kitten. He was painting on a dark eight-foot-high picture that had sweeps of black across it and a big look. That was early in '36. Soon Rudy Burckhardt and I kept meeting Bill at midnight at the local Stewart's, and having a coffee together. Friends of his often showed up, and when the cafeteria closed we would go to Bill's loft in the next street and talk some more and make coffee. I remember people talking intently and listening intently and then everybody burst out laughing and started off intent on another tack. Seeing the pictures more or less every day, they slowly became beautiful, and then they stayed beautiful. I didn't think of them as painting of the New York School, I thought of them as Bill's pictures.

These early ones are easy to get into now from the later point of view of the New York School. At the time, from the point of view of the School of Paris, they were impenetrable. The resemblances to Picasso and Miró were misleading, because where they led one to expect seduction and climax, one saw instead a vibration. To start from Mondrian might have helped. One could not

In the late fifties, Denby offered this memoir to introduce the catalogue of a show of New York paintings of the thirties.

1

get into the picture by way of any detail, one had to get into it all at once, so to speak. It often took me several months to be able to.

I remember walking at night in Chelsea with Bill during the Depression, and his pointing out to me on the pavement the dispersed compositions — spots and cracks and bits of wrappers and reflections of neon-light — neon-signs were few then — and I remember the scale in the compositions was too big for me to see it. Luckily I could imagine it.* At the time Rudy Burckhardt was taking photographs of New York that keep open the moment its transient buildings spread their unknown and unequaled harmonies of scale. I could watch that scale like a magnanimous motion on these undistorted photographs; but in everyday looking about, it kept spreading beyond the field of sight. At the time we all talked a great deal about scale in New York, and about the difference of instinctive scale in signs, painted color, clothes, gestures, everyday expressions between Europe and America. We were happy to be in a city the beauty of which was unknown, uncozy, and not small scale.

While we were talking twenty years ago, I remembered someone saying, "Bill, you haven't said a word for half an hour." "Yes," he answered, his voice rising like a New Yorker's to falsetto with surprise, "I was just noticing that, too." He was likely to join in the talk by vehemently embracing a suggestion or vehemently rejecting it. Right off he imagined what it would be like to act on it and go on acting on it. He didn't, like a wit, imitate the appearance of acting on it; he committed himself full force to what he was imagining. As he went on, characteristic situations in his life or those of friends came back to him as vividly as if they had just happened. He invented others. Objections he accepted, or circumvented, or shouted his opposition to. He kept heading for the image in which a spontaneous action had the force of the general ideas involved. And there he found the energy of contradictory actions. The laugh wasn't ridiculousness, but the fun of being committed to the contrary. He was just as interested in the contrary energy. Self protection bored him.

In the talk then about painting, no doctrine of style was settled at Bill's. He belligerently brought out the mysterious paradoxes left over. In any style he kept watching the action of the visual paradoxes of painting — the opposition of interchangeable centers, or a volume continued as a space, a value balancing a color. He seemed to consider in them a craft by which the picture seen as an image unpredictably came loose, moved forward and spread. On the

---

*Denby used de Kooning's perceptions in his poem "The Silence of Night" [page 11].

other hand, his working idea at the time was to master the plainest problems of painting. I often heard him say that he was beating his brains out about connecting a figure and a background. The basic connection he meant seemed to me a motion from inside them that they interchanged and that continued throughout. He insisted on it during those years stroke by stroke and gained a virtuoso's eye and hand. But he wanted everything in the picture out of equilibrium except spontaneously all of it. That to him was one objective professional standard. That was form the way the standard masterpieces had form — a miraculous force and weight of presence moving from all over the canvas at once.

Later, I saw in some Greek temples contradictory forces operating publicly at full speed. Reading the *Iliad,* the poem at the height of reason presented the irrational and subjective, self-contradictory sweep of action under inspiration. I had missed the point in the talks in 22nd Street. The question Bill was keeping open with an enduring impatience had been that of professional responsibility toward the force of inspiration. That force or scale is there every day here where everybody is. Whose responsibility is it, if not your own? What he said, was "All an artist has left to work with is his self-consciousness."

From such a point of view the Marxist talk of the thirties was one-track. The generous feeling in it was stopped by a rigid perspective, a single center of action, and by jokes with only one side to them. If one overlooked that, what was interesting was the peremptoriness and the paranoia of Marxism as a ferment or method of rhetoric. But artists who looked at painting were used to a brilliance in such a method on the part of the Paris surrealists and to a surrealist humor that the political talk did not have. Politically everybody downtown was anti-fascist, and the talk went on peacefully. Then when friends who had fought in Spain returned, their silence made an impression so direct that the subject was dropped. Against everybody's intention it had become shameless.

In the presence of New York at the end of the thirties, the paranoia of surrealism looked parlor-sized or arch. But during the war Bill told me he had been walking uptown one afternoon and at the corner of 53rd and Seventh he had noticed a man across the street who was making peculiar gestures in front of his face. It was Breton and he was fighting off a butterfly. A butterfly had attacked the Parisian poet in the middle of New York. So hospitable nature is to a man of genius.

Talking to Bill and to Rudy for many years, I found I did not see with a painter's eye. For me the after-image (as Elaine de Kooning has called it) became one of the ways people behave together, that is, a moral image. The beauty Bill's Depression pictures have kept reminds me of the beauty that instinctive behavior in a complex situation can have — mutual actions one has noticed that do not make one ashamed of one's self, or others, or of one's surroundings either. I am assuming that one knows what it is to be ashamed. The joke of art in this sense is a magnanimity more steady than one notices in everyday life, and no better justified. Bill's early pictures resemble the later ones in that the expression of character the picture has seems to me of the same kind in early and later ones, though the scope of it and the performance in later ones becomes prodigious.

The general look of painting today strikes me as seductive. It makes the miles of New York galleries as luxurious to wander through as a slave market. Room after room, native or imported, the young prosperity pictures lift their intelligent eyes to the buyer and tempt him with an independent personality. The honest critics, as they pass close to a particularly luscious one, give it a tweak in the soft spots. The picture pinches them in return. At the end of a day's work, a critic's after-images are black and blue. It takes more character to be serious now.

Twenty years ago Bill's great friend was Gorky. I knew they talked together about painting more than anyone else. But when other people were at Bill's, Gorky said so little that he was often forgotten. At one party the talk turned to the condition of the painter in America, the bitterness and unfairness of his poverty and disregard. People had a great deal to say on the subject, and they said it, but the talk ended in a gloomy silence. In the pause, Gorky's deep voice came from under a table. "Nineteen miserable years have I lived in America." Everybody burst out laughing. There was no whine left. Gorky had not spoken of justice, but of fate, and everybody laughed open-hearted.

At a WPA art occasion, I heard that La Guardia had made a liberal speech about art and society. After the applause, Gorky who was on the reception committee stepped forward unexpectedly and began, "Your Honor, you know about government, and I know about art." Short La Guardia looked at tall Gorky, who was earnestly contradicting him in a few sentences. I imagine he saw Gorky's seedy sportclothes and the exhilarating nobility of his point of view and valued them. Maybe he felt like laughing happily the way we did.

The last time I saw Gorky, not long after the war, he was sitting with Bill and Elaine in the diner that used to be at Sixth Avenue across from 8th Street, and I went in and joined them for a coffee. I told them I had just read in a paper that when the war was over there were 175 million more people in the world than before it began. He looked at me with those magnificent eyes of his and said quietly, "That is the most terrible thing I have heard." The beauty of Gorky's painting I understood only last year.

I began this train of thought wondering at the cliché about downtown painting in the Depression — the accepted idea that everybody had doubts and imitated Picasso and talked politics. None of these features seemed to me remarkable at the time, and they don't now. Downtown everybody loved Picasso then, and why not. But what they painted made no sense as an imitation of him. For myself, something in his steady wide light reminded me then of the light in the streets and lofts we lived in. At that time Tchelitchev was the uptown master, and he had a flickering light. The current painters seem for their part to tend toward a flickering light. The difference that strikes me between downtown then and now is that then everybody drank coffee and nobody had shows. Private life goes on regardless.

POEMS

The Climate

I myself like the climate of New York
I see it in the air up between the street
You use a worn-down cafeteria fork
But the climate you don't use stays fresh and neat.
Even we people who walk about in it
We have to submit to wear too, get muddy,
Air keeps changing but the nose ceases to fit
And sleekness is used up, and the end's shoddy.
Monday, you're down; Tuesday, dying seems a fuss
An adult looks new in the weather's motion
The sky is in the streets with the trucks and us,
Stands awhile, then lifts across land and ocean.
We can take it for granted that here we're home
In our record climate I look pleased or glum.

The Subway

The subway flatters like the dope habit,
For a nickel extending peculiar space:

You dive from the street, holing like a rabbit,
Roar up a sewer with a millionaire's face.

Squatting in the full glare of the locked express
Imprisoned, rocked, like a man by a friend's death,
O how the immense investment soothes distress,
Credit laps you like a huge religious myth.

It's a sound effect. The trouble is seeing
(So anaesthetized) a square of bare throat
Or the fold at the crotch of a clothed human being:
You'll want to nuzzle it, crop at it like a goat.

That's not in the buy. The company between stops
Offers you security, and free rides to cops.

City Without Smoke

Over Manhattan island when gales subside
Inhuman colors of ocean afternoons
Luminously livid, tear the sky so wide
The exposed city looks like deserted dunes.
Peering out to the street New Yorkers in saloons
Identify the smokeless moment outside
Like a subway stop where one no longer stirs. Soon
This oceanic gracefulness will have died.
For to city people the smudgy film of smoke
Is reassuring like an office, it's sociable
Like money, it gives the sky a furnished look
That makes disaster domestic, negotiable.
Nothing to help society in the sky's grace
Except that each looks at it with his mortal face.

Summer

I stroll on Madison in expensive clothes, sour.
Ostrich-legg'd or sweet-chested, the loping clerks
Slide me a glance nude as oh in a tiled shower
And lope on dead-pan, large male and female jerks.

Later from the open meadow in the Park
I watch a bulging pea-soup storm lie midtown;
Here the high air is clear, there buildings are murked,
Manhattan absorbs the cloud like a sage-brush plain.

In the grass sleepers sprawl without attraction:
Some large men who turned sideways, old ones on papers,
A soldier, face handkerchiefed, an erection
In his pants — only men, the women don't nap here.

Can these wide spaces suit a particular man?
They can suit whomever man's intestines can.

The Silence at Night

(The designs on the sidewalk Bill pointed out)

The sidewalk cracks, gumspots, the water, the bits of refuse,
They reach out and bloom under arclight, neonlight —
Luck has uncovered this bloom as a by-produce
Having flowered too out behind the frightful stars of night.
And these cerise and lilac strewn fancies, open to bums
Who lie poisoned in vast delivery portals,
These pictures, sat on by the cats that watch the slums,
Are a bouquet luck has dropped here suitable to mortals.
So honey, it's lucky how we keep throwing away
Honey, it's lucky how it's no use anyway

Oh honey, it's lucky no one knows the way
Listen chum, if there's that much luck then it don't pay.
The echoes of a voice in the dark of a street
Roar when the pumping heart, bop, stops for a beat.

First Warm Days

April, up on a twig a leaftuft stands
And heaven lifts a hundred miles mildly
Comes and fondles our faces, playing friends —
Such a one day often concludes coldly —
Then in dark coats in the bare afternoon view
Idle people — we few who that day are —
Stroll in the park aimless and stroll by twos
Easy in the weather of our home star.
And human faces — hardly changed after
Millennia — the separate single face
Placid, it turns toward friendly laughing
Or makes an iridescence, being at peace.
We all are pleased by an air like of loving
Going home quiet in the subway-shoving.

Meeting in the Postoffice

Was it you or myself I saw, white in the postoffice,
The white face hung in the air before the government marble —
Like the brutalized inmate who, questioned about his grievance,
Sees his own crazy face in the mirror and hears his speech garble.
A face, a face, mine, his, the President's, who cares whose face
Crazy alike, alike a horrible one-nosed lump,
The heart tied to the same known face of the human race
Goes into spasms of pain for a pet facial bump.
So we left that soapy government erection.

Dazed. Outside the day is filling the street and the farm
Equally. Heat and brightness and reflection
Play in the distance and in your look, doing no harm.
And now we coast like on the summer's crest
Seeing the east, and looking to the west.

The Poison

Here the primped housewife has the choice between
Being vain of her provider or of loathing,
The smooth college-boy in his generous dreams
Quakes to think of himself in cheap clothing.
The rich man is in terror of being taken advantage of,
The intellectual stews his affection in envy,
The poor girl's bliss is to humiliate the boy she loves,
And the feeble try at least to cheat in their own family.
Therefore I hope the human species is wiped out.
But my shame is not a pang a billion people share —
Listen to them giggle and whinny and roar and shout
Look at them squeeze and feed and stare and snore.
Expecting little of themselves or others
Dying scares them, but to suffer hardly bothers.

Irish American Song

Irish Yeats told of a barn, three men in there at night
One held a lock of hair up, two threshed by its given light
Did they know the woman whose it was? as remote as at a crime
The wan lock shone greenish and the men worked in that shine.
Here in New York where two or three persons lie asleep in a black
Room and the night lies in the airshaft on the bricks at the back
I know there is hair glowing like a weak bulb hung alone
But not what small manufacturing by its private light is done.

Young men with work, now lounging in a narrow luncheonette
In your underwear you get up from your bed without regret
Never will such a glow wake you at two in a hotel room
In the dead of night beside you, to use this monstrous bloom.
The fluorescence shed is like from my dead ma's radium clock
The man in the room with only a night his has his clock stop.
Tomorrow the people on the street will shine in the great light of day
Their bright young smiles will, which money gives and money takes away.

A Postcard

Elaine, Nini, Sylvia, Marjorie, Theda,
Each sends you happy wishes for your birthday,
Red and black Frances, Frannie, and Almavida,
Louise, gay Germaine too who is far away,
Kind Maggie, and Pit, Martha who prays gladly,
Jeannie, Ruth, Ernestine, Anne, Billie Holiday,
Husky Patsy, Ilse they love so madly,
And straightfaced Teddy — Dear Rudy, they all say.
And then Victor, and Bill, and Walter the mild,
And Frank, David, John, Aaron, Paul, Harry and
Virgil, the Photoleague, Oliver, Ebbie wild,
I and Gankie and the Shoe-man shake your hand.
Marieli and Susan come running at the end
And all of us send our love to you, our friend.

Mid-Day Crowd

When they build for a million a day to use it,
What is the point in, say, five hundred years,
Abroad they've still got the pyramid of Whoosis,
Would it last in New York? The answer is, who cares.

So many a day makes anything like forever:
So a hydrant is (the joke is on the designer)
So the shutter of a camera is open forever,
So how's the fuckin wife, christ, couldn't be finer.

Isolated, active, attractive, separated,
Momentary, complete, neat, fragmentary,
Ordinary, extraordinary, related,
Steady, ready, harried, married, cute, astute, hairy.

Created equal as they say, so where's the pity?
In a split second a girl is forever pretty.

FROM *MEDITERRANEAN CITIES* (1956)

Venice

She opens with the gondola's floated gloze
Lapping along the marble, the stir of swill
Open to night sky like in tenement hallways
The footfalls, and middream a bargeman's lone call;
Sideways leading to her green, like black, like copper
Like eyes, on tide-lifted sewers and façades
Festooning people, barges a-sway for supper
Under hunched bridges, above enclosed pink walls;
And crumbling sinks like a blond savory arm
Fleshed, a curled swimmer's pale belly that presses
And loosens, and moist calves, then while the charm
Subsides, Venice secrets pleases, caresses;
The water-like walking of women, of men
The hoarse low voices echos from water again

Rome

Pear-brown Rome, dyed for the days whose blue is sweet
Disencoils as a garden would the wreaths and noses

Waists and loose fountains it adores to prodigate
A fair-weather darling as loose as roses
Soft up to the scar, dead Imperial Rome's;
But an American in the exposed ruins
They meet him like a face unrecognized from home
The mute wide-angle look, to Europe alien;
A stare of big men worried about their weight
Gaze of bounty, but too clumsy to have mourned
Or held, listening to the heartbeat which was a fate
Sky-hues that will return, the slope of solemn ground;
And I to whom darling Europe is foreign
Look home from here, to its mystery, with longing

Villa Adriana

Who watched Antinous in the yellow water
Here where swollen plains gully, Roman and brown
Built for fun, before a flat horizon scattered
Fancies, such advanced ones, that lie overthrown;
Urbanely they still leer, his voided surprises
Curved reflections, double half-lights, coigns of rest
Embarrassing as a rich man without admirers
Peculiar like a middle-aged man undressed;
Over the view's silent groundswell floats a field
Enskied by one eerie undeviating wall
Far to a door; pointing up his quietude
Watchful Hadrian exudes a sour smell;
The ratty smell of spite, his wit, his laughter
Who watched Antinous smile in yellow water

Olevano Romano

Samnite, such a high hilltown made Romans cross;
Viewed below, April ledges of grape or rye

Slim greens, deeper green in the valley, and a voice
Chanting on the mountainside; Dante woke too
To dawn of rain, thrush, of farmers' and beasts' tread
Leaving the cold alleys tight about the keep
Driven diurnally from the mountainhead
Down to farm, at dusk resorbed upward to sleep;
They sleep close; clouds like hounds coil on the mountaintops
And the bare Spring, girl-like Olympian hunter
Sharp for our smell, shudders; so old the night drops
While people lie flaccid and covered grunters
Godless; a dream stirs one, she scents them again
And they flee like hares through wide delight and close pain

Naples

I feel of night streets as of a reef, squamous
Grotto-wash; entombed, claws loose, a Siren lies
Who bleeds, the phosphor-drift leaps in these Naples
Eyes, thousands of eyes, thousand and one night eyes;
By day, a crater; the oldest the island
Ischia, a solitary shire in an
Illuminated sky; stinking springs, birds silent
Oblique speech where is sand or a hoed vineyard;
For between volcanoes Naples tattered shelves
Loud dense mother sudden in adoration
Among children who hop among her themselves
Deck her screaming in variegation
Each a spell or a carnation
Pensive, when she calls like the moaning in a lie
Parthenope's lascivious guttural cry

Sant'Angelo d'Ischia

Wasps between my bare toes crawl and tickle; black
Sparkles sand on a white beach; ravines gape wide
Pastel-hued twist into a bare mountain's back
To boiling springs; emblems of earth's age are displayed;
At a distant end of beach white arcs piled
Windows, and in the sea a dead pyramid washed
As if in the whole world few people had survived
And man's sweetness had survived a grandeur extinguished;
Wonders of senility; I watch astonished
The old hermit poke with a stick the blond lame boy
Speaking obscenities, smiling weird and ravished
Who came from New York to die twenty years ago;
So at a wild farmer's cave we pour wine together
On a beach, four males in a brilliant weather

Syracuse

Are you Russians the boys said seeing us strange
Easy in grace by a poster with bicycles
Soft voices in a Baroque and Byzantine slum
Lemon pickers by swelling seas rainbow-fickle;
On the height drizzle, and among thyme and mint
A small shepherd, a large canvas umbrella
Leaps away down the crumbled ruins, timid
Where once they fought in moonlight, and Athens fell;
Up in sun, the Doric fort, stone blocks graceful
And fresh, erect as a statue in the air
Bright wind in our eyes, bright sea glittering peaceful
The dead come close trusting to embrace, and glare;
Beyond where rode an American fleet, Pindar's
Snowy Etna, pillar of Sicily, blows cinders

Delos

Dark pure blue, deep in the light, the sea shakes white-flecked
Foam-white houses sink, hills as dry as dried fruit
In a gale, in a radiance massive like sex
The boat bounces us and Greeks in business suits;
A thick-built landing stage; an isle low and small
And one old hill on it, cake-shapen; screening
Her solitude other islands bulge and sprawl
She lies dazzled, floating, as remote as meaning;
Left among the Hellenistic marble scum
Glistens a vivid phallus; marsh-born here before
At a palm, cleft-suckled, a god he first came
Who hurts and heals unlike love, and whom I fear;
Will he return here? quickly we pluck dry flowers
The sailor blows his conch; Delos disappears

Ciampino • Envoi

Flying from Greece to see Moscow's dancing girl
I look down on Alba Longa, see Jacob's house
And the Pope's, and already the airplane's curls
Show St. Peter's, and the Appian tombs' remorse;
But Jacob, a two-year-old American
Is running in the garden in August delight;
"Forum not a park, Forum a woods," he opines
In November quiet there on days less bright;
Now in New York Jacob wants to have my cat
He goes to school, he behaves aggressively
He is three and a half, age makes us do that
And fifty years hence will he love Rome in place of me?
For with regret I leave the lovely world men made
Despite their bad character, their art is mild

SONNETS

Out of Bronx subway June forest
A blue mallard drums the stream's reach
Duckling proud crosses lilyleaf
The thinnest of old people watch
And Brooklyn subway, Apt 5 J
Dozen young marvelous people
A painter's birthday, we're laughing
Real disaster is so near us
My joke on death they sweetly sink
Sunday follows, sleepy June rain
Delighted I carry icecream
A few blocks to friends' supper drenched
Baby with my name, old five weeks
I hold after its bath, it looks

Neighbor sneaks refuse to my roof
Cat snores — that's a winter landscape
Newcomers shining in the loft
Friends' paintings — inattention to cope
With the rest — the tap's voice, the street

Trucks, nextdoor coffee, gas from drain's
Hole, the phone's armorplated speech
Snow's hush, siren, rain, hurricane
Nature crowds, big time, into, out
The building and of the man I'm
I do with nature, do without
Penetrated, also sublime
I'd like the room mine, myself me
But as facts go, neither's likely

Born in my loft, dancer untame
A wilderness imagined, small
Cat, which we reached for real by plane
You stalked on the roof up the hall
Heart nursing six kittens, that grew
With them, long-tailed splendid-eyed cat
A disease struck the womb, left you
Savage fighter, playful at night
Lamed, ireful you prowled then; vet cut
Out the womb, so rage might subside
Telephone rings, speaks, I hang up
Cat-heart that knew me gone, I cried
It stopped beating drugged in a cage
Dear, mine will too, and let go rage

Writing poems, an employee
I lived here at nineteen, who I?
Current boys nineteen, their beauty
Of skin, all I can recognize
On this passport, soft vague boy's smile
Recalls few facts, does, his horror
Scale's abyss, void becoming real

A heart's force, he was going mad
Which I? — surviving forty years
Schizophrenia of a goof
I remember his savage tears
The kind reproof, the kind reproof
Vague-faced boy, he faced what was it?
A white old man, approved, I sit

Alex Katz paints his north window
A bed and across the street, glare
City day that I within know
Like wide as high and near as far
New York School friends, you paint glory
Itself crowding closer further
Lose your marbles making it
What's in a name — it regathers
From within, a painting's silence
Resplendent, the silent roommate
Watch him, not a pet, long listen
Before glory, the stone heartbeat
When he's painted himself out of it
De Kooning says his picture's finished

The size balls are saddens Lamarck
It's of no relevance to Marx
And Freud shoots his lunch at the fact
Dad's funny if he's just as small
July subway, meditate on
The decently clothed small male parts
Take the fabulous importance
Felt by homes, felt better by farts
They won't be missed, science will soon

Claim, parthenolatric more than
Religion, women left alone
To travel planets with women
In the lit subway gently shook
Imagine they've a goodbye look

The grand republic's poet is
Brooklyn Whitman, commuter Walt
Nobody else believes all of it
Not Harvard, that finds him at fault
I have, but first he broke my heart
He points to the moon and breaks it
I look for him, Twenty-first Street
Sleep against the push of a cat
Waking stumble to start coffee
At my back Walt in underwear
His head slants from unaltered day
Strokes my cat, the cheeks streaming tears
Sits on the bed, quietly cries
While I delay turning round, dies

Cold pink glowing above wakes me
Sky-light, ok, it's dawn, cat wants out
Outdoors I see skysea of pink
Blue pine bush, lightbrown goldenrod
Dazzle like baby cheek and hair
For acres, for miles of country
Each exposed brute so pure, so clear
Coolly on earth as in thought's joy
Me too, old man who pees adoze
Then dressed rereads Dante's Eden
One of dignified culture Joes
Lots of them take walks in Sweden

A me, free of himself at dawn
Sleeps, this me reads in noonday Maine

Inattentively fortunate
Have been pausing at lunchcounters
While what I most like, art that's great
Has been being painted upstairs
No homebuilder, even goofy
To virtue have been close as that
It I love and New York's beauty
Both have nodded my way, up the street
At fifteen maybe believed the world
Would turn out so honorable
So much like what poetry told
Heartbreak and heroes of fable
And so it did; close enough; the
Djin gave it, disappeared laughing

Disorder, mental, strikes me; I
Slip from my pocket Dante to
Chance hit a word, a friend's reply
In this bar; bare, dark avenue
The lunge of headlights, then bare dark
Cross on red, two blocks home, old Sixth
The alive, the dead, answer, ask
Miracle consciousness I'm with
At home cat chirps, Norwegian sweater
Slumped in the bar, I mind Dante
As dawn enters the sunk city
Answer a one can understand
Actual events are obscure
Though the observers appear clear

Nocturnal void lower Fifth, I
Stepped in that desert off the kerb
A roar spurting eighty whams by
What a pleasure, I wasn't killed
Laughed how dear the morose asphalt
Tail light at Sixth, waiting for a green
I'd recognized it, a friend's car
That like enraged had roared past me
Game unmentioned when we met, roar
Obscure he, I, have let alone
New York accommodates years more
Daily the unknown and the known
Sometimes I can't, madly gloomy
Recall that events are roomy

The meadow rolls slanting like the
Heave of a midocean wave; woods
Ensecret a mossgrown road, path
To our lake, the land a neighbor's
Shoes on grass, I slow in noon's silence
Step by step reach the water blindly
The torments of weakness disgust
They're so unreal, everyone kind
Greedy my soul upsidedown leaps
Into the deep sky under me
A more brilliant autumn it swims up
Rising inside the lake's mirror
It leaps back, ribbons of color
Impenetrably beautiful

A fall night, September, black, cold
Sheen on branches from lit windows
Thin fog; before sunset not a cloud

Surveyed the lake from its marsh end
Water, many leaves shone silver
A breeze blew, whitish brilliant sky
Dark hills, dark the landscape appeared
Minutely stereoscopic
Spongy dusk was more comforting
A door slammed, cooking, greasy pots
Night has me now, by itself from
Forever, go to bed a coward
Swum supine in brightness, raised my head
Immortal shone afloat in trunks

New York dark in August, seaward
Creeping breeze, building to building
Old poems by Frank O'Hara
At 3 a.m. I sit reading
Like a blue-black surf rider, shark
Nipping at my Charvet tie, toe-tied
Heart in my mouth — or my New York
At dawn smiling I turn out the light
Inside out like a room in gritty
Gale, features moving fierce or void
Intimate, the lunch hour city
One's own heart eating undestroyed
Complicities of New York speech
Embrace me as I fall asleep

In a hotelroom a madman
Breaks off armchair leg, brains me
Asleep; clever Paris surgeon
Extracts stomach; been killed nearly
Who hasn't, the much worse rents of love
Even of selfesteem survived

Left shamefully but glad to still live
Watch the rich hide, watch the poor hide
Death's dread; trapped I turn toward friends
Long dead when I found them, poets
Who when I'm crazed give my heart strength
By their tone of voice they do it
Some of that death-dread can be shook
Jumping across, eyes read a book

At first sight, not Pollock, Kline scared
Me, in the Cedar, ten years past
Drunk, dark-eyed, watchful, light-hearted
Everybody drunk, his wide chest
Adorable hero, mourn him
No one Franz didn't like, Elaine said
The flowered casket was loathsome
Who are we sorry for, he's dead
Between death and us his painting
Stood, we relied daily on it
To keep our hearts on the main thing
Grandeur in a happy world of shit
Walk up his stoop, 14th near 8th
The view stretches as far as death

Old age, lookit, it's stupid, a big fart
Messy what you are, it's preposterous
Cane slips on the kerb, helped up, he grins, part
Apologetic, watchful, vain, a mess.
And the flash phantom jumps transparent jumps
Rust flange loose, eye walked with walking sweet bees
Straw coin, sky's green pin, own heart's shrewd lumps
Its submiss trees and ancient evasive ease.
Child's shrieks left tied in the dark who falls bruised

Like a senile man's squeaks of rage at chess
Girl's gorgeous, ten feet tall, smile unconfused
I'm a fool cared for, thank you yes, age, yes, such a mess.
Cat and kittens each summer my sweetheart
Consciousness shrinks, leaves them the larger part.

[VERSION A]

DANCE WRITINGS

Nijinska's *Noces*

Noces in the choreography of Nijinska (revived this spring by the Monte Carlo Ballet) is, I'm sure, one of the finest things one can see anywhere. And if I could think of higher praise I would write it. *Noces* is noble, it is fierce, it is simple, it is fresh, it is thrilling. It is full of interest. It is perhaps an indication of the heroic age of Nijinsky. There is a realness in the relation of dance and music like a dual force, separate but inseparable. The movements, odd as they are and oddly as they come, often in counteraccent, are always in what theoreticians call "motor logic": that is, they are in a sequence you get the hang of, to your own surprise, and that has a quality of directness when performed. Amazingly few movement motives are used, and only the clearest groupings and paths, making the rhythmic subtlety obvious by contrast. That all these movement motives should be accentuating the direction into the floor leads to such interesting results as that ballet dancers, more familiar with the opposite direction, do these movements with a curious freshness; that the leaps seem higher; that the "pointes" get a special significance and hardness (almost a form of tapping), a hardness which all the performers, by the way, had not understood; and, as a further example, this general downward direction gives the heaped bodies a sense beyond decoration and gives the conventional pyramid at the end the effect of a heroic extreme, of a real difficulty. This sense of the realness of what is being done is underlined by the constant use of people at rest contrasted with people dancing—in the last part, people actually at rest on chairs. How often in other ballets have people stood about while others danced without adding by their contrast, because the contrast was not being used. And the stillness of the whole company at the end after all their frenzy is a climax of genius. During the whole last scene, the climax is a sort of steady inevitable expansion, a motion from the particular to the abstract.

Of the dancers themselves I would like to say that, though they seemed handicapped by insufficient rehearsal, they danced, especially at the last performance in New York, with a fine fervor. In fact the group of the Ballet Russe deserves every praise; the way they are overworked by the management is inhuman, because it is destructive of talent; and that they can still offer so much is a miracle.

Of the music of *Noces* I need not speak; it is as fine as the choreography. The scenery and costumes I find satisfactory, though I should like to see the four pianos on the stage, and the bed through the door of the house. The production is fifteen years old, and scenery and costumes belong more completely than choreography or music to that "abstract" fashion, the didactic heroics of the early twenties (those were Mary Wigman's best days, too).

Modern Music, May–June 1936

Nijinsky's *Faun;* Massine's *Symphonie Fantastique;* American Ballet Caravan

During the last six weeks New York has been a pleasant place for a person who likes ballet. I have seen one absolutely first-class piece, Nijinsky's *Faun;* Bérard's sets for the *Symphonie Fantastique,* the second and third of which are as good as the best ever made — probably the best we'll see all winter; and then a new dance group that is full of freshness and interest, the American Ballet Caravan. I have also seen other things I liked more or less, or not at all, and I have not by any means seen everything that has been done.

The revivals of the de Basil Ballet Russe are as carefully rehearsed and as freshly executed as its novelties. Last year's *Noces* and this year's *Faun* are things to be very grateful for. The *Faun* is an astonishing work. After twenty-three years it is as direct and moving as though it had been invented yesterday. It gathers momentum from the first gesture to the last like an ideal short story. From the point of view of a story, the way the veil is introduced and re-emphasized by the Nymph is a marvel of rightness. From the point of view of visual rhythm, the repetition of the Nymph's gesture of dismay is the perfection of timing. It is, of course, because so few gesture motives are used that one can recognize each so plainly, but there is no feeling of poverty in this simplification. The rhythmic pattern in relation to the stage and to the music is so subtly graded that instead of monotony we get a steady increase in suspense, an increase in the eyes' perceptiveness, and a feeling of heroic style at the climax.

It is true that most of the gestures used have prototypes in Greek reliefs and vase paintings, but, in addition to that intellectual association with adolescence, the fact is that when the body imitates these poses, the kind of tension resulting expresses exactly the emotion Nijinsky wants to express. Both their actual tension and their apparent remoteness, both their plastic clarity and their emphasis by negation on the center of the body (it is always strained between the feet in profile and the shoulders en face) — all these qualities lead up to the complete realization of the Faun's last gesture. The poignancy of this moment lies partly in the complete change in the direction of tension, in the satisfying relief that results; and the substitution of a new tension (the incredible backbend) gives the work its balance. But besides, the eye has been educated to see the plastic beauty of this last pose, and the rhythmic sense to appreciate its noble deliberateness. That it is so intensely human a gesture, coming after a long preparation of understatement, gives it, in its cumulative assurance, the force of an illumination. This force of direct human statement, this faith in all of us, is the astonishing thing about the *Faun*. It is as rare in dancing as in the other arts. These last moments of the *Faun* do not need any critical defense. But they have been so talked about that I am trying to point out for intellectuals that they are not a sensational tag, but that the whole piece builds up to them, and reaches in them an extraordinary beauty.

The de Basil company danced the *Faun* beautifully. Lichine in the title role excelled. It is a part that demands exceptional imagination as well as great plastic sense. And Lichine had besides these a fine simplicity.

His own ballet *Pavillon* (music by Borodin) was pleasant but left no definite impression as a piece. Its lightness was often commonplace, and its inventions often plastically ineffective. I hope he will show us a new ballet next year in which his admirable sense of dance will find a more definite form.

The other novelty, Massine's *Symphonie Fantastique* (music and book by Berlioz) was at the opposite extreme from *Pavillon* in point of definiteness and effect. Massine is without doubt the master choreographer of today. He has the most astonishing inventiveness and the most painstaking constructivity. He is an encyclopedia of ballet, character, specialty, period, and even of formulas from modern German dancing. In the *Fantastique,* for instance, his Musician runs the whole gamut of late romantic gesture, and the prison scene is glorified Jooss. Besides this gift of detail he has a passion for visual discipline, a very good sense of dramatic variety and climax, and one watches the whole *Fantastique* — except perhaps for the last finale — with a breathless attention. The prison scene in particular moves as fast as a movie thriller. In the *Fantastique* Massine uses even more successfully than in *Présages* or

Choreartium the device of a number of simultaneous entrées, giving an effect like a number of voices in music; and his gift for following the details as well as the main line of a score is remarkable.

But notwithstanding these many great attainments, I personally do not enjoy his work. For me, the activity of his ballets is an abstract nervousness that has no point of reference in a human feeling. The physical tension remains constant; it has no dramatic subsequence. The gesture motives are ingenious, but they allow no projection of any imaginative reality; they allow only the taut projection of a gesture in the void. His characters are intellectual references to types; they do not take on a mysterious full life of their own. And I imagine that it is this lack of humanity in his work that has limited such dancers as Toumanova and Jasinski, though he has developed a fine visibility in Zoritch.

For me the great treat of the *Fantastique* is the extraordinary sets of Bérard. Their proportion, both in themselves and to the dancers in the course of the scenes, their space, repose, and coloring are miraculous. Much of the lighting was fine too, among other things the dark opening of the ballroom scene, which disappeared in a later performance.

The American Ballet Caravan, composed of members of the American Ballet, presented, the evening I saw them, *Promenade* (Dollar-Ravel), *The Soldier and the Gypsy* (Coudy–de Falla), and *Encounter* (Christensen-Mozart). The Mozart was the best, with the right quality of definiteness and play, of stage magic and tender friendliness. The Spanish number had an interesting and appropriate attempt to combine dancing with parlando movement, so to speak; and the Ravel had a sense of style and several happy inventions. The costumes were interesting, those for the Ravel remarkable. But it is a shame they chose to dance against that old eyesore, black curtains. The company is well trained and unspoiled. They are pleasantly un-Russian. There is an American freshness and an American modesty that is charming. There may be as yet the usual faults of beginners — lyricism, too timid a dramatic attack, too little concentration choreographically, and occasionally by some dancers more projection than the moment warrants. But the important thing is that young talents get a chance and that the enterprise as a whole is lively and real and part of us. I regret that I missed the second program, which contained a ballet by a young American composer, Elliott Carter, *Pocahontas* (Christensen), and *Harlequin for President* (Loring-Scarlatti).

The novelty by the Jooss Ballet, *The Prodigal Son* (music by Cohen), was not a success, but I do not think it necessary to analyze it, as it may well be thoroughly revised. The Jooss Ballet, accurate as they are, could learn a good deal in theater effectiveness and in invention from Massine. From the standpoint of new music the season has not been very rich. *Concurrence* by Auric is nice but not new. Tansman's new version of his *Sonatine Transatlantique* for Jooss is excellent music and good for dancing. I didn't like Cohen's *Prodigal.* The best new ballet music I heard was Paul Bowles's score for *Horse Eats Hat.* This whole production is much the most interesting thing in the season's spoken theater from the standpoint of movement.

Modern Music, November–December 1936

Graham's *Chronicle;* Uday Shankar

In December Miss Graham presented a new heroic dance suite for herself and her group called *Chronicle.* It deals with division, grief, and final adjustment. I wish I had seen it again to clarify my own impression and to be able to point specifically to its more or less successful elements. As it is, I can only speak of it in general terms, and confusedly.

Seeing Miss Graham with her group and in solo recital, I was impressed by her courage and integrity. She believes in the biggest possible gesture; so she has trained herself to execute these extraordinary movements as accurately as a ballerina would her own most difficult feats. She believes in unexpectedness of composition, and she succeeds in keeping up an unremitting intellectual tension. There is no slack anywhere, physically or intellectually. She has, besides, an emotional steadiness in projection that binds together her constantly explosive detail, a determination which controls what might otherwise seem unrelated and fragmentary.

These are certainly rare qualities. I think anyone who likes dancing will admire her. But it seems to me her courage could go even further. She seems to watch over her integrity with too jealous an eye. She allows her dance to unfold only on a dictatorially determined level. But a dance unfolds of its own accord on a great many contradictory levels. And I miss the humanity of these contradictions.

To speak more in terms of dance, it seems as though Miss Graham were too neat. Her group is excellently trained. They do each motive given them with accuracy and decision. But from time to time, accidentally it seems, Miss Graham herself has a softening of contour between moments of emphasis where her natural subtlety of body substitutes shading, continuity, and breath for the geometry of constant tension; and it is at these very moments, which seem unintentional, that Miss Graham gets her audience most, gets them to feel something of the drama she is trying to tell about. I have the impression that Miss Graham would like to keep a dance constantly at the tension of a picture. She seems to be, especially in her solo dances, clinging to visual definition. Even her so-called angularity springs partly from a fear that the eye will be confused unless every muscle is given a definite job. The eye would be confused. But our bodily sense would not. Our bodily sense needs the rebound from a gesture, the variation of hard and soft muscle, of exact and general. As I said, Miss Graham herself has an instinct in this direction; but she seems to hesitate to rely on it in composition. I think it is this lack of confidence that she can communicate her tension directly to the body of anyone in the audience that makes her dances so "difficult." Isadora did not have this lack of confidence, and so her dances — though perhaps pictorially undistinguished — were always compelling, and gave the effect of beauty. But I don't want to go off on too theoretical a discussion, though Miss Graham is a controversial figure and important to us.

For musicians Miss Graham's programs are especially interesting because a number of modern American composers write for her, setting her dances to music after the dance has been composed. In general they seem anxious to stick literally to the rhythmic detail of her dance, the way many dancers — inversely — might try to stick to the rhythmic detail of music. It isn't a good method. Especially because Miss Graham's motives are so obvious, they need no reiteration in music, and they are structural body rhythms rather than ornamental gestures. For the musicians the result of following her is that instead of making their piece a whole, they divide it up into a series of brief phrases, each stopping on an accent. It seems to me that the rhythmic structure of dance and that of music are parallel but not interchangeable. Time in music is much more nearly a mathematical unit than in dance — in the dance-pulse, stress and recovery (the down- and upbeat of the measure) are often not of equal time length as in music, and stress in music is more regularly recurrent. A good dance goes along with a piece of music with plenty of points of contact but many of duality. A dance needs a certain rhythmic independence — similar in a sense to the rhythmic elasticity the voice is given in our popular songs. But to give this freedom to the dance the music must have a life of its own as music; and the more unassuming this life is, the more definite it should be. In any case it is no fun seeing a dancer dance smack on his *Gebrauchsmusik,* and he looks as dramatic doing it as a man riding an electric camel.

One very good kind of dance music is that of Uday Shankar. I do not mean to criticize it as music, much less as Hindu music. But to a lay ear it sounds pleasant, it sounds as though it made sense without being emphatic, it repeats itself without insistence. The Oriental music I have heard always has this independent friendliness toward the dancers. It may have something to do with the fact that the music is made in sight of the audience, and that the musician exists not only as an instrument but also as a person. To me it is theatrically much pleasanter to see the people who make the music for dancing. It puts the dancer into a human perspective; it takes the bombast out of his stylization, and instead shows its real reference to the more usual look of a body. Human beings don't look any better for being alone; on the contrary, their beauty is a relative thing, and even their solitude is more lonely when it is imaginary.

Uday Shankar is a fine dancer. What struck me most about him was that though he is a star, though he projects as vigorously as any Broadwayite, he still gives a sense of personal modesty. Many gifted dancers seem to say on the stage, "I am the dance." He says, "Hindu dancing is a beautiful thing and I like to do it as well as I can." We see him and admire him. His exact control of every gradation of dancing — fluidity or accent, lyricism or characterization, space movement or stationary gesture, virtuoso precision or vigorous generality — is marvelous. His intention is always clear and his surprises never offend. Within the limits of what may seem to us supercivilized and adolescent suavity, without either our classic footwork or our modern backwork, he finds it easy to run the whole gamut of dancing. Another style of dancing might have a different range, so to speak, but none can have a more complete expressiveness. Although he shows us all this in his own person as a dancer, we do not feel that he is showing us himself; he is showing us something that is beautiful quite apart from his own connection with it. He is a friend of ours who thinks we will enjoy too what he would enjoy so much if he were a spectator. As a result, he is glad to show us his company — the coquetry and wit of Simkie, the juvenile eagerness and delight in his own gifts of Madhavan. He shows us even the least expert of his dancers as they are — not subtle, of course, but agreeable. All these shades of dance personality are allowed to flower according to their nature, and add up to the sense of harmonious and natural completeness. I believe that this use in a troupe of whatever gifts are present — like the sense in a star that he is not the only person, that he is in fact only a detail in the whole of dancing — is the only thing that makes the theater real. Considerations of accuracy, of form for the group, of personal projection or style for the star are not secondary, they are an integral part of the artist's life. But they belong at home in the routine of preparation; they are his private life. In the studio the artist is more important than the whole world put together. On the stage he is one human being no bigger than any other single human being, even one in the audience. The big thing, the effect, is then at an equal distance from them both.

Modern Music, January–February 1937

Balanchine's American Ballet

Classic Ballet, the new work at the Metropolitan by Dollar and Balanchine (to the Piano Concerto in F Minor of Chopin), is excellent. It is swift, pleasant, interesting, and very well danced. And its moving quality (which a first night is bound to flatten out) will increase the more often it is repeated.

Beyond this, it shows that the American Ballet has grown up to be the first-class institution it was meant to be. George Balanchine has done more than anyone could have expected in so short a time. The company is at home on the huge stage. They are becoming brilliant in virtuoso passages. Without losing their freshness, they emerge as individually interesting — by which I mean that last, most exciting, and most dangerous phase in a dancer's development when he not only can do brilliantly what he is supposed to, but adds to that an illumination from individual feeling.

I admire Balanchine extremely for the way he fosters this personal quality in his dancers. It is real theater personality, in distinction to the fictitious kind common on Broadway, which consists of projecting yourself with a fanatic intensity regardless of anything else on the stage. There are moments when this is fine, and occasions besides when a performer has to do it to save a show, the way the boy stuck his arm in the dyke. But too many soloists appear only in this catastrophic role. And they never get or give the variations of intensity that make a whole piece, and the soloist, too, theatrically satisfying. It is worth pointing out that the projection Balanchine encourages is the satisfactory kind, and that he is beginning to get it.

Dollar's choreography shows an honest and well grounded talent. In style it reminds me of Balanchine's *Nocturne,* but Dollar's application is so intelligent, it speaks well for his integrity. Balanchine seems to have two styles. One, like his *Mozartiana,* is brilliantly complex, full of surprising realizations and poignant interchanges and a subtle, very personal fragrance. The other (to which belonged *Nocturne, The Bat,* and the "Abstract Ballet" in *On Your Toes*) looks like the opposite of the first. It minimizes detail for the soloist or the ensemble, and avoids technical feats. Instead it builds on unmistakable clarity of groupings and of directions; on rapid oppositions of mass, between single figures and a group; and above all on an amazing swiftness of locomotion. (The entrées are brief and, by simplifying the leaps, cover an astonishing amount of space.)

This style may have been due originally to the lack of training with which the American Ballet started. At any rate, Dollar now uses it very well. He has been able to add to it interesting feats, where they were worth doing. But he has not forgotten its essentials: mass, direction, clarity, and above all swiftness, a fine swiftness even in more complex passages that gives physical exhilaration to the whole. In addition, Balanchine has contributed a middle section which is more elaborate both in detail and in feeling, and which fits in astonishingly with the more abstract speed of the rest, heightening it with its greater warmth.

I think there is another reason besides Dollar's integrity as a dancer that makes this collaboration between teacher and pupil come off so agreeably. It is that Balanchine, no matter how odd some of his choreography may appear, has always composed in a way that is natural for a dancer to dance. He has no interest in effects which are not danced, which are merely seen. His poses are not arbitrary, they are the point at which a certain kind of gesture in a definite direction is arrested by a complementary tension. The method of movement may be classic ballet, and the source of material, intellectually speaking, the practice room, but the practice room is as much a part of life as the factory or the jungle, intellectually speaking. It is because all his movement has this living quality that it can have a continuation in someone else's, or combine with any other kind of living movement, I imagine, without anything being lost. It is also for this reason (that Balanchine's movement is natural to the body) that the technical training of the American Ballet has been so happy. Its members are now both exceptionally well grounded in the essentials of dancing and proficient in the technique of the ballet. Personally I am not a "balletomane." But dancing that makes sense is so rare it is worth being serious about.

Modern Music, March–April 1937

Balanchine's *Apollon;* American Ballet Caravan

Now that the Metropolitan does have a ballet masterpiece in its repertory — one as good as the very best of the Monte Carlo — there's a conspiracy of silence about it. It's true people ignored this ballet last year, too, when it came out, but I think they'd better go again, because they are likely to enjoy it very much. It's the Stravinsky-Balanchine *Apollon* I mean, which the Metropolitan is repeating this year, and which it does very well, even to playing the music beautifully.

It is a ballet worth seeing several times because it is as full of touching detail as a Walt Disney, and you see new things each time. Did you see the way Balanchine shows you how strangely tall a dancer is? She enters crouching and doesn't rise till she is well past the terrifically high wings; then she stands up erect, and just standing still and tall becomes a wonderful thing. Did you see how touching it can be to hold a ballerina's extended foot? The three Muses kneel on one knee and each stretches her other foot up, till Apollo comes and gathers the three of them in his supporting hand. Did you notice how he teaches them, turning, holding them by moments to bring each as far as the furthest possible and most surprising beauty? And it isn't for his sake or hers, to show off or be attractive, but only for the sake of that extreme human possibility of balance, with a faith in it as impersonal and touching as a mathematician's faith in an extreme of human reasoning. And did you notice the countermovement, the keenness of suspense, within the clear onward line of Terpsichore's variation (what the moderns call the spatial multiplicity of stresses)? The intention of it — the sense of this dance — is specified by a couplet quoted in the program, a couplet by Boileau which contrives to associate the violence of cutting, hanging, and pointing with an opposite of rest and law, and makes perfect sense, too:

> Que toujours dans vos vers le sens coupant les mots,
> Suspende l'hemistiche et marque le repos.
>
> [Let meaning in your verse that shapes each word,
> Always halve the line so that a rest is heard.   — Richard Howard]

Aren't you curious to see how incredibly beautiful this couplet is when danced? Or did you notice how at the end of a dance Balanchine will — instead of underlining it with a pose directly derived from it — introduce a strange and yet simple surprise (an unexpected entrance, a resolution of the grouping into two plain rows), with the result that instead of saying "See what I did" it seems as though the dancers said "There are many more wonders, too." And did you notice how much meaning — not literary meaning but plastic meaning — he gets out of any two or more dancers who do anything together? It's as though they were extraordinarily sensitive to each other's presence, each to the momentary physical strain of the other, and ready with an answering continuation, so that they stay in each other's world, so to speak, like people who can understand each other, who can belong together. And he combines this intimacy with an astonishing subtlety on the part of each individually. The effect of the whole is like that of a play, a kind of play that exists in terms of dancing; anyway, go and see if you don't think it's a wonderful ballet. The subject is the same as that of the music, which as you know is "the reality of art at every moment."

The dancers at the Metropolitan do these extremely difficult dances very well. Lew Christensen (from the Caravan) has, it is true, a personal style that is easy rather than subtle; but, besides being an excellent dancer, he is never a fake and at all times pleasant. The girls have a little more of the Balanchine tautness and they too are excellent dancers and appealing. The costumes are good.

The intelligentsia turned out in full for the All-American Evening of Kirstein's American Ballet Caravan; they approved the whole thing vociferously, and they were quite right. There was a happy community feeling about the occasion, a sort of church-social delight, that would have surprised the out-of-towners who feel New York is just a big cold selfish place, where nobody has any interest in anybody else. The ballets — *Show Piece* by Mc-Bride and Hawkins, *Yankee Clipper* by Bowles and Loring, and *Filling Station* by Thomson and Christensen — taken together show that an American kind of ballet is growing up, different from the nervous Franco-Russian style. From Balanchine it has learned plasticity, and openness, and I imagine his teaching has fostered sincerity in these dancers as in others he has taught. But our own ballet has an easier, simpler character, a kind of American straightforwardness, that is thoroughly agreeable. None of these ballets is imitative or artificial, and there is nothing pretentious about them. Hawkins shows us a good-humored inventiveness, Loring a warmth of characterization, and Christensen a clear logic of movement that are each a personal and also specifically American version of ballet. I think this is the highest kind of praise, because it shows the ballet has taken root and is from now on a part of our life. And the dancers themselves have an unspoiled, American, rather athletic quality of movement that is pleasant. As a group they are first-rate in their legs and feet and in the profile of the arms. I think they still lack an incisive stopping, and the expressiveness across the shoulders that will shed light through the correctness of movement; but their improvement in the last two years has been so phenomenal that these reservations aren't serious. At present the boys steal the show, especially Christensen, with his great ease, and Loring, with his human quality, but they don't try to steal it; and Albia Cavan and Marie-Jeanne show they intend to catch up with them. But one of the very good things about the Caravan is its homogeneity as a group. And I congratulate them all wholeheartedly, just as the audience did.

Of Balanchine's ballet in the *Goldwyn Follies* I would like to say that it is worth seeing if you can stand the boredom of the film as a whole (but don't leave before the mermaid number of the Ritz Brothers). It is worth seeing because the dancing is good, and one can see it; and because there's something moving left about the piece as a whole. But it is particularly interesting because you see a number of dance phrases that were composed into the camera field — an effective and necessary innovation anyone could have learned from Disney, but which nobody tried till now. It is the only way dancing can make sense in the movies.

Massine and the New Monte Carlo

The oddly written publicity for the new Monte Carlo states: "The arrival each year of the Ballet Russe de Monte Carlo automatically mobilizes the ballet fans of the nation, and the resulting enjoyment is prodigious." This sounds as though we were to derive prodigious enjoyment from being automatically mobilized — almost as though we were to plunk down our shekels, raise our right arms, and shout "Heil Hurok." Of course, the sentence quoted and others like it are ridiculous. It was a great pleasure to see the new Monte Carlo; it was a pleasure too that it was such a success. But it isn't yet all it set out to be: it hasn't kept as many of its campaign promises as it could have.

This new Monte Carlo is subsidized by our own money, so it isn't a gift horse; we have a right to look it over, and there are several front teeth missing. One of them is music by our own composers, whom we have a hard enough time hearing anyway. Thanks to the WPA and more to the Ballet Caravan, anyone interested in ballet music already knows that you can get it as satisfactorily here as abroad. We want it not for the pleasure of saying it's ours but because we are curious to hear it, and an American enterprise seems a natural place, especially an enterprise which promisingly entitles itself "Universal Art, Inc."

So much for propaganda; now to the pleasure of praising. Massine deserves the greatest praise for the company he has chosen. The freshness of the corps de ballet is wonderful. Especially the girls, as Wilis, as swans, as sylphides, as Parisiennes, as Transylvanians, are a constant pleasure. The soloists are excellent, with a clarity of profile and a physical zest that are first-rate; and the boys even outdo the girls. I particularly enjoyed the intelligence of Platoff and the limpidity of Guérard; and I remember half a dozen others in great moments. These soloists have not reached the completeness of personal projection that would transform them into stars, but they are all wonderfully free from faking either technique or personality; and with what wholeheartedness they all dance. In fact, I think the very best thing about the new Monte Carlo is this real sense of dancing it gives you all the time.

I saw two stars in the New York season — Danilova and Lifar — and for complete satisfaction two stars are not enough, especially as before the season was half over Lifar had left. (I missed Markova.) Danilova is not only a prodigious technician, but the way she points up a technical feat with a personal wit and distinction makes her the equal of any great actress. Her pointes, her ballonnés, and above all the poses in which she rests on her partner's shoulders are among the joys that genius gives us. Lifar is neither such an impeccable technician nor such a wit. He is frequently brilliant, but he can sometimes be awkward, and even dull. I seem to forget these lapses and only remember that more than any other dancer, he touches me. Look at his Faun standing next to the Nymph, look at his attempted flight in *Icare*. It is dancing, but something else is there too, a kind of naturalness in the part that goes beyond the gestures required, as though the character were as much alive as anybody living. As though on the stage, he seems to believe in the life that is going on outside of the theater in the present. He seems to believe that his part makes sense anywhere, that his part (in the words of cummings) is competing with elephants and skyscrapers and the individuals watching him. They all seem real at the same time, part of the same imagination, as they are really. There is something unprofessional about carrying reality around with you in public that goes straight to my heart. This is the kind of criticism it is hard to prove the justice of; I wish we could see Lifar more often so I could try. To me his ballet *Icare* seemed a strange real story sincerely told. It wasn't always successful (the percussion is quite bad), but it was far more warm and human than the agreeable cuteness of Fokine's new pieces, or the brilliantly calculated blatancy of Massine's. Massine is certainly brilliant, whether he appears as a performer or a director. He knows how to keep things going, how to make them look like a lot, how to get a big hand. He can get away with murder. If one took him seriously, he would be guilty of murdering the Beethoven Seventh, the Scarlatti, and even tender little Offenbach (though there wasn't much of Offenbach left in that new orchestration). There is of course no reason for taking Massine seriously; he doesn't mean to be, he doesn't mean to murder. Like a cigarette company, he is using famous names to advertise his wares. But I cannot help resenting it, because they are names of living things I have loved. It is hardest to bear in the case of his *Seventh,* where the orchestra is constantly reminding me of the Beethoven original.

Trying, however, to put aside this private resentment, I still am disappointed. Well, I'll exaggerate, and be clearer. I could see a kaleidoscopic succession of clever arrangements, but there was no thrill in the order in which they came. There was no sequence in the movement that awakened some kind of special feeling, some kind of urgency. It all occupied the eye as long as it lasted, and left no reality, no secret emotion behind. I missed the sense of growth and interplay, of shifting kinds of tensions, the feeling of drama, almost, that makes the best choreography mean much more than a string of effects. As a pictorial arranger Massine is inexhaustible. But dancing is less pictorial than plastic, and pictures in dancing leave a void in the imagination. They arrest the drama of dancing which the imagination craves to continue, stimulated by all the kinetic senses of the body that demand a new movement to answer the one just past. Until a kind of secret satisfaction and a kind of secret weariness coincide.

This dramatic progression of different qualities of movement is what means so little in these ballets. Take the *Seventh.* Every gesture is visually clear, but every gesture is at the same pitch, hit equally hard. The picture changes, but the tension remains the same. It's all very agitated. There are sometimes more, sometimes fewer people on the stage; they get on top of each other, lie down, run around, jump, crouch, whirl, pose, wave, or huddle, and they never give any sense of getting closer together or farther apart, of getting lighter or heavier, more open or more shut in, more soft or more hard. It is showmanship with a vengeance, it is a drill of automatons. Notice Massine's use of ballet technique. The extended silhouette is used as though it were a constant, like a military position, with none of the thousand subtleties of direction and intensity with which Balanchine gives it so much variety and purpose. And consequently with Massine it breaks in the middle, in the small of the back, instead of growing out from there by reaching up and down in a thousand human ways.

Because Massine's tension is static he can never make us feel the curious unfolding that is like tenderness. Like a Hollywood director, he gives us no sense of human growth (there isn't time); he keeps everything at a constant level of finish; everything is over as soon as it starts. He has no equivalent for mystery except to bring down the lights. So the *Seventh,* though danced with fervor and transfigured by the most wonderful sets and costumes in the world, leaves a sense of cheapness; and if you remember the mystery of Beethoven dynamics, it is unpleasant. *Gaîté Parisienne* seems just another empty revue number, where sex is a convention and not an emotion. Smarter, of course, than Broadway, and marvelously danced. And *St. Francis* seems a slinky posturing, a Sakharoff-Kreutzberg parody of illuminated Books of Hours and Minnelieder, with a grand finale of anthroposophic chorus girls.

No one but Massine could have got any theatrical effect out of this hodge-podge of minor pictorial devices, no one but he could have held the stage with a solo only half executed — but everyone acknowledges his stupendous gift of showmanship, and eminence, for that matter. We should miss a great deal if we were not to have a new Massine ballet; but we miss more by not having a new Balanchine ballet, or at least an old one like *Apollon,* a work of genius that reminds us of the sort of thing the greatest choreography is. The Monte Carlo has plenty of effective pieces; it should also have a great one.

All this schoolmastering leaves me only room enough to say that the purest pleasure I had was from the old *Coppélia,* which spread a kind of gentle radiance.

Modern Music, November–December 1938

Ashton's *Devil's Holiday*

The Monte Carlo, which I am always happy to see, began the season with a new ballet Diaghilev would have been proud of: *Devil's Holiday.* And Massine, who has been the Diaghilev for this production, deserves equal praise. I have seen it three times and I like it better each time. Everything about it is full of zest, sincerity, freshness, and charm. Tommasini, as Mr. Martin so well said, seems to have had the time of his life writing the music on Paganini themes, and the variations in the first half of the last scene struck me as particularly beautiful. Berman, from whom we had wonderful drops for *Icare* last season, has given us five more which are as brilliant as any baroque Burnacini, but full of a contemporary intimate and personal sentiment, and also scenically discreet; and his costumes are the most wonderful imaginable — just look at the two Servants of the Devil, at the Devil's horrible disguise, or at the farandole in the last scene, like a fashion show in heaven. (Judging from the published sketches, the drops were not as well executed as they should have been — especially the landscape — nor all the costumes; but even so they were wonderful.)

And I am delighted too with the new choreographer, Frederick Ashton, the young Englishman who several years ago did the dances for *Four Saints.* His style is original, and originality usually looks awkward at first, or unnecessarily complicated, or arbitrary, or something. His at first looks jerky, and you miss the large simple phrases you have come to like in Fokine, or the expert mass climaxes of Massine, or the incredible long moments of extension and tenderness of Balanchine, like speech in the silence of the night. But you can praise all that and still praise Ashton too. If he derives from anyone it is, I think, Nijinska, with her hasty, almost shy elegance, her hobbled toe steps. He derives too, it seems to me, from the kind of awkward and inspired dancing that young people do when they come back from their first thrilling ballet evening and dance the whole ballet they have seen in their own room in a kind of trance. The steps do not look like school steps (though they are as a matter of fact correct); they are like discoveries, like something you do not know you can do, with the deceptive air of being incorrect and accidental that romantic poetry has. But how expressive, how true to human feeling the dances are. The perverse solemnity of the betrothal guests, the noble and pathetic stiffness of the betrayed betrothed, the curious frenzy of cruelty after the scandal; these are real emotions. The lovers' dream dance is restlessly hurried, like a dream in which you know you are only dreaming; and what a final and brief conclusion it has into a deeper sleep. Like a Sitwell poem, the hunting number is fussy and witty to heighten the lonely and frantic despair of the lost lover, interrupted by a diabolically hysterical substitute love. And the last scene is a whirl of inventions, of young eagerness that can hardly stop for the tenderness it dreams of, and that is tender without knowing it. A choreographer who can call up so many sincere emotions, who keeps a steady line of increasing interest (and animation) throughout a long ballet and does not fall into conventional tags at important moments, is a real rarity who is worth being enthusiastic about, and, what is more, worth paying for a ticket to see. Personally, the only part I do not care for is the fox's dance, which, however, gets a laugh and a hand.

Devil's Holiday is probably difficult to dance and it is danced very well by everyone. The type of expression is not mimetic but like that in classic ballet, in which the entire personality illuminates a role that the dancer has to conceive without the aid of detail. Danilova is particularly fine, of course; Krassovska is brilliant; and Franklin is magnificent. Platoff, of whom I think very highly as a dancer, was good but not as good as he generally is. All the dancers in the divertissement of the last scene were splendid.

Modern Music, October–November 1939

Balanchine and Stravinsky: *Poker Game* and *Baiser;* The Monte Carlo Season

Balanchine's *Poker Game* (set to Stravinsky's *Jeu de Cartes*), revived this fall at the Monte Carlo, is a ballet in a minor genre but it is as good ballet as one can possibly have. And it creeps into your heart as unpretentiously as a kitten. To be sure, its range is limited. It is no more than a new twist to the animated doll subject, which by nature is witty, ironical, appealing, and playful, and rather likes to stay within the bounds of pleasant manners. Ballet certainly can have a wider range if it chooses; and *Petrouchka,* even though it starts with the doll idea, does choose. *Poker Game* doesn't, and yet it succeeds in becoming a "minor masterpiece." I think when you see it you will notice yourself how easy it is to look at, how agreeably it shifts from group to ensemble or solo, with an unexpectedness that is never disconcerting; how lively the relation is between still figures and moving ones; how distinct the action remains; how clear the center of attention, or the division of interest, so your eye does not take to wandering on its own and confuse the rhythm intended.

But besides being easy to look at, what you see is amusing. The steps emphasize a kind of staccato and a lateralness that may remind you of playing-card figures; many of the steps you recognize as derived from musical comedy. But the variety, the elasticity of dance impetus, the intelligent grace are qualities you never get in musical comedy routines. Nor does the musical comedy routine allow everyone onstage to project intelligent and personal good spirits. *Poker Game,* by allowing the dancers just this, makes you feel as if you were for a while in the best of company, with everybody natural and everybody interesting.

It is Balanchine's merit that all this is so. He keeps the dance placed in relation to the actual stage frame, which gives it a commonsense point of reference. He has the sense of timing, the sense of distances, which make the movement distinct. He has the wit which makes it amusing and the invention both plastic and rhythmic to keep it going in a lively way. He has the good sense to keep the numbers to their obvious subject: you see the Durante-like Joker egging on the silly Queens against the Aces, you distinguish between Jacks and Kings, you can tell who is winning or losing, and he does not make either too serious for the other. The subject in other words remains real and aboveboard; and the emotion it leads to, whether witty or sentimental, kept in relation to this subject, does not take on a faked or a private urgency.

But Balanchine has a profounder choreographic gift. His steps, no matter where derived, are steps that a ballet dancer specifically can do and do best, steps a ballet dancer can be brilliant in. His rhythms, however complex, are grateful to ballet dancers. He seems never to violate the real nature of a dancer's body, the part-native, part-trained relation of trunk and arms and head and feet; so that no matter how odd the movement required, the dancer still remains himself and does not congeal to an impersonal instrument. And so the choreography does not violate the dancer's best gift, which is his natural human warmth. It is a fact that Balanchine has been able to make the same dancers seem real and true in his ballets who have seemed conventional or stupid in others. All these qualities, being the best qualities of choreography there are, make a good Balanchine ballet as good ballet as you can get. It is true his style is very complex, and some people don't like complex dancing. There is also a joyous irony in his tenderest pathos, and irony in sentiment seems subversive to good people who like to think that sentiment is something comfortable, secure. But this issue does not arise in *Poker Game.*

I found the entertaining music of *Poker Game* wonderful to listen to and, thanks to the play of counterrhythm and counterdynamics on the stage, easy to follow. (The light orchestration, obvious accents, and sharp eighth notes seemed helpful for dancing, making counting easier.)

I cannot resist adding by way of footnote that I urge you to see and see again the Balanchine-Stravinsky *Baiser de la Fée,* now also in the Monte Carlo repertory. Unlike *Poker Game* it is ballet at its grandest. It has a range of expression that includes the brutality of the peasant dances, the frightening large mime gestures of the fortune-telling scene, the ominous speed-up of the wedding party, the hobbled tenderness of the bridal duet, the clap-of-thunder entrance of the veiled Fairy, the repulsive dissolution of the last scene — all of it fascinating and beautiful. Its images of destiny, its tragic illuminations, are as convincing as any I know in literature; but the lightness, the grace with which these dramatic scenes develop is peculiarly Balanchinian. *Baiser de la Fée* is poetic theater at its truest.

Balanchine's third piece for the Monte Carlo, a revival of *Serenade,* I was not invited to by the organization's publicity department; well, I remember liking it some years ago at the Stadium.

The other revival of the Ballet Russe, Petipa's* classic *Nutcracker,* has a charming and straightforward first scene, which is also a good example of ballet "recitative." In this scene Miss Lauret was very fine indeed, and Miss Etheridge also. The second scene is a virtuoso adagio and variation, in a noble and extensive style, beautifully composed; the dancers did it full justice technically but were unable to give the real presence of nobility. The third scene seemed pretty dull. I do not care for the décor of any of it. Which leaves the two actual novelties: Massine's *Vienna — 1814* and *The New Yorker.* *Vienna* (Massine-Weber-Chaney) is unfortunate in every way. *The New Yorker* (Massine-Gershwin) I thought entertaining, with many excellent caricatures (Danilova, Semenoff, Yazvinsky, Chamié, Lauret). It's nothing you remember as ballet. Nor has Gershwin's nice Bronx nostalgia (in a corny orchestration) anything to do with what goes on.

Looking back on this season and the repertory as a whole, I thought the dancers seemed better than ever in technique and verve. But I am disappointed that Danilova and Massine are still the only artists who seem to have got over the limitation and the prejudice of being invariably juvenile. Maybe I do Rostova, Lauret, and Krassovska an injustice; and Markova — whose second act in *Giselle* was so miraculous last year — showed real warmth this time as Queen of Hearts. But I believe that she and Franklin and Eglevsky are greater dancers than they have dared to prove in their repertory this season. I missed in general the performer's passionate and uninhibited belief in his part, which can give to a dancer the most luminous theater presence in the world.

And in another way, too, the season discourages me. It looks as if the Monte Carlo were reviving not the Diaghilev tradition of intelligent dancing but the Petersburg tradition of attractive performers. The last score one could be eager to hear was *St. Francis,* which was also the last time Massine took a chance with novel choreography; and that happened long before the war. *Devil's Holiday,* also prewar, is still the last interesting décor or choreography to be shown, excluding the Dali backdrop, which a year ago looked lonely enough in the foolishness in front of it. That isn't much of a record for so pretentious an institution.

---

*Here and elsewhere, Denby continues a frequent confusion concerning the appropriate attribution of the choreography for *The Nutcracker.* In 1892, Marius Petipa prepared a detailed scenario for *The Nutcracker* but, because of illness, he turned over the creation of the choreography to his assistant Lev Ivanov.

The American contributions, so condescendingly promised, have been pathetically stupid, and seem to have been chosen with a kind of inverted snobbishness — commercial art for commercial art's sake. Commercial art is, as Cocteau said of New York's Jewish and Negro populations, the rich manure of our intellectual life; but to dump that manure on the stage in full view is not the proper function of Universal Art, Inc. Broadway does it more naturally. Our local artists may not have the easy sweep of the great Paris period, but at least they are in the real art business, and they are the people to go to if you do want American art — they have all there is, and there isn't any more. This season the only local contribution that can be mentioned among educated people is Irene Sharaff's — the pretty costumes for *Poker Game;* and they were bought up from a previous show.

Nothing risked, nothing gained. Still, at this date, it's hardly such a risk. Thomson, Copland, and Bowles have all been on Broadway. As for painters, there is Stuart Davis, who is a ballet natural; Cristofanetti, with his exquisite taste; last year there was a show of ballet sets by New Yorkers at Valentine's, and the sketch of Rudolph Burckhardt, for instance, was far better ballet than anything the company commissioned this year; I have also seen two good ones by Lorna McIvor. But the organization of the Monte Carlo, it appears, pays for the pretense of intelligence, not for its reality. It is unjust, I think, to blame Massine. But it begins to make a stuffy atmosphere that I have no great pleasure smelling.

Modern Music, November–December 1940

Graham's *El Penitente* and *Letter to the World;* Balanchine's *Balustrade*

Martha Graham has now presented to New York her two dance works *El Penitente* and *Letter to the World,* which are full of interest and full of poetry. *El Penitente* looks like a mystery play. A young woman and two young men come on the stage carrying a bright banner. Their manner is collected and cheerful. You watch them act out a play which tells that though man's duty to Christ is hard, his pain is relieved by a Divine Grace visiting him in turn as a virgin, a seductress, and a mother. Sometimes they use their banner as a little curtain from which emerge supernatural apparitions; once, they strip off the cloth, and the frame suddenly is a cross. When the play is over, the three performers add a little dance of jubiliation in their character as farmers. The style of gesture reminds you of New Mexican primitives — the votive pictures and *bultos*. It suggests — as they do — a double emotion of unlimited space all around and of solid weight at the center, there where you are. There is an apparent naïveté of timing and placing which is charming in detail and carried through with distinction. All this might be true either of a real Catholic piece or of an exquisite tour de force. But the dance seemed to have a poignancy other than Catholic and a reality beyond that of charm. The gestures are not made so much for their symbolic meaning as for their shape and rhythm as dancing; the dancing does not exploit its own limpidity, invention, and restraint but moves you by its dynamics as a whole, a personal meaning which makes the form real, which makes the religious style real too, but in an oblique way. Partly because the scenes between the man and the woman are placed downstage, partly because they are the most expressive, partly because it is Miss Graham who dances in them, it was not the relation of man to the Divine but the relation of a man and a woman that seemed the true subject. On me the effect was that of a tender and subtle love poem, a real love held nearly in suspense by a remote terror. It was as though Miss Graham had used the Spanish-Indian farmers' expression of religious faith as a metaphor for her own faith in the strangeness love can have. It is a sincere and touching and very attractive work, whether you choose to describe it in these terms or find better ones.

Letter to the World is a longer, richer, and more uneven piece. Much of it is not clear to me after seeing it once. But it contains such astonishing passages that one is quite willing to forgive the awkward parts it also has, and remember it as a masterpiece. *Letter to the World* is about Emily Dickinson. There is a legend that Emily Dickinson fell in love with a married minister, whom she saw once or twice and might have run away with. On the stage you see the garden door to a New England house and a garden bench. You see a woman move about as though she were dancing to the rustling in the trees and with the odd swirl of the breeze. She appears and disappears mysteriously, suddenly, or delayed, like a leaf, or a mouse, or a word. Other figures, too, appear, sometimes one, sometimes several. You see a tall and dominating woman in black, you see a crowd of stiff boys and girls, you see a solemn and violent man, and a boy who is ironic to the heroine and exuberant alone. The heroine herself appears at one point in a funny dress with trousers under it, and plays games with herself like a schoolgirl, even upsetting the bench and doing happy stunts on it. Much later, the man pays little attention to her, and in the end, according to the program, "out of the tragedy of her loss will be born the poet."

The passages for the other characters, except the "Death" dance for Jane Dudley and the "March" leaping dance for Merce Cunningham, did not seem very interesting; but many of those for Miss Graham are extraordinary for their devious grace, their unpredictable and fascinating current. Often they have a round buoyancy like that of waltzing, with poignant gradations of greater and less airiness. Her funny dance, "The Little Tippler," is a sort of polka of impish pranks, like Thoreau's squirrel — "all of his motions, even in the depths of the forest, imply spectators as much as those of a dancing girl." And altogether wonderful is her sitting on the bench toward the end, half turned from the audience and reflective in a pure, Victorian attitude, with a passionate heroism of repose that has all the amplitude of Isadora Duncan. The continuity of a lyric line, the contrast of dynamics (the sense that a gesture is not always a thrust but often a caress) — both of these are a new development in Miss Graham's way of composing, as is also the use of different kinds of projection (the sense that she dances at times more publicly for the audience, at times more privately for herself). From many points of view *Letter to the World,* no matter how uneven it appears at first sight, is a moving and noble work one cannot praise too highly.

Miss Graham's technique is as always impeccable. And she has three fine dancers with her, Jane Dudley, Erick Hawkins, and Merce Cunningham, who by having dance characters of their own throw her personal quality into relief. Cunningham, the least finished dancer of the three, delighted me by his humor, his buoyancy, and his wholeness of movement, a singleness of impulse like that which makes Negro dancers so graceful. The empty lightness of his upheld arms when he leaps I have never seen elsewhere. I did not think the music for *El Penitente* (Horst) had much character of its own; but I liked that of *Letter to the World* (Hunter Johnson), which, though modest and gentlemanly, contributes another personality to the piece.

Balanchine's *Balustrade,* with a Stravinsky score and a Tchelitchev décor, was a ballet in the Diaghilev tradition, a collaboration of first-class artists where one can expect to feel movement, look, and listen with the same degree of sensibility. In such collaborations you can see the poetic quality of dancing better, because all the different aspects of the spectacle have been made by people who believe in its poetry. When there is only one artist working on a show at a time, there is mostly something pathetic and provincial about the theater; one feels too sorry for him to pay undivided attention. At any rate it is a fact that such collaborations created the Diaghilev tradition: the tradition that dancing can be as poetic (or, if you prefer, as serious) as any other art; the tradition that painters and musicians should not give up their character when they work for dancers; the tradition that a dance evening is a natural pleasure for a civilized person.

Balustrade is danced to Stravinsky's Violin Concerto, music that seems to me easy to go along with from the rhythmic side. The choreography too is easy to go along with from the rhythmic side, as it is full of references to our usual show dancing, the kind you see anywhere from a burlesque to a Hollywood production number. I noticed two elements, or "motifs": the up-stretch on the downbeat, and one knee slipping across the other in a little gesture of conventional shame. The first, syncopated element Balanchine enlarges into the liveliest and lightest ensemble dances; the second element, one of gesture, he elaborates into a long acrobatic trio in which all sorts of "slippings across" are tried — of legs, of bodies, of arms — and this trio ends by a separation, the girl looking reproachful, the boys hanging their heads in shame. How strangely such a concrete moment tops the abstract acrobatics before it — a discontinuity in one's way of seeing that is bridged by the clearness of placing and the sureness of timing.

Balustrade is complex (or "contradictory") in this way as the eye adds up its successive phases. Its novelty is that it is not complex at each moment in the manner we are accustomed to. The individual dance role has almost no countermovement, no angular breaking of the dance impulse or direction. The impulse is allowed to flow out, so to speak, through the arms and legs, which delineate the dance figure lightly, as it were in passing — as they do in our show dancing. This is all something else than the "European" style of the thirties. There is in this new "undissonant," "undeformed," or "one at a time" way of dancing a kind of parallel relation to Miss Graham's new modern-school manner in *Letter to the World*. Once more, dancing, like any living art, has moved ahead of what we had come to think of as the modern style, and this time without even any manifestos to warn us.

I must add that in *Balustrade* the costumes are elegant but annoying. Though they have imagination and a sort of super-Hollywood pruriency, the materials are such that after the first minute or so they look like a wilted bunch of rags cutting the line of the body at the knee, obscuring the differentiation of steps, and messing up the dance. And the trio costumes look too publicly sexy; they take away from this erotic dance its mysterious juvenile modesty. Still, it was right of the management to take a first-rate painter for a work of this kind; an artist's mistake is infuriating, but not vulgar.

Modern Music, March–April 1941

Kurt Jooss; The Monte Carlo Ballet

The season opened with the Jooss Ballet, presenting eight or nine pieces by Jooss and one brand-new one by Agnes de Mille. First, Miss de Mille's *Drums Sound in Hackensack.* It is about New Amsterdam, the fur trade, how the cheated Indians found a Dutch girl in the jungles of Jersey, and what happened then. To show us New Amsterdam, Miss de Mille begins with a folk dance, adds a Puritan hop and a de Mille wiggle, and we all get the joke and smile easily. When she comes to the serious parts, terrors of the forest and Indian savagery, she invents some gestures as simple as those an earnest child would hit on. Again everybody gets the point and is perfectly satisfied to go on watching until something else happens. So the piece comes out a hit. The stage Indians, either woodenly noble or tomtomish, I liked especially. I like Miss de Mille's work in general. Though her heroines are inveterate wigglers, she has a real sense of how the body dances, she composes properly, and she has a gift of rhythm completely congenial to Americans.

Jooss's works, however, one looks at very seriously. They are on the plane of "masterworks." Jooss has a great reputation, too, as a leader in serious theater dancing and as a systematizer of modern technique. Just the same, watching the stage, what I saw was one dud after another. There is one exception — the famous first scene of his *Green Table.* This is brilliant and curiously different from all the rest: different in rhythm, style, humor, and theatrical punch.

The Jooss dancers are engaging, accurate, lively, and devoted executants, without mannerisms or bad manners, dancers by nature. They were fine for Miss de Mille. But when they dance the Jooss choreography, what do you see them do on the stage? Well, the best thing you see is a controlled, clear, wide movement in the arms. (And they can stop an arm gesture more neatly than most good dancers.) Their hands and necks are plain and good. The breast-bone is held high and the chest is open. This upper third of the body is excellent. But below it, the belly is dull, the buttocks heavy, the small of the back sags in. Where is the shining tautness across the groin, a glory of Western dancing? These people might as well be sitting down, as far as the expressiveness of their middle goes. And below, the leg gestures are forced and heavy. The leaps are high and strong, but they have only bounce, they don't soar (except one boy in *Old Vienna*); they don't hang in the air, either. (The low wide leaps are the interesting ones but get monotonous.) The feet in the air look thick. On the other hand these dancers land better from a leap than most ballet dancers. Does this add up to a satisfactory new norm of technique? It does not. Neither does it exhaust the possibilities of the modern school. Because the Jooss norm of the outward chest and inward middle is fixed, and modern technique demands that any portion can vary at will from outward to inward. It's a terrific demand, but it's the essence of widening the expressive range beyond that of classic ballet.

Or take the Jooss stylization of rhythm. I see an emphatic pound (this is, a gesture stopped and held). Then comes an unaccented moment (no gesture, change of position). Then comes another equally emphatic pound (a new gesture, stopped and held). This keeps up all evening. In the pit the music pounds down on the beat at the same moment the dancer pounds out his gesture. The effect is very dispiriting.

What happens is that there is a systematic alternation between emphatic and unemphatic movement, like that between beat and nonbeat in a bar. There is also an unusual continuousness about the time quality of the move-ment. Many people are dissatisfied with a kind of hoppitiness in classic ballet. They point out that there is a fraction of a second between steps, between arm positions, that goes dead in the way a harpsichord goes dead, but not an orchestra, or even a piano. Jooss has stretched a movement to fill the time space completely; he uses a pedal. It was Dalcroze who thirty years ago made us most conscious of this possibility in moving.

When a dancer makes his gesture coincide as closely as possible with the time length and time emphasis of musical rhythm, he is apt to be as pleased as a hen is who has laid an egg. He tells everybody "Look how musical I am," and everybody cackles back "Isn't he just the most musical thing!" Ra-tionally it seems odd to confuse the metrics of music with musicality. And also to assume that the metrics of dancing are identical with those of music. It strikes me that there is in fact an inherent disparity. The proportioning of time, as well as the proportioning of emphasis, between the stress and the follow-through of a single metric unit is much more regular in music than it is in movement. Apart from theory, in practice this kind of measured gesture draws attention to itself and away from the body as a whole. In practice, too, the dancer loses a certain surprise of attack, which is one of his characteristic rhythmic possibilities.

Well, in point of musicality, listen to the music Jooss uses. True, the dancers obey the metrics of music, but the music in its rhythmic development obeys beat by beat the rhythmic detail of the dance. The piece makes no musical sense. It is merely a cue sheet for the dancers. It sounds as if it kept up a continuous gabble about the mechanics of the steps. It's like a spoken commentary in a documentary film that names every object we see while we're looking at it. Music that can't make any decision on its own is functioning on a bare subsistence level, and it is apt to be as glum as that. Poor Frederic Cohen's voluble cue-sheets for Jooss are utterly depressing; they reminded me most of cafeteria soup gone sour. I don't think much of the musicality of a director who makes me listen to such poverty. If this is collaboration, it must be the Berlin-Vichy kind. I detest a dancer who is satisfied with it.

I don't go to the theater to see a servant problem solved. Jooss of course isn't the only choreographer who has music in to do the dirty work and keeps all the dignity for himself. Modern dancers have made the same error often enough in the past. They commission a new composer, but when the piece is played it has (like a poet's advertising copy) no character, it only has manner. For a while it was fun enough to listen to a new manner, and affix at least an ideological, a historical meaning. But the historical significance of style is a parlor game that gets tiresome. I wish all kinds of dancers wouild let us hear pieces of music old and new, and do, while they are played, whatever they like to. I wish they would put themselves on the spot in the presence of serious music. When the dancer acts serious and the music is trivial, he can't escape seeming petty and provincial. Anyway, in the theater I want the dancer to dance, the orchestra to make music, and the décor to be a stage picture. If these three don't come out in accord, I am angry but still interested. If only one of them is allowed to speak up, the production isn't big time.

But the issue of dance music has led me away from the subject of Jooss. Besides technique, rhythm, and the use of music, there are many other aspects to choreography. In the Jooss ballets I did not see any I cared for. He has systematized grouping so that diagonals, cubes, and spheres cut across each other by the dozen. But they look stupid because they have no relation to the size of the human figure on the stage. He has systematized the representational aspect of movement, with the result that every gesture can be translated so exactly into words, the dance might as well be a series of signals for deaf mutes. You imagine it would have the same meaning if performed by nondancers. The dancers add neatness, but they don't by dancing create the meaning, a meaning which undanced would not exist. Looking at it another way, all the gesture is on the same level of signification. The wonderful shift possible from pantomime to lyric (like a new dimension of spirit), or the shift as in Spanish dancing from standing around to taking the stage — all this, with all the rest in dancing that is tender and variable and real only the moment it happens, has been systematized away.

A systematization of modern dancing, like the literary adoption of the heroic couplet, makes a great deal of sense to dancers floundering between the arrogant academicism of the ballet on the one hand and the uncompromising private language of some studio dancers on the other. I remember fourteen years ago in Germany the attempt to establish a new academy, a new order, seemed of the greatest importance, and we all watched Jooss's gradual discoveries (for he was the leader of the movement) with delight. The results shown here this fall are well worth acrimonious theoretical dispute. But what I actually looked at on the stage was a stodgy, self-satisfied, and petty solemnity, pretending to be serious and, worse, significantly ethical.

Modern Music, November–December 1941

Ballet Theatre

The reorganized Ballet Theatre presented a season that was timid and on the musty side. Only one new feature was a real pleasure: the presence of Alicia Markova, the great English dancer. . . . Markova has appeared here before, but the more you see her the higher you value her. Seen merely as a virtuoso she is extraordinary; the adagio movements "bloom in space," the allegros "scintillate evenly," the leaps soar and subside, when lifted she looks fluid — well, in every department of classic technique she is flawless. And she has all those peculiarities of physical structure that ballet enthusiasts gloat about — like the overlong arms, the lateral overmobility in the hip joint, the outward set of the shin, and of course the fabulously high arch — all of which add to the poignancy of the gesture because you seem to be seeing what it is impossible to do. Musically too she is a virtuoso, even to dancing an imperceptible fraction ahead of or behind the beat, for the special attack or pathos it gives to dancing. And she holds your eye on her. Not that she is sexy; she is very proper, but you watch her as intently as if you were perturbed.

Markova has power too as an actress. She alters her style to characterize her part, even to giving her virtuosity no special play. A few details of characterization, such as Giselle's mad dance, I do not agree with; but it is a disagreement of taste, not of principle. For she builds and holds a scene as steadily as an actor like Evans. And there is something more to it than the proper control. She does not make the part a vehicle for her own glamour. She takes it disinterestedly. And what you see is not Markova as Giselle, but Giselle in the figure of Markova. In this unself-consciousness, so to speak, her dancing becomes serious and sincere poetry. When you watch her, the whole body shows that unpredictable burning edge of movement that the living images of real life have, which continue so mysteriously to live inside our hearts, and out of whose inexhaustible light art is made. It is an equivalent of the absorbing "living line" in poetry and drawing. Out of hundreds of good dancers of all nationalities, there have been perhaps a dozen in whose dancing I have seen it continue as the characteristic of the whole body for minutes at a time.

The other star ballerina, also new to the Ballet Theatre, is the sumptuous Baronova, who used to be a very fine dancer indeed. Of her present style I can find nothing good to say. She hams with a heartlessness that is frightening. She ogles, flounces, capers, and cuddles, jumps, turns, and stands, slapping down each effect like a virago operating a cash register. She seems to want the title of "Miss Ironpants." I hope so intelligent a dancer as she is will quickly get over this phase, or else team up with the Three Stooges, where her present manner properly belongs.

Isadora Reconsidered; Graham's *Punch and the Judy* Revisited

The recital of Maria Theresa (one of the original Duncan dancers), who
danced several of Isadora's Chopin pieces, was interesting because it brought
up again some of the technical procedures of Isadora: the large plain phrases
in which a single gesture is carried about the stage; the large, clear contrast
between up and down, forward and back; and the way the body seems to yield
to the music and still is not passively "carried" by it, but carries itself even
while it yields. It seems to me the effect of these dances, technically speaking,
comes from the kind of support the gesture has, rather than from the interest
of each new gesture. The gesture in itself, in the softness with which it begins,
in the shape it takes and its accentual rhythm, is monotonous enough; but the
support it has is a kind of invention. The support seems continuously improvised and always active, always a little stronger than the gesture in energy
and just ahead of it in time. Such an accurate proportioning of energy, as it
decreases from a central impulse in the torso through the joints to the extremities, gives the limbs an especial lightness; the hands, head, and feet an
attractive, as if careless, bearing. It also gives the observer's eye a definite
center from which to appreciate the body movement as a whole, and a feeling
of following the dance continuously. It requires a technique on the dancer's
part, and no easy one. Just remember how even good dancers confuse your
attention by jerking your eye from one detail to another; how often even good
dancers give you the sense that their impulse to move operates by fits and
starts; how often they seem to be dancing now and then during their number
and the rest of the time merely executing according to plan. It struck me that
in the Duncan method the dynamics of movement (the flow and current of the
impulse) becomes intentionally the most carefully controlled and the most
expressive aspect of dancing. In ballet this aspect is not systematically taught;
it is left individual and instinctive. The modern-school method, from Mary
Wigman on, has tried to analyze dynamic control; but it replaced the Duncan
gesture with an infinitely more varied kind, and in consequence the problem
of making the dance coherent became far more difficult to resolve, technically. I am speaking here of technique in its gymnastic aspect; the Duncan
coherence, which derives from the coherence of the music you hear as you
watch, and the "modern" coherence, derived from the nondance ideas you
are invited to recall while watching — these I am not now considering.

I am less convinced than I was ten years ago that classroom instruction in dynamics is much use to the dancer. A panacea against absurdity, as many hoped it would be, it certainly has not proved; and even with Duncan dancers, her own method did not turn out to be foolproof. But I think Isadora's technical approach to dancing (I mean distinct from her unique greatness as a dancer) is an interesting subject to clarify. It seems to me nonsense to imagine that she could have had so sweeping a success with highly perceptive audiences, could have created so disinterested an enthusiasm by numbers that she performed over and over, without (as many affirm) having a technique. The photographs seem to me not to show very much, but in several one notices a neck and shoulder line that is strikingly plastic, strikingly aware of three-dimensional expression. On her last American tour I watched a program from up in the Carnegie Hall gallery, from where she looked, all alone on the stage and facing the full blare of a Wagnerian orchestra, very small indeed. But the slow parts of her Venusberg dance and her Siegfried Funeral March remain in memory two of the very greatest effects I have seen; I can still feel their grandeur and their force.

Incidentally, when you observe the early Chopin numbers of Isadora's which Maria Theresa now has revived, you get to thinking that Fokine's *Sylphides* (also to Chopin) is hardly at all characteristic of the dancing of Taglioni and Grisi, as often supposed, but instead is full of Duncanisms. I mean in the "sensitiveness" of its extended phrases; in the stress it gives to contrasts in space — downward, upward, forward, backward; in the yielding quality of many arm gestures and back bends. These last look correct as ports de bras and renversés, but the timing is unclassical. And maybe too the rose-petal hands, the loosely drooping fingers that Fokine or Nijinsky invented for the *Spectre,* were suggested by a gesture of Isadora's. It is of course equally true that the relaxedness of her manner superimposed on the solid leg and hip rigor of ballet created a very different effect from hers: an effect of inherent contradiction, a poignant sense of perversity that has gone to the heart of most civilized people during the last thirty years. . . .

At the first view I was puzzled by the emotional effect of *Punch and the Judy* (Graham) — what the piece really means. So I am coming back to it again, now I have seen it a second time: I leave you to judge, by comparing your own impressions with mine, whether I get it this time either.

The program says it is a domestic comedy. The dance opens with some silly words and foolish ornamental overlarge gestures by three unsympathetic ladies, billed as the Three Fates. Then you see a young wife waking up with a headache. Her husband on the other hand wakes up at the top of his form. You get the situation, the joke of the ensuing friendly roughhouse. You think it's a comedy. You see too that the characters move in marionette style: they are Punch and the Judy. But you notice that their movement has not merely a puppet style (familiar in dancing, and rather a bore); it also seems real human movement, with a motor force not outside but within the torso. You admire the subtle adjustment of the two opposite styles. You admire how clearly you can follow the "meaning" of the separate gestures, as in a pantomime, and how at the same time these gestures in cut, contrast, and rhythm form a dance sequence. Nor do the gestures repeat themselves, or mark time, or utilize clichés; they are packed with inventive detail. And a kind of brutal plainness in the stage spacing is very deftly suggested.

As the story continues, you notice that the other characters are less real than the protagonists; they are straight puppets. Their dances amuse you as gags, but they don't have any inner drive of their own. Even the Three Fates, though they dance witty parodies of decorative movement, don't become a dynamic factor. The Power of Dreams, which appears as Pegasus, has a mysterious airiness in dancing, but the influence remains remote and brief and plays an ornamental and not a dramatic part. The two central characters are left with only unreal puppet foils. They themselves, part puppet, part human, never can act toward the others humanly. I had hoped till the end that at least in conflict with each other they would break through their own stylization, become completely human, and that then the emotion would open up, become a real conflict with a real resolution. It did not happen. Their relation to one another is unchanged after they have gone through all their puppet antics. And the futility of the action is expressed in the last spoken words: "Shall we begin again?"

It is then that you realize the action you watched was not as aboveboard as you at first imagined. Was there a kind of slyness, the way you were lured on to a pointless result? No, you were warned by the unpleasant opening. But now the jokes have a bitter taste, when you find they were not real people who made them. It has been a puppet story; not a drama but a monologue. The gags were the author's wisecracks at life, and she didn't give life a chance to answer back. You expected to see the humor of man and wife living together, but what you have seen is the folly of it, the pointless folly. The folly might have found a point if it had had the contrast of sentiment, or if it had had the added force of fury to drive it into the vastness of the unconscious, where folly is at home. But the point this work gives folly is a different one; it is the very care of its workmanship and execution. It is a high-class folly. And so I found the piece easy to watch and hard to take. I found it not pleasant or open, but in its peculiar prejudice serious and interesting.

Modern Music, March–April 1942

Tudor's Dark Elegies; Swan Lake

Dark Elegies, danced to Mahler's *Kindertotenlieder,* is a work in which pauses, a naive solemnity, and the simplest of dance figures give a clear effect of pathos. The dance style is that of Northeast European folk dances; the style of expression is like the odd stiffness of English morris dancers. The relation of dance rhythm to the music, the timing of the accents, the spacing of the figures — these are, as always with Tudor, of an impeccable elegance and clarity.

It is true that the willful spareness of the movement — as if it were dragged out of the dancers — stands in contrast to the florid emotionalism of the music. And both dance and orchestra are far from the sweet domestic note that the words of the songs have. But none of this lessens the effect of the piece on the stage. It was another well-deserved triumph for Tudor. I thought the dancing of Miriam Golden and Hugh Laing especially fine, but the entire company danced, as this piece can only be danced, with oneness of feeling.

Swan Lake, opening the program, was a completely magnificent performance of one of the most poetic of stage works. This ballet makes little enough sense when done as a production number. It makes the best of sense if the three central figures can convey that the Swan Queen is really enchanted, the Prince really in love with her, and his Friend really his friend. Then the ballet turns out to be a tender and true poem about love where love is impossible; about the beautifully glittering ambiguity that is at the core of Victorian romanticism.

Last night's performance was perfect from this poetic aspect, as well of course as from the technical one. Markova's phrasing of a dance is a joy of intelligence. As an actress, she was by turns delicate as a pet bird, scintillating, trustful, and a girl imprisoned in a spell. Eglevsky was tender and modest and manly. His gesture of despair to his Friend in the pause in the midst of the central love duet was noble and true. In fact the brief pantomimic scenes last night between the Prince and the Swan Queen were of an extraordinary limpidity. The music to these moments was also exceptionally clear and it turns out to be very interesting.

New York Herald Tribune, Oct. 30, 1942

Massine's *Aleko*

The one big-time novelty of the Ballet Theatre is Massine's *Aleko.* It has the only Paris School décor of the season, by Chagall, and besides giving the satisfaction and having the fine presence of a great painter's work, it is also beautifully executed. The ballet is Massine's finest since *Fantastic Symphony.* It has lots of his expert stylization of local color (in this case, Russian gypsies and peasants), lots of his stylized dance-pantomime, lots of his ballet counterpoint (different dancers doing different things at the same time). It has as prize plum a long last scene with the breathless melodramatic thriller rush that Massine does better than anyone else. And it even has an admiring bow or two in the direction of Tudor choreography. For me, however, it has also plenty of the qualities I dislike in Massine's work — an agitation that seems senseless, a piling up of scraps of movement and bits of character like so much junk from Woolworth's, patterns but no room for them, accent and meter but no rhythm and flower of phrase. The duets are bizarre without intimacy; the man has to jerk from one position to another by turning his back awkwardly on his partner. For me *Aleko* has a real subject only in its décor; the dance is just a hectic show, and whenever it slows down it goes flat. Well, the public at any rate loves the hubbub of it, and it loves the junk. Anyone can very well love all the dancers of it; they work as hard as possible, and everyone dances his or her best.

Modern Music, November–December 1942

Balanchine and Tchaikovsky: *Ballet Imperial*

Ballet Imperial (Balanchine-Tchaikovsky-Doboujinsky; danced by and created in 1941 for Kirstein's American Ballet) was the single full-length ballet offered at the New Opera and it is the most brilliant ballet of the season. In intention it is a homage to the Petersburg ballet style, the peculiarly sincere grand manner which the Imperial Ballet School and Petipa evolved. We know the style here from the choreography of *Swan Lake, Aurora's Wedding,* and *Nutcracker,* even of *Coppélia,* though all of them have been patched out; we know it from glimpses of grandeur in the dancing of the Russian-trained ballerinas; from photographs, especially of the young Pavlova and the young Nijinsky; and from the legend that persists and which is distinct from the Diaghilev legend. Balanchine of course knows it thoroughly from having been trained in the actual school. But even with little knowledge, homage to this manner is natural for a dance lover. The Petersburg style was the one that vigorously continued our whole tradition of serious dancing during the increasing barbarism of 1850–1900. It was also the solid foundation for the extraordinary glory of ballet in the Diaghilev era, a glory which still pays the expenses of our ballet companies. And there is another attraction toward it, more compelling and more personal: it is the force of the mysteriously poignant images of the style — an expressive force which keeps returning them to the mind. And they so return, even after the context of them is gone and their outline altered, marked among other images by their singularity of expression.

Such images spontaneously arising are *Ballet Imperial*'s theme. It does not reproduce the period as a decorator would. You don't find the fairy-tale plot, the swans, the dance variations strung on a story. Instead there is a backdrop that makes you think of the concrete St. Petersburg, and in front of that a brand-new ballet with lots of novel steps. Actually you see a stage full of dancers who, say, arbitrarily disappear, who reappear in peculiarly rigid formations that instantly dissolve, or else stop and stand immobile. You see the vivacity of the star set over sharply against the grand pose of the ensemble, or else the solo dancer lost and still while the full company hastens happily. You watch the solo partners discover each other, two individuals in the noncommittal cheerful society of the company; you follow their touching individual response. And afterward you see them alter their natures from having been tender personages to being star performers, an inexplicable duplicity that leads to no heartbreak but culminates instead in the general dazzle of a virtuoso finale for everybody all over the stage at once. So described, *Ballet Imperial* might be a typical Petersburg ballet. But the fact is that each of these typical effects is arrived at by so novel a technical procedure that it comes as a surprise. We feel the effect first, we recognize the feeling, and from that we remember the old effect. One might say the new effect is as fresh as that of the Petersburg ballet was in its own time. Or that the past and the present seem to happen at the same time, as they do in the drama of personal memory.

As dancing, *Ballet Imperial* is full of freshness. In point of form, it is an abstract ballet interpreting Tchaikovsky's Second Piano Concerto. Interpretive dance reveals one of the structural aspects of a piece of music — Fokine is apt to show how the periods sit, Massine goes for the tangle of musical motives. Balanchine draws our attention to the expressive flow under the syntax, and we have a vivid sense of the free musical animation. I was delighted in *Ballet Imperial* at how the concerto, a showpiece I had thought forced, came to life and sounded fresh and direct. The dance focuses the interest like a good musician's playing: certain moments get an imperceptible emphasis, a long passage is taken in at a swoop, another is subdivided; and thanks to a happy interpretation the piece comes out as good as new.

In dance steps and dance figures Balanchine has always been inventive. But most people think of his choreography as full of specifically poignant detail — quick thrusts backward and sideways, odd pauses, hobbled leaps, extraordinary group poses, indecently upside-down lifts. Most of us recall how his dancers have looked torn in three directions at once, and so were we, and it was wonderful. *Ballet Imperial* has a certain oddness, but it isn't in that earlier manner in the least. It does have a slow middle section, a very beautiful one (it's in a free style of ballet movement derived from classic pantomime), which has for sentiment the pathos of a love story. A boy and girl find each other, they misunderstand, become reconciled, and lose one another. The tone is intimate. But there is not one indecent image or lift. The gestures are easy, the figures simple. And at the end the movement is brushed away, and the solitary "frustrated" emotion left in the air is very simply succeeded by a general comradely liveliness of tone in the next section, a long finale which like the long opening section has no pathos at all.

And in the slow pantomime part as well as in the rapid other two parts one comes to notice how the detail of gesture does not run counter to the main line of movement. It is not an accent, it does not draw attention to itself. The arms are easy, the dance is lighter, faster, more positive, presents itself more openly. The dance figures throughout are readily grasped. Balanchine maintains interest by an extraordinary flickering rapidity of dance steps and quick shift of dance figures. I found the speed, perhaps because it is still unfamiliar, at times confusing; but the positive style was unexpected and it had a pleasantly fresh aroma. And the brief solos in the last section reminded me of the bold large manner Petipa seems to have had, where the dance stands out so plain you see it right off with delight and you don't stop to think of the choreographer.

I was sorry the ensemble performing *Ballet Imperial* had the weakness that young dancers always show — an insufficient power of projection. It is hard to feel them if you watch from the back of the house. Looking at this question in another way, in inexperienced dancers the movement never quite comes to rest, so that the dynamic scale is a bit blurred, and the movement does not lift to its flower, shine, and subside completely, leaving a completed image in the mind. This is rhythm in dancing (as distinct from musical rhythm) and it is what gives to dancing the air of style. It is a quality of expression independent of choreographic or virtuoso effects (or of characterization) and much more communicative than they are. To have it a dancer must be unusually sturdy and self-possessed. But as *Ballet Imperial* progresses, the dancers do give you a sense of dance style. You begin to feel it in the air. You see it as vivacity and then you recognize that the freshness of movement comes from their personal animation. And you realize in the end how badly you missed, in the celebrated ensembles at the Met this fall, an air of intelligence that the sense of style gives to dancing. I remember too that dancers Balanchine rehearses, whether stars or students, always tend to show their natural dance intelligence. They have an indefinable grace in dancing that seems to come naturally to them, that seems extemporaneous. They look not so much like professionals but like boys and girls who are dancing.

Balanchine has an extraordinary gift for bringing performers to life on their own personal terms, so that the unconscious grace that is in each one of them can shine out in the work they do, giving it the momentary and mortal expression of beauty. The plan of a choreography is a great pleasure. But it is the brilliancy of young dancers entirely in the present, the unique liveliness of each dancer caught entirely in the present instant that at once, we all know it, will be past and irretrievable forever — it is this clear sharp sense of our own natural way of living that makes a moment of ballet speak to the complete consciousness that makes choreography look beautiful. As Balanchine's has again and again.

Modern Music, January–February 1943

Notes on Nijinsky Photographs

Looking at the photographs of Nijinsky, one is struck by his expressive neck. It is an unusually thick and long neck. But its expressivity lies in its clear lift from the trunk, like a powerful thrust. The shoulders are not square, but slope downward; and so they leave the neck easily free, and the eye follows their silhouette down the arms with the sense of a line extraordinarily extended into space, as in a picture by Cézanne or Raphael. The head therefore, at the other end of this unusual extension, poised up in the air, gains an astonishing distinctness, and the tilt of it, even with no muscular accentuation, becomes of unusual interest. Nijinsky tilts his head lightly from the topmost joint, keeping this joint mobile against the upright thrust of the other vertebrae. He does not bend the neck back as some contemporary ballet dancers do. Seen from the side or the rear, the upward line of his back continues straight into the uprightness of the neck, like the neck of a Maillol statue. But Nijinsky alters his neck to suit a character role. The change is striking in the *Schéhéra-zade* pictures — and Mr. Van Vechten, who saw him dance the part, describes him as a "head-wagging, simian creature." Another variation is that for *Petrouchka,* where the shoulders are raised square to break the continuity of the silhouette; to make the arms dangle as a separate entity, and make the head independently wobbly as a puppet's is, on no neck to speak of. The head here does not sum up or direct the action of the body; it seems to have only a minor, a pathetic function. But it bobs too nonsensically to be humanly pitiful. In the role of the Faun the shoulders are slightly lifted when the Faun becomes dimly aware of his own emotion; but the neck is held up firmly and candidly against the shoulder movement (which would normally press the neck to a forward slant); and so the silhouette is kept self-contained and the figure keeps its dignity. Notice, too, the neck in the reclining position of the Faun. Another poignant duplicity of emotion is expressed by the head, neck, and shoulder line of the *Jeux* photographs — the neck rising against lifted shoulders and also bent sideways against a countertilt of the head. The hero in *Jeux* seems to meet pathos with human nobility — not as the Faun does, with animal dignity.

Looking in these photographs farther along the figure, at the arms in particular, one is struck by their lightness, by the way in which they seem to be suspended in space. Especially in the pictures from *Pavillon* and from *Spectre,* they are not so much placed correctly, or advantageously, or illustratively;

rather they seem to flow out unconsciously from the moving trunk, a part of the fullness of its intention. They are pivoted, not lifted, from the shoulder or shoulder blade; their force — like the neck's — comes from the full strength of the back. And so they lead the eye more strongly back to the trunk than out beyond their reach into space. Even when they point, one is conscious of the force pointing quite as much as the object pointed at. To make a grammatical metaphor, the relation of subject to object is kept clear. This is not so simple in movement as a layman might think. A similar clarification of subject and object struck me in the bullfighting of Belmonte. His own body was constantly the subject of his motions, the bull the object. With other fighters, one often had the impression that not they personally but their cloth was the subject that determined a fight. As a cloth is a dead thing, it can only be decorative, and the bull edged into the position of the subject: and the distinctness of the torero's drama was blurred. Nijinsky gives an effect in his arm gesture of himself remaining at the center of space, a strength of voluntary limitation related, in a way, to that of Spanish dance gesture. (This is what makes a dancer's arms look like a man's instead of a boy's.)

An actual "object" to a dancer's "subject" is his partner. In dancing with a partner there is a difference between self-effacement and courtesy. Nijinsky in his pictures is a model of courtesy. The firmness of support he gives his partner is complete. He stands straight enough for two. His expression toward her is intense — in *Giselle* it expresses a supernatural relation, in *Pavillon* one of admiration, in *Faun* one of desire, in *Spectre* one of tenderness — and what a supporting arm that is in *Spectre,* as long and as strong as two. But he observes as well an exact personal remoteness, he shows clearly the fact they are separate bodies. He makes a drama of their nearness in space. And in his own choreography — in *Faun* — the space between the figures becomes a firm body of air, a lucid statement of relationship, in the way intervening space does in the modern academy of Cézanne, Seurat, and Picasso.

One is struck by the massiveness of his arms. This quality also leads the eye back to the trunk, as in a Michelangelo figure. But it further gives to their graceful poses an amplitude of strength that keeps them from looking innocuous or decorative. In particular in the Narcissus pose the savage force of the arms and legs makes credible that the hero's narcissism was not vanity, but an instinct that killed him, like an act of God. In the case of *Spectre,* the power of the arms makes their tendril-like bendings as natural as curvings are in a powerful world of young desire, while weaker and more charming arms might suggest an effeminate or saccharine coyness. There is indeed nothing effeminate in these gestures; there is far too much force in them.

It is interesting to try oneself to assume the poses on the pictures, beginning with arms, shoulders, neck, and head. The flowing line they have is deceptive. It is an unbelievable strain to hold them. The plastic relationships turn out to be extremely complex. As the painter de Kooning, who knows the photographs well and many of whose ideas I am using in these notes, remarked: Nijinsky does just the opposite of what the body would naturally do. The plastic sense is similar to that of Michelangelo and Raphael. One might say that the grace of them is not derived from avoiding strain, as a layman might think, but from the heightened intelligibility of the plastic relationships. It is an instinct for countermovement so rich and so fully expressed, it is unique, though the plastic theory of countermovement is inherent in ballet technique.

Nijinsky's plastic vitality animates the poses derived from dances by Petipa or Fokine. It shines out, too, if one compares his pictures with those of other dancers in the same parts. This aspect of his genius appears to me one basis for his choreographic style, which specifies sharply plastic effects in dancing — and which in this sense is related both to Isadora and to the moderns. Unfortunately the dancers who now take the role of the Faun do not have sufficient plastic discipline to make clear the intentions of the dance.

From the photographs one can see that the present dancers of *Faun* have not even learned Nijinsky's stance. Nijinsky not only squares his shoulders far less, but also frequently not at all. He does not pull in his stomach and lift his thorax. Neither in shoulders nor chest does he exhibit his figure. His stomach has more expression than his chest. In fact, looking at his trunk, one notices a similar tendency to flat-chestedness (I mean in the stance, not in the anatomy) in all the pictures. It is, I believe, a Petersburg trait, and shared independently by Isadora and Martha Graham. In these photographs, at any rate, the expression does not come from the chest; it comes from below the chest, and flows up through it from below. The thorax, so to speak passively, is not only pulled at the top up and back; at the bottom and from the side it is also pulled down and back. Its physical function is that of completing the circuit of muscles that holds the pelvis in relation to the spine. And it is this relation that gives the dancer his balance. Balance (or aplomb, in ballet) is the crux of technique. If you want to see how good a dancer is, look at his stomach. If he is sure of himself there, if he is so strong there that he can present himself frankly, he (or she) can begin to dance expressively. (I say stomach because the stomach usually faces the audience; one might say waist, groin, or pelvic region.)

In looking at Nijinsky pictures, one is struck by the upright tautness about the hips. His waist is broad and powerful. You can see it clearly in the Harlequin pictures. If he is posing on one leg, there is no sense of shifted weight, and as little if he seems to be bending to the side or forward. The effort this means may be compared to lifting a table by one leg and keeping the top horizontal. The center of gravity in the table, and similarly that of his body, has not been shifted. The delicacy with which he cantilevers the weight actually displaced keeps the firmness from being rigidity. I think it is in looking at his waist that one can see best the technical aspect of his instinct for concentrating the origin of movement so that all of it relates to a clear center which is not altered. He keeps the multiplicity, the diffusion which movement has, intelligible by not allowing any doubt as to where the center is. When he moves he does not blur the center of weight in his body; one feels it as clearly as if he were still standing at rest; one can follow its course clearly as it floats about the stage through the dance. And so the motion he makes looks controlled and voluntary and reliable. I imagine it is this constant sense of balance that gave his dancing the unbroken continuity and flow through all the steps and leaps and rests from beginning to end that critics marveled at.

Incidentally, their remarks of this kind also point to an extraordinary accuracy in his musical timing. For to make the continuity rhythmic as he did, he must have had an unerring instinct at which moment to attack a movement, so that the entire sequence of it would flow as continuously and transform itself into the next motion as securely as did the accompanying sound. To speak of him as unmusical, with no sense of rhythm, as Stravinsky has, is therefore an impropriety that is due to a confusion of meaning in the word "rhythm." The choreography of *Faun* proves that Nijinsky's natural musical intelligence was of the highest order. For this was the first ballet choreography set clearly not to the measures and periods, but to the expressive flow of the music, to its musical sense. You need only compare *Faun*'s assurance in this respect to the awkwardness musically of Fokine's second scene in *Petrouchka*, the score of which invites the same sort of understanding. But this is not in the photographs.

Nijinsky does not dance from his feet; he dances from his pelvis. The legs do not show off. They have no ornamental pose. Even in his own choreography, though the leg gestures are "composed," they are not treated as pictorial possibilities. They retain their weight. They tell where the body goes and how. But they don't lead it. They are, however, completely expressive in this role; and the thighs in the *Spectre* picture with Karsavina are as full of tenderness as another dancer's face. It is noticeable, too, that Nijinsky's legs are not especially turned out, and a similar moderate en dehors seems to be the rule in the Petersburg male dancers of Nijinsky's generation. But the parallel feet in *Narcisse* and *Faun,* and the pigeon toes in *Tyl* are not a willful contradiction of the academic principle for the sake of something new. They can, it seems to me, be properly understood only by a turned-out dancer, as Nijinsky himself clearly was. For the strain of keeping the pelvis in the position the ballet dancer holds it in for balance is much greater with parallel or turned-in feet (which contradicts the outward twist of the thigh); and this strain gives a new plastic dimension to the legs and feet, if it is carried through as forcefully as Nijinsky does. I am interested, too, to notice that in standing Nijinsky does not press his weight mostly on the ball of the big toe, but grips the floor with the entire surface of the foot.

I have neglected to mention the hands, which are alive and simple, with more expression placed in the wrist than in the fingers. They are not at all "Italian," and are full of variety without an emphasis on sensitivity. The hands in *Spectre* are celebrated, and remind one of the hands in Picassos ten years later. I am also very moved by the uplifted, half-unclenched hands in the *Jeux* picture, as mysterious as breathing in sleep. One can see, too, that in *Petrouchka* the hands are black-mittened, not white-mittened as now; the new costume makes the dance against the black wall in the second scene a foolish hand dance, instead of a dance of a whole figure, as intended.

The manner in which Nijinsky's face changes from role to role is immediately striking. It is enhanced by makeup, but not created by it. In fact, a friend pointed out that the only role in which one recognizes Nijinsky's civilian face is that of Petrouchka, where he is most heavily made up. There is no mystery about such transformability. People don't usually realize how much any face changes in the course of a day, and how often it is unrecognizable for an instant or two. Nijinsky seems to have controlled the variability a face has. The same metamorphosis is obvious in his body. The Specter, for instance, has no age or sex, the Faun is adolescent, the hero of *Jeux* has a body full-grown and experienced. Tyl can either be boy or man. The Slave in

Schéhérazade is fat, the Specter is thin. It does not look like the same body. One can say that in this sense there is no exhibitionism in Nijinsky's photographs. He is never showing you himself, or an interpretation of himself. He is never vain of what he is showing you. The audience does not see him as a professional dancer, or as a professional charmer. He disappears completely, and instead there is an imaginary being in his place. Like a classic artist, he remains detached, unseen, unmoved, uninterested. Looking at him, one is in an imaginary world, entire and very clear; and one's emotions are not directed at their material objects, but at their imaginary satisfactions. As he said himself, he danced with love.

To sum up, Nijinsky in his photographs shows us the style of a classic artist. The emotion he projects, the character he projects, is not communicated as his own, but as one that exists independently of himself, in the objective world. Similarly his plastic sense suggests neither a private yearning into an infinity of space nor a private shutting out of surrounding relationships, both of them legitimate romantic attitudes. The weight he gives his own body, the center which he gives his plastic motions, strikes a balance with the urge and rapidity of leaps and displacements. It strikes a balance between the role he dances and the roles of his partners. The distinction of place makes the space look real, the distinction of persons makes the drama real. And for the sake of this clarification he characterizes (or mimes, one might say) even such a conventional ornamental show-off, or "pure dance," part as that in *Pavillon*. On the other hand, the awkward heaviness that *Faun, Sacre,* and *Jeux* exhibited, and that was emphasized by their angular precision, was not, I believe, an anticlassic innovation. It was an effort to make the dance more positive, to make clearer still the center of gravity of a movement, so that its extent, its force, its direction, its elevation can be appreciated not incidentally merely, but integrally as drama. He not only extended the plastic range in dancing, but clarified it. And this is the way to give meaning to dancing — not secondhand literary meaning, but direct meaning. Nijinsky's latest intentions of "circular movement" and the improvisational quality *Tyl* seems to have had are probably a normal development of his sense of motion in relation to a point of repose — a motion that grew more animated and diverse as his instinct became more exercised. (An evolution not wholly dissimilar can be followed in Miss Graham's work, for instance.) And I consider the following remark he made to be indicative of the direction of his instinct: "La grâce, le charme, le joli sont rangés tout autour du point central qu'est le beau. C'est pour le beau que je travaille [The graceful, the charming, the attractive are all arranged around a central point, which is the beautiful. It is for the beautiful that I strive]." I do not see anything in these pictures that would lead one to suppose that Nijinsky's subsequent insanity cast any premonitory shadow on his phenomenally luminous dance intelligence.

In their stillness Nijinsky's pictures have more vitality than the dances they remind us of as we now see them on the stage. They remain to show us what dancing can be, and what the spectator and the dancer each aspire to, and hold to be a fair standard of art. I think they give the discouraged dance lover faith in dancing as a serious human activity. As Mr. Van Vechten wrote after seeing him in 1916: "His dancing has the unbroken quality of music, the balance of great painting, the meaning of fine literature, and the emotion inherent in all these arts."

Dance Index, March 1943

Markova's Dance Rhythm; Tudor's *Romeo and Juliet*

The great event of any Ballet Theatre season is the dancing of Markova. And this season she danced even more wonderfully than before. She appeared night after night, and even in two ballets on the same program. Once the papers said she had fainted after the performance. There is only one of her. I very much hope she is gratefully taken care of and prevented from injurious overwork.

When she dances, everybody seems to understand as if by sympathy everything she does. And yet her modesty is the very opposite of the Broadway and Hollywood emphasis we are used to. A Russian girl I know who works in a defense plant brought along her whole swing shift one Sunday into standing room. They had never seen ballet, and they unanimously fell in love with Markova. Markova has the authority of a star, but her glamour comes from what the English so well call a genuine spiritual refinement.

Watching her critically in Petipa's *Swan Lake,* in Fokine's *Sylphides,* in Massine's *Aleko,* or in Tudor's novelty, *Romeo and Juliet,* I am constantly astonished how she makes each of these very different styles completely intelligible in its own terms. None looks old-fashioned or newfangled. Each makes straight sense. Her new Juliet for instance is extraordinary. One doesn't think of it as Markova in a Tudor part; you see only Juliet. She is like no girl one has ever seen before, and she is completely real. One doesn't take one's eyes off her, and one doesn't forget a single move. It doesn't occur to you that she is dancing for an audience, she is so quiet. Juliet doesn't try to move you. She appears, she lives her life, and dies.

One of the qualities that strikes me more and more in Markova's dancing is her dance rhythm. Anybody who has been to the Savoy Ballroom knows what rhythm in dancing is. But once you get away from there and start watching the art of stage dancing, you find rhythm very rarely. You find many beautiful things — exact control, intelligence, energy, variety, expression — but they aren't quite the same thing as rhythm. Of course rhythm in art dancing is not so simple as in the Savoy "folk" form. But you recognize it wherever you find it. And as anybody can hear that Landowska has rhythm, so anybody can see that Markova has it.

Markova's rhythm is not only due to her remarkable freedom in attacking her steps a hair's breadth before or after the beat, a freedom in which she shows a perfect musical instinct. I think one gets closer to it by noticing her phrasing. And what we speak of as Negro rhythm is perfection of phrasing in a very short dance phrase. What strikes me equally about their two-beat phrases and her very long ones is how clearly each separate phrase is completed. It is perfectly clear when the phrase rises, and when it has spent itself. I feel the impulse has been completed, because I have seen the movement change in speed, and in weight. (In the lindy the thrust is hard and quick, but the finish — or recovery — of the step is light and seems even retarded; in Markova's incomparable *Sylphides* phrases she prepares during five or six steps with a gentle, uniform downward martellato for one slow, expressive, and protracted upward movement in her arms.) In musical terms there is a rubato within the phrase, corresponding to the way the balance of the body is first strained, then is restored.

Markova's way of dancing adds a peculiar quality to a ballet by Tudor. Other dancers can make his dramatic intentions clear. They show that each of his gestures carries a meaning: a nuance of emotion, of character, of social standing. They show his precision of timing and placing, so that one appreciates his extraordinary genius for visual rhythms on the stage. They are personally self-effacing, and give a thrilling intensity to the drama he intended. But Tudor's style includes many hampered movements, slow-motion effects, sudden spurts of allegro arrested incomplete, arm tensions straining into space, pelvic displacements, and shifts of carriage. They are fascinating effects. On the other hand I notice that in execution the movement looks forced. The dancers have trouble with their balance, they are apt to look laborious and lose their spring. Perhaps Tudor meant the dance to look off balance, but it also looks airless. Now I see that Markova can sense and can show the dance rhythm that underlies his visual phrases. She finds their point of rest. She is easily equal to his dramatic meaning and passion, but she also gives his drama the buoyancy of dancing. As I watch her, Markova — like Duse in Ibsen — seems to be speaking poetry to the company's earnest prose.

Tudor's *Romeo and Juliet* was the world premiere that Ballet Theatre presented in its spring season at the Met. It was a great success and fully deserved it. It has a few unconvincing moments, but it has a great many original and very fine ones. (One of the most delicate effects is the special use of toe steps in the part of Juliet; they take on a quality different from any pointes I ever saw.) As a whole, I found the piece fascinating.

The plot of *Romeo* is that of Shakespeare's play. Tudor follows the action almost faithfully, but the individual thing about it is that the poetic message is not the same. The ballet's conception of mutual love is far less impetuous, far less straightforward, far less dazzlingly radiant. The difference is clearest in the character of Romeo, who in the ballet is never quite frank; he is like an object of love rather than a lover. But he is a perfectly real young man. And Hugh Laing — always a dancer full of real character — dances him as one. Tudor's piece strikes me as a personal version of the story, a reverie on the subject, with muted and oppressed images. Shakespeare's openness is its foil. And it is precisely the private deformation Tudor has made which gives to the ballet its core of poetic reality, its odd spell.

That Tudor had no intention of copying Shakespeare is clear enough in his choice of Delius for the music. The various pieces that together form the score have not the theatrical incisiveness of ballet music. But they are used as background music, as soundtrack; as such they are of high quality.

But I think the big event and most telling effect of the *Romeo* production is the extraordinary décor the painter Eugene Berman has given it. I have never shared the complacency with which we New Yorkers accept window-dressing (be it functional or "camp") as ballet décor. I think ballet sharpens the eyes and opens the heart, and under these circumstances a vulgar set is carrying our cult of lowbrow manners too far. I am shocked to see *Giselle* danced in front of a powder-room wallpaper, or to see the swans in *Swan*

Lake troop out in so many little homemade Dutch outfits, just as if they had rolled up their sleeves for a bout of spring cleaning.

Berman's Italian Renaissance décor is a serious work of art, like Picasso's *Tricorne* or Bérard's *Cotillon,* like the works of the baroque designers. And I imagine later theater lovers who look at the record of it will marvel at the refinement of sensibility it presupposes in the audience. As a picture it is shut in and still it lifts and spreads, it comes forward, and it keeps its secret. As a stage design it has inventiveness and immense learning, everything has been made with tenderness and is useful. The blended perspectives, the contrasted weights of the materials, the originality of the colors, the animation of the proportions, the energy of the drops, all these show us the many kinds of visual pleasure the stage has to offer. And in *Romeo,* for once, the scene painting and the execution of costumes are superlative. . . .

A number of people have asked me the reason for the present wave of balletomania that is sweeping from coast to coast, and that packed the Metropolitan for the longest ballet season in our history. My personal opinion is that ballet — when it is well danced — is the least provoking of our theatrical forms. Nobody on the stage says a word all evening. Nobody bothers much about sexiness or self-importance. The performers are bright, tender, agile, well mannered, they are serious and perfectly civilized. It is good for one's morale, because it appeals to the higher instincts. You feel sociable and friendly and at the same time wide awake. I think that's why so many people are delighted. Civilization is really a great pleasure.

Modern Music, May–June 1943

Massine's *Capriccio Espagnol;* de Mille's *Three Virgins; Giselle*

Saturday night's performance of Ballet Theatre at the Lewisohn Stadium was a full success. The first two ballets (*Capriccio Espagnol* and *Three Virgins and a Devil*) have the boisterous qualities that register most easily in the open air. *Giselle,* the third ballet, is anything but boisterous. But the passionate precision of Miss Markova in the lead made its subtle values intelligible a block away. It was a startling experience to see so delicate, so intimate a piece appeal without effort to an audience of ten thousand. It was a triumph for Miss Markova as a theater artist.

Capriccio Espagnol in Massine and Argentinita's choreography is a lively arrangement of Spanish regional and Spanish gypsy dances. It does not try for the special strictness of real Spanish dancing. The steps are authentic, but the rush and swirl of movement is Massine's. Massine has the secret of the sure-fire number for a large ballet company, and *Capriccio* is a happy example. Massine himself appeared in the part of the Gypsy, a role he does more sharply than anyone else. Miss Kaye was his gypsy partner; her lightning turns, her hip shakes, her wrist movements in the air were vividly temperamental.

Three Virgins, Miss de Mille's little satire on virginal vanity, makes all of its jokes very clearly. The dances slip from old country dance forms into burlesque bumps and bits of lindy steps (Flying Charleston, Susy-Q, and Pecking). The meaning of the pantomime is unmistakable. The five dancers were all excellent; and particularly Miss Karnilova, in the longest part, proved herself a masterly dance comedian.

These two ballets are meant as light entertainment. But *Giselle,* which followed them, is a tragedy. It is a hundred-year-old classic in which the great dancer Carlotta Grisi conquered Paris in 1841. The theme was inspired by two romantic poets; the plot was fixed by a successful librettist; and the choreography, credited to Coralli, is probably largely due to one of the greatest of choreographers and classic dancers, Grisi's husband, Perrot. The ballet is still danced in Paris, London, and Leningrad. And all the great ballerinas of the past have appeared in it.

Though so brilliant a history may add to the prestige of a ballet, all this seems remote from Amsterdam Avenue, 1943. But it is not prestige, it is its quality that keeps *Giselle* alive. The story of the ballet has poetic reality. The dances are in a large, open style. They are not intended primarily as exhibitions of virtuosity; they are meant to tell a tragic story and create a mood. And the score of *Giselle,* by Adam, is direct and animated; the more closely one listens, the more one notices how carefully made it is. But above all *Giselle* gives a great ballerina a superb chance to captivate, to dazzle, and to touch the heart. *Giselle* is the Lady of the Camellias, the Violetta, of the dance.

Miss Markova succeeded in the role on Saturday as completely as she already had at the Metropolitan. She captivated, dazzled, and touched. In the mimed passages — for instance, the conventional gesture of madness, staring at the audience with hands pressed to frame the face — she is somehow thrillingly sincere. In the dance passages of the first act, she is gay and light with a sort of chaste abandon; in those of the second, she is partly unearthly, like a specter, partly gracious, like a tender memory. It is as hard to color correct academic dancing with emotion as it is to give emotional color to correct bel canto. Miss Markova makes it seem the most natural thing in the world.

One reason she succeeds is that one sees every detail of the movement so distinctly. The movement of other dancers is apt to look fuzzy or two-dimensional in comparison to hers, which looks three-dimensional. Only the greatest dancers have this so-to-speak stereoscopic distinctness. Markova also has a complete command of the impetus of dance movement. She hits the climax of a phrase — say, a pose on one toe, or a leap — without a trace of effort or excess drive. The leap, the pose, seems to sustain itself in the air of its own accord.

She does not strain either in movement or in theater projection. She is so straight upright, so secure, that she does not have to thrust her personality on the audience for an effect; the audience is happy to come to her. This makes her dance seem personal, intimate, even in the open air.

New York Herald Tribune, June 28, 1943

Tudor and Pantomime

Many people who are disappointed to find little meaning in ballet dancing are struck by how much meaning the ballet figures in Tudor's *Pillar of Fire* and *Lilac Garden* convey to them. In *Lilac Garden,* for example, an about-to-be-abandoned mistress sees her lover standing alone, facing her at a distance. Desperately she rushes at top speed across the stage; she seems to leap straight onto his shoulder. He holds her tightly by the waist; she crouches there above his head, tensely arching her neck. He does not look up. The action is as sudden as the leap of a desperate cat on moving day. But the pose also brings up the sudden sense of a private physical intimacy. It has that meaning.

Again, in *Pillar of Fire,* a chaste and frenzied young woman sees a vigorous young man. He looks at her suggestively. She leaps at him though the air in grand jeté. He catches her in mid-leap in a split and she hangs against his chest as if her leap continued forever, her legs completely rigid, her body completely still. How is it one notices the momentary pose so distinctly?

It is partly because the stopped leap has a startling effect — like a fast tennis ball that goes dead. And the shock of the stop is heightened by the contrast to an onward full surge of the music. The timing, the placing of the pose, its contrast to the direction, the speed, the stopping and starting of the dance figures that went before — in brief, all the resouces of what the cinema calls visual rhythm — have been used to direct the eye to this special instance of bodily contact. The attention is focused on the parts of the body, their relation to one another, the physical force involved in the leap and the lift, almost as if by a motion-picture close-up. And the moment so distinctly presented registers all the more, because it registers as a climax in the story, as a pantomime of a psychological shock.

One "reads" the climactic moments in these ballets in a pantomime sense because from the outset Tudor has emphasized the pantomime aspect of the dance. He begins with easily recognizable movements, gestures of greeting, of pushing back a strand of hair, of fiddling with clothes, of averting the glance, of walking or standing not as in a ballet but as in daily life. One's attention is caught by these gestures because they at once specify the characters of a story, the situation, the psychological tension. They are expertly stylized to fit the music and to form sequences of motion that please the eye. They combine smoothly with dance steps, and we unconsciously expect from the more complex dance figures that follow the same sort of narrative meaning, the pantomime exposition of story we have begun to look for. The two dance figures described above show how completely Tudor succeeds as a storyteller, using ballet images.

In fact, in these two ballets Tudor gives to the whole classic ballet system of movement a pantomime bias. He uses ballet technique to portray a particular attitude, an upper-class code of behavior. In *Lilac Garden* he purposely exaggerates the constraint of ballet carriage; the dancers dance rigidly, hastily, with dead arms — as beginners might. But the ballet constraint they show portrays the mental constraint of the characters in the story, who rigidly follow an upper-class convention of behavior. Artificial upper-class constraint is the theme and the pathos of *Lilac Garden*.

In *Pillar of Fire* Tudor goes further. He shows two different ballet styles: an improperly strained one that characterizes the anguished heroine, and a smooth, proper style for the nice untroubled neighboring boys and girls. In addition, both kinds of ballet are set against the nonballet dancing of the exciting lowlife crowd — they dance and whirl in a sort of wild rhumba style, swivel-hipped, explosive, and frenzied; while the calm hero, in contrast to everyone, comes on not as any kind of dancer, but walking across the stage as modestly as a Fuller Brush man. Tudor fuses these heterogeneous elements brilliantly, but the dance device I wish to call attention to is the use of ballet technique to describe a special kind of person, to represent a special habit of mind.

Tudor's meaning is admirably clear and his dramatic effects are intense. It is interesting, on the other hand, that the traditional ballet (whether of 1890 or 1940) tries for a radically different kind of meaning than that of pantomime description; it appeals to a different manner of seeing dancing and requires a different technical approach in the dancer.

New York Herald Tribune, July 11, 1943

On Meaning in Dance

Any serious dance work has an element of pantomime and an element of straight dance, with one or the other predominant. When you think about it, it is curious in how different a way the two elements appeal to the intelligence, how differently they communicate a meaning.

Tudor's *Pillar of Fire* is a brilliant example of contemporary pantomime ballet. It is as absorbing to us as Fokine's *Schéhérazade* was to our parents in its 1910 version thirty years ago. The difference between the two is striking: *Schéhérazade* was bright and luscious, *Pillar of Fire* is gloomy and hot; Fokine hacked at his subject with a cleaver, Tudor dissects his with a scalpel. But — apart from the big orgy they each work up to — the two ballets both hold the attention by a continuous, clear story. Both belong to the tradition of the stylized drama, and not (as *Coppélia* and *Ballet Imperial* do) to the tradition of the dance entertainment. The pantomime ballet focuses the attention on stylized movement; the dance ballet, on a suite of dances.

What is a "stylized movement"? It is a movement that looks a little like dancing but more like nondancing. It is a movement derived from what people do when they are not dancing. It is a gesture from life deformed to suit music (music heard or imagined). The pleasure of watching it lies in guessing the action it was derived from, in guessing what it originally looked like, and then in savoring the "good taste" of the deformation.

Stylized movement has always been a perfectly legitimate pleasure in the theater. Sometimes it's merely a little quiz game thrown in for variety. In general, though, a stylized passage adds a pretty color to any dance. And stylization is one of the best recipes for a comic effect.

But in the pantomime ballet, stylized movement is the main aspect of expression. It is what one looks at particularly, because it keeps making a serious dramatic point. Gesture by gesture, as if idea by idea, the drama is built up. The audience watches for each allusion in turn; it follows point by point. The interest becomes like that of a detective story. The audience peers eagerly, delighted to have caught on, anxious not to miss a clue. It solves harder and harder riddles. The storytelling gathers momentum; as in driving a car, it's the speed that is thrilling, not the incidental scenery. One is, so to speak, hypnotized by the future destination. One merely wants to know what happened, as in watching a motion picture.

On the other hand, a dance ballet (*Coppélia,* for example) has a very different kind of appeal. True, it also has a story and it has pantomime portions. But you don't take them seriously. The parts that show you the heart of the subject, that are the most expressive, are in the form of dance numbers, of dance suites. They are like arias in an opera. In a dance ballet the story is not a pressing one, and it can be delayed awhile for a lyric comment on the momentary situation. The audience has come to enjoy the dancing; it is in no hurry to get the heroine married or murdered and to be sent out of the theater again.

In a dance ballet there is a difference in the way the audience watches the movement. It does not identify the gestures with reference to real life; it does not search in each pose for a distinct descriptive allusion. It watches the movements in sequence as a dance. There is a sort of suspension in judgment, a wait and a wonder till the dance is completed, till the dancer has come to rest. When the dance is over one understands it as a whole; one understands the quality of the dancer's activity, the quality of her rest, and in the play between the two lies the meaning of the dance aria, the comment it has made on the theme of the ballet. One has understood the dance as one does a melody — as a continuity that began and ended. It is a nonverbal meaning, like the meaning of music.

The dancer in pantomime emphasizes what each of the gestures looks like, he appeals pictorially to intellectual concepts. The dancer in a dance number emphasizes the kinetic transformation, his dance is a continuity which moves away from one equilibrium and returns to another. Repose is as important to the meaning of a dance ballet as activity. But in pantomime a stop must be made to look active and pressing, it must keep the urgency of the history. This difference leads the dancer to a different emphasis in technique.

New York Herald Tribune, July 18, 1943

Ballet Technique

When they watch a ballet in the theater, some people can take ballet technique for granted as easily as school kids take the technique of basketball for granted while they watch a lively game in a gym. These ballet lovers see the dance impulses perfectly clearly.

Other people, however, are bothered by the technique. They watch the gestures without feeling the continuity of the dance; the technique seems to keep getting in the way of it. Ballet looks to them chiefly like a mannerism in holding the arms and legs, and in keeping the back stiff as a ramrod. They can see it must be difficult to move about in that way, but why try in the first place? Annoyed at the enthusiasm of their neighbors in the theater, they come to the conclusion that ballet technique is a snobbish fad, the perverse invention of some dead and forgotten foreign aesthetic dictator who insisted on making dancing as unnatural as possible.

But ballet technique isn't as unreasonable as that. Just as a dazzling technique in pitching, for instance, is an intelligent refinement of throwing a ball for fun (which everybody does somehow), so ballet technique is a refinement of social dancing and folk dancing, a simple enough thing that everybody has tried doing for fun in his own neighborhood. You know the main technical problem of dancing the first time you try; it's to move boldly without falling flat on the dance floor. You have to get the knack of shifting your weight in a peculiar way. Next you try to keep in rhythm, and then you try to give the conventional steps that extra personal dash which makes the dance come off. It's a question, of course, of doing all this jointly with others, sometimes in groups, sometimes in couples — when a little sex pantomime may be added, by common consent all over the world. And incidental acrobatic feats are welcome if they don't break up the dancers' happy sense of a collective rhythm.

Exhibition dance technique is a way of doing the same things for the pleasure of the neighbors who gather to watch. You see the simple elements of common dance technique refined and specialized, with a particular emphasis placed on one element or another. In recent generations we have seen our own normal folk and social dances evolve into professional tap dancing, into exhibition ballroom, and most recently into exhibition lindy.

Like these recent dance techniques, ballet, too, is the result of practical experiments by a number of exhibition dancers — a long line of professionals which in the case of ballet began in the seventeenth century and has not yet ended. The ballet dancers seem to have taken as their point of emphasis not the small specialty tricks but the first great problem everybody has in dancing — the trouble of keeping in balance. The problem might be described as that of a variable force (the dance impulses) applied to a constant weight (the body). The ballet technicians wanted to find as many ways as possible of changing the impetus of the movement without losing control of the momentum of the body. When a dancer is not sure of his momentum he is like a driver who has no rhythm in driving, who jolts you, who either spurts or dawdles and makes you nervous. Watching a dancer whose momentum is under control, you appreciate the change in impetus as an expression. You follow the dance with pleasure, because the dancer has your confidence.

The foot, leg, arm, and trunk positions of ballet, the way it distributes the energy in the body (holding back most of it in the waist and diminishing it from there as from a center) — this is a method of keeping the urgency of the movement in relation to a center of gravity in the body. The peculiar look of ballet movement is not the perverse invention of some dead aesthetic dictator. It is a reasonable method which is still being elaborated by experiment. On the basis of a common technical experience — that of equilibrium in motion — this method tries to make the changes of impulse in movement as distinctly intelligible as possible. There have always been great dancers who danced in other techniques than that of ballet. But there have always been great dancers, too, who found in ballet technique an extraordinary range of clear expression.

New York Herald Tribune, July 25, 1943

The Dance in Film

. . . Dance expression and dance recording are two separate functions in the cinema that rarely coincide. The motion picture is the only means of accurately recording dancing, but dance lovers are aware of how rarely it projects anything like the dance quality one knows from the theater. When we watch dancing anywhere, the more distinctly we can see the plastic quality — the three-dimensional quality — of the movement, the more clearly we feel the point of the dance. But the camera gives a poor illusion of volume; it makes a distortion of foreshortening and perspective, and it is plastic only at short range. A further trouble is the camera's narrow angle of vision. A dance on the stage becomes clearer by the relation of the movement to the architectural space around it — that is, to the permanent stage space and permanent stage frame in which the dance moves back and forth and right and left. Theater choreography is movement suited to a whole, fixed area. But the film cannot show the whole stage and also show the dancer large enough so we can see just what she is doing. When the camera moves up to her the stage frame is lost; when the camera follows her she seems to be flailing about without making any appreciable headway — she bobs around against a swirling, fantastically liquid background. Altogether, when a stage dance has been photographed from various distances and angles and the film assembled, the effect of the dance is about like the effect of playing a symphony for the radio but shifting the microphone arbitrarily from one instrument to another all the time. Listening at home, you can hear the noise all right, but the symphony doesn't make any sense that way.

When you watch the film version of a ballet intended for the stage, why should good dancers so often look unnatural in a way they don't in the theater? Well, for one thing, you watch a dancer on the cinema screen as you would if she were dancing for you in a living room. You see her close by, at a distance ranging from two to twenty feet. In the theater she makes her big effects across a distance of a hundred or three hundred feet. What looks expressive away on the stage looks absurdly overemphatic near at hand. The hard thrust with which a stage dancer attacks a movement, the spread-wide openness of gesture which is eloquent in the theater, the violent speed at which a dancer can cover a large stage space — these phases of dancing are effective only at a distance. They are proportioned to a large space and not to a small one; so is the physical effort involved in doing them, which looks unreasonable and unattractive at close quarters. (Even in the theater many people are disappointed when they watch a great dancer from the first row; they are embarrassed to see her work so hard.) In short, the present manner of filming a dancer close by puts her into an intimate relation to the audience; she is therefore restricted to intimate effects and cannot use the full dynamic range of serious theater dancing. She is most successful when she looks not like a dancer at work, but like a nondancer who incidentally does some winsome steps and when in expression she restricts herself to understatement.

A dance style like Astaire's, which makes a fine art of understatement, is for this reason the immediately effective style in a film. It looks natural a few feet away. It does so not merely for the psychological reason that tap dancing is what we think of as a natural way of dancing in this country, but much more because tap dancing lends itself technically to an exquisite salon style. The dynamic range is narrow but sharply differentiated; the dramatic miming is barely indicated but perfectly intelligible; the presentation is intimately charming; and the dance itself rarely needs much room. A complete dance phrase can generally be photographed close by in a single camera field, and the continuity to the following phrase is generally so casual that a shift in the camera between phrases does not interrupt very much. These are the technical advantages which allow Astaire — who is certainly a great dancer — to give a more complete sense of dance expression on the screen than good dancers in other styles can. But there are indications that dance expression of a less miniature sort may also be possible in films. In Chaplin's early pictures there were often dance numbers that were not salon pieces — such as his own acts on roller skates, as a boxing referee, as a drunk, or "choral movements" like those of the crowds in *The Cop*. The film technique of the day was not so obsessed with intimate nearness, and Chaplin often performed a full dance sequence in a single camera field, giving the complete continuity.

In the present film technique Disney's animals have been more successful than human dancers in giving a wide range of dance expression to movement; and Disney often composed the dance to fit the field, as a choreographer does for the stage. Balanchine (in *The Goldwyn Follies*) tried composing serious ballet dancing to fit the successive camera fields (and camera angles). And this procedure is the sensible approach to making dancing in the cinema more than a mere recording or more than an amiable incident; it is an approach that might make film dancing as variously expressive on the screen as theater dancing has become on the stage.

New York Herald Tribune, Aug. 1 and 8, 1943

Flight of the Dancer

If you travel all over the world and see every brilliant and flying dance that human beings do, you will maybe be surprised that it is only in our traditional classic ballet dancing that the dancer can leap through the air slowly. In other kinds of dancing there are leaps that thrill you by their impetuousness or accuracy; there are brilliant little ones, savage long ones, and powerful bouncing ones. But among all dance techniques only classic ballet has perfected leaps with that special slow-motion grace, that soaring rise and floating descent which looks weightless. It isn't that every ballet leap looks that way. Some are a tough thrust off the ground, some travel like a cat's, some quiver like a fish's, some scintillate like jig steps; but these ways of jumping you can find in other dancing too. The particular expression ballet technique has added to leaping is that of the dancer poised in mid-flight, as easy in the air as if she were suspended on wires. Describing the effect, people say one dancer took flight like a bird, another was not subject to the laws of gravity, and a third paused quietly in midair. And that is how it does look, when it happens.

To be honest, it doesn't happen very often. It is a way of leaping only a few rare dancers ever quite achieve. But it can be achieved. You can see it in the dancing of Alicia Markova, the English-born star of our present Ballet Theatre company; though no one else in this country — perhaps no one else in the world — can "fly" quite as perfectly as she does. No one else is so serenely calm with nothing underneath her. In *Pas de Quatre* she sits collectedly in the air, as if she were at a genteel tea party, a tea party where everyone naturally sat down in the air. There is something comic about it. That is because Miss Markova, who in the part of Giselle is a delicate tragic dancer, also has a keen sense of parody. *Pas de Quatre,* a parody ballet, represents the competition in virtuosity of four very great ballerinas at a command performance before Her Majesty Queen Victoria. (It actually happened in 1845.) In the ballet, Miss Markova takes the part of the greatest of the four, Marie Taglioni — Marie *pleine de grâce,* as she was called — who was a sallow little lady full of wrinkles, celebrated not only for her serene flight through the empty air, but also for the "decent voluptuousness" of her expression. Watching Miss Markova's performance, one feels that not even the eminently respectable British queen could have found any fault with the female modesty of such a look as hers. And that "refined" look is Miss Markova's joke on Victorian propriety, and a little too on the vanity of exhibiting technique just for its own sake.

Her expression is parody, but the leap itself is no parody of a leap. It is the real, incredibly difficult thing. Taglioni's leap couldn't have been any better. A leap is a whole story, with a beginning, a middle, and an end. If you want to try it, here are some of the simplest directions for this kind of soaring flight. It begins with a knee bend, knees turned out, feet turned out and heels pressed down, to get a surer grip and a smoother flow in the leg action. The bend goes down softly ("as if the body were being sucked to the floor") with a slight accelerando. The thrust upward, the stretch of the legs, is faster than the bend was.

The speed of the action must accelerate in a continuous gradation from the beginning of the bend into the final spring upward, so there will be no break in motion when the body leaves the ground. The leap may be jumped from two feet, hopped from one, or hopped from one with an extra swing in the other leg. But in any case the propulsive strain of the leap must be taken up by the muscles around the waist; the back must be straight and perpendicular, as if it had no part in the effort. Actually, the back muscles have to be kept under the strictest tension to keep the spine erect — the difficulty is to move the pelvis against the spine, instead of the other way around; and as the spine has no material support in the air, you can see that it's like pulling yourself up by your own bootstraps.

But that isn't all. The shoulders have to be held rigidly down by main force, so they won't bob upward in the jump. The arms and neck, the hands and the head have to look as comfortable and relaxed as if nothing were happening down below. Really there's as much going on down there as though the arms and head were picnicking on a volcano. Once in the air the legs may do all sorts of things, embellishments sometimes quite unconnected with what they did to spring up, or what they will have to do to land. And if there are such extra embellishments during the leap, there should be a definite pause in the air before they begin and after they are finished. No matter how little time there is for them, the ornaments must never be done precipitately.

But the most obvious test for the dancer comes in the descent from the air, in the recovery from the leap. She has to catch herself in a knee bend that begins with the speed she falls at, and progressively diminishes so evenly that you don't notice the transition from the air to the ground. This knee bend slows down as it deepens to what feels like a final rest, though it is only a fraction of a second long, so short a movie camera will miss it. This is the "divine moment" that makes her look as if she alighted like a feather. It doesn't happen when she lands, you see; it happens later. After that, straightening up from the bend must have the feeling of a new start; it is no part of the jump, it is a new breath, a preparation for the next thing she means to do.

In other words, the action of a leap increases in speed till the dancer leaves the ground. Then it diminishes till it reaches the leap's highest point up in the air. From then on it increases again till the feet hit the ground, when it must be slowed down by the knee bend to a rest; and all these changes must be continuously flowing. But most important of all is the highest point reached in the air. Here, if the dancer is to give the feeling of soaring, she must be completely still. She must express the calm of that still moment. Some dancers hold their breath. Nijinsky used to say he just stopped at that point. But however he does it, the dancer must project that hair's-breadth moment as a climax of repose. The dancer must not be thinking of either how she got up or how she is going to get down. She must find time just then to meditate.

When Nijinsky exited through the window in the *Spectre de la Rose* thirty years ago it was the greatest leap of the century. He seemed to the audience to float slowly up like a happy spirit. He seemed to radiate a power of mysterious assurance as calmly as the bloom of a summer rose does. Such enthusiastic comments sound like complete nonsense nowadays, when you go to the ballet and see a young man thumping about the stage self-consciously. But the comments were made by sensible people, and they are still convinced they were right. You begin to see what they mean when you realize that for Nijinsky in this ballet the leaps and the dance were all one single flowing line of movement, faster or slower, heavier or lighter, a way of moving that could rise up off the ground as easily as not, with no break and no effort. It isn't a question of how high he jumped one jump, but how smoothly he danced the whole ballet. You can see the same quality of technique today in Miss Markova's dancing.

In one respect, though, Nijinsky's way of leaping differed from hers: in his style the knee bend that starts the leap up and the other one that catches it coming down were often almost unnoticeable. This is a difference of appearance, of expression, but not really of technique. Nijinsky could make the transitions in speed I spoke of above with an exceptionally slight bending of the knees — a very unusual accomplishment indeed. When a dancer can do this it gives an expression of greater spontaneity to the leap; but several modern ballet dancers who try to do it aren't able really to land "light as a sylph or a snowflake," as Nijinsky could. The slight jolt when they land breaks the smooth flow and attracts more attention than the stillness of the climax in the air. And so the leap fails to concentrate on a soaring expression. The correct soaring leap is a technical trick any ballet dancer can learn in ten or fifteen years if he or she happens to be a genius. The point of learning it is that it enables the dancer to make a particular emotional effect, which enlarges the range of expression in dancing. The effect as we watch Markova's pure flight can only be described as supernatural, as a strangely beneficent magic. It is an approach to those mysterious hints of gentleness that occasionally absorb the human mind. It is a spiritual emotion; so Nijinsky's contemporaries described it, when he danced that way, and so did the Parisian poet Théophile Gautier when he saw first Taglioni and then Grisi take flight a hundred years ago.

It was a hundred years ago, most likely, that the trick was first perfected, together with that other trick so related to it in expression, the moment of airy repose on one toe. (Toe dancing, like leaping, has many kinds of expression, but the suggestion of weightless, poised near-flight is one of its most striking.) Toe dancing, like the technique of aerial flight, took a long series of dance geniuses to develop. The great Mlle Camargo two centuries ago, in Paris and in London, was already "dancing like a bird." But it seems likely that she fluttered enchantingly, rather than soared calm and slow. Certainly Camargo's costumes didn't allow some technical resources that are related to our technique of flight; they allowed no horizontal lift of the leg, no deep knee bends, no spring and stretch of foot in a heelless slipper.

In the next century, soaring of a different kind was being perfected. They literally hung the dancer on wires, and hoisted him or her through the air. Theaters had machinery called "flight paths," one of them fifty-nine feet long — quite a fine swoop it must have made. Maybe these mechanical effects gradually gave dancers the idea of trying to do the same thing without machinery. In an 1830 ballet, girls dressed as woodland spirits bent down the lower boughs of trees and let themselves be carried upward into the air on the rebound, which sounds like some wire effect. And in 1841 the great dancer Carlotta Grisi — Taglioni's young rival — opened in the ballet *Giselle,* in the second act of which there was one passage at least where her leaps were "amplified" by wiring. (She was supposed to be a ghost in it, and it was meant to look spooky.) In the little engraving of her in this part she certainly floats over her grave in a way no ballet star ever could; but probably the pose is only an imaginary invention by the artist. The same *Giselle* is still being danced today both in America and Europe, and, according to report, in Paris, in London, and in Leningrad, at least, this particular hundred-year-old wire trick is still being pulled.

Mademoiselle, October 1943

About Toe Dancing

To a number of people ballet means toe dancing, that is what they come to see, and they suspect that a dancer only gets down off her "pointes" to give her poor feet a rest. But toe steps are not what ballet is about. They are just one of the devices of choreography, as the sharp hoots of a soprano are one of the devices of opera. Toe steps were invented, the historians say, "toward 1826" or "toward 1830." And the historians also explain that ballet during the century and more before the introduction of toe steps was quite as interesting to its audience as performances at the Metropolitan are nowadays to us. It was fully two hundred years ago that the audience enjoyed the difference between Mlle Camargo, that light, joyous, brilliant creature, and Mlle Sallé, the lovely, expressive, dramatic dancer. In 1740, too, the public was applauding with enthusiasm the plastic harmony of M. Dupré, "who danced more distinctly [*qui se dessinait mieux*] than anyone in the world." There was evidently plenty to watch before there were any toe steps. Still without toe steps choreography became so expressive that first Garrick and later Stendhal compared dance scenes they saw to scenes of Shakespeare. And long before toe steps Noverre's *Letters on Dancing* discussed the aesthetics of ballet so clearly that ever since, ballet has been judged by the general standards of art, or has not been judged at all. You can see that toe steps are not the secret of ballet.

I do not mean that the feature of toe dancing is foreign to ballet — quite the contrary. As a matter of fact the principles of ballet technique — its gymnastic as well as its plastic principles — were accurately defined shortly before toe steps were invented, and their addition did not require any revision of the fundamental exercises or postures. Toe steps are an application of an older ballet device, the rigid stretch of knee, ankle, and instep to form a single straight line. During the eighteenth century this special expression of the leg was emphasized more and more, though used only when the leg was in the air. Finally a girl discovered she could put her whole weight on two legs and feet so stretched (as in an 1821 ballet print), and even support it on one; that became our modern toe step.

Perhaps toe technique was due to the exceptionally severe exercises to which the dancer Paul Taglioni subjected his brilliant daughter, Marie; certainly it was her expressive genius that made the trick a phenomenal one. But she was a great dancer before she did toe steps, and she had at least six and perhaps ten years of success behind her when the new fashion began. The uncertainty of history over the exact date suggests that these initial toe steps were far less precise than ours. In any case, in the 1830s other dancers besides Marie Taglioni learned them, though, done as they then were in a soft slipper darned across the toe every evening, they were often uncertain and dangerous. Now of course any student learns them painlessly and with no heartbreak at all.

But to do them expressively, as Taglioni, Grisi, and Elssler did, is still not common. Gautier, the poet-critic of a hundred years ago, described expressive "pointes" as "steel arrows plunging elastically against a marble floor." Unfortunately we have all seen dispirited performances of *Sylphides* where they have been merely a bumpy hobbling. Toe steps inherently have a secret that is not easy for either the dancer or the public: it is the extraordinary tautness of the completely straight leg-and-foot line which seems to alter the usual proportions of the body, not only the proportion of trunk and leg but also the relation of hard and soft. Dancing on and off the toes may be described in this sense as an expressive play of changing proportions.

But "pointes" have a psychological aspect, too. There is a sense of discomfort, even of cruelty in watching them, a value that often shocks sensitive persons when they fail to find in the emotion of the dance a vividness that would make this savage detail interesting. Well, from a psychological point of view, toe steps have here and there a curious link to the theme of a ballet. In *Giselle* they seem consistent with the shocking fascination of death that is the core of the drama; in *Swan Lake* they are a part of the cruel remoteness of the beloved; in *Noces* they hammer out a savage intoxication. Elsewhere, in scenes of intelligent irony, they can look petulant or particular, absurd or fashionable.

But it would be a complete mistake to tag toe steps in general with a "literary" meaning. Their justification is the shift in the dance, the contrast between taut and pliant motion, between unexpected and expected repose, between a poignantly prolonged line and a normal one. Toe steps also increase the speed and change the rhythm of some figures. On paper these formal aspects sound less dramatic than psychological ones; but they are what one actually sees on the stage, and out of them, seeing them distinctly, the better part of the dance emotion is made.

New York Herald Tribune, Oct. 3, 1943

How to Judge a Dancer

When you watch ballet dancers dancing you are observing a young woman or a young man in fancy dress, and you like it if they look attractive, if they are well built and have what seems to be an open face. You notice the youthful spring in starting, the grace of carriage, the strength in stopping. You like it if they know what to do and where to go, if they can throw in a surprising trick or two, if they seem to be enjoying their part and are pleasantly sociable as performers. All this is proper juvenile charm, and it often gives a very sharp pleasure in watching dancers.

But you are ready too for other qualities besides charm. The audience soon notices if the dancer has unusual control over her movements, if what she is doing is unusually clear to the eye, if there are differences of emphasis and differences of urgency in her motion. Within single slow movements or within a sequence, you enjoy seeing the continuity of an impulse and the culmination of a phrase. Now you are not only watching a charming dancer, she is also showing you a dance.

When she shows you a dance, she is showing how the steps are related, that they are coherent and make some sense. You can see that they make some sense in relation to the music or in relation to the story; and now and then the dancer shows you they make sense also as dance phrases purely and simply. You may notice that a dance phrase holds together by its rhythm in time (a rhythm related to that of music), as a sequence of long and short motions set off by a few accents. Again in other passages you may be most interested by the arrangements in space, motions that make up a rhythm of large and small, up and down, right and left, backward and forward. You watch dance figures that combine several directions, done by single dancers or by groups, in place or while covering distance. Such dance phrases are plastically interesting. But at still other moments you notice especially the changes in the dancer's energy, the dynamics of a sequence, which contrast motion as taut or easy, active or passive, pressing or delaying, beginning or ending. Dynamics, space, and time — the dancer may call one or another to your attention, but actually she keeps these three strands of interest going all the time, for they are all simultaneously present in even the simplest dancing. But a dancer who can make the various factors clear at the proper passage so as to keep you interested in the progress of the dance is especially attractive because she is dancing intelligently. She makes even a complicated choreography distinct to see.

Intelligent dancing — which might as well be called correct dancing — has a certain dryness that appeals more to an experienced dance lover than to an inexperienced one. In any case, everyone in the audience becomes more attentive when he recognizes a personal impetus in an intelligent dancer's movement, when she has a way of looking not merely like a good dancer, but also different from others and like her own self.

Her motions look spontaneous, as if they suited her particular body, her personal impulses, as if they were being invented that very moment. This is originality in dancing — and quite different from originality in choreography. The original dancer vivifies the dance — plain or complicated, novel or otherwise — that the choreographer has set. She shows a gift like that of an actor who speaks his lines as if they were being uttered for the first time that very moment, though they have been in print a hundred years or though he has spoken them a hundred nights running.

Such vitality in dancing is not the same thing as that punch in projection sometimes called a "dynamic stage personality." A lively dancer does not push herself on the audience, except, of course, during curtain calls. Projection in serious dancing is a mild and steady force; the dancer who goes out to the audience with a bang cuts herself off from the rest of the stage action. Galvanic projection is a trick appropriate to revue, where there is no drama to interrupt. But in serious dancing the audience must be kept constantly aware of the complete action within the stage area, because the changes — and, therefore, the drama — of dancing are appreciated clearly in relation to that fixed three-dimensional frame. So the best dancers are careful to remain within what one may call the dance illusion, as an actor remains within the illusion of a dramatic action — when you cannot help imagining he is a young man speaking privately to a girl in a garden, though you see perfectly well he is middle-aged, that he is talking blank verse for you to hear and standing on a wooden floor.

And just as you become really absorbed at a play when Romeo is not only distinct and spontaneous but also makes you recognize the emotion of love, which has nothing to do with the actor personally or with acting in itself or with words in themselves, so the dancer becomes absorbing to watch when she makes you aware of emotions that are not make-believe at all. Some of my friends doubt that it is possible to give so much expressive power to dancing, though they grant it is possible to performers of music or of plays. To recognize poetic suggestion through dancing one has to be susceptible to poetic values and susceptible to dance values as well. But I find that a number of people are and that several dancers — for example, Miss Danilova and Miss Markova — are quite often able to give them the sense of an amplitude in meaning which is the token of emotion in art. I myself go to dancing looking for this pleasure, which is the pleasure of the grand style, and find a moment or two of satisfaction in the work of a dozen dancers or more. In these remarkable flights the choreographer may be admired even more than the dancer, but here I am describing the merits of dancing only.

What I have said applies to any dance technique, and now that the ballet season is opening, it is a simple matter for anyone to go to the Metropolitan and check for himself the accuracy of it or the mistakes.

New York Herald Tribune, Oct. 10, 1943

Tudor's *Lilac Garden;* Lichine's *Helen of Troy*

Saturday night's Ballet Theatre performance at the Metropolitan was brilliantly executed throughout. First came the new *Fair at Sorochinsk,* the choreography of which has been previously reviewed. Dolin, as the Devil of the Ukraine, danced his part (which, if I saw right, includes even two gargouillades) at astonishing speed. His toe steps — Caucasian style — make him look as if he were dancing on a claw. Eglevsky, in the part of young Gritzko, did a pirouette followed by a triple tour in the air as if it were the most natural thing in the world. His simplicity in the part is admirable.

The men in the piece do all the hardest varieties of those Russian dance steps done in a crouching position, and they do them with bravura and enthusiasm.

Second on the bill came *Lilac Garden* in an especially fine performance. The choreography in this case is full of carefully adjusted detail, rushes cut short, impulses constrained, half gestures, lightning lifts and reversals. The detail suits perfectly the story, and also the music's constantly shifting emotional stress; but it requires of the dancers the most meticulous control in execution. The entire cast in *Lilac Garden* danced not only so that every detail was defined, but with an impetuosity that was theatrically convincing. Miss Kaye and Laing in particular were thrilling to watch.

Interesting, too, is how different the two dancers make the characters they portray in *Lilac Garden* from those they do, for instance, in *Pillar of Fire*. It is to their credit as actors and equally to Tudor's as choreographer; but I point it out to balletgoers as a striking example of characterization by dancers.

The evening closed with David Lichine's *Helen of Troy*. The newspaper deadline usually prevents this reviewer from seeing the last ballet on the bill, and I had not seen the piece this season. In fact it happened that I had not seen it since the first performances here last spring, and so had missed the many changes that had been made in the dances and the stage business. Though I am way behind the other ballet fans, I should like to say that I was quite surprised Saturday night and that I found the piece in its present form sunny, civilized, and very enjoyable. The story is well told, the characters are clear, the jokes are amusing. The solos are pretty, and the love duets even have a little tenderness, so that the sweetness of Offenbach's humor is not — for once — wasted on a ballet.

The cast for *Helen* couldn't be better. Everyone on the stage deserves praise for the happy charm the piece has, and the audience loves them all. Jerome Robbins, as Mercury, has of course the most original part, and he does it beautifully. It is a part in straight American — real Third Avenue, in fact. One of the interesting things about it is that, where everyone else dances with a particular vivacity, he moves with an American deliberateness. The difference is as striking as it used to be in peace time abroad, when a stray American youth appeared in a bustling French street, and the slow rhythm of his walk gave the effect of a sovereign unconcern. So Robbins on the stage, by being very natural, looks different enough to be a god; and that a god should be just like someone you see any day on the street is a nice joke.

New York Herald Tribune, Oct. 18, 1943

Argentinita's *Pictures of Goya;* Tudor's *Judgment of Paris*

Last night's performance of Ballet Theatre at the Metropolitan was — like that of the night before — full of verve, and the crowded house applauded the dancers in the friendliest spirit.

The program brought the second performance of Argentinita's new suite called *Pictures of Goya,* danced by herself; her sister, Pilar Lopez; and their two partners, José Greco and Manolo Vargas. It was a distinct hit with the audience.

At the first performance of the piece, I had found it too unclear in its phrasing to be effective as dancing, and it did not seem one of the successful creations of Argentinita. Last night it was danced with more precision and more expression and its effects — which are small ones — carried. Argentinita's Fandango is an interesting number, and the Jotas at the end by all four dancers are charming. The piece is not a very original one; it has neither the lambent grace of the Goya tapestries nor the exacerbation of his *Caprichos;* it is a modest and agreeable number.

Tudor's satiric *Judgment of Paris* followed on the program. Miss Reed danced Juno; Miss Karnilova, Venus; Miss Chase, Minerva; Tudor himself was the Customer; and Laing, the Waiter. This little picture of three ladies of the oldest profession trying despite their varicose veins and their boredom to stimulate the interest of a seedy and sodden customer is as elegant in its horrid detail as it is virulent in its humor. The dancers put across each of its points with phenomenal accuracy; and I am surprised that the audience seems to take it all as good clean fun. It's a ghastly little piece.

New York Herald Tribune, Oct. 18, 1943

The de Mille "Touch"

Miss de Mille's dances for *One Touch of Venus* shine by their good sense. Among our choreographers she has always had in particular that touch of nature that the title of the piece suggests. It is a striking virtue in musical comedy, where nature is the last thing you expect. Miss de Mille has not this time the chance for human warmth she had in *Oklahoma!* but she certainly makes the most of what opportunity she has; and in *Venus* she again succeeds in touching the heart of the average audience through the dance numbers in a way no other musical comedy dance director can. The specialized dance lover, on the other hand, who naturally has special standards in the originality and the emotional interest he expects from dancing, will readily recognize in the course of these dances the intelligence of a fine choreographer.

Most interesting of the four numbers is the "Venus in Ozone Heights" ballet in the second act, which depicts what goes on in Venus's mind when she faces the possibility of becoming a suburban housewife. It begins lightly with children playing, they gradually get to be a nuisance, they grow up and start leading their own lives. The goddess remembers more and more distinctly the nymphs and fauns who do not change with time; and finally, with a last salute to human romance, she reassumes her divine majesty. Here at the end, when Mary Martin enters upstage, tall and remote, when she tosses with a quick, high gesture a handful of spangles as a blessing to the Aviator and his Girl, and then paces unperturbed across the luminous stage with a retinue of flying immortals, the dance reaches a clear statement of why a goddess is simply undomesticable — a statement that is vital to the plain story of *Venus,* and which is Miss de Mille's (and Miss Martin's) contribution.

The effect is a true one, and the change of mood from comic and intimate to remote and grand is convincing. It is achieved not so much by novel dance detail as by a change in the rhythm and a change in the bearing of the dancers. It is made possible by the fact that the entire dance is serious in the sense that the dancers represent an action; they do not — as musical comedy dancers generally do — exhibit their personal charm. They have a clear story to tell, and they tell it. And this successful change of mood gives (in *Venus* as in *Oklahoma!*) a direct dramatic life to Miss de Mille's ballet.

Among the other dance numbers "Forty Minutes for Lunch" is a new version of the city traffic theme that modern-dance groups used to like. But the topical introduction of the French sailor, the simple intelligibility of the action, and the absence of an overearnest straining make it a pleasant number, if not a novelty.

The prodigious success of Sono Osato as the star of the dance company is good news to her many admirers who know her in her former ballet roles, but it doesn't come as a surprise to them. In the first act she dances with a precise sharpness in every limb and a rhythmic punch that startles; she is a galvanic comedian. In the second act, she then transforms herself into a glamorously alluring comic Nymph, who at the end is quite serious and beautiful.

The jitterbug number in the first act, arranged, I believe, by Lou Wills, Jr., for Miss Bond and himself, is a particularly original and happy one. The way they dance it, it stops the show too.

There is no doubt that the public loves any show Miss de Mille touches. And, personally, I look forward to the humanization of musical comedy, which her successes are bringing about, with the greatest enthusiasm.

New York Herald Tribune, Oct. 24, 1943

Billy the Kid and Its Dance Faults

The ballet *Billy the Kid* is a peculiar piece. Any sensible person can point out its absurdities, yet sensible people like it. It bobs up year after year in one company or another, always in inadequate performance, but it keeps on the boards. It is not satisfactory while you look at it, it is obscure and pieced out awkwardly; but something of it stays with you, something original that it alone has. I find its flavor very different from that of *Rodeo,* our other serious American ballet. *Rodeo* is about the West as it is lived in; *Billy* is about the West as it is dreamed of, as it is imagined by boys playing in empty lots in the suburbs of our cities. And for this reason *Billy* is unreal in its local description, but real in its tragic play. An anthropologist would recognize it as an urban puberty ritual; I like it because there is somewhere in its folderol of stylization the sense that tragedy is natural, and this is, after all, the most interesting emotion that the theater can present.

Because *Billy* as a theater piece has a sense of the tragic, because the music is of the finest quality, and because *Billy* was frankly conceived as a serious artistic collaboration, I admire it sincerely. All the more because it was made around the corner and talks about things I know. Of course, if our big ballet companies could afford it, we should have, after all these years, more than merely two American ballets that are meant as a serious and touching image of the spirit. But till we get more such pieces we should at least pay attention to the two we have, watch and criticize and generally participate in their existence. Both ballets have naive faults of choppy, gesture-by-gesture pantomime; just the same, both of them, in their main overall expression, appeal to the imagination and get across a suggestion of reality to the audience. They are truer, in this respect, than many more adroit and more celebrated ballets.

Looking at the pantomime movements that Loring invented for *Billy,* I find them more interesting when they tend to be literal than when they tend to be symbolic. The storytelling gestures — those of the cowboys riding or strolling, the gun play, the sneaking up on the victim, Billy's turning away from his sweetheart or lying down — all this has more life as dancing than the gestures meant as "modern dance." The latter pound a beat, but often they don't add up to a dance rhythm.

The eye gets snagged on them, one at a time, as by sign language. In the "March," for instance, the energetic horizontal arm thrusts with open palms look as if our ballet dancers were mimicking "pushing back the frontier." The "Come on out West" gestures back to the electricians offstage, the praying, digging, running, housekeeping, ever westward, ever westward are meant as a frieze of history; but it is history like that shown us in the slick-paper ads.

The technical fault is that the gesture does not lead out into space and relate to the full dimensions of the stage; it only leads back into the dancer's figure. It makes the stage close in on the dancer, instead of showing him boldly taking possession. Only the double turns in the air at the end of the "March" give an effect of real vigor.

On the other hand, the "Street Scene" that follows is most interesting. The wandering individual floor patterns by not emphasizing a fixed place on the stage and the gestures by not emphasizing a climax in rhythm give the sense of unfenced spaces and of all the time in the world. Nothing could be more characteristically American or more original as a dance conception.

But it is the lack of emphatic grouping, of a compact center of attention, which makes the "Macabre Dance" a foolish letdown — much later on in the ballet. The center-stage ladderlike floor pattern of the "Gun Battle" just before has been so insistent that it would refresh the eye (and indicate a new scene) if there were a sudden focus on a new, completely different grouping off center. Instead, there is just a wavering lineup. (I wish, too, that the scene were danced straight as a naive celebration; the "macabre" element is mere la-dee-da. The steps themselves are all right.)

The halfhearted placing at this point blurs also the wandering scenes that follow. Then, just in time, the climax is saved by the interpolated waltz adagio, which is especially effective if the girl seems to spin out the distances of her dance from Billy's fixed position downstage right. Billy's death itself is excellent as a scene and very much in character, particularly if there is no nervousness in his movements, only wariness.

The character of Billy derives its interest not from his murders but from his attempts at human contact, contact with his mother, with his friend Garrett, the sheriff, and with his sweetheart. His feeling for them is reciprocated. When this is clear then the story of his solitary fate becomes tragic — really tragic because he never appeals to us for sympathy or considers himself wronged. He accepts his isolation and lives the life he has. Billy's real enemy is the plain crowd of frontiersmen, who being a crowd can ignore him and whom he ignores by an act of pride. Billy's friend, Garrett, is at ease in the crowd, but different from it; Billy and he are both individualists, but of opposite social types. I regret that the crucial dispute between the two — over a card game at night on the prairie — no longer expresses either their natural interest in one another or their profound difference. And I regret that in the crowd scene (Billy's first murder) Garrett does not — now that Lew Christensen no longer dances the role — remain distinct enough from the crowd either in the sustained smoothness of his movement or in his stage presence.

Often Loring's contrasts between relaxed American movement and jerky, accentuated, Massine-style gesture are effective, often they seem accidental. But there is no doubt that Loring was the first to bring this different quality in movement into a ballet. It is this that gives *Billy* its core of dance sincerity, its fascination. And its further tragic implications, though obscure and hesitant, are perfectly real if you look closely, and they make the ballet a very remarkable American theater piece. I haven't mentioned in this the role the Copland score plays, but it is a masterpiece, at every point a decisive help to realizing the poetic meaning of *Billy*.

New York Herald Tribune, Oct. 31, 1943

Some Faults of Ballet Theatre

In the recent Ballet Theatre season the new choreographies were — except for the fair scene in Lichine's *Fair at Sorochinsk* — disappointing. I am not referring to the disappointing roughness of execution of the opening nights, but speaking of the ballets as they look at their best. At its best, a little of Massine's *Mademoiselle Angot* was amusing in a sort of overcute, opéra-bouffe style; and all of Tudor's *Dim Lustre* was a competent dance version of a modern English drawing-room play. They both had less conviction than manner, and both tried too anxiously to play safe; they were meant to look elegant, but the effect they made was only a trivial one. Luckily we know Massine and Tudor well enough as choreographers so that we needn't judge them merely by what disappoints us.

Lichine, however, has not yet established a choreographic reputation. He has shown several ballets, and besides four inconclusive ones, I remember with sincere pleasure the comedy *Graduation Ball,* done by the de Basil company. *Helen of Troy* in its present state is an excellent farce, and he is officially responsible; but after its many changes and after the persistent rumors of large-scale collaboration, one hesitates to judge him by it. The qualities in the fair scene of *Sorochinsk,* however, are distinctive and add a new style to our ballet repertory. In this scene Lichine too plays safe (as do Massine and Tudor), but he does it in more innocent a fashion. For there is obviously never anything oblique about it, in intellectual or choreographic manner. The sentiment is straight, the dancing vigorous or plain, and the sequence of it is determined by dance contrasts. The points it makes are simple, but they are not stupid: in the moonlight dance, the way the girls sail easily across the stage when the boys have bowed to them, the moment of hesitation (against the music) before the boys grab the girls, the moment of delay (also against the music) when they all face toward the moon and lift their arms — these plain effects ring true after the multiple exuberance of the folk dances before. It is no use looking for an intellectual intentness or refinement in these dances; but it is a pleasure to find that whatever there is is aboveboard: the dancing carries as dancing, the sentiment carries as sentiment.

I am not speaking here of the foolish (witches' sabbath) scene in Lichine's ballet, but only of the fair scene. The good scene is so long and complete that the bad one in the same ballet doesn't change my high opinion of Lichine's capability; but the bad one does, I am sorry to say, add to the other choreographic disappointments of this particular season. Incidentally, the Mussorgsky music for the fair scene is magnificent to dance to; the *Bald Mountain* music of the witches' scene isn't as good for dancing, and unless the dancers keep clear of the music's rhythm and beat they look dwarfed by its force.

The great disappointment of this ballet season's dancing was that Alicia Markova could appear only briefly. It was to be expected that we should miss her technical brilliance, but we missed even more her brilliance of characterization, as Giselle or Odette or Juliet or Zemphira, or in her two comic parts as Elora and as Taglioni. She alone can make each of these different characters convincing, she alone can keep them wholly within the dance illusion, where we believe in them. She has the art of never attracting attention to her private self, and the art of expressing in her role a kind of love that makes the character a rare being we watch with complete attention as long as it appears on the stage before us.

Instead of repeating once more the praise already given the various excellent dancers of the company, I should like to criticize what I think of as Ballet Theatre's general dance intention. Ballet Theatre has always stressed — so it has seemed to me watching the dancers — the obvious dramatic expression in dancing. The method has the advantage of emphasizing decision and energy in the dancer's movement, of making him try to get across a specific point to the audience, of bringing him out of the secluded studio and onto the public stage. But it has the drawback of encouraging his stage vanity, because it tempts him to be personally a focus of attention. It also makes him think his dance part unimportant unless it has a logical and special narrative function. Many dance parts have an illogical atmospheric function. In many ballets old and new it is the delicate finish of the ensemble dancer's simple movements that makes the audience appreciate the poetic intention of the piece. These parts have dance meaning rather than dramatic meaning. And most solo parts have more dance meaning than dramatic meaning, if one looks closely.

Ballet Theatre in recent seasons has developed a fine rush and verve in dancing; they disregarded, I thought, the sensitive articulation of movement which people call elegance. Ballet Theatre got across to the audience boldly; at times I have seen them overdo their parts, though, and try to top each other till the effect has been silly and vulgar. This season I feel that the company as a whole has a new interest in the ballet classics, and an interest in them is the best corrective for the faults I have mentioned. For though the classics need dance verve and stage presence in dancing to bring them to life, they also need dance elegance and personal reticence; a classic dancer doesn't spill his personal glamour all over the stage and orchestra, as a dancer in a character part is sometimes tempted to. I notice that the audience also is getting more and more interested in these old ballets. The more they are danced, the sharper the audience's eye and the clearer the dancers' execution become, so that a choreographer finds himself after a few years with a more sensitive instrument and a more sensitive public, too.

New York Herald Tribune, Nov. 14, 1943

Anna Sokolow

Anna Sokolow's modern-dance recital brought back to mind the striking impression she had made a few years ago in intense numbers evoking proletarian adolescence. Her figure with the small head, the solid neck, the small sloping shoulders and elongated limbs was immediately touching. Her hands and wrists were lovely, her arms light. Her dancing had the directness of a child's motions. When she lifted her forearm, when she ran and leaped, you watched the action itself. It was the action in itself that moved you. In composing, the way she derived dance gestures easily from pantomime, her simple formal arrangements — these "naive" qualities suited her adolescent atmosphere. And when she danced her numbers with subjective intensity the confusion between herself and her dance heroine did not bother anyone.

Conscious of Miss Sokolow's originality, I was puzzled to find her recital unsatisfactory. Her figure is still the ideal one for a dancer, her way of moving as graceful and distinct as ever. She worked with intensity; in fact, she often forced out an angry little grunt that sounded like an impatient Spanish "Eh!" — as if she were whipping herself on. But the atmosphere of her presence had changed; this time her own presence was not that of an adolescent. It was that of a lady, of an adult.

Unfortunately, Miss Sokolow's present adult subjective fervor no longer suits the girlish simplicity of her former compositions; the more intense she becomes the more she hides their real character. And so the old numbers dealing with such themes as slum childhood, juvenile delinquency, or Loyalist Madrid — numbers that once seemed natural as adolescent reflections — now, seen in an adult atmosphere, look artificial and false to their terrible themes.

In addition to old numbers, Miss Sokolow also showed a new long work, *Songs of a Semite* (for four dancers, a musician, a singer, and a speaker). It presents a Jewess who feels homeless and lost; she remembers — in the form of dance episodes — the courage of several women in the Old Testament, and then she finally joins them in a brave march. The theme is a special one and the audience applauded the piece. But, though I thought it rounder in movement and maturer in tone than the earlier numbers, it seemed confused in its storytelling and repetitious in gesture, and it seemed inadequate as an evocation of legends so heroic, or an emotion so religious. To me Ruth's dance looked only a little tender, Miriam's only a little exultant, and Miss Sokolow, as the meditating figure, seemed to move more like a torch singer than a real person. The truest moments, I thought, were small and sweet ones.

What about the big moments? I believe the trouble is that Miss Sokolow has not developed enough variety of expression in dancing, a wide enough variety in its technical resources, to represent a complex theme from an adult point of view. Technically, the dancer's trunk is loaded with energy, but the energy remains latent. It is not used in muscular actions that would give the torso plastic variation, not in weight in the arms, not in lightness in the thighs, not in the play of the feet with music. You don't see the impetus increase or decrease, the body soften or harden, the movement float or break, the figure gain expression by its path on the stage. Such qualities are only hinted at. But they are the expressive material of dancing, and it is to make their contrasts clearer to the audience that modern dancers, from Isadora on, have preferred to abandon the tradition of ballet forms.

Whatever the dance form (ballet, modern, or as yet uninvented), the actual realization of such expressive effects is what constitutes the dance tradition. A tradition is not a police regulation, nor is it a device for repetition. It is a practical aid to an artist. It is useful for suggesting practical methods, for reminding him of expressive possibilities, for encouraging him by showing him that other persons have been faced with similar difficulties. A tradition is an artist's home base; or, to reapply Wordsworth's remark, it is the "tranquillity" in which the event that is the artist's subject is "recollected." And his tradition also is, as Auden has said, what he can judge himself by.

Miss Sokolow's own *Songs of a Semite* has, at least in intellectual intention, this same point in view, since it draws the moral that a tradition is a good thing for an adult individual.

New York Herald Tribune, Dec. 12, 1943

Graham's *Deaths and Entrances* and *Salem Shore*

Martha Graham, no doubt the greatest celebrity in the American dance world, appeared last night at the Forty-sixth Street Theater, giving her first Broadway recital in two seasons. The house was sold out the first day of the ticket sale, and the performance is to be repeated January 9.

Miss Graham presented two new works, *Salem Shore* and *Deaths and Entrances. Deaths and Entrances* is a piece for ten dancers — six women and four men — and is described in the program as "a legend of poetic experience rather than a story of incident. It concerns the restless pacings of the heart on some winter evening." In performance it is long, obscure, of intense interest and extraordinary richness of invention.

The action concerns three sisters. The memories and fantasies that pass through their ardent hearts are personified by other dancers, whom they move among and touch, so that reality and imagination are no longer two distinct experiences. The Brontë sisters, who used to pace in the firelight on winter evenings at Haworth, imagining the passions of their novels, are a kind of model. But the piece is in no sense biographical.

One might describe it instead as a poem in the associative or *symboliste* technique, a sequence of tightly packed and generally violent images following a subconscious logic.

But it is Miss Graham's own performance that is the extraordinary and fascinating focus in which one sees this irrational world as a real experience. The intensity with which she projects agitation, wonder, fury, or — at the end — a heroic acceptance of fate is a unique quality. Unique, too, is the extraordinary technique with which she makes every movement seem that of an actual person, not of a performer. The other dancers, accurate and excellent though they are, cannot give their movement this sharp immediacy. Miss Graham constantly controls not only the active driving portion of a gesture, but also its passive, unemphatic phase. She changes the speed of a gesture after its instant of fulfillment, and so gives the motion a living rhythm that is wonderfully dramatic. This is in all kinds of dancing a perfection of technical intelligence, and you hardly ever see it.

The other novelty, *Salem Shore,* is a solo for Miss Graham, describing the longing of a young wife for her husband's return from the sea. It is not at all the wildly dramatic number one might expect; it is a discreetly poignant piece. By presenting her heroine as a reticent young lady of Salem, a girl who remembers playing on the shore as a child but knows she is now an adult, Miss Graham makes the character an interesting and real one. The handling of stage properties is particularly "natural," and quite unusual in that sense. Miss Graham looks wonderfully young in this piece.

The orchestra, under Louis Horst, performed the specially composed scores by Paul Nordhoff, Hunter Johnson, and Robert McBride. They were useful accompaniments, and their quality was generally good.

The costuming of the novelties by Edythe Gilfond was excellent, and the stage sets by Arch Lauterer effective, modest, and useful. The lighting by Jean Rosenthal was superb.

Among the dancers in the company Merce Cunningham's long dance phrases, his lightness, and his constantly intelligent head are very fine. Erick Hawkins and Nina Fonaroff shone particularly in the last number, *Punch and the Judy,* a sardonic comedy of white-collar married life first seen two seasons ago. In this Miss Graham can make the house laugh by a flick of the wrist, so accurate is her timing and her emphasis. As a comedian too her distinction is extraordinary.

New York Herald Tribune, Dec. 27, 1943

Deaths and Entrances Revisited

It isn't often I've seen the lobby in the intermission so animated in its discussion of a ballet as it was after Martha Graham's new *Deaths and Entrances.* The piece is a harsh one: it has neither a touching story, nor a harmonious development, nor wit and charm to help it along. But at both its recent performances it has held the audience spellbound. What fascinates is the movement itself as it takes place on the stage — the rapid succession of curiously expressive and unforeseen bursts of gesture, the urgency they have, and above all the intense vividness of Miss Graham's own dancing.

Her dancing does not look stylized or calculated; it looks spontaneous as movements do in life or as Markova's motion does on the stage. Miss Graham's effect of spontaneity comes from attention to that part of the gesture which is like the following-through in athletics, the part which restores the body to balance after an effort, which relaxes the tension after an outward stress. Most dancers do this mechanically and their dance, though accurate, looks wooden. Miss Graham, by making the speed of the unemphatic and relaxing movements just a little different from what one would have expected, gives animation and a personal rhythm to the ebbing of energy, too. It makes all her dance look elastic, fresh, and ungloomy. Such an unexpectedness of rhythm is what delights us in the playful motions of children and animals; in the calculated clarity of dancing only the great stars can look as free as children.

A spontaneous look has little to do with novelty in the general shape of a gesture. In fact, the more novelty of gesture, the less freedom of movement is the common rule. Just the same, Miss Graham wants every movement to be a novel one. She finds new varieties of hobbling, kicking backward, sinking in one's steps, going with a bounce; she finds caressing undulations, flights looking downward, reactions to the touch of a hand, spidery dartings of the arms, possessed shoulder-shakes, or a group of deformed graces holding hands. One has the impression of not having seen any of the movements the ten dancers do before, of never having seen bodies take these odd shapes.

Such extreme originality is shocking, and it is suited to the shocking subject of the piece. *Deaths and Entrances* is a homage to Emily Brontë, the stoic young woman who conceived the terrors of *Wuthering Heights.* It is meant in one sense as an image of her heart, and in the dance we see reflected some of the strange wonders that absorbed her — incestuous family love-and-hate, the duplicit need in a woman for both a brutal and a tender contact, "perverted passion and passionate perversity" mounting to real madness and ending heroically sane. Like the actions in Emily Brontë's novel, the movements of the dance look frantic, but not at all indecent.

The current of *Deaths and Entrances* is frenzied, and one is never at one's ease in it. One is never prepared for the next moment. What holds the piece together is the lucid concentration of Miss Graham in the central role, a personage to whom all the actions on the stage are completely real. They are images she contemplates within herself and also sees independently active outside her; and her mobile face lights up at the objective impressions. She is adolescently tender dancing with her two Beloveds at once; she is terrifying and horrible in her mad scene; her final gesture is adult, like tragedy. Very strange, too, is the mysterious elegance which never leaves her.

I hope that Ballet Theatre (or the Monte Carlo) when it comes to town will invite Miss Graham and her company to perform *Deaths and Entrances* as a guest production on its programs. As it is the most extraordinary novelty of the season, the general public will be curious to see it and to form its own opinion of it.

New York Herald Tribune, Jan. 16, 1944

The Rockettes and Rhythm

The Rockettes at the Music Hall are an American institution and a very charming one. Their cheerfulness is sweet as that of a church social. Their dancing is fresh and modest, their rhythm accurate and light, and everyone can see that they accomplish what they set out to do to perfection. At the end of their routine, when the line of them comes forward in a precision climax, the house takes all thirty-six of them collectively to its family heart. It is a very pleasant moment of contentment all around.

The Music Hall has a charming chorus of classic-ballet girls too, who, like the tap-dancing Rockettes, are perfectly accurate in their timing and exact in their motions. They too dance without affectation in a graceful and modest manner. Just as the Rockettes avoid what is "hot" and disturbing in taps, so the toe dancers avoid what is intensely expressive in ballet; instead they are phenomenally neat, they never blur anything they do, and everyone can see they fully deserve their applause.

The ballet doesn't, to be sure, establish a family feeling in the house as the Rockettes do, but then you rarely see toe dancing in the living room and you often see tap dancing there. Ballet is meant to be seen at a distance, it isn't relaxed or familiar in its bearing. But there is a further reason why the ballet is less effective at the Music Hall than the tap routine. In both of them the dramatic punch of the number lies in the unique (and apparently effortless) synchronization of all the dancers and of the entire dance with the music. While this feat heightens very much the sense of rhythm you get from the Rockettes, it doesn't somehow heighten the sense of rhythm you get from the ballet; though it's just as difficult a feat for the latter, it doesn't carry so in ballet.

The fact is that tap and ballet rhythm are different to start with, in the way they connect with the music. The tap dancer plays with the beat, he plays around it and he never leaves it alone. Whatever else he does in the way of elegant ornament, it's the beat that interests him, and each beat does. You see his relation to it in his motion and you hear it in his taps, and his relation to it is the excitement in the dance. The "hotter" he is, the more intimate and dramatic his relation to it becomes; but he can hold your interest just by showing a cool and a sure relation. And a tap-dancing chorus can by complete synchronization fix with a kind of finality the relation of the dance to the music and so reach a satisfying expression. You know what to follow and at the end you know where you are.

But you don't follow a ballet beat by beat. Ballet dancing probably once had a good deal of this percussive quality — so eighteenth-century dance music suggests. In 1890s ballet you can see a percussive dance number in the Cygnet quartet in *Swan Lake.* Contemporary American ballet tends to use this device more sharply — you see it in parts of *Rodeo* and particularly in *Concerto Barocco.* Here the sound of the dancers' toe steps is part of the effect. But these passages are details. More generally the rhythmic interest in ballet dancing isn't fixed on the beat or on the dancers' relation to it; the interest is in their relation to the musical phrase, to the melody, to the musical period. At such times their rhythm is a "free" one, more like that of a singer in its variety of emphasis than like that of a tap dancer.

Like the blues singer, the ballet dancer takes a freer emphasis for the sake of more intense dramatic (or lyric) expression, so he can change his speed against the steady music, so he can make more kinds of effects with his body and travel more freely about the stage. The spring that is the life and rhythm of taps is not tied to the beat in ballet; it has been extended, so to speak, into a lift in the expression of the dance; you follow the rhythm not by separate steps but by the rise and fall of extended phrases.

In taps you see and hear two different rhythms, both of them in the same strict musical meter. In ballet you often look at a free meter and listen to a strict one. Complete synchronization of ballet and music is a special effect that works by contrast to other rhythmic possibilities and it satisfies only when used for such a contrast. People accustomed to strict acoustic rhythm often take a while to get used to ballet rhythm so they can follow it, but there are many too who can't follow a tap dancer, who lose track of any dance rhythm unless it pounds the downbeat. Well, that's why there are several kinds of dance rhythm to suit different types of the human receiving set.

New York Herald Tribune, Feb. 20, 1944

Humphrey's *Inquest*

Doris Humphrey's new *Inquest* is a dance that leaves no doubt as to its story or its point. The story is clearly told by a speaker, who reads a newspaper report of an inquest held in 1865 in a London slum. We hear of a destitute family, father, mother, and son, who lived in a squalid room. The son began to go blind; finally the father died of starvation. As we listen to the words we also watch the scenes they tell us of, they are acted out in quiet pantomime upstage, in a small space like a room. When in between the pantomime scenes a number of persons pass in files across the darkened stage it is easy to think of them as neighbors passing along the streets. When the story has been told and the neighbors begin a rushing dance sequence to music, it is clear that this dance is their emotional reaction to the story.

But the story has made a further specific point. By quoting sentences spoken by the two survivors at the inquest, the news account has shown us the devotion of the three central characters to one another and to their home. In the pantomime scenes Miss Humphrey, Mr. Weidman, and Mr. Hamilton, who portray the three, give the sense of the dignity of a united family very strikingly. They make us realize that the theme of the piece is the destruction of a home. And so when the movement, which during the story portion was slow and repressed, then bursts into rushing violence in the dance sequences, with stamps and clenched fists, we are quite ready to accept it as expressing our own anger and grief. And at the end, when it grows calm and sustained, we take it as expressing a firm and valid reproach. The piece has pointed out that poverty destroys humane values we all believe in. We applaud it as a sincere and eloquent sermon on the theme of the freedom from want.

If a dancer feels like preaching he has as good a right to do it as any other citizen, and the theater has always liked a sermon now and then. *Inquest* is a piece that appeals to our moral sensibility; it aims to be clear and its aesthetic appeal is secondary. The audience approved of it very much indeed. For my part, I was also interested in something that has often struck me in dances with an excellent propaganda purpose: the difference in speed between getting the ideas and following the dances. One grasps the moral implications quickly and agrees with them. But the full rhetorical exposition of these ideas in dance form takes a good deal longer. The result is that one's response is complete before the dance is finished; and at *Inquest,* too, I was ready for a new idea while, for the sake of emphasis, the dancers were still dwelling on the old one. As the secondary, purely aesthetic appeal was slight, there was a gap in the interest.

Intellectually speaking, an interesting dance is a continuous discovery. The ideas it presents do not precede it, they are formed after one has perceived the movement. And because an interesting dance creates new ideas, it is often not at all easy to understand nor in accord with what one would reasonably expect. This, of course, does not do for propaganda.

Inquest is concerned with reminding us of an idea we all approve and urging us to act on it — and that it does rationally, with complete clarity. It begs the question of how a dance creates its own novel meaning as it goes along.

New York Herald Tribune, Mar. 12, 1944

A Note on Dance Intelligence

Expression in dancing is what really interests everybody, and everybody recognizes it as a sign of intelligence in the dancer. But dancing is physical motion, it doesn't involve words at all. And so it is an error to suppose that dance intelligence is the same as other sorts of intelligence which involve, on the contrary, words only and no physical movement whatever. What is expressive in a dance is not the dancer's opinions, psychological, political, or moral. It isn't even what she thinks about episodes in her private life. What is expressive in dancing is the way she moves about the stage, the way she exhibits her body in motion. A dancer's intelligence isn't shown by what intellectual allusions she can make in costume or pantomime, or, if she is a choreographer, in her subject matter. It is shown by how interesting to look at she can make her body the whole time she is on the stage.

In the coming ballet season you may be able to compare Alexandra Danilova, Nana Gollner, and Alicia Markova, each as the Swan Queen in *Swan Lake* and each one celebrated in that particular part. Each will be interesting to look at the whole time she will be on the stage, but the effect they make will be different. Watching the three in turn you may see what differences in their physical movement parallel their difference of expression and see how the dance intelligence of each leads her to a slightly different visual emphasis in identical steps and gymnastic feats.

Far apart from questions of choreography, it is variety of visual emphasis that we see when we feel variety of expression. And there are many resources for visual emphasis in dancing. There are the shifts in the pacing of a sequence, the points where the dancer hurries or delays. An identical step or arm gesture can be attacked sharply or mildly, it can subside or be stopped short. These differences draw the eye to one phase of motion rather than another, to one line of the body rather than another, or to the dancer's partner, or else to her momentary position on the stage, or even to a moment in the music which sharpens our sense of her movement.

But the most interesting resource for visual emphasis is the heightened perception of the dancer's body not in a line or silhouette, but in its mass, in its all-aroundness. A dancer can emphasize a passage in the dance by emphasizing the shape her body takes in the air. When she does this she does not call attention merely to the limb that moves, she defines her presence all around in every direction. At such moments she looks large, important, like a figure of imagination, like an ideal human being moving through the air at will. The great dancers seem to do this throughout a dance, but they vary it in intensity.

These are some of the physical characteristics of dance expression, and the brilliant use of them to arouse our interest, to thrill and to satisfy us, is proof of an artist's exceptional dance intelligence. She may have several other sorts of intelligence besides, but it is of no consequence to the public if she has not. It is the boldness and tenderness of her dance intelligence that the public loves her for.

New York Herald Tribune, Mar. 26, 1944

A Forum on Dance Criticism

Agnes de Mille, speaking on a forum on dance criticism recently, made a point I should like to pass on to other dancers as the wisest advice I know on the relation of the dancer to the critic. She spoke of the alternate confident and uncertain periods through which artists pass and how in his uncertainty the dancer longs for assistance and clarification. He is tempted then to turn to the critic to lead him out of his confusion by an authoritative estimate of his individual creative gifts. But Miss de Mille warned against relying on reviews in such moments of doubt. A good critic will tell the dancer which elements in a work get across and which do not. But that alone does not necessarily indicate the most productive, the most sincere direction for the dancer to take. An artist will find his own real strength not by listening to what is said about his work, but in the creative process itself. And it is safer for him to rely on himself to find his own identity; for it is unlikely that anyone else can find it for him.

The forum at which Miss de Mille spoke so brilliantly was held at the YMHA during the storm last Wednesday night in a large comfortable crowded room. The other speakers were Mary Jane Shea, the very gifted choreographer of *Sailor Bar,* B. H. Haggin of *The Nation,* George Beiswanger of *Theatre Arts, Dance Observer,* and *Dance News,* and Milton Robertson, a young radio writer; I acted as chairman. The audience took a lively part in the discussion, which turned on the function of the dance critic, what one can expect of him and what he is good for.

Mr. Robertson affirmed that a critic should be a propagandist, that it is his function to create a movement in the right direction, to popularize good art and teach as large an audience as possible what and how to enjoy. But this radio-minded view met with opposition. Not one of the other speakers, and few, it seemed, of the audience, could see the critic as a glorified teacher with all a teacher's classroom authority. Most of those present agreed with Mr. Haggin, who stated that the best critic is a man of exceptional perceptiveness who reports as clearly as possible to his reader. His merit does not lie in dictating what is to be right or wrong. It lies in animating the reader's own perceptions, so that he can see the work more distinctly for himself. This much one can expect of a good critic. But to direct new movements, to popularize the appreciation of masterpieces, to encourage artists, these are not the critic's function; he has no power and no authority to affect them.

On the subject of the critic's lack of authority, Mr. Chujoy, the ballet critic, remarked from the audience that for ten years each season every dance critic has condemned *Schéhérazade,* but *Schéhérazade* continues to be given and is as popular as ever.

For myself, I too quite agree with Mr. Haggin's realistic view of what the critic at best accomplishes. I find the critic looks ridiculous in the role of a dictator of taste and also in that role against which Miss de Mille warned, that of a fortune teller for artists. And yet in practice both roles are constantly being assigned him. With charming good humor, some members of the forum audience, after agreeing that the critic was not a teacher, asked if he couldn't, though, teach just a little. I guess a critic won't quite avoid being a bit of a pedagogue and a bit of a charlatan. But I'm all for everybody's recognizing that these are not his functions, that his function is as Mr. Haggin

said: to notice, to order, to report; or as Virgil Thomson has said: to put down
a sort of portrait of what went on.

New York Herald Tribune, Apr. 2, 1944

Merce Cunningham

At the small Humphrey-Weidman Studio in the darkness of Sixteenth Street,
Merce Cunningham and John Cage presented a program of solo dances and
of percussionist music last night which was of the greatest aesthetic elegance.
The audience, an intelligent one, enjoyed and applauded.

It was Mr. Cunningham's first solo recital, though he is well known to
dance audiences as soloist in Martha Graham's company. His gifts as a lyric
dancer are most remarkable. His build resembles that of the juvenile *saltim-
banques* of the early Picasso canvases. As a dancer his instep and his knees
are extraordinarily elastic and quick; his steps, runs, knee bends, and leaps
are brilliant in lightness and speed. His torso can turn on its vertical axis with
great sensitivity, his shoulders are held lightly free, and his head poises
intelligently. The arms are light and long, they float, but do not often have an
active look. These are all merits particularly suited to lyric expression.

As a dancer and as a choreographer of his own solos, Mr. Cunningham's
sense of physical rhythm is subtle and clear. His dances are built on the
rhythm of a body in movement, and on its irregular phrase lengths. And the
perfection with which he can indicate the rise and fall of an impulse gives one
an aesthetic pleasure of exceptional delicacy. His compositions too were in
no way derivative in their formal aspect, or in their gesture; they looked free
and definite at the same time.

The effect of them is one of an excessively elegant sensuality. On the other
hand — partly because they are solo dances, partly because they lack the
vigorous presence of the body's deportment characteristic of academic ballet
style — their effect is one of remoteness and isolation. This tone may well be
due to the fact that Mr. Cunningham is still a young dancer, who is only
beginning to discover his own dramatic resources. But I have never seen a
first recital that combined such taste, such technical finish, such originality of
dance material, and so sure a manner of presentation.

Mr. Cage accompanied the six dances on "prepared" piano and his compositions for them were perfect as dance accompaniment. He also played six piano solos of his own, accompanied Juanita Hall in two songs (one to a text from *Finnegans Wake*), and directed his quartet *Amores,* performed at the Modern Museum last year. The new pieces were applauded — as had been those heard last year — for the delicate sensuality of their odd timbres, for their rhythmic subtlety, and their willfully remote tenuousness of construction. His music, like Mr. Cunningham's dancing, has an effect of extreme elegance in isolation.

New York Herald Tribune, Apr. 6, 1944

Serenade

Balanchine's *Serenade* was beautifully danced last night by the Monte Carlo at the City Center, and it is a completely beautiful ballet.

George Balanchine is the greatest choreographer of our time. He is Petipa's heir. His style is classical: grand without being impressive, clear without being strict. It is humane because it is based on the patterns the human body makes when it dances; it is not — like romantic choreography — based on patterns the human body cannot quite force itself into. His dance evolutions and figures are luminous in their spacing, and of a miraculous musicality in their impetus. Sentiment, fancy, and wit give them warmth and immediacy. But as the audience actually watches, it all looks so playful and light, so unemphatic and delicate, it doesn't seem to call for noisy applause. Ten years later, when noisier successes have faded, one finds with surprise that his have kept intact their first freshness and their natural bloom.

Serenade is a kind of graduation exercise: the dancers seem to perform all the feats they have learned, both passages of dancing and passages of mime (or plastique). There is no story, though there seems to be a girl who meets a boy; he comes on with another girl and for a while all three are together; then, at the end, the first girl is left alone and given a sort of tragic little apotheosis.

I was delighted to hear some giggling in the audience at the parts where all three were together — it showed how well the point got across; the audience at plays giggles too when the sentiment becomes intimate, it is our national way of reacting to that emotion. After giggling last night they gasped a little at some particularly beautiful lifts and then began applauding them.

New York Herald Tribune, Apr. 15, 1944

A Monte Carlo Matinee

At the City Center, at the Saturday matinee, the Monte Carlo gave their three-scene version of *The Nutcracker,* and the children in the audience were impressed when little Clara — no older than they — came on in the third scene and all the dancers bowed to her and she to them. But at the jumping Chinaman they crowed and burbled with pleasure all over the house. Later, they approved the rodeo scene in *Rodeo* as audibly, especially when the heroine fell off her imaginary horse and rolled over on the floor. A few of them, I imagine, will remember many years from now the gently wonderful radiance of Danilova and Youskevitch in the *Nutcracker* duets, and will be in doubt if dancing could really have been as beautiful as that. But it was.

In *Rodeo,* Vida Brown took Miss Etheridge's part as the Cowgirl heroine. Miss Brown's version of the part is more open, more assertive, more horsey. She looks healthy and attractive, she puts the pantomime points across clearly, and she has no trouble filling a star role. On the other hand she does not give — as Miss Etheridge so brilliantly does — the sense of a girl who only gradually discovers what it means to be a girl. It is this gradual, painful, and at the end happy discovery that is the dramatic heart of the piece. And you realize that Miss Etheridge's Cowgirl is really in love with the honest and openhearted Champion Roper whom she gets, while Miss Brown's seems to take him good-naturedly as a second choice in place of the dark and fascinating Chief Wrangler.

New York Herald Tribune, Apr. 16, 1944

Fancy Free

Jerome Robbins's *Fancy Free,* the world premiere given by Ballet Theatre last night at the Metropolitan, was so big a hit that the young participants all looked a little dazed as they took their bows. But besides being a smash hit, *Fancy Free* is a very remarkable comedy piece. Its sentiment of how people live in this country is completely intelligent and completely realistic. Its pantomime and its dances are witty, exuberant, and at every moment they feel natural. It is a direct, manly piece: there isn't any of that coy showing off of "folk" material that dancers are doing so much nowadays. The whole number is as sound as a superb vaudeville turn; in ballet terminology it is perfect American character ballet.

Straight character dancing has to do with lowlife characters. *Fancy Free* deals with three sailors on shore leave who come into a bar. They pick up one girl who happens by, then a second girl. That makes two girls for three sailors. The three sailors first show off, and then they fight: result, they lose both girls. Now, too late, a third girl shows up. They decide it isn't worth getting into another fight about her. And then comes a tag line, so to speak, and a blackout.

If you want to be technical you can find in the steps all sorts of references to our normal dance-hall steps, as they are done from Roseland to the Savoy: trucking, the boogie, knee drops, even a round-the-back done in slow motion. But the details aren't called to your attention. Or when each of the sailors to show off does a specialty number you may take John Kriza's turn (the second) as a Tudor parody and Jerome Robbins's rhumba as a dig at Massine mannerisms. But they are just as effective without an extra implication. Most effective of them was the first dance of the three, Harold Lang's brilliant acrobatic turn, with splits like those of the Berry Brothers. It was in this number that the house took fire, and from there on the ballet was a smash.

Leonard Bernstein, the young composer of *Jeremiah,* wrote the score for *Fancy Free* and conducted it brilliantly. It has complex nervous rhythms and violent contrasts of thin and thick orchestral texture. I thought it a little overcomplicated, and not quite charming enough; but it was a hit, too, and the musicians I spoke to commented on the brilliance of its orchestration. I liked best the rhumba for Robbins's solo. Oliver Smith's set is in the style of vaudeville sets; it is a perfect space for the seven characters of the piece to dance in, but it is less interesting to look at than his previous sets. It, too, was applauded. Kermit Love's costumes for the three girls were perfect. So were the girls.

New York Herald Tribune, Apr. 19, 1944

Pearl Primus

Pearl Primus, the young Negro modern dancer, who has attained celebrity via ten months at Café Society Downtown, gave a solo recital at the Ninety-second Street YMHA last Saturday and repeated the program on Sunday. Both dates were sold out long ahead. Since her last recital in January (jointly with Valerie Bettis) Miss Primus has made striking progress in the technical finish of her dancing, and the revisions she has made in her numbers are all of them interesting choreographic improvements. Now her magnificent natural dance impulse is seen even better than before.

Strange Fruit and *African Ceremonial* were on Saturday especially impressive. In these dances the detail was exactly defined, the continuity consistent throughout, and in *Strange Fruit* the pacing was brilliantly contrasted. There were three new numbers on the program, of which *Study in Blues,* a little joke, was the most finished.

In one serious piece, the reiterated leaps were so fine that the house broke in with applause. And in *Hard Time Blues* Miss Primus did another leap that by its drive and height made the audience gasp. It happened that the second and third similar leaps in this number did not succeed so well: the second one, because it was turned the wrong way; the third, because when she came to it she missed her breath and so the run up to the leap was not sharp. It is proof of Miss Primus's taste that she does these startling leaps only rarely, and only for the sake of their expression at that moment in the number.

Miss Primus has astonishing gifts of movement — for flow, for lightness, for power; and her powerful body is beautifully plastic on the stage. With constant stage experience, her stage personality grows sweeter and more direct. Though the dance effect of almost any young dancer's solo recital is repetitive and strained, Miss Primus's seemed varied and easy. She seemed, too, to rely less on the moral sanction of her themes to awaken sympathy and interest, and more on the buoyant drive of her dance; and in the theater, whatever the theme, it is not the theme, it is the actual dancing that really wins the audience's faith.

New York Herald Tribune, Apr. 24, 1944

Dark Elegies

Tudor's *Dark Elegies,* on yesterday's program at the Metropolitan, is Ballet Theatre's *Parsifal.* A sort of *Weihefestspiel* given only once or twice a season, it is said to be Tudor's favorite among his works, and Miss Kaye and Mr.

Laing, the stars who interpret his work so brilliantly, are said to consider it his masterpiece. The reviewer feels respect for these opinions, but he does not share them.

Dark Elegies is set to Mahler's *Kindertotenlieder,* a luxurious, slightly overstuffed symphonic setting of the touchingly intimate poems by Rückert on the death of children. In the orchestra a man sings the words. On the stage seven young women and four young men, dressed in the Youth Movement fashions of Republican Germany, dance a stylized version of Nordic folk dances. The dance figures have the flavor of a vestigial ritual and the solemn expression of the dancers is ritualistic also. They look a little like modern dancers of some years back doing a symbolic number.

The actual dance detail of *Dark Elegies* is willfully spare, but it is also of a remarkable elegance in its arrangement. The timing of the accents, the placing of the dancers, the correspondences of dance phrases to musical ones, the variety of invention — all this is completely interesting. The look of helplessness in the men's arm movements, in the women's toe steps, and in the remarkable lifts has a distinct pathos. The running circles at the climax are very effective. But the fact that this helpless and impoverished tone is continued so long, and continued even during the consolatory last section, leaves me with the feeling that at the end there has been no dramatic progress, that the stage characters have exhibited their suffering and have gone off content with that. It gives the ballet a faintly stuffy, holier-than-thou expression.

New York Herald Tribune, Apr. 26, 1944

A Tribute to Youskevitch

The Ballet Russe de Monte Carlo closed its spring season at the City Center Saturday night with a program consisting of *Etude, Cuckolds' Fair, Pas de Deux Classique* ["Black Swan"] (danced by Alexandra Danilova and Igor Youskevitch), and *Red Poppy.* It was the pas de deux that was the event of the evening, and it was Seaman Second-Class Youskevitch — dancing on the last night of his shore leave — who made it so.

At the moment Youskevitch is at the peak of his classic style. His style is calm, rich, and elastic. It is completely correct. You see easily what the action is, how the trunk takes the main direction of the dance, and how the limbs vary the force and the drive by calculated countermovements. The changing shape of the dancing body is vigorously defined. The weight of the body and the abundant strength of it are equally clear; and the two aspects blend gracefully in the architectural play of classic sequences. The distribution of energy is intelligent and complex. In his leaps, for instance, the noble arm positions, the tilt of the head sideways or forward, make you watch with interest a whole man who leaps; you don't watch, as with most dancers, only the lively legs. And while most dancers leap for the sake of the bound upward only, Youskevitch (like Markova) leaps for the entire trajectory, and for a mysterious repose he keeps as he hangs in the air.

The completeness of his dance education is unique among our classic male dancers. His rhythm is free, his characterization economical, his lift gracious. His stage presence has none of that hard insistence on attention that breaks the illusion and the flow of a classic ballet. It is unanxious and gentle confiding. True, he has neither blazing temperament not dazzling edge; at times I find his romantic miming a trifle too politely eager; I prefer Franklin's Hussar in *Danube* to Youskevitch's. But if Igor hasn't every quality imaginable, I, at least, know of no dancer anywhere who is nearer than he to perfection.

And now he is returning to his base, it is hard to think how the Monte Carlo can long continue as a first-class company without him.

New York Herald Tribune, May 1, 1944

Markova's Giselle: Ballet Theatre's Glory

Alicia Markova in *Giselle* is Ballet Theatre's greatest glory. Last night was the second of three performances of *Giselle* on this season's programs; and it was a gala evening at the Metropolitan. Miss Markova danced once again with incomparable beauty of style — dazzlingly limpid, mysteriously tender.

There is no other dancer whose movement is so perfectly centered, and who controls so exactly the full continuity of a motion from the center to the extremities. There is no other dancer whose waist and thighs are so quick to execute the first actions that lead to an arm gesture and to a step, or who diminishes the stress so precisely as it travels outward along the arms and legs. It is this that gives her dancing figure its incomparable clarity, its delicacy, and its repose. It is this, too, that makes her dance rhythm so clear to the eye and so full of variety.

This superlative dance intelligence makes her dance fascinating, both as pure motion and as motion to music. The fragility of her figure, the dramatic conviction of her characterization give her dance another and equally strong expressivity. Her physical and intellectual concentration confer on her a mysterious remoteness and isolation, and this tragic dignity makes her expressions of tenderness extraordinarily touching.

All her qualities, of dancing, of mime, of presence, find a perfect use in the part of Giselle; the extraordinary effect Miss Markova creates in this part is obvious to the thousands who watch her, whether they are familiar with ballet or not. Last night again she received a unanimous ovation.

New York Herald Tribune, May 6, 1944

Where Are the New Serious Ballets?

The April "war" between Ballet Theatre and the Monte Carlo would have been more exciting to watch if it had been a competition between artistic directions instead of a competition for customers. There were plenty of customers everywhere, so both companies won. Ballet Theatre, of course, had the smash hit, *Fancy Free,* and it had all through the smarter public. But it didn't allow its great choreographer, Mr. Tudor, to produce a new serious work; nor had the Monte Carlo allowed its guiding artist, Mme Nijinska, also a great choreographer, to create a serious new piece. Though the dancing was often superb and the audience got its money's worth, neither company can boast of a new production an intelligent citizen can get excited over; with all their rich resources neither company produced anything as remarkable as Martha Graham's *Deaths and Entrances.*

Ballet Theatre has given native-born choreographers a chance as long as they would entertain. The Monte Carlo has tried to get the foreigners to be cute. No doubt the heavy touring schedules of both organizations make it impossible for them to rehearse with concentration. And no doubt the general public likes light pieces. But it is striking how the daily public here in town responds to the heavy ones, the abstract ones, the classic ones. Both companies underestimate the intelligence, the sensibility, and the curiosity of the public. And they have no faith in the special power of a disinterested creation. One can't win an artistic victory without taking an artistic chance. And without such a special kind of victory no amount of success can counterbalance the decline of prestige.

Artistic prestige is ballet's chief economic asset. In order to survive, ballet has to keep in competition with the classics — as contemporary serious painting, music, and poetry do. It can't compete with commercial entertainment. This is not a matter of snobbishness, it is strictly a money matter. Ballet is too extravagant an apparatus to exist without subvention, public or private; it is as extravagant as a museum, or a symphony orchestra. In their artistic policy all of these enterprises must sell themselves to the kind of money that can pay for them — in their case the solid fortunes of trusts, foundations, and states. Once our ballet succeeds in interesting such money, it can stop living from hand to mouth and present itself in its proper splendor.

And it is the solid world of the classics and of their serious contemporary competitors — representing as it does long-term artistic capital — that is most congenial to such long-term fortunes; while the world of commercial entertainment — strictly short-term artistic capital — normally appeals to short-term fortunes as a congenial field for their erratic spending.

But there is a simpler argument in favor of a disinterested artistic policy. It is that a ballet company is a company of artists, and artists lose their vitality when they cannot feel around them an atmosphere of artistic conviction.

For the moment success is enough to give our dancers vitality. And though I feel that the glamour of momentary success is no solid foundation on which to build an American ballet, I am full of admiration for their freshness, their earnestness, and their unremitting intensity. Their own artistic integrity is unimpeachable.

New York Herald Tribune, May 7, 1944

Graham's *American Document* and *Primitive Mysteries*

Last night's program of Martha Graham and her company at the National consisted of *Primitive Mysteries, Punch and the Judy,* and *American Document. Primitive Mysteries* is a gentle work of ten years ago which many recall with pleasure. Suggested — like several other of Miss Graham's works — by the Spanish-Mexican art of the Southwest, it is consciously naive in its gesture. It contrasts the rigid, heavy, underslung stance of the group of girls with Miss Graham's delicate refinement; she is a Madonnalike figure who sheds her grace gently on her peasant worshippers. The sense of communion on the stage is touching, and unforced. Only the repeated processional entrances and exits exaggerate the pseudo-naive stylization; as a whole the work is distinctly a happy one. The music by Louis Horst is flowing, beautifully shaped, and reticently expressive. Of all Miss Graham's scores his are by far the most musical and apt.

American Document, on the other hand, is in its present form a complete failure. Originally it seemed at least to conceal some sting of protest and to present our history as much for its disgraces as for its strength. At present it seems intended merely as smug glorification. It is monotonous as dancing and in sentiment varies from hollow solemnity to mawkish sentimentalism. The opening of Miss Graham's Indian solo and one sentence quoted from Jonathan Edwards are the only thirty seconds of interest; the rest seems as insincere as those patriotic full-page advertisements in color in the slick-paper magazines.

One can see that Miss Graham's intentions were to make the movement open, plain, and buoyant. Perhaps it is her own natural subtlety that defeated her. The movement turns out to be inelastic, it strikes poses, and it pounds downward. The company performed the piece very handsomely, and one failure is not a disgrace to any choreographer.

New York Herald Tribune, May 12, 1944

A Ballet Lover's View of Martha Graham

Any one of Martha Graham's highly intelligent pieces would gain in theatrical brilliancy if she and her company could present it singly, say, as an item on a Ballet Theatre program. Her particular genius would flash more strikingly right next to the genius of other choreographers and dancers who excel at other aspects of dancing. Some of my friends are shocked by this genius of hers and they tell me she has no style, that she fascinates merely as heretics do, by her contrariness. But I keep being struck in all her work by its intellectual seriousness, its inventiveness, and its exact workmanship; and these are qualities I can't think of as heretical or contrary. They offer a moral basis for style. I see no reason why one shouldn't try to place her work in relation to the ballet tradition and see what is special in her dance method.

The special thing about Miss Graham is not that she is a modernist. Almost no one nowadays is anything else. Modernism in dancing is really a conservative tendency. Its first victories through Isadora and Fokine, its boldest ones through Nijinsky and Mary Wigman, its general acceptance in the twenties — these are facts of history. Inside and outside of ballet, modernism has emphasized the interest in bit-by-bit gesture, gesture deformed, interrupted, or explosive. It has done everything possible to break up the easy-flowing sequence of a dance.

But through all these modernisms well-trained ballet dancers made any gesture, however odd, with reference to their traditional center of motion, and so still gave to a series of disjointed gestures a logical dance continuity. And through all these modernisms, too, ballet retained its traditional formula of the architecture of a piece, with the long dance aria (like the central adagio in *Swan Lake*) as the basic type of an expressive climax. Ballet dancers had sound models for dance coherence and for dance rhythm all around them.

The modern-school dancers, however, had no models for long, serious poetic forms: for them the fundamental questions of dance rhythm and dance continuity could not be referred to a traditional type. Miss Graham, for instance, began with the decorative attitudes and the connecting walks of Denishawn "exotica"; her formal point of departure was an actor's loose gesture sequence, not a dancer's logically sustained dance sequence. But against this enormous handicap she did succeed in discovering for herself a sound basis on which any sequence of gesture can keep a strictly logical continuity.

She has done this, I think, by developing an acute sense of the downward pull of gravity and of balance, and an acute sense, too, of where the center of pressure of a gesture is. By concentrating motion on these two elements, she can exaggerate or deform a gesture as far as she chooses without blurring it, and she can retract or transform a gesture without breaking the continuity of movement. She is the only one of our modern dancers who has really solved this fundamental problem in all its aspects.

Ballet began, one might say, on the basis of lightness, elevation, and ease; it could add modernism (which was an increased heaviness and an oddity of gesture) for its value as contrast. Miss Graham, beginning with modernism, made of heaviness and oddity a complete system of her own. Brilliancy in heaviness and oddity became her expressive idiom. This is one way of explaining why much of her style looks like ballet intentionally done against the grain, or why she has used lightness and ease not as fundamental elements but for their value as contrast. But Miss Graham's system keeps expanding, and this season her entire company now and again seemed to be using nonmodernist dance qualities not merely for contrast but directly.

Judged by what I look for in ballet, Miss Graham's gesture lacks a way of opening up completely, and her use of dance rhythm seems to me fragmentary. It does not rise in a long, sustained line and come to a conclusion. I find she uses the stage space the way the realistic theater does, as an accidental segment of a place, not the way the poetic theater uses the stage, as a space complete in itself. And I do not feel the advantage to dancing in these qualities of her style. But I am intensely curious to see what her next works will look like, and where the next ten years will lead her. I find watching her not a balm for the spirit, but certainly a very great pleasure for the intelligence.

New York Herald Tribune, May 28, 1944

Balanchine's *Danses Concertantes*

The Monte Carlo's new *Danses Concertantes* is a glittering little piece, brilliantly animated and brilliantly civilized. As a production it combines the talents of Stravinsky, Balanchine, and Berman — a ballet composer, a choreographer, and a ballet decorator so eminent that each in his field can be called the best in the world. A new piece involving any one of them is something to look forward to; a piece that involves all three at once and allows each to do his sincere best is that rare luxury, a ballet production in the grand style — in the grand style Diaghilev insisted upon and thanks to which ballet acquired its peculiar artistic prestige. *Danses Concertantes,* with fourteen dancers onstage for twenty minutes, is a ballet quite small in scale. But as a new ballet by three great artists it is a big event, an event of interest to London, Paris, and Moscow, an event the American ballet world can take pride in.

The first thrill of *Danses Concertantes* is that of Berman's costumes and drops. Before an inner curtain the dancers cross over quickly by twos and threes, bowing to the audience, looking as brilliant as scarabs, if scarabs came in several colors. Then the inner curtain rises. Now the dancers stand assembled, glittering sharply against a black drop, but it is a drop that is as atmospheric as the open sky of night. You peer into nocturnal distance. And in this lofty blackness every motion of the dancers coruscates. Berman has emphasized their limbs and molded their bodies with black ornaments and with rhinestones so that each motion is distinct in itself.

The dancing is a suite of brief numbers, classically correct in steps but in surprising sequences that contrast sharply and have a quick effervescent invention. The changes from staccato movements to continuous ones, from rapid leaps and displacements to standing still, from one dancer solo to several all at once follow hard on one another. The rhythm is unexpected. But the shift of the figures and the order of the steps is miraculously logical and light, and so even fitful changes have a grace and a spontaneous impetus. What had first seemed separate spurts, stops, and clipped stalkings turn out to be a single long phrase or impulse that has risen and subsided in a group of dancers simultaneously. The line of the large phrase is seen in their relations to one another, and each dancer independently remains open and free in bearing, the arms natural and elegant.

One notices how each dancer in all this coruscating complexity remains a charming and a natural person. They are like characters in a garden, individuals who communicate, respond, who modify and return without losing their distinctness. The dance is like a conversation in Henry James, as surprising, as sensitive, as forbearing, as full of slyness and fancy. The joyousness of it is the pleasure of being civilized, of being what we really are, born into a millennial urban civilization. This is where we are and this is what the mind makes beautiful. *Danses Concertantes* makes it beautiful by presenting a sumptuous little garden pastoral, a highly artificial, a very exact, and a delicately adjusted entertainment.

The dancers performed the piece to perfection. Even those of them just out of school danced like soloists, with a light and civilized deportment. And Danilova and Franklin, the stars whose happy flirtation is the central theme of the piece — and a birdlike duet it is — characterized their parts charmingly and lightly, he with the fatuousness of a happy male, she with the willfulness of a tender woman.

New York Herald Tribune, Sept. 17, 1944

Coppélia Tells the Facts of Life

The Monte Carlo *Coppélia* might well be more celebrated than it is. With radiant Miss Danilova and either Franklin or Youskevitch in the leads, and given in its entirety — as it wasn't this fall — it is a very happy version of a delightful classic. The score Delibes made for it so carefully has lost none of its charms. And in the Monte Carlo production the choreography and the decoration are — like the music — distinguished, gracious, and light. *Coppélia* is a modest little comedy, but it has a peculiar grace, an 1870 secret, a bouquet as fresh as a summer morning in the country. The Monte Carlo dancers dance it clearly, they do it gaily and they do it straight. And thanks to their lack of affectation, I noticed with some surprise that if you follow the action quite literally it isn't a silly story, as people claim it is. A part of *Coppélia*'s secret is the serious good sense with which it treats a serious subject — the basis for a good marriage.

This is the action you watch: Two very lively and very real young persons love each other and are about to marry. But the boy is struck by the sight of a mysterious stranger, the beautiful Coppélia, who sits on a balcony. Naturally, his first girl is vexed and hurt. That night the mysterious Coppélia turns out to be only a mechanical doll. The flesh-and-blood girl breaks the doll, she harries the old dollmaker, she even rescues the boy, whom the dollmaker has drugged with a sinister intent. The boy acknowledges his fault, and the next day there is a celebration at which the local duke pays for everything, the boys and girls all get married and get money, and everybody watches dancing and dances happily, too.

Critics have claimed that the celebration scene added nothing and could as well be omitted. It cannot, because you haven't until then seen the boy and girl dance together and exhibit all their virtuosity, their combined dance power at its highest pitch. When you see their motions and physical proportions beautifully balanced, when you see them harmoniously overcoming impossible difficulties, you have seen a convincing image of what would make two young lovers happy in marriage.

And the divertissement that clusters round this grand duet bears logically on the same subject. The dances are entitled "Dawn" (a solo), "Prayer," "Work," and "Follies" (several of them); and taken together the series represents rather well the nonsexual basis for a happy domestic life. On the other hand, the pitfalls that prevent marriage are told in the earlier action, when the boy is infatuated by a beautifully mechanical ideal: he wants a real girl and he wants an ideal one in addition. In this psychological dilemma, like a man, he goes to sleep. But the girl, like a Shavian heroine, solves the dilemma by her independent courage. And then the boy proves his real worth by his strength and his gentle control in the nuptial dance duet. All these ideas of marriage are reasonable ones, though the lightness, the wit and tenderness they have in dancing are lost in retelling.

As you watch the dance you notice how the more perturbing the emotion becomes, the purer becomes the movement of dancing and the more open and free the dancer's bearing. You see the magic of the heart's sincerity, its most urgent necessity, transforms a village girl into a grand and gracious ballerina. And what a solace the transformation is! But *Coppélia* has only two such really serious episodes; it shifts easily to a pantomime scene, to a folk dance, to a sparkling parody. Its theme is domestic, and it ends with a modest circle of dancers enclosing the stars in a running ring. I only wish the young Monte Carlo would take some lessons in classic pantomime; it is a charming game when dancers play it right. And I wish I had space to tell you about Danilova, who is the most wonderful *Coppélia* heroine in the world.

New York Herald Tribune, Sept. 24, 1944

Pearl Primus on Broadway

Pearl Primus, the justly celebrated young Negro dancer, and her troupe opened a ten-day season last night at the Belasco with a show that came across completely only in a few numbers. She has proved herself a quite exceptionally gifted and thrilling dancer before, and it is likely that later performances will not have the self-consciousness that she and her somewhat disparate troupe showed again and again in their first contact with the Broadway theater public.

The program, elucidated by a speaker, begins with "primitives" — that is, dances derived from African or Haitian origins. A second part brings dances of protest from the point of view of the Negro in the United States. And a final portion, more or less on a jazz basis, begins with several playful dance inventions and ends with more protest.

It is the playful dances, *Afro-Haitian Playdance, Study in Nothing, Rock*

Daniel, Mischievous Interlude (the last a very brilliant solo danced by Albert Popfull), which delight the audience. They are witty, warm, and well made. Of the serious numbers *African Ceremonial* and *Hard Time Blues* are thrilling dancing. But a number of the other serious ones fail of complete effect because the audience agrees beforehand with the protest they make. An artist can protest passionately to a hostile audience and win them over; but there is little drama where the audience is quite amenable. In that case the propaganda can't excite the public, but only the elegance of the execution, and the dignity of the protest is compromised by no longer being the dramatic center of attention.

But it is Miss Primus's privilege to attempt these very earnest themes. One regrets that she hammed them occasionally last night. As a dancer, she has a unique power and unction in her hips, knees, and instep. The leaps can be thrilling, the quickness of the feet a delight. Waist and torso are strong and often beautifully pliant. She has the gift of motion, which controls the body easily in flow. The arms are uninteresting in formal movements, but charming when they play a subordinate role. One wishes she would dance more with a partner, less in the correctly "modern" manner and more in her personal, playful way, where her invention is most brilliant and free, and her personality warm and charmingly dignified.

Miss Primus's troupe consists of four male dancers, two excellent drummers (Messrs Cimber and Koker), Frankie Newton and his four-piece band, two pianists, two singers, and a speaker. The jazz drummer was excellent also.

New York Herald Tribune, Oct. 5, 1944

Ballerina Trouble at Ballet Theatre?

The Ballet Theatre company, in the first five days of the season, has seemed to suffer from a drop in its morale, unknown before in this admirably steady ensemble. The trouble has been, I imagine, that Ballet Theatre has had to change classic ballerinas in midstream and that this delicate operation was not at once successful. For a ballerina is not only a superacrobat with extra publicity. She is also an artist whose performance shows you the heart of a ballet. She sets the tone; the other dancers can add to it but cannot go counter to it, and so her quality is of crucial importance to them. Indeed, company, ballerina, and chief choreographer need to have a sort of affinity, an unconscious confidence in one another if they are to become completely effective. The mutual adjustment comes by working together and there is no way of forcing it.

In Ballet Theatre's case the adjustment is especially delicate because the repertory has two tendencies, classic and modern. It was a stroke of luck that Tudor, the modern choreographer, and Markova, the classic ballerina, were united not only by mutual admiration but also by a common nationality. Even so it took some time for each of them to get what they needed at Ballet Theatre, to feel at home and shine in a homogeneous and confident company.

There is no way of replacing this particular confidence now Markova has left. Miss Toumanova, if she is to take the place of permanent classic ballerina at Ballet Theatre, will have to grow used to a company with a special tradition. And to start with she has further difficulties. She is cast in Markova's classic roles, and these are all on the serene side. Toumanova has in the past been superb in the opposite manner, the dramatically intense (as in the Black Swan, a role that is the evil counterpart of the serene Swan Queen). In the lyric roles she has taken these first few days, coming after Markova's gentle radiance and Danilova's warm and lovely presence in the same parts, Toumanova's manner seems a little grim. Technically she has not yet shown the control of arms or the sure phrasing Markova has led us to expect; on the other hand, her grand leg extensions and sharp toe steps have been phenomenal to see — especially last Thursday in the first section of the *Nutcracker* duet, where she was well supported by Dolin. Whether Toumanova can suit her temperament to these particular roles or will be given others, she is certainly a dancer of exceptional style and interest. And it is to Ballet Theatre's credit to be bringing her back to ballet.

The two new pieces Ballet Theatre has added to its repertory so far have been very agreeable ones and that is also to its credit. Lichine's revived *Graduation Ball* is a pleasant ballet comedy set to Strauss waltzes. Balanchine's new *Waltz Academy* is classic dancing so unselfconscious and spontaneous in its elegance it is art without a capital A. These novelties, Miss Toumanova's return, and two roles for two other great dancers, Miss Riabouchinska and Mr. Lichine, were calculated to open Ballet Theatre's season with brilliance. But the mistake has been to begin by presenting Miss Toumanova, as prospective ballerina, in parts in which she was not at her own best. That has put a jinx on these first few days, I think. But I feel sure that by the time this appears our leading ballet company will have recovered from this moment of uncertainty and will be dancing again with the verve it has consistently shown, in the three years since it has been appearing at the Metropolitan. That's the way it has always solved its troubles.

New York Herald Tribune, Oct. 15, 1944

Riabouchinska and Toumanova

The general impression over the weekend is that Ballet Theatre is headed up again. Sunday night's performance at the Metropolitan was lively and accurate, the best evening so far. The new *Waltz Academy* looked as it should have on its opening night, gay, unpresuming, and beautiful. Miss Alonso was dancing with new animation in her perfect neatness, Miss Gollner with a new simplicity in her fine feats, a directness we have waited for for two years. And the audience enjoyed the charming piece and the company cordially.

The bill included the Grand Pas de Deux from *The Nutcracker,* danced by Toumanova and Dolin. Miss Toumanova, with a prettier coiffure, this time superimposed a different manner on her dazzlingly perfect leg action, smiling and giving ecstatic little tosses of the head before big effects. I imagine a great classic choreographer like Balanchine could best correct the miscalculations of manner that mar her superb capabilities.

Sunday afternoon's *Sylphides* and Saturday night's *Aurora* billed both Toumanova and Riabouchinska, the guest celebrities of Ballet Theatre. Miss Riabouchinska, though no great technician in movement, has so warm and true a presence, so clear a sense of the musical enchantment that surrounds her, and so keen an instinct for a natural characterization that one watches everything she does — even her faults — with pleasure. Her greatest fault is a tendency to raise her shoulders too much, which gives her torso a dumpy look. But when you see her dancing with the happy absorption of a little girl, you wish other dancers in classic pieces would learn from her to believe in their imagination.

In *Sylphides* she seems to be one of the chorus dancing by accident; in the Bluebird she is a sparkling princess with a wonderful bluebird of her own; in *Graduation Ball* she is a little girl, mischievous, sweet-natured, and well-mannered. She creates a magic world around her — a very rare dancer indeed.

Graduation Ball on Sunday afternoon brought Harold Lang in Lichine's part, and he danced it with a fine natural charm and clarity, perfectly in character. He is developing particularly well this season. This piece is, happily, losing the strident stress that spoiled it at first.

New York Herald Tribune, Oct. 16, 1944

Toumanova in *Giselle*

Miss Toumanova with her large, handsome, and deadly face, her swordlike toe steps, her firm positions, her vigorous and record-high leg gestures — and with her bold and large style of dancing — by nature makes a very different figure from delicate Miss Markova, whose star role in *Giselle* she undertook for the first time last night. Dancing at the Metropolitan as guest of Ballet Theatre in the familiar Ballet Theatre version (including Mr. Dolin as the star's partner), Miss Toumanova was very striking and was properly cheered. But Miss Markova's Giselle is still incomparable.

In Toumanova's performance, this Markova fan missed the sustained otherworldly floating quality and the calm completion of each pose and phrase that were Markova's specialty, and that helped make this ballet in particular extraordinarily thrilling. But Miss Toumanova not only gave her best performance of the season, she showed some of her dramatic gifts as well as her technical ones. She sustained the first act and built up an atmosphere of threat that might well lead into the second. And in the second act she gave her supported adagio section a very interesting sensual overtone, which might, if developed in the role, add to this whole act an unusual (but perfectly possible) macabre intensity.

Later in the second act, at the allegro climax, in the famous series of little leaps on both toes, Miss Toumanova leaped too far to keep her lightness, and she did not reach a sort of desperate quality she may have intended. In the lifts that follow she was too large for Dolin quite to create an effect of lightness. Indeed, Dolin's overpowering assurance in the part is now becoming his most serious qualification; he has to substitute a theatrical pose for dance brilliance. But he supported Miss Toumanova very handsomely.

The company was excellent indeed in the second act; here Miss Hightower as the Queen was at her very finest, with magnificent leaps, beautiful arm gestures.

New York Herald Tribune, Oct. 17, 1944

Toumanova's Show

Dazzlingly handsome to look at in *Black Swan,* effervescently and girlishly temperamental in *Three-Cornered Hat,* Tamara Toumanova sustained and put across last night's Ballet Theatre show at the Metropolitan as a star performer should. Ballet can be more gracefully poignant and the Spanish style more controlled; but last night one was happy in the vigorous theatrical impetus Miss Toumanova gave both pieces she appeared in.

Black Swan is the grand pas de deux from *Swan Lake,* Act Three. The most correct version of the duet was the Monte Carlo's of 1941, danced then by Toumanova and Eglevsky, and a performance unparalleled that was. Mr. Dolin's present version is a straight bravura exhibition number, and Miss Toumanova rose to the occasion. The grand abundance of force she had in all she did was stunning; and her accurate line, her half-turn recovery from a deep back bend, her ballonnés and circle of turns — each effect was driven home magnificently. The house rightly gave her an ovation.

The same duet in its context in *Swan Lake* has an overtone of vicious evil; it can be danced with more reference to the ballerina's partner and projected less hard at the audience. It is more moving that way. But done as Miss Toumanova did it — a brilliant feat of unique prowess — it affords an honest theatrical thrill; and no other dancer could have delivered it with such physical magnificence.

Mr. Dolin was Toumanova's partner, and what he did was neatly done. His showmanship put it over successfully.

Three-Cornered Hat, with Toumanova and Massine in the leads, and David Lichine as the Governor, had a star cast. Here Miss Toumanova was very touching in the brief hand-fluttering solo after the Miller's arrest; and if her

Spanish is awkward in the arms and vague in the feet, if her silhouette is diffuse — as Massine's even now is not — still the way she plays her role with conviction and dances with impetuosity brings back a long-lost freshness to this excellent little ballet. The Picasso drop and costumes are each time a joy to see. One wishes Ballet Theatre would also restore the Picasso front curtain. Lichine was amusing and discreet, though he does the role as impish comedy without any Spanish dignity to give it an extra sharpness.

New York Herald Tribune, Oct. 24, 1944

A Fault in Ballet Theatre's Dancing

Each Ballet Theatre season, the more often I go, the more I admire the company. As a group they are gifted, strong, conscientious, untiring dancers; as individuals they are lively, attractive young people. Each season, as the weeks pass and they recover from the strain of touring and from the interruption of ballet classes on tour, you see first this one and then that one begin to blossom in their dancing. Just now they are better than ever, and among the soloists, warmhearted Miss Hightower, Miss Alonso, and Mr. Kriza are often even strikingly expressive. And yet, despite all this, the general tone of Ballet Theatre's dancing has long had a tendency to seem heavy-footed and wooden. Watching Miss Riabouchinska and the illusion of animation she gives, I wondered what the technical secret of it might be.

For in the technique of a step, a leap, or a lift most of Ballet Theatre's company is far more accurate than she is. She fakes and she has no tautness. But when she dances she has a miraculous instinct for the atmosphere of a piece, so that her number fits naturally into the poetic illusion of it. Her dance makes sense in terms of the piece and it also makes natural sense as a dance. Her naturalness in action comes from the fact that she shows you so clearly the sustaining impetus, the dance impulse which carries her lightly through from beginning to end. Because the impetus is exactly right she strikes you as dancing her whole number on an impulse, spontaneously for the joy of it.

Ballet Theatre, by comparison, looks as if it tried manfully to do its duty. It doesn't dance as if dancing were easy; it doesn't quite seem to believe that a dance is a joy in itself. Instead of letting the number take wing and deploy in the make-believe atmosphere of the piece, Ballet Theatre is afraid to let it go at that; it "theatricalizes" a dance by mugging or glamorizing. Often it acts as if a dance were an argument, a string of points to be put across by fair means or foul. It hits hard one step or gesture, goes dead, and then with an effort begins the next one. You don't feel that the waist and the thighs are ready for dancing ahead of the feet and arms; the slight knee and ankle bend which connects steps isn't agile; the muscles around the small of the back aren't quiet enough. And so the feet stick and the arms drag. I am of course drawing a caricature here, but though I exaggerate the failing, it exists.

Ballet Theatre has, I think, trained itself too little in the physical basis for continuity in dancing and it has not trained, either, the instinctive gift for it that dancers have. They have not been trained to sense accurately the dance impetus which will best carry them through all the detail they are called on to perform, which will give it coherence and expression. But it is when he discovers the appropriate impetus for his part that the dancer begins to look light and natural and captivating.

Unfortunately Ballet Theatre's repertory doesn't suggest lightness and naturalness to a young dancer. In spirit, its nineteenth-century revivals are often too self-conscious; its light modern pieces are often too smart-alecky — they comment on comic characters selfconsciously from the outside. And in technique Tudor's complex serious ballets are obviously hard to dance with spontaneity. Spontaneity in dancing requires, among other things, personal changes of pace which animate the prevalent rhythm, but Tudor's main rhythm is hard to get hold of, it has no beat or lilt. So it is difficult for the dancers to sense where their instinctive changes of pace (their rubato) would be proper. Much rehearsed, *Romeo* and *Lilac Garden,* thanks to the brilliant example of rubato that Markova and Laing have given, have recently been danced with a striking increase in animation. And the company is dancing the new *Waltz Academy* with a new naturalness, too. It gives hope that Ballet Theatre will plan its future repertory (and its future ballet classes) with an eye to remedying its faulty tendencies in dancing.

Ballet Theatre is our strongest dance company. Its accuracy and its steady drive are quite exceptional. But it might look lighter and more spontaneous and more unselfconscious. As a company it still needs more of the physical sincerity, the warmheartedness that it admires readily and generously when it sees its own home-grown ballerina, Rosella Hightower, dancing.

New York Herald Tribune, Oct. 29, 1944

Toumanova and Dolin at Ballet Theatre

What really thrills in Toumanova's dancing is its horizontal and downward drive — the velocity with which she travels perfectly stiff, the force with which she rams her squared-off toe shoe into the floor, the solid slowness with which her free leg deploys its mass from the leg she stands anchored on. These are thrills where her prowess and her dance instinct coincide. She can simulate the motions of airiness — she did it perfectly in her second *Giselle* performance and in *Sylphides* — but she does not sustain for any length of time the impulse upward, the lyric breathing on which these roles are based. On the contrary you see her natural genius in *Tricorne,* when she sits down grandly and massively like a Roman river deity on the floor and waits for the farucca to begin. The true expression of her dancing comes from her passion for the floor, and its rhythm is one of pressure and explosion. The tone is an unexpected one in ballet, it even recalls Mary Wigman at her best. Toumanova has some of Frau Wigman's scorn for the amenities of the theater, her force of self-isolation on stage, her hectic smashing rhythm. A ballet in which Toumanova could oppose her record feats and her quasi-Wagnerian grandeur to the airiness of the rest of the company would be completely sensational; what she needs is a choreographer to show her as she is.

She has, I believe, been presented this season mostly as she is not. Unable to use her natural expressiveness, she has improvised a fake stage personality and with that, with her unfaked acrobatics, and with her face, she has been wowing the customers in the old vaudeville way.

Mr. Dolin as her partner in classic numbers, equally unable to prove his real theater virtue, has resorted to the same vaudeville attack. He is not technically a classic dancer anymore. He can get applause, to be sure, merely by looking lovingly at his own right hand or by doing a leap (entrechat) in which his feet paddle in the air like Donald Duck's; but this is no proof of his classic technique, it is a proof of his genius and experience as a showman. Dolin is a first-rate showman and comedian. His natural wit, enthusiasm, great charm, and sense of caricature give a parody point to everything he does; they assure him of an immense success on the speaking stage, and those of us who sincerely admire him would like to see him add a fresh legitimate glory there to his former great glory in ballet. It is distressing to see two artists as fine as Toumanova and Dolin, both miscast, competing in a ballet number as to which will be the more audience conscious and stagey.

High-class vaudeville is not ballet. Ballet Theatre is a company of very fine dancers. If the management encouraged their native sincerity as artists, if it encouraged sincerely poetic dancing above vaudeville auto-exhibitionism, the management would be astonished at both how its neglected classic ballets would increase in value and how its intellectual prestige would soar.

New York Herald Tribune, Nov. 5, 1944

Ballet International at Two Weeks

Ballet International, our new company, has several strong points which should not be overlooked. In the first place, it is a resident company. The dancers will not be exhausted by touring and their regular training will be less interrupted. Ballet dancers are athletes and they respond to a reasonable hygiene as much as other athletes do; they are also artists, and artists need a quiet place where they can work and they need an unconscious participation in the daily life of a city as anybody there lives it. A resident company can eat and sleep at home; it can practice and rehearse with concentration; it can be happy and unhappy in the same familiar drug store or elevator. International already shows a trace of the easy family feeling sensible working conditions induce. There is a serious and cheerful tone on the stage that a ballet company should have; there is no desperate anxiousness for personal applause that stage people resort to, as to a drug, when their vitality and self-respect are low.

But good points at International have been obscured by bad mistakes in artistic judgment. Of the nine pieces shown so far even the four more or less interesting productions — *Constantia, Sentimental Colloquy, Sebastian,* and *Sylphides* — have not been satisfactorily produced all around. The general impression of the repertory to date is that the new choreographies begin well, but instead of developing further they turn repetitious; the choreographers needed more discerning encouragement to go on. The new orchestrations of old scores are not dry, but they tend to banalize (and rather sour) the music they set out to amplify. Hardly any of the new costuming is properly calculated for the small stage; it takes up too much room. The cut is awkward (*Swan Lake* bodices) or conceals the gesture (*Sebastian*) or suggests foolish associations (*Constantia*), or the colors break up the dance (*Brahms Variations, I*). The problems of orchestral balances, of how a lot of costumes will add up in dancing, of how drawing and color in a drop create or destroy space onstage — these technical problems are outside of the professional experience of Broadway because they are vital only in ballet production. And so instead of commissioning Broadway stylists, International might have appealed for new scores and sets to the composers and painters in town who are perfectly familiar with ballet production from experience with ballet here and abroad; their boldness and accuracy would have started the new repertory right.

When International started, the town was looking for a bold venture and it found a timid one. What we expected and missed was a clear sign of artistic direction, of intellectual drama and decision, of the nerve that creates style. Style can be created only at a risk; it is a form of courage, it is an exposed and often indefensible position. Stylishness even in the serenest classicism has a now-or-never edge and thrill, and even at its most playful it doesn't ask for a second chance. International has not been bold in style.

New York Herald Tribune, Nov. 12, 1944

About Ballet Decoration

Because ballet dancers keep moving all over the stage and because in looking at them you keep looking at all the scenery all the time, ballet decoration is observed in a livelier way than play or opera decoration. In fact as a ballet unfolds and your interest in watching it grows, you become more susceptible to visual impressions and so more sensitive, too, to the decoration. In plays or operas you forget the scenery for long stretches while the performers stay still and you listen, more and more captivated, to their voices. The real dramatic power of a play or opera is felt to such an extent by listening that you can be thrilled even when you sit at the radio with no stage to watch at all. But the dramatic power of a ballet is in its visual impact. You feel it by seeing just how the dancers move, seeing their impetus in relation to each other and also their force in relation to the entire stage — how far they choose to go in contrast to how far they might go.

The force with which dancers approach, touch or separate, come forward toward you or retire, take possession of stage center or pause isolated near the wings, these changing intensities are meant to have a cumulative effect. You appreciate this best if you sit far enough back to view the whole stage at a glance, so that its height and width can act as a fixed frame of reference. Ballet scenery and costumes are meant to make the action of the dance distinctly visible at a distance and also to give a clear coherence to its variety, a livelier common term to its action than the mere empty stage area.

For this purpose a décor so busy that it confuses or so stuffy that it clogs the animation of the dances is of no use. But it cannot be timid. It must have power enough to remain interesting and alive as the dancing gradually sharpens the visual susceptibility of the audience. One of our finest sets — Pierre Roy's *Coppélia* — does this without attracting any notice to itself at all. The effect of a décor is right when as the ballet gathers momentum the dancers seem to have enough air all around to dance easily; when you see their long dance phrases in clear relation to stage center; when the flats keep the force of the gesture from spilling aimlessly into the wings; then the dancers — no matter how odd they looked at first — can come to look natural in the fanciful things they do, the natural fauna of the bright make-believe world they move in.

The present standards for ballet decoration were set by Picasso, whose *Three-Cornered Hat* is still pictorially alive after twenty-five years. The reason easel painters are better designers for ballet than anyone else is that they are the only craftsmen professionally concerned with what keeps pictures alive for years on end. When they know their trade they make pictures that hold people's interest for hundreds of years, so making one that will be interesting to look at for twenty minutes is comparatively easy for them.

A ballet set has to stand up under steady scrutiny almost as an easel painting does. At first sight it tells a story, it has local color or period interest or shock value. But then it starts to change the way a picture in a museum does as you look at it attentively for five or ten minutes. The shapes and colors, lines and textures in the set and costumes will act as they would in a picture, they will seem to push and pull, rise and fall, advance and retreat with or against their representational weight. The backdrop may tie up with a costume so that the dancer's figure seems to belong in it like a native, or it may set him plainly forward, where he has a floor to dance on. A good ballet décor, like a good painting, does different and opposite things decisively; like a painting, it presents a bold equilibrium of pictorial forces. And when the bold equilibrium in the décor corresponds in vitality to that of the dancing and that of the score, then the ballet as a production is alive and satisfactory.

The decorations by Picasso, Roy, Berman, and Chagall in our current repertory (Bérard's and Tchelitchev's are at the moment in storage) set a satisfactory standard — the highest in the world. It is a standard worth keeping for the time when other native American easel painters join Oliver Smith in working for ballet, as, despite management and union, they obviously should. Painters as they are, they will enjoy furnishing the pictorial power and nobility of presence ballet thrives on; and to see their American invention so openly presented would be a great pleasure to them and to us.

New York Herald Tribune, Nov. 26, 1944

Meaning in *The Nutcracker*

Thinking of Christmas, I remembered the Christmas tree conspicuously onstage and the Christmas party in the first scene of *The Nutcracker,* the venerable fairy-tale ballet that Petipa's collaborator Ivanov set long ago to Tchaikovsky's lovely score. Has the action anything to do with Christmas? What is its nonsense plot really about, and how does *The Nutcracker* create its mild and beneficent spell? This serene old vehicle, complete with all the 1890 ballet conventions — pantomime scene, ballroom dance, grand pas de deux, divertissement, and ballabile, all of them strung in a row on a story nobody pays attention to — still works as a theater piece. It does even in such a form as the Monte Carlo's three-scene version, which though cut, patched, and mauled by years of hard wear keeps the formal continuity of the original three acts. At the Monte Carlo most of the young dancers show no manners in the pantomime part and they may do their stint in the dance scenes as if they were reciting "Thanatopsis." But the great Danilova as the Sugar Plum Fairy (especially with Youskevitch as partner) has a radiant and tender presence that lets you see the heart of the ballet and convinces you of its expressive power. Through her performance the choreographic intentions of the work emerge once more. If you are curious about choreography, you find that the dance logic of *The Nutcracker* is solid and that the nonsense plot — its idea content — has a rational structure too. The intentions of *The Nutcracker,* when you do catch on, are humane and sensible, and its 1890 formal method is highly intelligent.

What is the method? This is what happens on the stage. The long first scene is a clear pantomime story. The dance is plain, realistic, without embellishments, it does not lead to leaps; it is all terre-à-terre. The second and third scenes, in contrast to the first, tell hardly any story; instead they are dancing that clearly looks like dancing, with steps in patterns, leaps and lifts, dancing with "elevation." The two dance scenes are made up of successive dance numbers, each with a beginning and an ending, each a set piece, all of them together arranged in a suite ending with an ensemble finale.

The suite method in ballet, as in opera, does not have the urgency of the continuous, symphonic method. The suite ballet does not try so hard to get somewhere. The emotional tone is stable, it changes en bloc from number to number. The series of emotions that constitute the whole work are grouped in clear rubrics, the imagination dwells on one at a time and then proceeds satisfied to the next. The momentary detail is seen in relation to the number it appears in; when the number is finished one has a complete image, and the detail loses its insistency. There is a sense of repose in action, a control of the emotion that is both modest and noble. In short, the set-piece structure is not at all a foolish device.

The Nutcracker is not foolish in form, nor is it foolish either in its literal content. It is a fairy-tale ballet and certainly looks like nonsense. But nowadays, with psychoanalysis practically a household remedy, grown-ups take the nonsense of fairy tales more seriously than children. We call them narratives in free association and solve them like crossword puzzles. *The Nutcracker* is an easy one — the title gives it away. The story begins on Christmas Eve in an upper-class home, the locus classicus of ambivalent anxiety. An elderly bachelor with one eye gives a preadolescent girl a male nutcracker (the symbols and inversion couldn't be more harrowing). Her young brother tears it away from her by force and breaks it. But she takes it up from the floor and nurses it; she loves it. She dreams that the nutcracker turns almost into a boy. Then she dreams of a deep forest in winter with restless girl-snowflakes and a handsome young man who keeps lifting up a young lady (and who is this lady but the little heroine's own dream image?). And after that she dreams she is watching a lot of dancing Chinamen and Russians and oddly dressed people — all of them somehow "sweets" — and at last the previous young man and the previous young lady turn up again, too. They furnish a brilliant climax, and that leads to a happy dazzle for everything and everybody everywhere at once.

You can see that the suite of dancers presents an intelligible association series, operated with unconscious sexual symbols; that the piece makes sense enough as a subconscious reverie beginning with a cruel sexual symbol, the nutcracker, which is also its literal title; and in this sense the various subjects of its pantomime and dance scenes are intelligible, too. It is the kind of sense one expects of a fairy-tale plot, since it is how fairy tales are rationally understood. But what you see on the stage is a suite of well-mannered dances, graceful and clear. The clarity of the dance-suite form controls the pressure of the unconscious theme and by easy stages brings on a pleasing change of emotion. Using the methods of 1890, *The Nutcracker* reaches an unconsciously satisfying final goal by a series of choreographic effects; and even in what appear to be merely formal evolutions, this old-fashioned dance entertainment follows a sincere emotional logic.

At the start of the piece, the effect of the pantomime scene — sadistic in content for all its upper-class Christmas party manners — is gloomy and oppressed; the dancers don't really get off the floor. What a relief when the dancing begins with leaps and airy lifts in the next snow scene. But the choreography here preserves a coolness and a remoteness that don't quite satisfy. The third, last scene is friendlier, lighter, more open to the audience, more animated, more playful in detail, and in the end there is a happy sense that everyone on the stage has leaped about freely and sufficiently. So they can all stop and smile straight at you, looking pretty without the least embarrassment.

And there is another unconscious satisfaction in the sequence of the dances. For the strictness of bodily control inherent in dance virtuosity, a strictness that grows more exacting as the dance becomes more animated and complex, seems at the end a satisfactory sublimation for the savagely cruel impulses suggested in the disturbing pantomime opening of the piece. And so *The Nutcracker* is really a dream about Christmas, since it succeeds in turning envy and pain into lovely invention and social harmony.

Compare this conciliatory dream libretto with the dream libretto of the Dali-Massine *Bacchanale*. The latter proceeds from anxiety to disgust and hysteria and bogs down in a pile of umbrellas. If one took the *Bacchanale* seriously one would find it a very unsatisfactory story.

No doubt Ivanov, the choreographer of *The Nutcracker,* didn't look for symbols in a fairy tale; he was interested in dancing that one could see clearly and that would have a cumulative effect. He would find my account of his ballet absurd, and so would the many thousands who like it and don't ask for a reason. Thousands of people all over the world find *The Nutcracker* touching and comforting without knowing why. My point is simply that if you look for a reason, if you are interested in what ballet means rationally, you can find a great deal of meaning in *The Nutcracker* and excellent reasons for its peculiar effect.

It is not quite by chance either that they are to be found. *The Nutcracker* was derived in one way or another from a long fairy tale of E. T. A. Hoffmann's, "The Nutcracker and the King of Mice." The ballet has a little of the story and much of the tone of Hoffmann, his special note of hurt and tender assent. Hoffmann was one of the brightest of men and master of the free-association device. The free-association device was as familiar to educated persons in 1820 as it is to us, and practiced by them with more sense of humor. Their joke was: as long as the association of images is free, why not make it come out pleasantly? Perhaps this is the secret connection between Hoffmann's conciliatory fairy tale and the emotional control of the set-piece ballet form; and the connection, too, between the quality of the score Tchaikovsky composed and that of the dancing and the story. At any rate, story, score, and choreographic style join very beautifully in this academic ballet.

New York Herald Tribune, Dec. 10 and 17, 1944

Deaths and Entrances

Martha Graham and her company made their first metropolitan appearance of the season last night, presenting *Salem Shore, Deaths and Entrances,* and *Every Soul Is a Circus. Deaths and Entrances* was the most absorbing dance work that opened in New York last season, though it competed with plenty of ballet novelties. If its original shock value no longer operates, both the piece itself and Miss Graham's dancing in it have lost none of their first fascination.

Suggested originally by the life and works of the Brontës and by their atmosphere of passionate intellectual sensuality, heroic in despair, *Deaths and Entrances* in its dance gesture evokes the romantic stage tragedies of a hundred years ago — the ferocity, tenderness, and grandiloquence, the ancestral manor, the duel, the ball, the mad scene, the garland of wildflowers, the goblet, and the cushion with an embalmed heart in it.

Our forebears when they saw these tragedies started with horror and wept. They sensed their secret obscenity. Miss Graham brings back the true romantic impact and effect; it is as immediate now as then, and this is an achievement of genius. If we had expressive tragic actors they would go to *Deaths and Entrances* to learn their trade. For the general theatergoer, the ballet is an absorbing experience.

In recapturing romantic fervor Miss Graham has reinvented the gestures, the poses, the rhythms it needs, and made them startling afresh. Her tumultuous dance sequences are clear and firm. She herself never loses the ladylike elegance, the womanly look that makes formal tragedy communicative. And she does not force her private emotion into the passionate role she impersonates.

Her own role strikes me as the only completely rounded one in the wordless drama. The two men, though handsomely danced last night by Hawkins and Cunningham, are expressive only in their relation to the heroine; they have no independent existence as real characters would. The parts of the three little girls, though small, seem more autonomous than last year. The heroine's two sisters, danced so brilliantly last year by Miss Maslow and Miss Dudley, done now with care by Miss Lang and Miss O'Donnell, have become sketchier.

New York Herald Tribune, Feb. 6, 1945

Ballet Imperial

In *Ballet Imperial,* the novelty that the Monte Carlo presented at its opening last night at the City Center, the company looked miraculously renewed. It danced with an animation, a lightness and neatness that was far from the disheveled young valiance it showed only last September. The transformation that the dancing in Balanchine's *Danses Concertantes* then suggested is now in full view in his brilliant *Ballet Imperial.* And Mary Ellen Moylan, the leading ballerina of the piece, is a lovely jewel and a joy.

Ballet Imperial, which was first danced here by Private Kirstein's American Ballet a few years ago at the New Opera, is a vivacious, exacting, inexhaustibly inventive classic dance ballet, a ballet that evokes the imperial dazzle of the St. Petersburg style in all its freshness. It is no period parody. Everything is novel in its effect. But you recognize the abounding inner gaiety, the touch of tenderness, the visual clarity and elegance, the bold dance impulse that exist — often in only vestigial form — in the Petipa-school classics still in our repertory. Balanchine has re-created the spirit of the style which was its glory. And you look at *Ballet Imperial* with the same happy wonder that our grandparents may have felt in the nineties, when the present classics were novelties.

Ballet Imperial is a ballet without a plot, as luminously incomprehensible as the old classics were. It begins with a solemn, pompous, vaguely uneasy mood, groups and solos that turn into brilliant bravura; then comes a touching pantomime scene, with softer dances, a scene that suggests a meeting, a misunderstanding, a reconciliation, a loss; and then a third section succeeds, even more vertiginously brilliant than the first, in which everybody shines, individually, in clusters, the boys, the girls, the stars, and all in unison. The musicality of the choreography is as astonishing as its extraordinary ease in affording surprises and virtuoso passages.

Young Mary Ellen Moylan, dewy in diamonds, delicate, long, and with a lovely pose of the head and a beautiful freedom in her correctness, was the star. But Maria Tallchief, brilliant in speed and with a steely exactness, and Nicholas Magallanes, easy, sincere, and animated, were real stars as well.

The handsome backdrop, by Doboujinsky, suggests the architectural glories of Petersburg. The score, Tchaikovsky's Second Piano Concerto, was brilliantly conducted by Mr. Balaban. Rachel Chapman was ideal for dancers in the piano part, and the orchestra, too, was exact and strong, as it was all evening.

New York Herald Tribune, Feb. 21, 1945

Balanchine's *Mozartiana*

Mozartiana,* the new Balanchine ballet that the Monte Carlo presented last night at the Center, is in atmosphere light and subtle; it is as full of personal

---

*George Balanchine's first version of *Mozartiana,* designed by Christian Bérard, was produced in Paris for Les Ballets 1933, with a cast that included Tamara Toumanova and Roman Jasinsky. This version, in reduced form, was first shown in the United States in June 1934, performed by students of the School of American Ballet and a year later performed by the American Ballet in White Plains, New York, with a cast headed by Holly Howard, Charles Laskey, and Gisella Caccialanza. The production Denby is reviewing was produced by Ballets Russe de Monte Carlo and was closer in

life as an ancient town on the Mediterranean on a holiday morning in the bright sun. In point of form, Balanchine recaptures the flavor of an old-style grand ballet like Petipa's *Don Quixote,* recaptures in novel terms its variety of playfulness, tenderness, and virtuosity, and he does it with only four principals and a chorus of eight girls. *Mozartiana* is another of his unassuming pocket masterpieces which restore to ballet its classic clarity and joyousness.

Mozartiana is a straight dance suite without a plot set to Tchaikovsky's Suite No. 4, an orchestral arrangement of Mozart piano pieces. Against an airy backdrop that suggests a crossroad at the edge of an Italian town, you see a young man in an eighteenth-century abbé's costume, dancing full of vivacity by himself. Enter a chorus of girls that are classic ballet's version of villagers, whom he joins in a little game.

They are followed by a girl who appears to be very sad and comes in carried by two veiled figures, a bit comic in their emphatic mysteriousness. She dances a touching Prayer. And after that comes a series of lively dances by the stars, by individuals from the chorus, by the first young man and the sad lady, now very gay in a tarantella costume. Then a poignant grand adagio by the stars, now crowned with gold leaves. And last comes a blithe little country-dance finale.

Full of novel sequences and novel bravura effects as all this is, it is striking how the variety of character in the principals becomes perfectly clear and how happily the chorus contrasts with them. Balanchine presents all the dancers at their best, and the Monte Carlo shines in *Mozartiana* once more. Danilova, both in her first pizzicato allegro and her second earnest and beautifully dramatic adagio, is a very great ballerina. But Franklin's joyous lightness, Lazowski's happy vivacity, and Miss Etheridge's serious grace and clear quickness are all wonderfully effective. And the little chorus is a chorus of soloists in achievement. *Mozartiana* was first produced by the Ballets 1933 in Paris; I thought I recognized some of the dances — they are all said to be the same — but the open, clear, and sunny tone of it now seems very different, very new.

New York Herald Tribune, Mar. 8, 1945

---

form to the original version than the previous American productions. It premiered in New York, on March 7, 1945. In 1981, Balanchine rechoreographed the ballet for the New York City Ballet's Tschaikovsky Festival, and the leads were Suzanne Farrell and Ib Anderson.

Coppélia: Ballet's Masterpiece of Comedy

Fokine's *Prince Igor* dances, looking as pleasant as a newly weeded victory
garden in August, reappeared nicely cleaned up in the Monte Carlo's repertory at the Center on Thursday. The event of that evening, and an event of
local dance history, was the *Coppélia* performance which preceded *Igor.* It
was all through in spirit and in style the finest presentation of an old-style
classic that this reviewer has seen. Had it been shown in the flattering frame
of the Metropolitan instead of the impossible one at the Center, it would have
been not only the success it was, but the unique triumph it deserved to be.

If *Giselle* is ballet's *Hamlet, Coppélia* is its *Twelfth Night* — its masterpiece
of comedy. Less effective dramaturgically than *Giselle,* it has more variety
and vivacity. *Giselle* is grandiose and morbid. *Coppélia* is captivating and
unneurotic. It treats of love and marriage, and beginning with adolescent joys
and troubles, it suggests in its radiant last grand pas de deux an adult happiness. The range of its leading role is equal to *Giselle*'s, its incidental dances
have far more fancy, and its score is far lovelier.

Last night's Monte Carlo performance was at nearly every point an extraordinary one. Alexandra Danilova, incomparably brilliant in coquetry, wit,
warm feminine graces, and warm intelligence, was last night miraculous in
classic clarity, in subtlety of rhythm, in darting and soaring elevation, in the
biting edge of her toe steps and the wide, strong line of her wonderful extension. Her dancing of the "Ear of Wheat" and of the succeeding number with
the village girls in the first act was both in its lightness and its nobility the most
glorious dancing in the world; the elegance of her playfulness in this act and in
the second were that of a peerless ballerina. The third act had here and there a
trace of tiredness, but the grandeur and limpidity of the greatest ballet were
there, and the last lift, for instance, to Franklin's shoulders, was entrancing.

But the unique merit of the Monte Carlo performance was the company's
natural grace all through. Franklin, as the hero, shone happily with the incomparable vitality he has, and in classic passages he was clean in style,
manly, and imaginative. Quite extraordinary in their beauty of style were the
eight girls who are the heroine's friends — the Misses Boris, Goddard, Chouteau, Lanese, Etheridge, Riekman, Svobodina, and Horvath, of whom I noticed the first four in particular. Never has such a chorus been seen here. But
the rousing folk dances, the doll dances, the mimed passages, the divertisse-

ments all delighted by the sense of a happily inspired company. And on this occasion Miss Chouteau celebrated her sixteenth birthday by dancing alone a Prayer that was lovely in every way.

New York Herald Tribune, Mar. 10, 1945

Balanchine's *Pas de Deux*

Balanchine's new *Pas de Deux,* which Danilova and Franklin introduced last night at the Center, is a lovely incident in the grand manner but too brief a one. When you see these two stars dancing beautifully on the stage you want them to go on dancing; and though the piece isn't called a "grand" pas de deux, the audience nonetheless was hoping for solo variations and a coda to come when the curtain went down.

Not that the piece itself is fragmentary in feeling or in form. It is set to entr'acte music from Tchaikovsky's *Sleeping Beauty,* music composed to carry a mood of suspense through an interval required for a scenic transformation, but omitted in the original production at the suggestion of Alexander III, who thought it more amusing to speed up the machinists. Balanchine's duet too is a sort of transformation scene, an episode between conclusive actions. A prince appears with a lovely princess, he holds her gently, and as she flutters and turns and bends, he lets her free, and she returns to him, and they exit together. Their intimacy is that of young people in love and engaged, and their dance figures express the dewiness, the sense of trepidation in the girl and the generous strength of the man.

Technical feats are an integral part of the delicately nervous rhythm, of the romantic suspense that the music, too, has. And at every point the plastic clarity of the two figures in their many relations is as surprising as it is unemphatic. The style for the ballerina — the piece is hers — is not the bold but the gentle grand manner, the manner that requires delicate toe steps, lovely arms, a pliant back, and extensions that are not stressed. The marvelous Danilova, lovelier to look at than ever, is as perfect in this new field as if she had never danced in any other way. Franklin held and supported her perfectly, too, with his natural generosity of stage presence.

The bolder grand style they had both shown earlier that evening, in the completely different and equally beautiful second pas de deux they have in *Mozartiana.*

New York Herald Tribune, Mar. 15, 1945

Balanchine: Ballet Magician

At the Center last night the Monte Carlo presented the first of two all-Balanchine programs, celebrating his twenty-fifth anniversary as a choreographer. (He was born in 1904.) At the conclusion of the second ballet of the evening the curtain rose again on the company, some of them in the costumes of *Danses Concertantes,* which they had just danced brilliantly, some of them already dressed for *Ballet Imperial* — a brilliant performance of which followed — the rest in street clothes, with Mr. Balanchine standing among them. Everyone applauded, the audience calling "Bravo!" Then Mr. Denham, the company director, made Mr. Balanchine an affectionate little speech and presented him with a package of Chesterfields and something to put them in. Enthusiastic applause, and a curtain call with Danilova and Franklin on either side.

The astonishing transmutation of the Monte Carlo this season is evidently the latest of Mr. Balanchine's amiable miracles. The five excellent new productions of his works added to its repertory this year have made the current season the most satisfying artistically in many years. But in the few months since the fall he has transformed the dancers as well. None of them has danced with such spontaneity, clarity, and modesty as now; and even Danilova, after twenty years of triumphs, has marvelously surpassed herself in these last weeks. The whole season has been properly a Balanchine festival.

And it is not only the delightful surprise of a single season that ballet lovers owe him. By showing us that the young Americans, who form most of the company, can dance straight classic ballet without self-consciousness — as naturally as people speak their native tongue — he has proved that ballet can become as native an art here as it did long ago in Russia; and it can develop, as it did there, a native and spontaneous brilliance. Balanchine is indeed the founder of American ballet as an art, and ballet lovers in this country are happy to have an occasion to express their sincere admiration.

He has laid sound foundations for its development here by insisting on its integrity as an art, on its inheritance as a bicentennial tradition of expressive movement, and by working with Americans — in all our theater forms, for that matter — continuously for eleven years. He shows no nostalgia for Europe, either in his work or in his teaching. And his unique genius as a ballet choreographer — he is the greatest and the most advanced of choreographers anywhere — has already made and will continue to make American ballet the envy and admiration of dance lovers all over the world. We hope they get a chance to see it soon and share with us one of our most civilized pleasures.

The second all-Balanchine evening, which the Monte Carlo presented last night at the Center, was once again a happy triumph of George Balanchine's magic. *Bourgeois Gentilhomme, Mozartiana,* the new *Pas de Deux,* and *Ballet Imperial* (all brilliantly danced), which composed the program, are in their striking variety of sentiment and form an indication of his inexhaustible classic invention; in their clarity and spontaneity, the dancing grace and wit, they prove his easy choreographic mastery. But the special secret of his magic is to make you forget the choreographer for the dancers you see before you, dancing in their lovely young freshness onstage.

Their freshness comes from the fact that they understand completely the classic dancing they are asked to do, understand it in dancers' terms. Classic dancing is what they chose as a vocation and carefully learned, what they are happy to do. For Balanchine they need not understand a dance by rationalizing psychologically, they need not put it over by emoting their role or glamorizing their personality. When they get the physical feel of a dance sequence, the bodily rhythm of the movement (and this is a profoundly personal and instinctively emotional recognition), they know they are right and that nothing will fail to carry. The audience will love them.

Nothing will fail to carry because Balanchine, by accepting the classical system of body balance (foot positions) and the steps based on it, has — for all his exciting invention — taken care of the flow of the dance phrase and the line of the deployed human figure. He has placed the gesture of the dancing figure in space so that you see it in positive relation to the visible stage center or the wings and to the figures of the other dancers. And you see it too in happy relation to the music you hear, to its formal as well as its emotional stress or ease. So the dancer dances lightly, distinctly, rhythmically, and is constantly the natural focus of attention and the source of a happy excitement.

If clarity in excitement is one of the classic tenets, the other is human naturalness of expression. Balanchine, by asking his dancers to do what they best can, by allowing each to be independently interesting, by combining the figures easily and following the emotional overtones of the rhythm and line of a human body in action, leaves the dancer his naturalness, his freshness, his dignity. The secrets of emotion he reveals are like those of Mozart, tender, joyous, and true. He leaves the audience with a civilized happiness. His art is peaceful and exciting, as classic art has always been.

New York Herald Tribune, Mar. 17 and 23, 1945

Massine's *Moonlight Sonata*

Poor Toumanova. Poor Ballet Theatre. With a kind of numb dismay, your reporter watched them submitting to a new choreographic indignity when Massine's *Moonlight Sonata* was shown Saturday night for the first time at the Metropolitan. Slick the performance was; but "Russian ballet" can hardly sink any lower than it does in offering us this clammy hallway chromo. And to have the great Massine and our fine Ballet Theatre responsible is ignominious for everyone.

Massine himself appeared as that stock chromo character "The Poet." Against a chromo backdrop representing a lake in the moonlight — it looked like an inexpensive Swiss lake in the off-season — he stuck out his chest, waved his arms importantly, and kept having to go somewhere offstage. Miss Toumanova was that other stock chromo character "The Young Girl." Unbecomingly dressed for her hip formation, she was still much the handsomest girl staying at the same deserted Swiss hotel as he. They seemed to realize stonily that there just wasn't anyone else to go around with — which is pretty much the expression of lovers on chromos.

Later, while Miss Toumanova was sitting in the moonlight alone upstage — and sitting very beautifully, really — two further characters came on, a Cupid and a Dark Lover. Cupid, in a ginger-ale-colored spotlight, turned out to be Miss Kavan, who hastily acted like the Cupid in Dolin's parody *Romantic Age.* The Dark Lover was less conventional. He turned out to be Mr. Petroff without a toupee, dressed in an old-fashioned black bathing suit several sizes too small, so that he could get it up over one shoulder only. For propriety's sake, he also was wearing long black stockings. He looked as if he were employed at the local bathing establishment, though the program billed him as a figment of fancy. Fancy or no, he made persistent advances to Miss Toumanova and finally succeeded in lifting her so that she faced the audience in the air with — oddly enough — his backside on view just below her. Cupid came back and cleared up matters.

The orchestra all this while had been playing a fantastically brutal orchestration of Beethoven's so-called *Moonlight* Sonata, which, as everyone knows, has nothing to do with moonshine on Lake Lucerne or anywhere else. They had begun disemboweling it long before the curtain went up, clammy strings appropriating the left hand and loud brass the right. Beethoven expressed his views on orchestral transcription of his piano pieces the same year this sonata was published; you can imagine what they were.

New York Herald Tribune, Apr. 9, 1945

Markova at Ballet Theatre

There are only two real ballerinas in the country; the senior one is the great Alexandra Danilova and the junior one is the great Alicia Markova. Miss Markova, appearing last night with Ballet Theatre at the Metropolitan in two of her former ballets, *Romeo and Juliet* and *Pas de Quatre,* transformed this sadly disoriented company at a stroke into the splendid one it was during her marvelous final week with them last spring. She did it by showing them the quiet simplicity of a great style, by believing completely in the piece she was performing. They glowed, they danced, they were all wonderful.

Miss Markova's delicacy in lightness, in rapidity; the quickness in the thighs, the arrowy flexibility of the instep; her responsiveness in the torso, the poise of the arms, the sweetness of the wrists, the grace of neck and head — all this is extraordinary. But her dancing is based on a rarer virtue. It is the quiet which she moves in, an instinct for the melody of movement as it deploys and subsides in the silence of time, that is the most refined of rhythmic delights. The sense of serenity in animation she creates is as touching as that of a Mozart melody.

She is a completely objective artist. Who Markova is, nobody knows. What you see on the stage is the piece she performs, the character she acts.

She shows you, as only the greatest of actresses do, a completely fascinating impersonation, completely fascinating because you recognize a heroine of the imagination who finds out all about vanity and love and authority and death. You watch her discover them.

Markova's Juliet is a miracle of acting. Every nuance of pantomime is poignantly clear and every moment is a different aspect of the cumulative tragedy. Her shy loveliness in the balcony scene, her moment watching Romeo die — but one would like to enumerate them all minute by minute. And the restraint of them all, the slow-motion continuum from which they each arise as dance gestures and which flows so steadily through the whole hour-long ballet are wonders to have seen.

The entire performance of *Romeo* was everywhere a glory. Laing, that beautifully poetic dancer, was an inspired Romeo. Mr. Orloff as Mercutio was distinguished indeed. And at the end, when Markova and Laing with the great Sir Thomas Beecham, who conducted the score with miraculous fluidity, and Tudor the choreographer (and Tybalt in the piece) took a joint bow, the enthusiastic audience applauded our quartet of British genius with the sincerest enthusiasm.

Later Miss Markova's Taglioni in *Pas de Quatre* was — as it used to be — a delight of sweet wit and stylistic brilliance. But I must add a word of sincere praise, too, for the semi-novelty of the evening, Argentinita with her enlarged company in *Café de Chinitas.* It is her best creation at the Metropolitan — in style, in sequence, in atmosphere — and it is fine to have it in the repertory. The Dali set and front curtain are grandiosely handsome, and the dancing (and Miss Miralles's fine singing) have true Spanish charm and distinction.

New York Herald Tribune, Apr. 9, 1945

Tudor's Undertow

Undertow, Tudor's new ballet which Ballet Theatre is giving at the Metropolitan, is well worth seeing. Though not so effective theatrically as *Pillar of Fire* or *Romeo,* it is a highly interesting, a very special piece, and a notable credit to the season. *Undertow* tells a story which appears to happen more in a young man's mind than in objective reality. The first scene presents quite realistically an image of his birth and his later interrupted breast-feeding. In the second, he stands, a shy and gentle adolescent in an imaginary city, and watches with increasing excitement the suggestive actions of passers-by. Other figures, innocent ones, which include a sort of innocent "brother" of his own self, try to divert his attention; and he, too, would like to ignore the horrid excitement he feels. He even persuades a girl, as excited as he, to join him in a kind of prayer meeting. But she breaks away, she invites his passion, and in an irresistible paroxysm of desire he strangles her. The next scene, set against a backdrop of clouds, shows him frenzied with terror and alone, while some of the previous characters, with a noncommittal air, stroll past. He realizes his guilt, he sees his innocence lost in the symbol of a balloon that escapes from a child's hand. And as he becomes conscious of the town once more, this very child, whom he had scarcely noticed before, points an accusing finger at him; the other characters, whether good or bad before, join her and point at him. An outcast, as if going to his execution, he walks slowly and resignedly off.

The theme of *Undertow* is that of an adolescent's neurosis, the terrifying dilemma which presents to him the act of manhood as equivalent to murder. The hero of the piece cannot find the normal solution of this, according to psychology, normal dilemma; the image of murder is so powerful in him it dominates and petrifies him, and in his impotence he kills. But despite Hugh Laing's completely sincere and sustained impersonation of the adolescent, the motivation does not convey itself to the audience; one doesn't identify oneself with him. The trouble is, I think, that the decisive initial scene, presenting a bloody birth, brilliantly shocking though it is, does not seem to be a part of the hero's inner life; it is not placed anywhere in particular. Later, at the climax, after the shockingly instantaneous murder (brilliantly duplicating the birth image), we see the hero trying to escape in vain an unseen force mightier than he; but we should have to see this antagonist of his moving in an active shape on the stage to know what the hero knows and feel as he feels. Because *Undertow* lacks such a physical release of opposing forces, it remains intellectual in its effect, like a case history, and does not quite become a drama of physical movement.

Indeed one keeps watching the movement all through for the intellectual meaning its pantomime conveys more than for its physical impetus as dancing. Its impetus is often tenuous. But its pantomime invention is frequently Tudor's most brilliant to date. The birth scene, an elderly man's advances to a prostitute, a hysterical wedding, drunken slum women, several provocative poses by the hero's victim, and quite particularly the suggested rape of a vicious little girl by four boys — these are all masterpieces of pantomime, and freer, more fluid, more plastic than Tudor's style has been. Brilliant too is his individualized use of the dancers, and wonderful the way each one of them rises to the occasion. *Undertow* is worth seeing just for Miss Alonso's horrifying bit; and though not a successful drama, it suggests in many details that Tudor's style is more powerful at present than ever before.

New York Herald Tribune, Apr. 15, 1945

The Toumanova Problem

Ballet Theatre's current season closes next Sunday; judging by the improvement the company has shown this last week the final one may well be brilliant. Thanks to *Undertow* the company's spirits have recovered and so has attendance. During the first fortnight, however, Ballet Theatre looked generally demoralized. Poor its houses were, due to a general slump in theater business, but an experienced company is not bowled over by a week of poor houses. I shouldn't wonder if Ballet Theatre's jitters are serious and are due to an aggravated case of ballerina trouble. Ballet Theatre often seems like a tight little republic of soloists; though they once accepted Miss Markova as their queen ballerina, they have not accepted Miss Toumanova as her successor. And miscast as she has been — in absurd novelties, too — she has had the misfortune of not being fully accepted by the public either. Since she dominates the classic repertory, however, everybody is under an unhappy pressure, the general style of the company suffers, and the public is disappointed.

If this is so, it would seem that the solution would be to run Ballet Theatre without a queen ballerina until one emerges by public recognition of her merit. Miss Alonso, Miss Hightower, Miss Kaye have all been granted a joint first rank with Miss Toumanova and Miss Gollner by ensemble and public alike — in fact, despite the billing, this season has turned out to be more Miss Alonso's than Miss Toumanova's. It would be fine to see all five of them taking turns in starring.

Miss Toumanova is no doubt a more striking figure than the others. Her fascinating prowess is even more startling than in the fall; her aura of fanaticism, the impression she gives of devouring the stage, suggest how thrilling she might be in a part suited to her. Even in the way she is now presented, as an athletic prodigy of incomparably powerful leg gestures, she supplies a special excitement welcome on special occasions. It is only in her current false position as the central dynamo of the company that she is lost.

For in classic ballet the queen ballerina of a company is its central dynamo; she sets the style, she exemplifies it at its most completely expressive. It is through watching her that the audience understands the style of a piece, and the style creates the poetic illusion in which the drama becomes real. She projects not only her own role, but the entire world of fancy in which that role becomes dramatic, in which everybody and everything onstage can play a part. Stage stars of all kinds project such imaginary worlds; Miss Holm and Miss Merman, for instance, do it in musical comedy, Miss Cornell and Miss Taylor in spoken drama. In ballet Miss Markova showed this quality preeminently two weeks ago in *Romeo.* Miss Kaye showed it last Monday in *Lilac Garden,* and Mr. Laing has it very strongly among male dancers. It is a quality that ballet language recognizes by saying that a real ballerina dances not a part but a ballet, not the Swan Queen but *Swan Lake.* I imagine that if Toumanova had shown this quality as steadily as Markova used to — as convincingly for the general ballet public — they would crowd to see her and give her similar ovations. And for myself, I notice she often gives me the impression of a phenomenal sleepwalker moving isolated among dancers who are performing a different piece.

Her isolation comes, perhaps, from the special nature of her dance style, which has little in common with that of the other dancers, for all its apparent classicism. Her blocklike torso, limp arms, and predatory head position, her strangely static and magnificent leg control, set her apart from the others. Her action looks not like what everyone does, done more subtly and naturally (which is a ballerina's function), but it looks like something radically different from her classic surroundings. It makes her seem less a classic heroine than an outcast.

And sometimes one wonders if Miss Toumanova doesn't play up her gift of chilly isolation onstage for an effect of exotic glamour, for a solemn impersonation of the foreign ballerina as Hollywood would type the part. It seems a foolish pose for her to take. Danilova, Krassovska, Riabouchinska, all as Russian as she, are all of them far too busy dancing to emphasize their Russianness among the Americans who surround them. But perhaps forcing her all at once into the position of top ballerina with Ballet Theatre — instead of letting them gradually become acclimated to one another — has been the real cause of a "Toumanova problem." Now, as I see it, the problem both threatens to disrupt the company and misemploys this great dancer's native genius.

Ballet Theatre's Season

Though Ballet Theatre's season has proved disappointing on several counts, the individual performances of its soloists have frequently been very fine, and a phenomenal performance among them has been Miss Alonso's as Ate in *Undertow.* In devising the part Tudor was at his most brilliantly horrid in the special angle of the head, the slightly lopsided ports de bras, the shoulder thrusts, the nasty accents of toes and knees, the fingering of the dress — all reminiscent, if you will, of the Youngest Sister in *Pillar.* Miss Alonso might have done all this as a series of striking gestures and given the impression of an acid caricature. Instead, by subordinating the separate detail to a continuous fluidity of movement, she gives you the sense of a real girl's instinctive rhythm of motion, she creates a real and living character. The coherence of her phrasing is as perfect as Markova's, and Alonso's classic precision and lightness give the part an air of distinction which makes it all the more frightening dramatically. Miss Alonso's gift for distinction is as evident for that matter in *Lilac Garden, Pillar of Fire, Peter and the Wolf, Sylphides,* or *Waltz Academy* (a moment of which is even a laughing little hint of her role in *Undertow*). Watching her, one wonders if a pointer or two from the older great Russian ballerinas on the large impetus of movement the famous classic sequences have in their finest phrasing would not be all Alonso now needs to triumph in them, too.

Rosella Hightower has shown, this season especially, a largeness of line Alonso still sometimes lacks, and Hightower's long-limbed Diana-of-the-chase figure is a handsome one to deploy. She still missed the edge that rapid translations give to slow extensions in classic phrases; her ankles do not respond sharply enough in these moments of an adagio. And in her readiness to meet the audience, she neglects, I think, the fairy-tale mystery which belongs to a classic-role. But her sense of freedom, the beauty of her yielding movements, her cordiality, humor, and courage make her Ballet Theatre's best-loved dancer. Miss Kaye (if I may extend the term soloist for the moment), though finer than ever in *Pillar* and *Lilac Garden,* in other dramatic parts sometimes begins a gesture too hard and too fast, so that the rest of the movement has no carrying power, and because the moment of repose at the end of the phrase is blurred, she sometimes gets a rather busy look in action. She still lacks full confidence in her femininity. But her strength, her boldness, her accurate classicism, her growing sense of a large rhythm and of the stylistic unity of a piece have been increasingly remarkable. Miss Gollner has won a triumph in *Undertow* in the first part really suited to her natural looks and temperament, and in *Swan Lake* she performed a few calm développés in a lift that looked like real développés — nobody else at all seems able to do them just now. Miss Reed has been as successful a soubrette as ever.

In smaller parts Miss Adams, Miss Sabo, Miss Eckl, Miss Fallis, Miss Banks have struck me particularly this season for their clean style and graceful personality, and Miss Tallchief, as a comic mime. The little trio of bathers in *Aleko* — Hightower, Alonso, and Adams — is a moment when one sees clearly how fine an ensemble Ballet Theatre disposes of; or, for instance, the little trio in *Waltz Academy* — Miss Adams, Miss Eckl, and Mr. Kriza. Kriza has now a straight, free sweep and clarity of movement, a fine posture, and a friendly modesty of manner that are all first-rate; a little attention to ankles and feet is all he seems to need. In last Wednesday's *Fancy Free* he danced his solo with a sudden instinct for continuity in phrasing that showed very sharply his rich real gifts as a dancer, and Robbins, who followed him, quite as instinctively took his cue from Kriza, and phrased his own solo handsomely, too. This season Orloff's unfailing elegance has seemed to me very striking, as well as F. Alonso's clean style and charm. Kidd, though highly talented, has suffered, I think, from hasty timing. Young Lang is rumored to be leaving. He will be badly missed in all his parts, exceptionally fine dancer as he is.

Hugh Laing is, of course, among the men the special star of the company, and, in his style, in a class by himself. His exactness of gesture, his fine intellectual fervor, and his almost Sinatralike suggestion have been as compelling as ever, and his balance has improved. Also in a class by himself, Eglevsky showed what great classic male dancing is like. He surpassed himself this spring in simplicity and power of style, and in his later appearances he has had a grandeur of rhythm that has made them great dance moments of the season.

Looking back on the two recent ballet seasons, I find that the Monte Carlo at the Center left an exhilarating impression despite its faults, and Ballet Theatre at the Metropolitan, despite its merits, left a depressing one. Wondering why so strong an array of dancers and a number of fine performances should leave a ballet lover depressed, it struck me that Ballet Theatre's season had seemed like a number of disconnected efforts that had no guiding conviction to give them coherence and collective power. The performances of individual dancers had often been very fine, but too often they had had no dance contact with the rest of the ensemble onstage. Everybody did his job, but each worked for himself. Too often I missed the collective inspiration in dancing, the mutual dance response, that had been so exhilarating at the Monte Carlo. Ballet Theatre was slick, but not inspired. And most of its fine moments reminded me of the fine moments of a good jazz soloist playing with a high-class commercial band; slick the band is and it has a showy punch, but it can't pick up the animation of his rhythm.

The expressive virtue of any dancing is its rhythm, and its rhythm is felt only in continuity. Lightness and heaviness, the start and stop of a gesture or step, the thrust and return of a limb form the alternating rhythm of dancing, its stress and nonstress. But the two elements must not be so different in interest that they cannot combine into a continuity; and so to be able to combine them a dancer learns light-footedness, elasticity, and grace.

Classic dancing is our most expressive development of dance rhythm. It builds long continuities (or phrases) of movement that offer the audience variations of bodily impetus clearly set in relation to a fixed space. And these long phrases of movement convey the specific meaning of the ballet — its drama. As the impetus of successive phrases of music suggest to the hearer a particular quality of emotion and thought, so the successive phrases of a ballet suggest to the observer a particular quality of human action. When you watch a girl moving about a room you sometimes guess what the quality of movement "means." It is not that she expresses herself by making handies, she does it by the rhythm of her actions. We often understand animals that way and they us. And in love we all know how dramatic such a moment of understanding is. It seems to tell more than any words and say it more irrevocably. And this is the natural phenomenon on which the art of ballet is built as a convincing human expression.

I think it was this power of expression through rhythm that I missed at Ballet Theatre so often this spring, for, as a company, their dancing was convincing only now and then. It seemed somehow too heavy-footed, over-stressed, discontinuous. I think it did because they defined the stress of the gesture emphatically but took no interest in the unstressed part. Perhaps they were thinking in dancing terms of key effects rather than in terms of a continuous melody. But they missed giving the exhilarating sense of dance rhythm that only the projection of a complete movement — stress and non-stress — can begin to create.

One can see that while it is possible for a dancer to smash the stress of a gesture at the public, he cannot do the same with the gesture's weaker phase. A complete movement (both parts of it as a rhythmic unit) gets its carrying power by a different attack — by being projected in relation to the stage space and the other dancers. This method has an air of modesty that doesn't catch the public as quickly, but it has the advantage of drawing the audience steadily into the illusion of situation and character which can exist only back of the proscenium. That is why the dramatic illusion and the dance illusion of ballet are broken by the punch of the hyperactive showman and are secured by the gentle-mannered and luminously calm ballerina.

If Ballet Theatre's fine company would aim for the continuity of movement of classic dancing and for the rhythmic power such dancing has, it wouldn't need to worry whether the ballet craze is over yet in America or not.

New York Herald Tribune, May 13 and 29, 1945

Graham's *Herodiade*

Herodiade, a tragic dance scene for two characters which Martha Graham presented for the first time in New York last night, was first seen like her new *Appalachian Spring* at the Coolidge Festival last fall in Washington, for which both works — their score and choreography — had been commissioned. And here at the National, like *Appalachian Spring* on Monday night, yesterday's *Herodiade* was another complete audience success. But apart from that, the two pieces resemble each other not at all.

The scene of *Herodiade* as the program states is "an antechamber where a woman waits with her attendant. She does not know what she may be required to do or endure. Fragments of dreams rising to the surface of a mirror add to the woman's agony of consciousness. With self-knowledge comes acceptance; as she advances to meet the unknown, the curtain falls."

This is an accurate outline. *Herodiade* is an immolation scene and might take place in the antechamber to the Cretan labyrinth. It has the tone of a mythological rite and a classic sense of the grandeur of destiny. Miss Graham's motions are passionately and nobly contained, and marvelously natural as she makes them. A few large static gestures of tragic splendor and a few small desperate outbursts in complex hammered rhythms are enough to express the richness and dignity of the protagonist's fate. Her slow entrance; a later passage in "archaic" profile; a few crouching insane and blinded steps in which she approaches and touches the attendant; a twisting walk from the back with her feet parallel to the footlights; another with one hip thrust wildly sideways and held so; two grand poses heroically reminiscent of Isadora at the Parthenon: that is what gives to *Herodiade* its sustained wonder, its amazing human power and sense of human knowledge.

The second role, that of the Attendant, is far less interesting. It has a kind of coarseness that contrasts with the leading character's exquisite elegance. And the moment when Miss Graham, who is the victim of the action, turns to console the attendant is like a hint from the *Phaedo*. But one wishes this other woman had more character, either as a rude jailer or even as a comic foil. But this dramatic weakness in the piece is counterbalanced by the brilliant inventiveness of the chief role and the superbly restrained performance of Miss Graham in it.

The score of *Herodiade,* by Paul Hindemith, is a beautiful work, full, flowing, and somber, and the orchestra played it very well indeed. The title *Herodiade,* incidentally, is the title of the score — Mr. Hindemith chose Mallarmé's celebrated poem of that name for his subject. Though the ballet has very little relation to that poem, Miss Graham, who first had called her work *Mirror Before Me,* now uses Hindemith's title.

Miss Graham's second costume, an underdress, was beautiful too. The decor by Noguchi, however — in a sort of Bonwit Teller surrealism — added nothing. It looked to me like a doctor's office in a Hollywood fantasy.

New York Herald Tribune, May 16, 1945

Appalachian Spring and *Herodiade* a Second Time

On seeing Martha Graham's new *Appalachian Spring* a second time a quality which touched me particularly was the fresh feeling of hillside woods and fields the piece conveys. It does it partly in the way the still figures look off as if at a horizon of hills. The horizon is not the treetop garden horizon of *Letter to the World* nor the expanse of summer sky and sea of *Salem Shore,* but it is the real open air that is suggested in all three. *Herodiade* and *Deaths and Entrances,* on the other hand, happen in a room of some kind, and in these pieces, when Miss Graham suggests in her gesture a great space about her it is, so to speak, the intellectual horizon of the character she depicts. The precision of such differences in suggestion is one of the fascinations of watching her repertory.

Appalachian Spring describes the landscape not only in terms of its contour, but also in terms of living conditions. The separateness of the still figures, one from another, which their poses emphasize, suggests that people who live in these hills are accustomed to spending much of their time alone. Their outlines don't blend like those of townsmen. "In solitude shall I find entertainment" ("Einsam und allein soll mein Vergnügen sein") is painted on an early Pennsylvania Dutch bride chest, and the Bride in *Appalachian Spring* might well have read it. It is touching how gently the piece persuades you of the value of domestic and neighborly ties by giving you a sense of rural isolation.

The Appalachian isolation of the pioneer farmhouse in the piece is suggested even more imaginatively by a note of wildlife that keeps cropping up in the dances. A passage of Miss Graham's first solo looked to me as if she were a hillside girl darting after the little beasts her playing flushed from cover. And the Revivalist's four ecstatic girl Followers suggested in their fluttering and breathless darting the motions of chipmunks and birds on the ground, as if they were four small wild animals that were not frightened away by people; the Revivalist, too—part St. Francis, part Thoreau—seemed to treat them like tame wildlife rather than like girls. And the way his part merged evangelism with animism served in the ballet to join domestic ties to nature magic.

After seeing *Herodiade,* Miss Graham's other new piece, a second time I think Virgil Thomson's account of it in his article in today's music section more accurate than mine of last Wednesday. The secret of the piece lies much more in the complex and completely individualized elegance of the heroine than it does in the classic allusions of her gesture. Her elegance of motion is her private integrity. We watch it in conflict with her instincts, we watch her transform their force and gain in grandeur; and to watch so desperate a conflict being fought in middle age makes the drama the more poignant, the more heroic. But what makes it real in the first place is the real situation — a lady getting dressed by her maid. It is a pity the maid isn't some sort of real woman too; even her obscene gestures toward the floor look merely wooden.

New York Herald Tribune, May 20, 1945

Concerto Barocco

Concerto Barocco, the Balanchine novelty of the current Monte Carlo season at the Center, is an unpretentious and good-tempered little ballet and it is also the masterpiece of a master choreographer. It has only eleven dancers; it is merely straight dancing to music — no sex story, no period angle, no violence. It does not seem to be trying to win your interest, but before you know it, it has absorbed your attention and doesn't let it go. It has power of rhythm and flow; in a wealth of figuration it is everywhere transparent, fresh, graceful, and noble; and its adagio section is peculiarly beautiful.

Concerto Barocco was recognized as a masterpiece at once when it was shown here in dress rehearsal four years ago by Lincoln Kirstein's American Ballet. It had just been created then for the Rockefeller-sponsored South American tour of that company. And though this ballet tour has recently been spoken of as one of Mr. Rockefeller's inter-American mistakes, as a ballet critic I can say that in showing *Concerto Barocco,* he was showing our neighbors choreography of the best quality in the world — showing a United States product that no country of Western Europe could have equaled. A mistake such as that does anyone honor.

It is a pleasure to report that the Monte Carlo production of *Barocco* is excellent both in the dancing onstage and in the playing in the orchestra pit. Unfortunately, though, the piece has in the present production been given a backdrop of meager, dirty blue and a set of harsh black bathing suits for the charming girls. Meagerness and harshness are not in its spirit; some of the

wonderful clarity in its spacing is dimmed and in so poverty-struck a frame the rich title of the ballet strikes one as absurd.

But *Concerto Barocco* comes by its fancy title quite honestly. The name might lead you to expect an evocation of baroque dancing or baroque mannerisms; still, what the title actually promises is a baroque concerto, and that is just what you get. Balanchine has set his ballet so happily to Bach's Concerto for Two Violins that the score may be called his subject matter. The style of the dance is pure classic ballet of today, and the steps themselves follow the notes now strictly, now freely. But in its vigorous dance rhythm, its long-linked phrases, its consistent drive and sovereign articulation, *Concerto Barocco* corresponds brilliantly to this masterpiece of baroque music.

The correspondence of eye and ear is at its most surprising in the poignant adagio movement. At the climax, for instance, against a background of chorus that suggests the look of trees in the wind before a storm breaks, the ballerina, with limbs powerfully outspread, is lifted by her male partner, lifted repeatedly in narrowing arcs higher and higher. Then at the culminating phrase, from her greatest height he very slowly lowers her. You watch her body slowly descend, her foot and leg pointing stiffly downward, till her toe reaches the floor and she rests her full weight at last on this single sharp point and pauses. It is the effect at that moment of a deliberate and powerful plunge into a wound, and the emotion of it answers strangely to the musical stress. And (as another example) the final adagio figure before the coda, the ballerina being slid upstage in two or three swoops that dip down and rise a moment into an extension in second — like a receding cry — creates another image that corresponds vividly to the weight of the musical passage. But these "emotional" figures are strictly formal as dance inventions. They require no miming in execution to make them expressive, just as the violin parts call for no special schmaltz. And this modesty of stage presence combined with effects so strong and assured gives one a sense of lyric grandeur.

The adagio section is the only movement with a lyric expression. The introductory Vivace is rather like a dance of triumph, strong, quick, and square; while the concluding Allegro is livelier and friendlier, with touches of syncopated fun and sportive jigging. Both these sections have sharply cut rhythms, a powerful onward drive, and a diamondlike sparkle in their evolutions. There are, for instance, many lightning shifts in the arm positions and yet the pulse of the dance is so sure its complexity never looks elaborate. The eight girls who execute the little chorus and the two girl soloists are precise and quick and their grace is wonderfully natural. They are all so earnestly busy dancing, they seem more than ever charmingly young, and their youth gives an innocent animal sweetness to their handsome deportment.

New York Herald Tribune, Sept. 16, 1945

To Argentinita

The death of Argentinita brings to many Americans who loved to see her dance a grief like that of a personal loss. Only the greatest dancers can awaken so personal a response by as restrained an art as hers was. Her spell as a star was that of a special Latin bearing, discreetly sensible and delightfully polite; she seemed a lady vivaciously entertaining her guests, and one could imagine that her expertness as host was only the reflection of the pleasure she felt in seeing her friends. Her dances had the effect of captivating anecdotes about Spanish style easy for us North Americans to appreciate and enjoy. By her amiable gaiety of spirit, her wit, her tact in sentiment, her perfect grace and perfect courtesy, she established a sure contact, so that in her case the classic reserve of Spanish dance forms seemed even to sentimentalists like ourselves neither remote nor haughty. Argentinita was in this sense a triumphant popularizer of the Spanish style among us; and through her easy and charming approach she opened the eyes of thousands of Americans to the nature of the Spanish tradition she worked in, to its vitality of rhythm, its subtlety of expression, and its high sense of personal dignity.

Argentinita's knowledge of the Spanish dance tradition was prodigious. An accurate scholar, she knew it in all its historical, regional, and racial diversity, folk forms and theater forms, the special techniques as well as the special deportments. She knew it from living with gypsies, from traveling in the mountains, from talking to poets. But she did not try to reproduce this material literally. Like the circle of poet-scholars and musicians she belonged to in Madrid, from Benavente and Martínez Sierra to Falla and, greatest of them all, García Lorca, her aim was to keep the full savor and amplitude of local traditions in freely invented and consciously shaped personal works of art. Argentinita's personal nature as a dancer was, by witty edge and lyric grace, essentially Andalusian, and she was too honest an artist to falsify it. And so if her Peruvian Indian dance, for instance, or her music-hall studies or even her flamenco became her own graceful versions of these dance forms, they were nonetheless each completely different from the others, each composed in its own specific dance idiom and danced with its characteristic rhythmic impulse and its own dance attitude. And you would scarcely have imagined, watching her in recital, on how strict a discipline in characterization her charming little numbers had been built.

Argentinita's dances as you saw them had a charmingly ladylike air, with no athletics and no heroics. Sometimes the steps and patterns seemed naively plain and the best ones were never very elaborate, but her group numbers were always completely transparent and their comedy points rarely failed to register. Argentinita chose a small range of force as a choreographer, but she was a master in economy of detail, in proportion of emphasis, in sustaining interest and flow. Her gift for continuity and coherence (of impulse and of silhouette) made of slight variations distinct contrasts. Her own manner of dancing was suited to such delicate devices, for it was completely graceful, completely defined, and her rhythm was infallible. Her special glory as a dancer were her little slippered feet, in their tiny, airy dartings and in their pretty positions on the floor. Argentinita's dancing naturally included more spectacular elements, but it was in the clarity of small details that one appreciated best the classic craft of her dance technique.

A classic cameo artist she was in technique, in choreography, in characterization. But she was a born star in the quick grace of her movement and a born star in the vivacity of her theater personality. Though she knew for years she needed rest and care, she could not bear to stop dancing. And though her tours overtaxed her, though she was handicapped by halls too vast for her special quality, and sometimes perhaps by the illness she heroically ignored, her hold on the public increased with each appearance. Last spring she seemed more scintillating and more amusing than ever, and her last production, *Café de Chinitas* at the Metropolitan, was her happiest work in a larger form. From the peak of her success she has now slipped away into silence.

At Argentinita's funeral were many who had known her only across the footlights but who loved her. And many more, all over this country, will keep their memories of how delightfully she danced, surrounded by her charming company, by her high-spirited and witty sister, Pilar Lopez, and by Greco and Vargas, the young men she had trained so brilliantly.

New York Herald Tribune, Sept. 30, 1945

Apollo: The Power of Poetry

Ballet Theatre covered itself with a real glory at the Metropolitan last night by bringing back to us Balanchine's *Apollo* and by dancing it completely beautifully. *Apollo — Apollon Musagète* is the title of the Stravinsky score — has been performed in New York now and then by various companies during the last ten years, and each time its serene and sensuous poetry has won it a spontaneous acclaim. It is an untarnished masterpiece. Last night, too, there were bravos, and not bravos merely for the virtuosity but for the poetic beauty of the dancing. For myself, seeing *Apollo* last night has left me — for the first time in the current season, I'm afraid — happily and unreservedly enthusiastic.

Enthusiastic about the piece, which moves me and delights me each time I see it; enthusiastic about last night's performance, in which Alicia Alonso, Nora Kaye, and Barbara Fallis were brilliantly delicate, brilliantly strong, and André Eglevsky magnificently powerful. Virtuoso they were, all four of them — Alonso's extensions, Kaye's speed, and Eglevsky's sweep were in detail dazzling; but the sweet earnestness, the classic modesty, the poetic naturalness of all four throughout the piece made one forget the unhappy tendency to a more foolish kind of solo showmanship that seems to be creeping more and more into Ballet Theatre's everyday performances. Last night Ballet Theatre was dancing seriously again, and beautiful was the result.

Apollo is about poetry, poetry in the sense of a brilliant, sensuous, daring, and powerful activity of our nature. It depicts the birth of Apollo in a prologue; then how Apollo was given a lyre, and tried to make it sing; how three Muses appeared and showed each her special ability to delight; how he then tried out his surging strength; how he danced with Terpsichore, and how her loveliness and his strength responded in touching harmony; and last, how all four together were inspired and felt the full power of the imagination, and then in calm and with assurance left for Parnassus, where they were to live.

Balanchine has told this metaphysical story in the concrete terms of classic dancing, in a series of episodes of rising power and brilliance. Extraordinary is the richness with which he can, with only four dancers, create a sustained and more and more satisfying impression of the grandness of man's creative genius, depicting it concretely in its grace, its sweet wit, its force and boldness, and with the constant warmth of its sensuous complicity with physical beauty. *Apollo* is a homage to the academic ballet tradition, and the first work in the contemporary classic style, but it is a homage to classicism's sensuous loveliness as well as to its brilliant exactitude and its science of dance effect.

What you see onstage is strangely simple and clear. It begins modestly with effects derived from pantomime, a hint of birth pangs, a crying baby, a man dancing with a lute, and it becomes progressively a more and more directly classic dance ballet, the melodious lines and lyric or forceful climaxes of which are effects of dance continuity, dance rhythm, and dance architecture. And it leaves at the end, despite its innumerable incidental inventions, a sense of bold, open, effortless, and limpid grandeur. Nothing has looked unnatural, any more than anything in Mozart sounds unnatural. But you feel happily the nobility that the human spirit is capable of by nature.

New York Herald Tribune, Oct. 23, 1945

Alonso and Eglevsky in *Giselle*

Alicia Alonso danced Giselle Tuesday night with Ballet Theatre and both Havana and New York crowded into the Metropolitan to cheer, in enthusiastic ballet fashion, Markova's heiress apparent in the company. Young, unaffected, and often very brilliant the performance was, on Alonso's part and on André Eglevsky's, who danced the great partner role of Albrecht magnificently. Both of them broke through the familiar Markova-Dolin interpretation with a sincere youthful fervor of dancing and of love that even the mystery beyond the grave could not repress. You can imagine how the audience cheered.

Alonso is a delightfully young and a very Latin Giselle, quick, clear, direct in her relation to her lover. She is passionate rather than sensuous. She is brilliant in allegro, not so convincing in sustained grace. Her plié is not yet a soft and subtly modulated one and this weakens her soaring phrases. She has little patience for those slow-motion, vaporous effects that we Northerners find so touching. But there is no fake about her, no staginess. Her pointes, her young high extensions, her clean line, her lightness in speed, her quick balance are of star quality.

Her first act was the more distinguished of the two in its dramatic interpretation. She is no tubercular ballerina-peasant but a spirited girl who stabs herself. The dance solo was hidden from me by latecomers, but loudly applauded. The confrontation scene and the mad scene were convincing, simple and large in their miming. In the second act the first whirls were thrilling, and the famous passage of lifts with the following solo of échappés and spins stopped the show by its cumulative bold, clear speed. If there was little that was spectral in the second act, there was nothing that was not vividly young and straightforward.

But it was Eglevsky's dancing in the second act that was a superb revelation to those New Yorkers who have only seen Dolin in it of what this part is really like. Eglevsky's grandeur of rhythm, his magnificently easy elevation, his masterful, clean, and unstressed beats, and even more than that his modesty and young sincerity show how stagey, fidgety, and absurdly weak, technically, Dolin's Albrecht has recently become. Eglevsky's "fish leaps" (pas de poisson) near the end were beautiful indeed. And though he is clearly happier dancing than miming, and though the more difficult the passage the more beautifully he dances it, there is in his naive acting none of the empty showmanship of Dolin's. The way Eglevsky sustained an atmosphere of remoteness in his second-act solos showed that these passages can heighten the mystery of the second act and need not smash it in pieces as Dolin does each time he gets set for a solo. Eglevsky's Albrecht is something for ballet lovers to see.

The Ballet Theatre company danced *Giselle* Tuesday with a happy and spontaneous animation, particularly the first-act ensembles, and the second-act scene with Hilarion. Their interest in the mad scene, done so differently this time, was vivid, and the general support they gave Alonso made the company charming, too. I hope we shall have many more such bright Alonso-Eglevsky *Giselle*s.

New York Herald Tribune, Oct. 24, 1945

Apollo

Balanchine's *Apollo* is a ballet so simple in story, so rich in dance imagery, so exciting in invention, I should like to describe a little what happens. The piece calls for a string orchestra to play the Stravinsky score and for four superb dancers; it has beyond that only three small parts, no chorus, almost no scenery. It is quite unpretentious as theater. The scene is on Delos,

Apollo's birthplace, and the action begins a moment before his birth, with Leto, his mother, high on a rock in a sharp ray of light, tossing grandly to and fro in the labor of a goddess. Then Apollo appears standing wrapped rigid in swaddling clothes. Two nymphs bring him forward and he bawls infantlike. The nymphs begin to unwrap him, but with a godlike vigor before they are done he makes a ballet preparation and whoosh! spins himself free. Free, he makes a grandly clumsy and babylike thrust and curvet or two, and the prologue is over.

When the lights come on again, he is grown to boyhood and alone. The nymphs have brought him a long-necked lute and he tries to make it sing. But his solitary attempts, first entangled, then lyrical, then determined, look inconclusive. Three young Muses appear and the four of them dance together. They dance charmingly and a little stiffly, reminding you of the inexpressive seriousness and shy, naive fancy of children. But as they end, the boy gives the three girls each a magic gift, a scroll of verse to one, a theater mask to the second, a lyre to the third. And holding these emblems of poetry, each seems to be inspired beyond her years. The first girl dances flowingly with an airy and lyric delight. The second bounds with dramatic speed, with sudden reversals of direction as if in mid-leap; just at the end one hand that has seemed all through to be holding a mask before her face seems to sweep the mask away, and she is herself again and frightened. The third Muse, Terpsichore, invents the most adventurously brilliant dance of all, boldly cutting her motions in startling divisions, as if isolating the elements of her art, without in these diamond-clear stops breaking the cumulative drive. She combines suspense with calm. And as she ends, Apollo gently touches her bright head. But, the dance over, she ducks away like a child and runs off.

Then Apollo, his strength awakened, dances by himself, leaping in complex virtuoso sequences, in a grandly sustained sweep of powerful motion. It is no showoff number, it is a masculine surge of full dance mastery. Terpsichore returns just as he ends and together they invent a series of adagio surprises, extremes of balance and extension, boldly large in line, boldly intimate in imagery, and ending with a tender and lovely "swimming lesson" that he gives her. And now all three Muses dance together in darting harmony and dance inspired by poetry's power, swinging from Apollo like birds, curving from his body like a cluster of flowers, driven by him like an ardent charioteer, and ending, when immortal Zeus has called through the air, in three grand accents of immolation. Then calmly and soberly, in Indian file, all four ascend the rock of the island and a chariot comes through the sky down toward them as the curtain falls. They will go to Parnassus where they will live ever after.

You see as *Apollo* proceeds how from a kind of pantomimic opening it becomes more and more a purely classic-dance ballet. More and more it offers the eye an interplay of lines and rhythms, of changing architectural balances, the edge of which becomes keener and keener. In this sense *Apollo* conveys an image of increasing discipline, of increasing clarity of definition. It grows more and more civilized. But the rhythmic vitality of the dance, the abundance of vigor, increase simultaneously, so that you feel as if the heightening of discipline led to a heightening of power, to a freer, bolder range of imagination. Since the piece is about the gods of poetry, and how they learned their art, it seems, too, to be describing concretely the development of the creative imagination.

And as the dance images grow more disciplined, more large, and more vigorous, they also grow grander in their sensuous connotations. As Apollo and the little Muses grow up, the intimate contact between them seems to develop from an innocent childlike play to the firm audacity and tender inventiveness of maturity.

Suggested in no sense mimically but purely by dance architecture, the range and richness of *Apollo*'s sensuous imagery is marvelous; and because of this consistent honest but unself-conscious sensuousness, the "abstract" classicism is at no point dehumanized or out of character with the dramatic situation. So for example the taut ballet extension of a girl's leg and toe — used in *Apollo* as an insignia of poetry itself — grows increasingly poignant to watch as the piece proceeds; and you experience everywhere the cool sensual luminosity of civilized art.

So *Apollo* can tell you how beautiful classic dancing is when it is correct and sincere; or how the power of poetry grows in our nature; or even that as man's genius becomes more civilized, it grows more expressive, more ardent, more responsive, more beautiful. Balanchine has conveyed these large ideas really as modestly as possible, by means of three girls and a boy dancing together for a while.

But the immediate excitement of watching does not depend on how you choose to rationalize it. *Apollo* is beautiful as dancing and gloriously danced.

New York Herald Tribune, Oct. 28, 1945

Robbins's *Interplay*

Robbins's *Interplay,* once in Billy Rose's *Concert Varieties* and now a success in Ballet Theatre's repertory, is of serious interest both for being young Robbins's second work and for being, of all the ballets by American-trained choreographers, the most expertly streamlined in dance design. *Interplay* looks like a brief entertainment, a little athletic fun, now and then cute, but consistently clear, simple, and lively. You see four boys come out and then four girls and all eight join in improvised games (such as follow-the-leader) done in dance terms; there is a boy's joking showoff solo, and a duet with a touch of blues sentiment in the air, and then all eight together play another game, competing in leaps and spins with the effect of a collective speed-up finale. It looks rather like an American outdoor party where everyone is full of pep and naively rough and where the general unfocused physical well-being is the fun of the occasion. Still, it isn't always clear from the way the dancers behave to each other if they represent twenty-year-olds being cute or ten-year-olds on their good behavior.

But leaving aside the subject matter (which the program doesn't clarify either) what immediately captures your attention is the pace of the piece, the clear drive of its dance impetus, and the athletic verve of the cast — a perfect cast, in which Harold Lang is especially brilliant. The physical spring of the athletic phrases obviously suits the dancers and the impetus of the movement obviously suits that of the score as well; and the whole continuity is perfectly clear to the eye as dance architecture. There is nothing subtle about the dance — nor about the score, Gould's *Concertette,* for that matter; the texture and the expressive accents are commonplace, but nowhere does the piece break down and become fragmentary, fussy, or thick. And this is a serious achievement. Robbins alone of our native choreographers has grasped at one stroke that the basis of ballet logic is a view of time and space as a closed entity. The time of a ballet is that specified by the musical architecture of its score and the space is that of the stage area as a static whole. These two architectural frames of reference, so to speak, give to the mazes of a ballet its coherent and cumulative distinctness. And the cumulative distinctness in spacing and timing that *Interplay* has in action is of serious ballet quality.

Not of serious ballet quality is *Interplay*'s specific dance technique. Robbins does not show the resource of deploying the body unself-consciously, of a sustained and a natural soaring and sailing; the foot positions are only approximate and this spoils the buoyancy and sharpness of floor contact and of phrase construction; he tries for vivacity by again and again overspeeding pirouettes: his jokes are sometimes too coy; he does not distinguish between the timing of pantomime and of dance gesture; and the accents of the dance are likely to be energetic thrusts expressing a shot-in-the-arm vigor rather than an individual response to a dramatic moment.

But perhaps Robbins feels that both the score and the subject matter of *Interplay* call for a general vigor rather than for a modulated and individual grace. The characters of *Interplay* seem to be urban middle-class young people having a good time, who know each other well and like being together but have no particular personal emotions about each other and no special keenness of response. They know about sex as a jive joke or as a general blues sentiment; they don't know it is an individual focus of passion. From a hint of personal sincerity they turn untroubled and vague with a coltish playfulness, expert in strength but blunt in edge.

In this unpersonal aspect of *Interplay* there might be the poetic subject matter of an American flavor of sentiment. And Robbins has, I think, a poetic love for the air of rudeness and unresponsiveness in our national manners. But in *Interplay* he has glossed it over by a general mutual amiability that is humanly unconvincing and a bit goody-goody; he has for the moment confused love of America with flattery. Such criticism is nonsense if *Interplay* is taken as passing entertainment, but not if it is taken as some sort of serious ballet. And the intellectual vigor, the clear focus of its overall craftsmanship suggest — as *Fancy Free* suggested in another way — that Robbins means to be and can be more than a surefire Broadway entertainer, that he can be a serious American ballet choreographer.

New York Herald Tribune, Nov. 4, 1945

Markova's Failing

Ballet Theatre's season, which closes tonight, has been very successful commercially, but artistically it leaves a disappointing impression, and one of its unexpected disappointments has been the lessening of Markova's marvelous magic. Sunday night in *Romeo* and the night before in *Giselle* she was an exquisite figure to watch, clearly Ballet Theatre's loveliest dancer. But she who in her own miraculously fragile way used to illuminate the meaning of an entire ballet and spread a radiance over the rest of the cast and the entire stage seemed too often to be upstaging the company and to be dancing her own steps merely to look as deliciously graceful as possible, not for the sake of a larger dramatic expression. This has often been her failing this season.

Graceful she still is, and incomparably so, in the lovely bearing of the head, the beautifully effaced shoulders, the line of arms and wrists, the arrowy ankles and feet. Her variety in speed, her general exactness of positions, the limpidity with which she reveals the contrasting accents in direction of a dance sequence without breaking the smoothness of its flow are all of ballerina quality. Her leaps, her way of soaring and gliding, her wonderful lightness in downward motions are unique. But one notices that she tends this season to preserve these graces by lessening the vitality of her dancing, by understating the climaxes. It is as though a singer were to get the mannerism of taking fortissimos in half-voice, a kind of crooning in ballet.

One sees climaxes this season (in *Nutcracker* and *Aurora*) that are tricked out with flicks of the head in pirouettes, with flicks of the wrist in poses; one notices (in *Giselle,* too) the wrists beating time in sustained passages, and broad smiles held throughout a classic number. She seems, no doubt unconsciously, to indicate a discourteous aversion to dancing with Eglevsky and Kriza; and in dancing with Dolin she sometimes gives the effect of a private understanding between them — as is customary and proper in exhibition ballroom dancing but hardly in great classic roles.

These are no doubt inadvertencies which can be blamed on her year's absence from serious ballet. But they are unfortunate mannerisms in a great ballerina. They give an impression of sufficiency that is especially not in keeping with Markova's shy style. And though the audience still applauds her wonderful moments of grace, it does not now thrill to her performance as it used to and as it will again when she gives herself wholly to her parts. I don't doubt that so great an artist will soon tire of the effects she now toys with.

New York Herald Tribune, Nov. 5, 1945

Ballet Theatre in Decline . . . and a Farewell

Ballet Theatre is on the decline and its decline is due to mistakes in its management. That is the impression the recent season has left despite the crowds at the Metropolitan. Fine performances there were, bright moments of glory. But the defects which last spring grew less marked as the season progressed, this fall became more pronounced and new ones joined them. Many people noticed this time the increasing rudeness and heaviness of Ballet Theatre's general dancing; they noticed more than ever dancers in solo passages drawing attention to themselves at the cost of dance style and dramatic illusion, and a growing laxness in executing the older pieces in the repertory. People noticed too that the production routine was more careless — in hanging and lighting the sets, in replacing old costumes, in dragging out intermissions — and that the orchestra was more than usually unreliable. And even Markova, whose return to Ballet Theatre had been eagerly looked forward to, did not thrill the public as she used to.

Last spring Ballet Theatre had been saved only by *Undertow.* Last spring, too, the company was overtired and discouraged; but with *Undertow* they felt they had accomplished something worthwhile and had justified their existence as artists. So their morale soared and everybody — including those who had no roles in that piece — danced everything in the repertory with a new zest. But the management did not learn from that example. This time its novelties — though worthwhile as the first steps of new choreographers — were too timid as ballet to give the season a lift. There was no large risk in them. The management took only three other risks this fall, and though none was brave enough to lead to a decisive victory, in each case it spoiled even the small victory it could have won with them. They were the Chagall décor for *Firebird,* which had no choreography of interest to go with it; the Alonso-Eglevsky *Giselle,* which was done only once and in Alonso's hardest week; and the revival of Balanchine's 1928 *Apollo* — the high point of the season but marred at the two repeat performances by insufficient orchestra rehearsal. Poor management indeed.

And that was not all. When the recent season was planned last spring, the management saw it had no challenging novelty, and so it scheduled the best of its former repertory. It could so have presented a respectable season if it had also planned in advance for the best performances possible. Obstacles were the departures, some certain, some threatening, of Hightower, Gollner,

Dorati, Tudor, Laing, and a number of others; the cost of rehearsals needed for many changes of cast in so large a repertory; and the strain such a season would put on Kaye and Alonso. But if money had been spent on understudy rehearsals last spring (with Tudor) and on several weeks of extra rehearsal for the company this summer, the dancers would not have been exhausted by trying to learn everything in a hurry. It was poor management to save the money and instead to show Kriza, Kidd, and Lang at short notice and manifest disadvantage in Laing's crucial and complex roles; to wear out Kaye in trivial parts that added nothing to her range or her value; and to lead tired Alonso to save herself in *Swan Lake* and *Waltz Academy,* which she could otherwise have done brilliantly. It was poor management to present the whole company overtired, often underrehearsed, with a conductor who had to keep his eyes on the score and with awkward stage management.

Under such handicaps any dancers spoil their style, and their best style is what a performance depends on for its vitality and thrill. When she is tired, even Alonso, that meticulous stylist, falls into the great Toumanova's error of exhibiting prowess or the great Markova's error of seeming to snub the company and the piece. Even ardent Kaye — who, like Alonso, far bettered her previous best this season when she was rested — when she is tired begins to turn in and to hitch up an arabesque after it has been extended. This has become a general failing with Ballet Theatre's girls, and when tired they dance — it's not their fault — with a violence that reminds one more of a tennis game than of limpid ballet. Perhaps, too, the insistent self-assertiveness of Marjorie Tallchief and the undisciplined roughness of Rall, besides spoiling these two very gifted dancers, give a bad example to the rest. The young dancers who came through this strenuous season most happily were, I thought, the Misses Fallis, Adams, Eckl, Lanese, and Herman, the Messrs Tobias, Beard, and Dovell. Eglevsky — who wasn't used so hard — was magnificent when possible, though his facial miming is overdone; Orloff was remarkable. But John Kriza, overworked as he was, was everywhere Ballet Theatre's brightest mainstay, and his verve in his final Romeo woke up Zlatin and the orchestra to a fine musical performance and even almost woke Miss Markova out of her season's trance.

Ballet lovers are distressed by the wasteful handling of so fine a company of dancers as Ballet Theatre during this last season. The rumor that a new international company is being formed by De Basil, De Cuevas, and De Hurok is no palliative to watching the demoralization of so much of our most valuable native talent. Mr. Kirstein tells me our ballet ensembles are stronger than any he saw abroad. The future of American ballet depends on them, and their growing powers should not be frittered away by poor management.

With this article I end my duties as dance reviewer for the *Herald Tribune* and turn the department over to Walter Terry, back from more than three years of service in the Army.

New York Herald Tribune, Nov. 11, 1945

Wigman After the War

Harald Kreutzberg danced here a week ago, and tried out some new, decoratively surrealist numbers that looked silly to me; but I'm not a Kreutzberg fan. The public here was divided much as at home — he's a success but not with dance lovers. At the recital I saw Mary Wigman, light-eyed, red-haired, with a wild, ruined face and a wonderful human warmth; she was in Locarno (the next town) for a few days' vacation after giving a two-week course in Zurich (with Kreutzberg) and before going back to her school in Leipzig (Russian Zone). She was having a wonderful time staring at all the luxury of the West: clean trains, meals on the lawn, whipped cream and coffee on the sidewalk, and the palms and flowers and mountain peaks of this place. She told me she has a school and a new dance group formed since the war, and it toured in a program she made for them called *Aus der Not der Zeit (Out of the Rubble* is a free translation). She also was director at the Leipzig Opera for *Orpheus* (two months of rehearsals), doing it with a dance group onstage continuously almost. It was considered the best production in Germany since the war. She stopped dancing in 1942; the Nazis were always hard on her, and finally forced her to sell her school.

She says that modern dance didn't evolve under the Nazis or produce a new crop of dancers, and it's still too early since the defeat. A class of young people of hers to whom she mentioned the word "Olympus" didn't know what it meant, not one in thirty. Of course there is hardly any money for lessons, also no food. She was wearing a gray dress sent from New York. She is not well. But she had been sent a book of photographs of Martha Graham and wanted to hear all about her. She thought Graham must be marvelous and also so intensely American, an embodiment of the country. And she spoke of

Martha's having described the Grand Canyon to her — those subterranean mountain ranges — long ago in New York, and of the American landscape she remembered, and how her American pupils each one sooner or later danced a dance of spreading out into space.

A former pupil of hers, Pola Nierenska, was here too, said to be the best modern dancer in England.

Unpublished, ca. 1947

Ashton's *Cinderella*

The big hit of Ashton's *Cinderella* is its pair of Ugly Sisters, Helpmann and Ashton himself, and it is the one Ashton plays, the Second Ugly Sister, who becomes the charmer of the evening. She is the shyest, the happiest, most innocent of monsters. She adores the importance of scolding, the fluster of getting dressed up — in a rush of milliners, hairdressers, jewellers, violinists. To do a little dance transports her, though she keeps forgetting what comes next. At the Prince's she is terrified to be making an entrance; a few moments later, poor monster, in the intoxication of being at a party she loses her heart and imagines she can dance fascinatingly — in the way Chaplin at a fashionable tango-tea used to imagine he could slink like a glamorous Argentine. But after the slipper test she accepts the truth as it is, she makes a shy state curtsy to the princely couple, to the power of Romance and Beauty, and paddles sadly off. No wonder such a monster wins everybody's heart. Ashton does it reticently, with the perfect timing, the apparently tentative gesture, the absorption and the sweetness of nature of a great clown. He acts as if he never meant to be the star of the show and very likely he didn't. He cast Helpmann, England's greatest mime, as the First Stepsister and gave that part the initiative in their scenes; he himself was only to trail along vaguely, with one little solo in the second act. After all, he was busy at the time choreographing the three acts of the piece, his and England's first full-length classic ballet, and doing it in six weeks. Ashton's unexpected triumph onstage is the sort of accident that happens to geniuses.

The farce mime in the ballet is so amusing and so long in each act it is in danger of killing the dance scenes; as choreographer of it, Ashton keeps the clowning gentle and, what is more, all the pantomime completely comprehensible — a lovely feat. As dance choreographer his great moments are a set of classic variations for girls representing the Four Seasons (the Good Fairy calls each in turn to attend Cinderella), and a number of entrances for the Jester during the ball. What a Harlequin-Jester was up to in the piece and how he got so big a part I didn't find out till several days later, but I was so delighted with the vitality and style of all he did, I never thought of wondering about it while I watched. The part is Alexander Grant's, the company's most interesting male dancer. Like a jet of force he darts forward in deep plié, in renversé, bent sideways, bent double, leaping down a flight of stairs, springing into the meager dances of the guests with a smiling threat. In the Jester's leaps Ashton has timed the rhythm to the leap's arrival (instead of to its departure from the ground) and because your ear anticipates the rhythm, the crouching dancer's downward course through the air keeps the beautiful suspense of an animal pounce. More delicately Ashton uses the same device in the feminine Seasons variations and there too it gives the dancer an other-than-human presence. These four classic solos in their conciseness and grace of style, their freshness of fancy and purity of evocation are Ashton's master-piece. They don't look like Petipa or Balanchine and are worthy of either. The Seasons' passage is also the best incident in the score and in the decoration, as if composer, choreographer, and decorator each drew a breath of relief at being free for once of the logic of the libretto.

Seasons, Jester, Second Stepsister are Ashton's most expressive figures but they aren't in a position to carry the central action. *Cinderella* is a three-act ballet in the grand manner — it consists of miming, of classic, demi-caractère, and character dancing, of processions, lineups, tableaux, and apotheosis, all of them (including farcical female impersonation) traditional elements of the form. Ashton has composed in each style easily, correctly, clearly, without oddity, camp, or other subterfuge, each kind true to its nature and function (so he keeps the farce to mime, never extends it to classic steps). Such a piece leads straightforwardly to the entrances of the ballerina, of the ballerina and her partner, as its moments of intensest poetic illumination around which the piece revolves and re-echoes. The critic, delighted with Ashton's openness, is eager for the big climaxes ahead. He wants to love the ballerina not only for her dancing but even more for what the imagery of her dances can tell of her nature as a human heroine. And the libretto of *Cinderella* is so direct, her dances have to be logical parts of the story. An anxious critic is willing to excuse that in the first variation early in Act One (she is daydreaming of the ball at her housework) she looks mostly ornamental and not-quite-naively playful. She doesn't dance again till at the climax of Act Two, she enters, meets the Prince, and is in love. They have a pas de deux and each a variation. The two solos are bright and lovely — like youthful talk, the girl's more original, the boy's more amiable; but after this they could still fall in love with someone else. And when they dance together the rhythm is nervous, hasty, the figures crowded but not intimate — two people being obliging in a difficult situation. Aren't they in love? The eye doesn't catch any luminous movement-image of a dazzling encounter, a magic contact, and release of romance. Even the three-act form hasn't world enough or time for so many preliminaries. After that, when the third act opens and Cinderella in a morning-after variation remembers the ball, instead of retrieving the situation by a radiant kind of *Spectre de la Rose* recollection, she fiddles with her broom again and offers an adroit, ingenious anthology of bits from Acts One and Two. What a cold fish she is! Even here in private she won't give a hint of the marvel she has seen, of the kiss she has felt. Her shy Ugly Sister has more heart than that, and the smoldering, demonic, horsey First Stepsister has more vitality. Here they are — wonderful again — with the slipper, and what a lively family scene it becomes with its motley swirl of characters! Poor, silly Prince, of course the slipper fits only his ballerina! But they haven't danced yet in this act, by rights we'll get another pas de deux. Transformation, rapid procession of our old friends the Seasons and attendant Stars — the magic powers of time that create the bloom of beauty — and here we are in the bridal pas de deux. Noble style, calm rhythm. And here a lovely dance figure — the Prince kneels and she tenderly touching his bent shoulders extends away from him a lovely arabesque — a shy moment of forbearance in contact, a moment of clarity once more worthy of Petipa. Now the ice is broken, they can begin to really dance together — but no, the pas de deux is over, it's all over, they will never get any closer. Bitterly disappointed in them, I watched them get into a galleon the size of a telephone booth and sail off, while the Stars and Seasons and all Beautiful Powers sank back and subsided in a brief sweet pianissimo close like a gentle sigh. Curtain.

From the special standpoint of dramatic impact or drive, *Cinderella* would be more exciting if its central characters were more expressive, if it had a joyous ensemble dance in Act Three and a livelier one in Act One. (I even wished the First Stepsister's grim limp at her last exit could be dramatized to a scene of hatred and eternal horror.) The piece's success in impact is the long ensemble dance climax at the ball and the claustrophobic crowd that ends it during the fatal strokes of midnight.

But *Cinderella* hasn't the disharmony of a piece that can't do what it wants to, and impact and drive are not its method of being interesting. The fun of the farce keeps relaxing the hold of the central story and in the story the dances don't try for intensity and fail, they don't look silly, they look agreeable. Ashton's sense of character is a true one as far as it finds expression but he doesn't strain for drama any more than he does for humor. Comfortable in the pace of its developments and transitions, always amusing or attractive to watch, never embarrassing or insistent, the piece succeeds very well in what it chooses to do. In that so-to-speak domestic key is its harmony, the harmony of an untroubled voice at home telling once more the same fairy tale.

The fact is *Cinderella* lasts two hours and a half and doesn't seem long. The current that carries it is easy and gentle. Its hold on one's attention is so mild that an American like myself is hardly aware of being in the theater. The spell it creates doesn't crystallize in a climax or a specific dance image but no mean gesture breaks the continuity of it. English in the lightness of its fragrance, the charm it holds is a grace of spirit, an English sweetness of temper. It doesn't excite, it ever so mildly refreshes. To keep in a three-act ballet such a tone, to sustain it without affectation or banality, shows Ashton's power, and he shows this in doing it as simply as possible, by keeping the dancing sweet.

The dance impetus of his piece, mild though it is, is open and confident. The variety of ballet styles blend without a blur, each springing as fresh as the other from the score, and the spell of being inside the imaginary world of music where dancing is natural doesn't break all evening. The processions and lineups, for instance, don't disturb the dance pulse of the action, nor does the action jump in and out of the music when the ballerina dances right after the mimes have been funny or when a flurry of character dancers dance in the farce scenes. The jokes come easy, and the miming looks free, it isn't stylized or Mickey Moused to fit the notes, but it derives its phrasing and the emphasis from the shape and the stress of the musical phrase as spontaneously as the dancing does. Ashton responds to whatever is buoyant in a musical phrase as a whole, he responds to a musical phrase with a dance phrase and he takes the spring and momentum from the precise form of the other. So the score flows easy and clear and the dancers in motion look fresh and airy. They don't exhaust the music, nor vice versa; they can be many or alone, they can stop or continue. Ashton is sometimes too relaxed and then, though the impetus in the trunk still is right, the arm shapes and step shapes don't count for much; but if he is wary of dramatic tension it is that an expression which isn't in the phrasing clutters a dance and depresses it. The drama of his best ones is in their harmony and pulse. Even when his dances are slight they have in passing a spontaneous air of grace. They look on pitch, they make up a tune. He has disciplined his gift to sincerity, to an inability to fake or strain or impress or aggrandize, all of them uncivilized practices, that make successes but take the fun out of dancing. He could reach grandeur, but he is in no hurry to get there. The pleasure he offers is that of ballet classicism, which says what it does say in a tone at once civilized and innocent, a tone which is personal to him. In such a tone even a slight message makes an evening one is glad to have spent at a theater.

But the fact is, too, that for all the pleasure *Cinderella* gives, it is too slight to hold one's interest a second time. It has enough passages fascinating to see repeatedly, mime effects and dance effects, to make a brilliant one-act piece; but they don't make sense by themselves because they are those of secondary figures. In their own secondary range they express the idyllic human message or tone of the ballet; but the rest of it doesn't widen the range of feeling, doesn't make the idyllic feeling more poignant at the climaxes or more ample in the main ensembles. One may say that Ashton has been weak as a dramatist, weak in the contact between figures. But I think his fault has been an uncertainty of emphasis in the structure of many passages. It seems to me that a dance simultaneously with its impetus develops a quality of human motion contained in a phrase of classic movement, that a dance does this in the way a piece of music develops its "thought" by developing and refracting an expressive cadence contained in the harmony of music. The spontaneous emphasis of a dance falls at any rate on one phrase of movement more than another, an emphasis which makes a momentary look in motion of a thigh or flank or forearm or instep or neck more dramatic as it passes, with an effect like an unconscious characteristic gesture. These transiently emphatic images reverberated in the harmony of their context determine the particular expression of a dance, its poetic character, its human implications. When they appear large, free, and clear, a dance is fascinating, it is expressive. (I don't mean that expression is necessarily rationalizable — the Waltz of the Flowers in *The Nutcracker,* for instance, is completely expressive.) Though the dances of *Cinderella* are clear in many ways — but the emphasis of them is not always clear — the emphasis doesn't make luminous the special kind of motion that is the dance's subject matter. This is why the ballet seems slight. But because *Cinderella* shows that Ashton, in the many passages where he has expression, has it without oddity, without forcing his gift or his discipline, it shows his natural power and his achieved craftsmanship. I think the piece shows these qualities further developed than *Symphonic Variations* or than *Scènes de Ballet* (his best), though these two are better theater, more sustained in brilliance. Because of its slightness and its length the good qualities of *Cinderella* are likely to be overlooked when the sameness of its gentleness in everything it does, even in its clowning, begins to make itself felt more strongly than the harmony of its tone. And for people not susceptible to its charming transparency the piece must seem a weak one the first time they see it.

It may be Broadway hawks would find so transparent a piece invisible. For myself, I might have been less open to *Cinderella*'s shy spell had I been in an audience less forbearing than that of Covent Garden. Even at the premiere they looked at the ballet so to speak discreetly, almost as one watches family theatricals, as if the dancers weren't professionals. Afterward in the lobby I was to find that they saw as clearly as any other audience, but while the performers were working they gave the impression of seeing only the good things. The rules of first-night sportsmanship are very different in New York and Paris. But at the *Cinderella* opening, the audience's county family serenity (wonderfully exotic, so it seemed to me as a foreigner) was also due to the influence of a local ritual I knew nothing of, of which I became aware only a few days later when I saw another *Cinderella,* this time at the Palladium. Watching my first Christmas pantomime, with piping children around me and elders beaming at everything, with slapstick-clowning Dames and Cinderella in the same costume as Moira Shearer, and a Good Fairy to wave her wand (the same model as at Covent Garden) and start transformation scenes, and with a Harlequin-descended Buttons — and what a good one! — who "placed" for me the Jester in Ashton's piece, I realized how many childhood echoes the ballet awakens in its public which a foreigner can't share. To the British public *Cinderella* is not in a revived ballet form; as soon as the curtain goes up, the travesty Ugly Sisters at their sewing make everyone feel safe at home in the living pantomime ritual the audience has known all its life.

Thanks to the ritual Ashton was able to use two of the company's three stronger theater personalities — Helpmann and himself — in long parts which made the ballet's success. Margot Fonteyn, the greatest of the three, was cast for Cinderella, and her presence when she dances again will of course change the value of the central figure. Shearer in Fonteyn's part is lovely to look at, graceful and true in movement, and her legs are fine; Violetta Elvin in the same part is more interesting and alive on stage, and while she isn't more proficient, she has a grander kind of schooling (a more forceful bearing and thigh action); but she creates at best her own role, she has not the imaginative radiance by which a ballerina creates a world of romance on the stage all around her. Somes is a clean dancer and is unusually vivid at his first entrance. Nerina's Spring is charming. No part is done poorly, the whole company is attractive, bright, and well trained (though in too small-stepping a style) and they did all Ashton asked. He could have given them more had they developed in themselves more boldness and vivacity, qualities which involve a love of acting as well as dancing. But their general outlook of honesty, their sense of good manners, and their reticent willingness to dance has a touching quality of its own. Helpmann in the piece is a model of generosity and intelligent good taste. He gives everyone, particularly Ashton, every chance, knowing very well he could upset the balance at any moment by a single gesture delivered full force.

The costumes by Malclès are pretty; his decoration, though less stiff than the décor of several British ballets I have seen, aims for a homey-timid charm that only partly comes off. The Prokofiev score is in a homey style too, but not in the least timid. It is much more vigorous theater than the ballet. It is completely adroit in continuity, always ready with tunes and lively rhythms, never dull or thick, and also with no noticeable counterpoint, completely danceable, brilliantly sustained for the ball. All this can't be praised too highly and it helps Ashton immensely. But a facile and casual irony in it, suited no doubt to the brilliant Moscow production, doesn't suit the quiet London one. The score doesn't ever gather in a nonnarrative, a contemplative climax, an expression of the faith in a marvel which a fairy tale has. It wasn't Prokofiev's intention to repeat what Tchaikovsky had said so well already, but for all the score's large-scale vitality its character seems guarded compared to the innocent sweetness of nature of Ashton. Ashton's spontaneity is nearer to Haydn.

So Ashton has made *Cinderella* well and made it fun; it isn't a great ballet but he is a great choreographer, and proves it in this piece; and that it is a complete popular hit is a pleasure too.

Ballet, February 1949

Against Meaning in Ballet

Some of my friends who go to ballet and like the entertainment it gives are sorry to have it classed among the fine arts and discussed, as the other fine arts are, intellectually. Though I do not agree with them I have a great deal of sympathy for their anti-intellectual point of view. The dazzle of a ballet performance is quite reason enough to go; you see handsome young people — girls and boys with a bounding or delicate animal grace — dancing among the sensual luxuries of orchestral music and shining stage decoration and in the glamour of an audience's delight. To watch their lightness and harmonious ease, their clarity and boldness of motion, is a pleasure. And ballet dancers' specialties are their elastic tautness, their openness of gesture, their gaiety of leaping, beating, and whirling, their slow soaring flights. Your senses enjoy directly how they come forward and closer to you, or recede upstage, turning smaller and more fragile; how the boys and girls approach one another or draw apart, how they pass close without touching or entwine their bodies in stars of legs and arms — all the many ways they have of dancing together. You see a single dancer alone showing her figure from all sides deployed in many positions, or you see a troop of them dancing in happy unison. They are graceful, well mannered, and they preserve at best a personal dignity, a civilized modesty of deportment that keeps the sensual stimulus from being foolishly cute or commercially sexy. The beauty of young women's and young men's bodies, in motion or in momentary repose, is exhibited in an extraordinarily friendly manner.

When you enjoy ballet this way — and it is one of the ways everybody does enjoy it who likes to go — you don't find any prodigious difference between one piece and another, except that one will have enough dancing to satisfy and another not enough, one will show the dancers to their best advantage and another will tend to make them look a little more awkward and unfree. Such a happy ballet lover is puzzled by the severities of critics. He wonders why they seem to find immense differences between one piece and another, or between one short number and another, or between the proficiency of two striking dancers. The reasons the critics give, the relation of the steps to the music, the sequence of the effects, the sharply differentiated intellectual meaning they ascribe to dances, all this he will find either fanciful or plainly absurd.

Has ballet an intellectual content? The ballet lover with the point of view I am describing will concede that occasionally a soloist gives the sense of characterizing a part, that a few ballets even suggest a story with a psychological interest, a dramatic suspense, or a reference to real life. In such a case, he grants, ballet may be said to have an intellectual content. But these ballets generally turn out to be less satisfying to watch because the dancers do less ballet dancing in them; so, he concludes, one may as well affirm broadly that ballet does not properly offer a "serious" comment on life and that it is foolish to look for one.

I do not share these conclusions, and I find that my interest in the kind of meaning a ballet has leads me to an interest in choreography and dance technique. But I have a great deal of sympathy for the general attitude I have described. It is the general attitude that underlies the brilliant reviews of Théophile Gautier, the French poet of a hundred years ago, who is by common consent the greatest of ballet critics. He said of himself that he was a man who believed in the visible world. And his reviews are the image of what an intelligent man of the world saw happening on the stage. They are perfectly open; there is no private malignity in them; he is neither pontifical nor "popular"; there is no jargon and no ulterior motive. He watches not as a specialist in ballet, but as a responsive Parisian. The easy flow of his sentences is as much a tribute to the social occasion as it is to the accurate and elegant ease of ballet dancers in action. His warmth of response to personal varieties of grace and to the charming limits of a gift, his amusement at the pretensions of a libretto or the pretensions of a star, his sensual interest in the line of a shoulder and bosom, in the elasticity of an ankle, in the cut of a dress place the ballet he watches in a perspective of civilized good sense.

Ballet for him is an entertainment — a particularly agreeable way of spending an evening in town; and ballet is an art, it is a sensual refinement that delights the spirit. Art for him is not a temple of humanity one enters with a reverent exaltation. Art is a familiar pleasure and Gautier assumes that one strolls through the world of art as familiarly as one strolls through Paris, looking about in good weather or bad, meeting congenial friends or remarkable strangers, and one's enemies, too. Whether in art or in Paris, a civilized person appreciates seeing a gift and is refreshed by a graceful impulse; there is a general agreement about what constitutes good workmanship; and one takes one's neighbors' opinions less seriously than their behavior. Gautier differentiates keenly between good and bad ballet; but he differentiates as a matter of personal taste. He illustrates the advantages the sensual approach to ballet can have for an intelligence of exceptional sensual susceptibility and for a man of large sensual complacency.

Gautier assumes that all that people need do to enjoy art is to look and listen with ready attention and trust their own sensual impressions. He is right. But when they hear that ballet is an elaborate art with a complicated technique and tradition, many modest people are intimidated and are afraid to trust their own spontaneous impressions. They may have been to a few performances, they may have liked it when they saw it, but now they wonder if maybe they liked the wrong things and missed the right ones. Before going again, they want it explained, they want to know what to watch for and exactly what to feel. If it is really real art and fine great art, it must be studied before it is enjoyed; that is what they remember from school. In school the art of poetry is approached by a strictly rational method, which teaches you what to enjoy and how to discriminate. You are taught to analyze the technique and the relation of form to content; you are taught to identify and "evaluate" stylistic, biographical, economic, and anthropological influences, and told what is great and what is minor so you can prepare yourself for a great reaction or for a minor one. The effect of these conscientious labors on the pupils is distressing. For the rest of their lives they can't face a page of verse without experiencing a complete mental blackout. They don't enjoy, they don't discriminate, they don't even take the printed words at face value. For the rest of their lives they go prying for hidden motives back of literature, for psychological, economic, or stylistic explanations, and it never occurs to them to read the words and respond to them as they do to the nonsense of current songs or the nonsense of billboards by the roadside. Poetry is the same thing — it's words, only more interesting, more directly and richly sensual.

The first taste of art is spontaneously sensual, it is the discovery of an absorbing entertainment, an absorbing pleasure. If you ask anyone who enjoys ballet or any other art how he started, he will tell you that he enjoyed it long before he knew what it meant or how it worked. I remember the intense pleasure reading Shelley's *Adonais* gave me as a boy — long before I followed accurately the sense of the words; and once, twenty years later, I had two kittens who would purr in unison and watch me bright-eyed when I read them Shakespeare's sonnets, clearly pleased by the compliment and by the sounds they heard. Would they have enjoyed them better if they had understood them? The answer is, they enjoyed them very much. Many a college graduate might have envied them.

I don't mean that so orderly and respectable an entertainment as that of art is made for the susceptibilities of kittens or children. But consider how the enormous orderly and respectable symphonic public enjoys its listening, enjoys it without recognizing themes, harmonies, or timbres, without evaluating the style historically or even knowing if the piece is being played as the composer intended. What do they hear when they hear a symphony? Why, they hear the music, the interesting noises it makes. They follow the form and the character of it by following their direct acoustic impressions.

Susceptibility to ballet is a way of being susceptible to animal grace of movement. Many people are highly susceptible to the pleasure of seeing grace of movement who have never thought of going to a ballet to look for it. They find it instead in watching graceful animals, animals of many species at play, flying, swimming, racing, and leaping and making gestures of affection toward one another, or watchful in harmonious repose. And they find it too in seeing graceful young people on the street or in a game or at the beach or in a dance hall, boys and girls in exuberant health who are doing pretty much what the charming animals do, and are as unconscious of their grace as they. Unconscious grace of movement is a natural and impermanent gift, like grace of features or of voice or of character, a lucky accident you keep meeting with all your life wherever you are. To be watching grace puts people into a particularly amiable frame of mind. It is an especially attractive form of feeling social consciousness.

But if ballet is a way of entertaining the audience by showing them animal grace, why is its way of moving so very unanimal-like and artificial? For the same reason that music has evolved so very artificial a way of organizing its pleasing noises. Art takes what in life is an accidental pleasure and tries to repeat and prolong it. It organizes, diversifies, characterizes, through an artifice that men evolve by trial and error. Ballet nowadays is as different from an accidental product as a symphony at Carnegie Hall is different from the noises Junior makes on his trumpet upstairs or Mary Ann with comb and tissue paper, sitting on the roof, the little monkey.

You don't have to know about ballet to enjoy it; all you have to do is look at it. If you are susceptible to it, and a good many people evidently are, you will like spontaneously some things you see and dislike others, and quite violently too. You may be so dazzled at first by a star or by the general atmosphere, you don't really know what happened; you may on the other hand find the performance absurdly stiff and affected except for a few unreasonable moments of intense pleasure; but if you are susceptible you will find you want to go again. When you go repeatedly, you begin to recognize what it is you like, and watch for it the next time. That way you get to know about ballet, you know a device of ballet because you have responded to it, you know that much at least about it. Even if nobody agrees with you, you still know it for yourself.

That the composite effect of ballet is a complex one is clear enough. Its devices make a long list, wherever you start. These devices are useful to give a particular moment of a dance a particular expression. The dancers in action give it at that moment a direct sensual reality. But if you watch often and watch attentively, the expressive power of some ballets and dancers will fascinate, perturb, and delight far more than that of others, and will keep alive in your imagination much more intensely long after you have left the theater. It is this aftereffect that dancers and ballets are judged by, by their audience.

To some of my friends the images ballet leaves in the imagination suggest, as poetry does, an aspect of the drama of human behavior. For others such ballet images keep their sensual mysteriousness, "abstract," unrationalized, and magical. Anyone who cannot bear to contemplate human behavior except from a rationalistic point of view had better not try to "understand" the exhilarating excitement of ballet; its finest images of our fate are no easier to face than those of poetry itself, though they are no less beautiful.

Ballet, March 1949

Dance Criticism

People interested in dancing as a form of art complain that our dance criticism is poor. Poor it is but not poor in relation to its pay. Anyone who writes intelligently about dancing does so at his own expense. As a matter of fact the sort of semi-illiterate hackwork that oozes out shamelessly and pays off modestly in books and articles about music — educators recommend it — is hardly profitable when it deals with the dance. Almost all our dance criticism appears in the form of newspaper reviewing. But almost all papers would rather misinform the public than keep a specialized dance reporter. Even rich ones delight in skimping on costs by sending out a staff music critic who covers ballet as an extra unpaid chore.

In the whole country only three exceptionally well-edited papers have made a practice of employing specialized dance critics — the *New York Times,* the *New York Herald Tribune,* and the *Christian Science Monitor* — and a fourth, the *Chicago Times,* joined them in 1947. These four jobs, the best that specialists can hope for, carry an average salary below that of a trombonist in the pit and hardly comparable to that of a minor, not very reliable soloist onstage. If the profit motive is a sacred American right, it is easier to account for miserable performances by our writers than for acceptable ones. Nevertheless, among the mass of nonsense printed each year about dancing a few specialists and gifted amateurs do produce on their own initiative a trickle of vivid reporting, of informed technical discussion, of valuable historical research and striking critical insight. The conditions and the average quality of dance criticism seem to be similar the world over. Ours is no worse than that elsewhere, except that there is more of it packaged for breakfast.

Most of our criticism is poor but many readers hardly mind how foolish it is; they read it too inattentively to notice. Some of them glance at a review only to see if the verdict on a show is for or against their going. Others, who have opinions of their own, are eager to quote what the paper said either with rage or with pride. In their eagerness they often misquote what they read and catch the meaning of written words as vaguely as a playful dog does that of speech. Anyone who writes for a paper is expected to satisfy the canine eagerness of many readers. They love to be bullied and wheedled; to be floored by a wisecrack, excited by gossip, inflamed by appeals to bigotry or popular prejudice; they love a female critic to gasp or fret and a male critic to be as opinionated as a comedian. At this level the difference between good and bad criticism is slight; and if you have to read foolish criticism this is as much fun as you can get out of it.

There are, however, many people too who like to find sense even in a dance column. They expect a critic writing as an educated American to give them a clear picture of the event and to place it in its relation to the art of theater dancing. When good criticism appears in a large newspaper many people welcome and appreciate it. Many all over the country know very well what ballet is about and follow intelligent reviewing, not necessarily with agreement but with spontaneous interest. They realize that a good editor can give it to them and that one who doesn't is in this respect slovenly.

To judge a ballet performance as attentively as a work of imagination is judged and by similar standards is nowadays normal enough. To be sure, everyone doesn't respond to a high degree of imagination in dancing, and not every intelligent person is convinced that dancing can create the peculiar spell, intimate, sustained, and grand, a work of art does. But in the course of the last two centuries enough intelligent people have been convinced it can, so that now the possibility is normally accepted. Our stage dancing is less abundant an art than our music, painting, or literature; but its claim to serious attention is that it belongs like them to the formal world of civilized fantasy. In recent years ballet has been the liveliest form of poetic theater we have had.

Dancing that is pleasing and neat, that shows ingenuity and a touch of fancy, is no news in a luxurious city. But dancing that by its sequence of movements and rhythm creates an absorbing imaginative spell is a special attraction a journalist must be able to recognize and describe. The prestige position of a ballet company depends entirely on how well its performances maintain, for people who know what art or poetry is about, a spell as art and a power as poetry. It is these imaginative people who can watch with attention — there are many thousands of them in New York — whose satisfaction stimulates general curiosity and influences wealthy art patrons to pay the deficits. They go for pleasure, just as they might go to a concert by Gold and Fizdale at Town Hall or else read Stendhal or Jane Bowles at home. Dancing delights them where they see it become an art and it is to see this happen that they like to go. What they want to find out from a review is, Did an event of artistic interest take place, and if it did, what particular flavor did it have? And because they are the readers really interested in what only a dance reporter can tell them, it is his business to answer their questions distinctly.

If his report interests them, they will go and see for themselves, and incidentally they will notice the sort of news they can rely on him for. If his remarks often turn out to be illuminating, he is judged a good critic; too many foolish or evasive reports on the other hand make him lose his status as a valuable observer. They expect him to recognize and formulate the point at issue in a performance more quickly and sharply than they would themselves. But without considerable experience in several arts, and of dancing and its technical basis too, the observer has no standards by which to measure and no practice in disentangling the pretensions of a ballet from its achievements. That is why a newspaper that wants to inform its readers on interesting dance events has to keep a reporter with the particular gift and training needed for the job.

A dance journalist's business is to sketch a lively portrait of the event he is dealing with. His most interesting task is to describe the nature of the dancing — what imaginative spell it aims for, what method it proceeds by, and what it achieves. In relation to the performance, he describes the gifts or the development of artists, the technical basis of aesthetic effects, even the organizational problems that affect artistic production. The more distinctly he expresses himself, the more he exposes himself to refutation and the better he does his job. But beyond this the dance public wants him to be influential in raising the level of dance production in their community; to be enlightening on general questions of theater dancing, its heritage, and its current innovations; and to awaken an interest for dancing in intelligent readers who are not dance fans already.

What awakens the interest of an intelligent reader in a dance column is to find it written in good English. Even if he is not used to thinking about dancing he can follow a discussion that makes its point through a vivid picture of what actually happens onstage. On the other hand he loses interest if a dance column offers him only the same vague clichés he has already read elsewhere in the paper. After reading a movie review or a political commentator he is not thrilled to find that a ballet too is challenging, vital, significant (significant of what? challenging or vital to whom?). When a ballet is called earthy he recognizes the term as a current synonym for commercial-minded. Inappropriate visual images are suggested to him when he reads that a dance is meaty: or that dancers onstage were rooted in the soil and clung bravely to their roots; or that young choreographers are to be admired for their groping. No sensible person can want to watch a dancer brooding over a culture, or filling her old form with a new content, or even being stunningly fertile; or if he wants to watch, it isn't because of the dancing.

Our unspecialized dance reporters can't in sensible terms tell the public what is interesting and original in current dancing. Since 1942, for instance, strict classic ballet has become widely appreciated and acclimated in this country. It has changed so far from the prewar Ballet Russe manner that it has now a new and American flavor. But the nation's dance journalists have been notably unenlightening on the subject of classicism, its meaning, and its new development (some journalists even confuse classicism with stylized movement). To take another example, in the same period the modern dance has been trying for a new style, a new rhythm, and a different sort of theater appeal than before. Various aspects of the change have been due to Martha Graham's example, to her own shift in technique, to a new supply of male dancers, to the Party Line, and to contact with ballet; a new modern style shows particularly in the work of Shearer and of Cunningham. The nation's press knows that something has happened to our dancing in the last five or six years, but it doesn't yet know what.

During the same period the nation's press has not demonstrated its influence for raising production standards, either. All the New York critics together, for instance, have been unable to reform the miserable ballet company of the Metropolitan Opera. Neither they nor their colleagues elsewhere have been able to get the big ballet companies to keep fresh and clean the good productions (like *Romeo*) or purge the hopeless ones (like *Schéhérazade*). They have been unable to arrest the recent (1946–47) deterioration of dance standards, to protect dancers from being exhausted by overwork or demoralized by slipshod artistic policies. They have not ridiculed the illiterate English on ballet programs. They have even been unable to keep unmannerly latecomers in the audience from clambering over the rest of the public in the dark or to shush the bobby-soxers and showoffs who brutally interrupt a dance scene by applauding in a frenzy at any passable leap or twirl. If dance critics are meant to function as watchdogs of the profession they review, they will have to have sharper teeth and keener noses, too.

If only another half-dozen specialized and intelligent dance critics were writing on metropolitan papers, the public all over the country would profit considerably. Not that well-informed critics would agree on all details — far from it — but they could with a sharper authority insist on an improved general level of current production.

A special question of dance journalism is its usefulness to the choreographers and dancers who are reviewed. The point concerns few newspaper readers, but those it agitates bitterly. Ignorant criticism is naturally resented by professionals; but intelligent criticism when adverse often is, too. All critics would like very much to be helpful to a good artist. They love the art they review and everyone who contributes to it; they know the many risks of the profession. They are constantly trying to help, but the occasions when they are actually helpful seem to be happy accidents.

The professionals of the dance world are of course the most eager readers of dance reviewing, but they do not read their own reviews very rationally. For one thing a poor notice upsets them the way an insult does other people. For another, they argue that it endangers their future jobs. But in the touring repertory system of ballet the critics do not "make or break" a ballet or a dancer; managers do. To a dancer's career a bad notice is a much less serious occupational hazard than a poor figure, laziness, poor hygiene, tactlessness toward fellow professionals, or solipsistic megalomania — none of which a dancer who suffers from them complains of nearly so loudly.

A choreographer or a dancer, as he reads his notices, often forgets that they are not addressed to him personally but are a report to the general public. They are a sort of conversation between members of the audience on which the artist eavesdrops at his own emotional risk. What he overhears may make no sense to him; it may shock or intoxicate him; but it is astonishing how rarely, how very rarely it is of any use to him in his actual creative activity. It will sometimes corroborate a guess of his own, but it is generally silent on points he feels vital. Reviews cannot replace his own conscience, much less his driving instinct. A great dancer after twenty years of celebrity spoke of two reviews that had been valuable.

In my opinion reading reviews about oneself is a waste of time, like smoking cigarettes. To read reviews of rivals is more likely to be of use. Hardworking artists are refreshed by a rave for their "art," whether it makes sense or not, but blame is exhausting to deal with. Serious professionals often limit the value of reviews to the recognition of good craftsmanship and of technical innovations; and according to Virgil Thomson — great artist and great critic too — opinions beyond the recognition of these facts are pure fantasy. But for the audience — to whom the critic reports — the fantasy spell of art is that of conscious device multiplied by unconscious meaning. As long as the critic's fantasy remains intelligible to read, its forces and its scope are what give the reader a sense of the power and value of the work reviewed.

An intelligent reader learns from a critic not what to think about a piece of art but how to think about it; he finds a way he hadn't thought of using. The existence of an "authoritative critic" or of a "definitive evaluation" is a fiction like that of a sea serpent. Everybody knows the wild errors of judgment even the best critics of the past have made; it is easier to agree with contemporary judgments but no more likely they are right. It seems to me that it is not the critic's historic function to have the right opinions but to have interesting ones. He talks but he has nothing to sell. His social value is that of a man standing on a street corner talking so intently about his subject that he doesn't realize how peculiar he looks doing it. The intentness of his interest makes people who don't know what he's talking about believe that whatever it is, it must be real somehow — that the art of dancing must be a real thing to some people some of the time. That educates citizens who didn't know it and cheers up those who do.

When people who like dancing say a critic is right they mean he is right enough and that his imaginative descriptions are generally illuminating. He can hardly be illuminating or right enough unless he has a fund of knowledge about his subject. In theory he needs to know the techniques and the historical achievements of dancing, the various ways people have looked at it and written about it, and finally he needs a workable hypothesis of what makes a dance hang together and communicate its images so they are remembered. In practice he has to piece together what he needs to know; experience as a dancer and choreographer is an invaluable help to him.

The best organized and by far the most useful chunk of knowledge a critic has access to is that about the technique and history of classic ballet, in particular as ballet dancers learn it. Its gymnastic and rhythmic technique is coherent enough to suggest principles of dance logic — as expressive human movement in musical time and architectural space. But so far the best informed of specialized ballet critics have not formulated these clearly. And French ballet criticism as a whole, though it has had for several centuries nearly all the best dancing in the world to look at, though it has had since as far back as 1760 (since Noverre's *Letters*) a brilliant lesson in how to write about dancing, hasn't yet been able to bring order and clarity to the subject. Though they have been writing steadily for two centuries and more — and often writing pleasantly — the Paris critics have left us as reporters no accurate ballet history, as critics no workable theory of dance emphasis, of dance form, or of dance meaning.

The handicap to method in dance criticism has always been that its subject matter — dancing that can fascinate as an art does — is so elusive. Other arts have accumulated numerous wonderfully fascinating examples in many successive styles. Dancing produces few masterpieces and those it does are ephemeral. They can't be stored away; they depend on virtuoso execution, sometimes even on unique interpreters. They exist only in conjunction with music, stage architecture, and decoration in transitory, highly expensive performances. It is difficult to see the great dance effects as they happen, to see them accurately, catch them so to speak in flight, and hold them fast in memory. It is even more difficult to verbalize them for critical discussion. The particular essence of a performance, its human sweep of articulate rhythm in space and in time, has no specific terminology to describe it by. Unlike criticism of other arts, that of dancing cannot casually refer the student to a rich variety of well-known great effects and it cannot quote passages as illustrations.

This lack of precision, of data, and of method is not without advantages. It saves everyone a lot of pedantry and academicism, and it invites the lively critic to invent most of the language and logic of his subject. Its disadvantages, however, are that it makes the standards of quality vague, the range of achieved effects uncertain, and the classification of their component parts clumsy. Dance aesthetics, in English especially, is in a pioneering stage; a pioneer may manage to plant a rosebush in his wilderness next to the rhubarb, but he's not going to win any prizes in the flower show back in Boston.

The aesthetics of dancing — that is, a sort of algebra by which the impression a performance makes can be readily itemized, estimated, and communicated to a reader — is vague and clumsy. The dance critic's wits have to be all the sharper; he has to use aesthetic household wrinkles and aesthetic common sense to help out. And he has to pull his objectivity out of his hat. The poverty of his dance-critical heritage makes it hard for him to get a good view of his personal blind spots. A critic in the other arts learns to recognize his blind spots and develop his special gifts by finding out how he personally reacts to a wide range of much-discussed masterpieces. If he is annoyed by Mozart or Vermeer or even by Picasso and Stravinsky, he can read intelligent opinions different from his own. That way he learns who he is, what he knows and doesn't know. Gaps and crudities of critical technique are of concern to a professional critic; they are questions of his craft.

The earnest craftsman must hope that once a dance notation has become established, once the various hints toward a critical method (including those by modern-dance theoreticians and of exotic traditions) have been collected, sifted, and codified, dance critics will seem brighter than they do now.

At present a critic has to risk hypothesis. He can try, for instance, to distinguish in the complex total effect of a performance the relationships between dance effect and story effect, between expressive individualized rhythm and neutral structural rhythm, dance impetus and pantomime shock, dance illusion and dance fun, sex appeal and impersonation, gesture which relates to the whole architectural space of the stage and has an effect like singing and gesture which relates to the dancer's own body and so has the effect of a spoken tone. And there are of course many possible relationships of the dancing to the structure or momentum of the music which, by creating in the visual rhythm illusions of lightness and weight, impediment or support (for instance), affect the meaning of a passage. Dance criticism would be clearer if it found a way to describe these and other relationships in theater effect, and to describe just what the dancers' bodies do, the trunk, legs, arms, head, hands, and feet in relation to one another. The expression of a reviewer's personal reaction, no matter how violent or singular, becomes no immodesty when he manages to make distinct to the reader the visible objective action onstage he is reacting to.

Nowadays, however, a critic doesn't screen a dance performance according to such distinctions. What he actually does is to work backward, so to speak, from the dance image that after the event is over strikes him as a peculiarly fascinating one. He tries to deduce from it a common denominator in what he saw — a coherent principle, that is, among uncertainly remembered, partly intense, partly vague, partly contradictory images. It takes boldness to simplify his impressions so they add up clearly to a forthright opinion; and it sometimes takes a malicious sense of fun too, to trust to his instinct where he knows he is risking his neck. But the intelligent reader need not be at all sorry that dance criticism is in a rudimentary or pioneering stage. It makes it more inviting to poets than to schoolteachers; and though its problems and possible discoveries are not colossal ones, still — if it succeeds in attracting poets — it should be for a century or so to come fun to write and to read.

An intelligent reader expects the critic — in his role of schoolteacher — to distinguish between good and bad dance technique, to distinguish between good and bad choreographic craftsmanship, to specify technical inventions and specify also the gifts that make a choreographer or a dancer remarkable despite defects in craftsmanship. Here the writer shows his fairness. But what one enjoys most in reading is the illusion of being present at a performance, of watching it with an unusually active interest and seeing unexpected possibilities take place. Reading a good critic's descriptions of qualities I have seen, I seem to see them more clearly. If I don't know them, I try looking for them in performances I remember or try to find them next time I go to the theater. And when you look for qualities a reviewer has mentioned, you may find something else equally surprising. For your sharpened eye and limberer imagination is still a part of your own identity — not of his — and leads you to discoveries of your own. The fun in reading dance criticism is the discovery of an unexpected aspect of one's own sensibility.

In reading the great ballet critics of the past one is impressed not by their fairness but by their liveliness. In reading Noverre or Gautier or Levinson, I find accounts that strike me as so unlikely I interpret them — by analogy to contemporaries — as blind spots, or propaganda and rhetoric; even if some of these accounts are accepted as facts of dance history. But it is not the partisan spirit with which they can blindly propagandize their own aesthetic views that differentiates them from lesser critics; it is the vividness of their descriptions that is unique. Gautier, who of the three gives a reader the most immediate sense of the sensuous fluidity and physical presence of ballet, expresses theory in terms of chitchat and ignores choreographic structure and technical talk. He seems to report wholly from the point of view of a civilized entertainment seeker; the other two, from the backstage point of view of the craftsman as well.

Noverre and Levinson advance theories of dance expression which are diametrically opposite. The force with which they are formulated gives their writing an elevation Gautier avoids, but makes them both far easier than he to misunderstand. Here in a nutshell is the dance critic's problem: the sharper he formulates a theory of the technique of expression, of how dance communicates what it does, the further he gets from the human vivacity of dancing without which it communicates nothing at all. And yet it is difficult to consider the central question of dancing — I mean, the transport and sweep that dance continuity can achieve, the imaginative radiance some moments of dancing are able to keep for years in people's memory, the central question Balanchine in his illuminating "Notes on Choreography" brings up in speaking of "basic movements" — unless the critic finds some way to generalize and to speak vividly of general as well as of particular dance experience.

I trust a future critic will be well informed enough to discuss such generalized principles of dance expression clearly. He could begin by clarifying our specific ballet tradition — the tradition called classic because its expressive intentions and technical precisions were long ago in some sort modeled on the achievements of ancient classic literature. It seems to me the elements of this theater-dance tradition, if they were vividly appreciated, are various enough to include in one set of critical values both what we call the modern dance and our present classic ballet — though at the moment the two are far apart in their gymnastic, rhythmic, and expressive structure and in their theater practicability as well. It seems to me that a vivid sense of such an inclusive tradition would set the merits of a choreographer or of a dancer in a larger perspective and would offer a way of describing his scope as craftsman and as artist in the light of all the achievements of past theater dancing.

So I should like to read a critic who could make me appreciate in dancing the magic communal beat of rhythm and the civilized tradition of a personal and measured communication. I expect him to sharpen my perception some-times to an overall effect, sometimes to a specific detail. I should not be surprised to find in some of his descriptions general ideas stimulating in themselves, even apart from his immediate subject, nor to find in other de-scriptions technical terms of dancing, of music, of painting or theater craft. I should like him to place a choreography or a dancer with his individual deri-vations and innovations in the perspective of the tradition of theater dancing. I am far more interested, though, if a writer is able, in describing dancing in its own terms, to suggest how the flavor or the spell of it is related to aspects of the fantasy world we live in, to our daily experience of culture and of custom; if he can give my imagination a steer about the scope of the meaning it communicates. But as I read I want to see too the sensual brilliance of young girls and boys, of young men and women dancing together and in alternation onstage, the quickness and suavity of their particular bodies, their grace of response, their fervor of imagination, the boldness and innocence of their flying limbs.

A writer is interesting if he can tell what the dancers did, what they com-municated, and how remarkable that was. But to give in words the illusion of watching dancers as they create a ballet in action requires a literary gift. An abstruse sentence by Mallarmé, the rhythmic subtlety of a paragraph by Marianne Moore, a witty page-long collage of technical terms by Goncourt can give the reader a sharper sense of what dancing is about than a book by an untalented writer, no matter how much better acquainted with his subject he is. Such examples lead to fallacious conclusions, but I am drawing no conclu-sions, I am stating a fact. A dance critic's education includes dance experi-ence, musical and pictorial experience, a sense of what art in general is about and what people are really like. But all these advantages are not enough unless they meet with an unusual literary gift and discipline.

Now and then in reading dance criticism one comes across a phrase or a sentence that suggests such an ideal possibility. It is to emphasize these passages to people who wonder what good dance criticism is that I am writing. The fact that no criticism is perfect doesn't invalidate its good mo-ments. Granted it is brilliant far less often than the dancing it commemorates;

the fact that it is after all occasionally brilliant is what makes it as a form of intellectual activity in a modest way worthwhile.

The Dance Encyclopedia, 1949

An Open Letter About the Paris Opéra Ballet

I wanted to write you* an article about ballet at the Maggio Musicale as you suggested, but I couldn't, so I started a letter and then began to rewrite it to find out what I meant; here it is, it turned out to be just about the Paris Opéra.

What I most looked forward to at the Maggio was my first sight of Vyroubova. I agree with you about her entirely. After three steps I loved her — delicious figure, limpid style, sweet absorption. To be sure by the time she had done four ballets I didn't love her as much more as I had looked forward to when she first began; but there was no reason either to love her any less.

She has the sweetest Russian-style virtues. A long foot, quick thigh, delicate bust, small head far from the shoulder. The step has edge, the arms are a classicist's dream, the carriage of the head has distinction, the face makes sense. She is unusually accurate and musical. I thought her best number here was that in *Suite en Blanc* (Vaussard's part, I think), which she did with a kind of demi-caractère liveliness in grace that suited the steps perfectly. She did each of her four parts as if it were a different woman dancing, discovering the impersonation in the impetus of the steps, sustaining it without a break from the first move to the last, with no mannerisms of her own showing ever. (Her other ballets were *Mirages, Dramma per Musica,* and *Divertissement,* all Chauviré parts.) It was adorable to see how she — a dancer of little experience dancing new parts in a company new to her — by instinct at once accepted the complete responsibility for the piece; to see her go straight for the main thing, the reality of her role and of the imaginative world in which it can be real; to see her conceive of the importance of a character not in terms of rank but in terms of purity of motive, and impersonate beauty in the cleanest steps she could make. Her decision on all this was unhesitating. And it gave her that lovelier authority onstage which I am sure Margot has always had.

---

*Denby framed his contributions to the English journal *Ballet* in the form of letters to the journal's editor, Richard Buckle.

It's all there, but on the other hand not yet pronounced enough. Her technique is well rounded and sufficient but not virtuoso. Her waist is weak. And the last two nights here she tired. Nor did she show the variety of accentuation, the nuance in phrasing a finished dancer can; in this particular Chauviré was more interesting than she. And Vyroubova, at least here, did not make her parts magnificent with those movements of complete climax, of lovely stillness that a ballerina is born to express. She is a darling, but she should turn into a marvel, a complete marvel. I wish she could join Sadler's Wells and have the benefit of all you discreet idealists; and since she is the brightest hope in Europe for another great ballerina five years from now, in a sense it's your duty. I think, too, that in a couple of years Balanchine could make her long legs twice as long and give her a stunning elegance of attack.

Toumanova was here too, just the opposite of all V.'s virtues, and wonderful. She was at her worst: careless feet, limp and wormy arms, brutally deformed phrasings; in allegro she was a hoyden, in adagio it was a bore waiting for her to get off that stubby toe; she waddled complacently, she beat time, she put on a tragically wronged stare (Second Avenue style — lower Second Avenue), she took absurdly graceless and completely unconvincing bows. It upset me while I was in the theater; but the next day it seemed only ridiculous, I'd half forgotten it, and it had no connection with moments I couldn't help remembering the grandeur of: a few terrifying extensions, a few incisive strokes that counted phenomenally. At those moments she had so much vitality she made everyone else look as if they merely crept or scuttled about her while she danced. It wasn't ballet she did, it wasn't any kind of dancing anybody ever heard of, but it was dancing on some sort of grand scale, it was the real thing in that sense.

I liked Renault very much. His acting is naive, his waist wiggles and his wrist-flaps are silly, he has learned no distinction (Blasis ports de bras and head positions, effacés and harmonies of contrapposto — men look raw without them). But each time the steps grow difficult and strenuous, he forgets his foolishness, and I don't care about his faults. He whirls and leaps in the rush of action, he likes pouring out his strength, he dances on a big scale, and the joy of it then is contagious. And when he looks honest, simple, and sweet natured.

The season as a whole was received in a friendly way, not with the enthusiasm I had seen here last year for Sadler's Wells.

I enjoyed *Palais de Cristal,* though friends who know the New York version complained bitterly of the slow tempos which they told me disfigured it. Lifar's ugly edition of *Sleeping Beauty* (*Divertissement*) makes me cringe like a knife scraping on a plate. His own works at their best have a curious antimusical and desperate pound; apart from this personal quality — at its strongest in *Suite en Blanc* — I can see no interest in them that lasts. With poor choreography ballet loses for me its nerve; but usually I am happy anyway watching a good company dance.

As companies go, the Paris Opéra one seems to me very good, and here the credit is Lifar's; they looked fresher, better disciplined, and better rehearsed than when I last saw them a year and a half ago. I liked them all very much as professionals. They are attractive, well built, loyal, and gifted. They believe in doing what they do with attention and individual imagination. When they begin they suggest a kind of glitter of stylishness onstage that fills me with happy expectation. They show at once that they are going to have variety of expression, that they are not going to do the immature juvenile charm act far too many adult Anglo-Saxon dancers do. So I look forward to the dance action to come when their interesting expressions will become an interesting grace of movement, when it will bloom and shed a radiance over the stage as a dancer's expression does in dancing.

Instead, what I see is different. The dance action looks small and con-stricted and close, it makes the dancers become short-limbed. In the general effect of shrinkage, the dancers keep their pointed expressions, and the result is arch. Affectedly so, it often seems to me. When I see them stepping out gingerly, when I see a large bold step modestly diminished and a stabbing rapid one becomingly blurred, see the girls separate their thighs as if reluctant to do that in public, the world of decent domesticity it conjures up appals me. And when I catch fretful flappings and crookings of elbows, dissatisfied glances of the girls toward each other and irritated ones at the conductor, a fluster of waist wriggles, wrist flicks, and head tosses, the expression reminds me of a nervous woman who can't resist tidying up her furniture and her person after the guests have already sat down. The boys seem to take the feminine flurry with a slightly superior or interestingly sullen male detach-ment, though their own action is not free of what look like fatuous flourishes and they promenade about with a tight bouncy step that looks silly. All this is my first impression and at this point I realize I have misunderstood every-thing so far and missed the point completely. So I look more closely at what is happening.

The dancers are well built and strong; but I begin to see that the Opéra style transforms them according to its own ideas of grace. It makes their figures in action look thick and droopy in the middle, stumpy and brief at the ends. The figure doesn't hold its shape in the air as it moves. Necks shrink in, shoulders hunch, waists sag and bob, thighs seem to take on weight. The step becomes unresilient, timid, and short; the tempo spurts nervously and drags. The pulse of the rhythm is weak. The style makes the dancers look like sedentary persons dancing.

They are painstakingly trained to. They do the step correctly, but they do it only from the hip joint down. Similarly they do arm motions from the shoulder out. (The ports de bras are altered as a rule from a correct shape into a resemblance to expressive gesture.) The Paris Opéra style avoids using the tremendous strength of waist and back to move with, to move the thighs and upper arms freely and equally. The Ballet Russe or Russian-derived style uses the full strength of the back to initiate, to sustain, and to reabsorb a movement, as Negro dancing does too. It gives these styles a kind of follow-through effect, an ease in flow; it gives the dancers a straight but not stiff back, a long neck. In ballet, without the full strength of the back their figures bunch up awkwardly in motion, they lose the carriage in large steps, they don't deploy fully in the air. They lose their speed, their spring, their impetus, their vigor in resilience. They don't sustain the continuity, they don't reach the large-scale virtuosity or the large-scale vitality they otherwise would. The Paris Opéra dancers don't, not through weakness, but because the style avoids such effects.

The style's idea of musical grace in dancing is as peculiar as its idea of grace of movement, I mean equally puzzling to a balletgoer used to the Russian-derived style. The Opéra dancer likes to put the dance stress where the shape of the musical phrase gives it no support; so it gets a petulant look. She likes to begin a shade behind the beat as if prettily taken unaware, and end a little ahead as if in confusion; then she adds a vigorous flip of the wrist on the last note, which by being synchronized makes the wrist suddenly look disproportionately big, as big as a leg. I speak from the standpoint of the Russian style, which treats the score like a glorious partner on whose strength the dancers soar and dart and effortlessly end. By contrast the Opéra style has the music run along beside the dancer like a stray dog — it keeps shying away from her when she stops and getting underfoot when she goes on again. An accomplished Opéra dancer is one who makes one forget what a nuisance it is.

But such a view is based on the assumption that the Paris Opéra style is doing worse what the Russian style does better. Looking at it closer, the Opéra style indicates on the contrary that its intentions are different to begin with. Its conception of rhythm and of phrasing inclines away from that of the music and toward that of speech. The general effect is not unlike that of speech rhythm. The dancer shapes her phrases by giving them point, as one would in speaking. She selects a step in the sequence and points it up, giving it a slight retard and a slight insistence, and she lets the other steps drop around it so to speak casually and a shade hastily, much as a glittering conversationalist stresses the telling word, delivers his epigram and seems to throw the rest of the sentence away. Following the step rhythm as speech rhythm — and as speech rhythm set against music — one can find virtuoso subtleties and ingenuities in the phrasing of an Opéra soloist, odd little vivacities, implications, hesitancies, bursts of rhetoric, tiny gusts of inspiration that hurry her onward. We Anglo-Saxons think a dancer looks like a lady when she dances divinely; but that is our lack of realism. The Paris style doesn't mean to transport you so far from the appearances, from the awkward graces and characteristic reserves of normal sedentary city life. The point of unprofessional carriage and unmusical rhythm is to make the dancer look less like a marvelous vision and more like an opinionated Parisian with all her wits about her whom one might meet in a room full of conversation.

Other traits of the Opéra style seem to resemble characteristics of French conversation, too. Ranking dancers are expected to dance against each other as acute conversationalists are expected to talk each other down. Agreement is not considered interesting and when everybody dances it's like everybody talking at once. To pause awhile onstage is like keeping still; it's a sign of respect, not of listening. Listening doesn't count, it's nothing to make a point of; and a dancer doesn't make her stillness a part of the rhythm of the general dance — in the way a singer makes her silence as well as her voice a part of the music.

The Paris Opéra style has its own view of what a performance is about. The dancers do not present a ballet as though it were a stage drama. There is no collective attempt to create the illusion of a poetic event taking place before our eyes. They don't come on as imaginary characters whose fate is unknown but foreordained. They come on instead in their official character as Opéra dancers. The ballet is a ceremony which offers them an occasion for the exhibition and the applause suitable to their various ranks. The excitement of the official ceremony is in the suggestion they individually convey of being people it would be delightful to know at home. And that is perhaps why the dancers scatter in all directions a great many of those little shakes, peckings, and perks of the head that look so pretty around a Paris dinner table, though coupled to the foot activity of ballet they unfortunately give an effect of witlessness.

I am under the impression that Parisians of taste (who can remember Diaghilev) take the Opéra style far less seriously than I have. They are surprised anyone should. They know there is no one onstage who does it with the acuteness of wit, the stylishness of presence it calls for, or with imaginative scope; and that there are many whose airs and graces are more respectable than stylish. The best Opéra dancers try to Russianize their dancing, and even the Opéra fans encourage them to.

And as for me, I see that by instinct I can hardly be fair to the style. The weak rhythm it has by choice depresses me as I watch. The fun of ballet is in the feet — in the feet and the bearing and the mutual response of the bodies in motion. The spring and edge and lift of ballet is in its relation to the beat — and to the beat in the full variety and extension which the musical animation of a piece of music gives it through musical structure. Of course, dancers are actors too, and their acting gestures can be delightful, noble, even thrilling. But their most wonderful moments of all come when they are in the middle of dancing. Their expression then looks unintentional. The wit or the sentiment it communicates, the ravishing lyric flight or sweeping collective transport is in the impetus of the dancing bodies, in the sustained pulse of their motion in space. The force of the communication, its imaginative scope, is in a kind of reverberation with which the resilient pulse of a rhythmic stream enlarges the hint of natural behavior that appears in a momentary movement of dancing, transfiguring it in the exhilaration of sustained buoyancy into a poetic image as innocent as the action of fate. I love the thrill of such a grace in meaning. But large-scale vitality in ballet, even apart from any meaning, is also a pleasure, deeper than it seems. The Paris Opéra style has too weak a pulse, too weak a dance rhythm for these two kinds of exhilaration.

Poor Lifar. He looks older onstage than Dolin or Massine. He has had the misfortune to put on weight all over him except between knee and ankle. (And he insisted on leaving no doubt in the matter by appearing as a Greek statue.) Dolin and Massine at least have extraordinary stage presences and are able to conceal some of the weaknesses of their dancing. Here in Florence

Lifar wasn't able to conceal any weakness of his; but what surprised even more, he had no stage presence at command with which to pull his performance together. He worked harder than anyone and completely in vain. I haven't the heart to blame him, remembering his beauty and his genius; but if one doesn't, one has to blame Hirsch.

And one has to blame Hirsch too for not suppressing the three recent short ballets of Lifar which were shown here, *Pavane, L'Inconnue,* and *Entre Deux Rondes.* The first might have been devised for an end-of-the-year party at a desperate dancing school. The other two looked just as batty. One was earnest about the Decay of Western Civilization and resembled an apache number; the other was gay about Our Enduring Cultural Values and offered gambols by a Greek Statue and a Degas Ballet Girl. Tudor could have made wonderful little pieces out of both by making them loathsome intentionally.

There was a piece of business in Lifar's *Giselle,* Act Two, which was new to me. Mourning at her tomb, he seemed for some time unwilling to part with the flowers he had brought. He held them out, snatched them back, looked at them appreciatively. Mastering his emotion, he sacrificed them and fainted. But Giselle, dead as she was, rushed out from the wings with a much bigger bunch and pelted him with it headlong. So prompt, so sweet of her, so fitting. He lay drowned in flowers. If only the audience had given way to its impulse, had leapt to its feet in rapture and tossed hundreds of bouquets more, aiming them from all over the house, what a perfect moment of art it would have been for all of us to share with him!

Still, I believe Lifar inspires his company. Their devotion to him, their faith in virtues of his no longer visible onstage, is touching. A few company mannerisms seem imitations of mannerisms formerly his own as a dancer; that is foolish but not meretricious. Distasteful, however, is the way his choreography keeps making the dancers look pompous.

Ballet, July–August 1950

A Letter About Ulanova

About Ulanova. She is a very great dancer, no doubt of that, even seeing her as we did very awkwardly presented. What we all saw first was the magnificent schooling and the admirable personal discipline. You know how touching that is when you see a dancer not allowing herself to monkey with the rules. What we saw was a wonderful flow of movement sustained and sustained, a sort of cantilena style of dancing with beautiful legs (marvelously shaped arabesques of all kinds, and so clearly differentiated too), and beautiful elbows. The very beginning of a movement is fresh and quick and almost at once the motion so begun slows down to a strong full velvet flow; and before the flow has stopped, without any break (like a fresh current that appears from below in a wide even stream of water), the new next motion begins, clear and decisive, and that one too seems to be already flowing calm and sustained. It isn't the bird or dragonfly style of dancing, it's a kind of aspiration upward: lightness as a longing and a dream rather than as a possession. I can't think of any one dancer we know who has that particular quality; nor is it one that goes with being a model pure-classicist: it's romantic. Ulanova makes herself more heavy and more light, too, like a romantic. And another quality she shows is that of not presenting herself to the audience, of being like someone who is dancing for herself, a sort of half-in-shadow-in-the-deep-woods quality. There isn't much conscious response between her and her partner, I mean all those conscious little consciousnesses. In the same way that the pulse of the rhythm is broad and slow, so the characterization or flavor or key of the dance is barely noticeable; it's there but it's only appreciable after a while. There's something covered, a sort of inner life unconsciously revealed, that carries her more than it directs her. (I'm speaking not of her personally but of the kind of stage personality that comes across.) Of course one can fall in love with such a special creature; or else not. Some people were crabby — I mean a few ballet fans I spoke to.

Of course it's nonsense to pass judgment after seeing her dance half a dozen numbers with piano accompaniment in front of black curtains, awkwardly costumed, without a company or a ballet to set her off, and with a foreign audience, who probably expected a triumphant beauty and saw instead a modest little-girl-style creature. The general theater style that was indicated — I mean the kind of overall performance atmosphere or manner, which is different according to whether the dancers are Parisian, Danish, British, or from New York — that theater style was quite different from any of our various ones; which makes a confusion too. Just as what Parisians think pretty New Yorkers are likely to think affected, and just as Parisians think mechanical what we see as unaffected and friendly, so there was about the Soviet atmosphere a strange absence of chic or bite or risk or individualized projection. It struck us who were foreign to it as homey, and goody-goody. And sometimes this tone made Ulanova seem a bit puss-in-the-corner, which I imagine one wouldn't think in a big long piece where she can gradually make the character clear.

Her weaknesses as a dancer seemed at this performance to be a kind of thickness, a kind of lack of ease at the base of the neck and all round there in the region of the breast and shoulders. This makes her neck look short, and doesn't give her head that queenly port that is so lovely; but then queenliness isn't her style. Her feet aren't delicately placed when she steps, nor are the hands and wrists so good. But the arms don't suffer, and she has a marvelous lightness in the knees. Though her pas de bourrée weren't beautiful, her feet stretched in the air always were. And particularly beautiful were all her poses in lifts. Really beautiful lifts. I liked a few mime gestures she made very much too.

I liked her second number immensely — for the lifts, much more exact than we make them, and more varied. It's practically the *Sylphides* pas de deux. Next best I liked the *Casse-Noisette*. Number three, *Chopin,* to music from Schumann's *Carnaval,* was a Greek supported adagio with veil, by Chaboukiani, absurd in style to us. The final Rubinstein waltz was an allegro with bunches of flowers and a very pretty saut de poisson, I couldn't find out by whom; but this also looks to us very démodé in style. The style it resembles is a sort of super dinner-dance adagio couple style; of course it's done so very prettily. *The Dying Swan* I liked least, but she got an ovation for it. The choreography of the two other pieces, the Rubinstein and the *Red Poppy,* was uninteresting, but the style is too different to judge at a glance.

Perhaps what I missed in Ulanova's dancing was the want of those moments that affect me so, those moments of rest in a dance when a movement resolves for a hair's breadth of time into repose and finishes, and there is like a sense of eternity from which the dancing and the movement re-arise. I didn't see this completion of repose in her dancing.

Her partner, Kondratov, was a pleasant young man, with no intentions as to what we think of as style or grace, a trifle muscle-bound, completely unaffected. He was a marvelously sure partner, and one who could support her on one upstretched hand, and so forth. Her balance wasn't sure at this performance, and his support was both unnoticeable and pleasing. I don't approve of dancers who don't dance like dancers, but it was interesting to see one so well trained and so simpatico. The Parisians, however, were utterly dismayed by such an apparition.

The musical part of the program was bad. The dance accompanists were wonderful as such. (A good deal of rubato, but never noticeable.)

Oh yes, I forgot to mention Ulanova's wonderfully lyric entrances and exits, so soft, merging into an infinite continuation.

This is what I saw so far; I'm coming again to her second concert. (I came back from Greece for her, and was so excited the afternoon before she danced I had to go to bed with a fever.) Maybe next time I'll see more calmly. Beryl de Zoete exclaimed afterward that she'd never seen dancing before, which was the reaction I hoped to have, but didn't. That she belongs with the half-dozen great geniuses we know is obvious too.

Ballet, August 1951

A Letter About Ulanova and the Royal Danish Ballet

I went back to Florence for Ulanova's second recital. She danced, I think a critic would have said, even better: the same large clear strong movement, the same calm lightness of strength, and the wonderful velvet flow. The timing is perfection: each phrase of movement, of the step or arm gesture, materializes at the exact speed and with the right urgency to make it visible in itself and coherent in the sequence, as movement and as plastic image; a perfectly proportioned continuity or dance phrase. Great musicians play music with a similar absolute clarity of proportions in the continuity, so you follow it completely, and it makes sense. Whether that sense is interesting as sense is not what I am speaking of at the moment; the quality of making sense of a dance as dancing is in itself rare and beautiful in the extreme degree in which she has it.

In details of action I saw again the same beautifully distinct and sure arabesques and attitudes, the same beauty in lifts and complicated lift sequences, a beautiful small développé (her style is so much in the développé spirit that I wish she had had occasion to do lots of large slow ones). She did a very pretty quick five- or six-turn finger pirouette. She did very clear large renversés, but I liked some small ones even better. She did some nice bourrées this time, but they aren't apparently one of her great gifts; nor did balance seem to be. I didn't get an impression of her gifts in second position; I saw (at the first performance) a pretty leap, but not how much bounce she has in a series; that wouldn't seem her style, but then her Giselle is famous. The shape of the knee is perhaps not quite ideal by nature, but the leg extension and stretched foot in the air are always beautiful.

I was left in doubt on one major point of the schooling, that impression of opaqueness I mentioned in the chest and shoulders (the line of the body in motion doesn't seem to travel through the upper thorax up into the neck and head easily; the head doesn't seem to have enough—how shall I say?— harmonious dignity). I didn't see the effects of schooling in Blasis's head positions, which is another way of putting it, perhaps. And floor contact and hands (wrists) seemed to have been understressed in schooling. Here in Italy, where in daily life one sees so much elegance and ease of carriage, so many pretty hands and feet, one's eye notices these things more than elsewhere. Neither Ulanova nor her partner has a "sensuous" grace of movement, or any intention of having it.

The number I liked best on the second program was a dance from *Cinderella;* she was completely pervasively "in character." I don't mean that she was an English or an Italian Cinderella, but she was her own kind. She was first gently pleased to be waltzing with him, then gently sportive in a sort of period step; gently she refused a crown he offered and then was gently proud when after she'd put it on him he nicely put it on her; and she was happy, oh! so mildly blissful; then, resuming the waltz at a quicker tempo, she was gone. It was all completely clear and convincing, touching and sweet; her head was too sweet in its little gestures. And yet I wondered that the contact between the two of them seemed so generalized that it didn't seem an extraordinary, unique event, it seemed too blunted to me in its particularity, in its keenness.

Partly, I thought, from the lack of keenness of definition in the movements of the extremities; partly from the plainness in the plastic images of the choreography. As plainness, the choreography was excellent: every stage of the encounter entirely clear in statement, smooth in flow, and convincing in development. Their spiritual intimacy was expressed by supported arabesques and attitudes. (Her promenade en arabesque is marvelous, especially penchée.) But I thought of those encounters in Balanchine, those extraordinary images of unique moments of fate, Shakespearean in the startling brilliance they have, and with such delicacy in the power of their imagery as contacts.

She repeated *The Dying Swan,* and though she did it even more meticulously than the first time (and received an even louder ovation) I wondered that I saw neither the uniqueness of the swan creature nor the image of death. I saw a pang and then it was over; I was puzzled. The execution had been so careful. She also did a "Danse Russe" (mixed character and classic), which she began as a smiling village beauty and, gradually becoming mystical, ended as a sort of icon figure. It seemed neither suited to her (she isn't "earthy" or "abundant") nor a good dance. Even so, the timing of the execution couldn't have been better.

As for Kondratov, he had an opportunity of being more varied in style, and he was suiting the style to the number, characterizing (as she did) in a pervasive rather than a scintillating manner, but staying completely in the role. In *Cinderella* he had, in particular at the climax, a kind of free manly courage in the pose of the head for a moment that was very good. He also did a fine Russian dance (big leaps, a pirouette that slowed down, rousing rush and all), which was a great pleasure. He couldn't have been more straightforward, and the audience at his second time liked him very much; so did I. I don't care for the opaque look about the shoulder blades or the walk with not-quite-stretched hip joints (vaguely hurt style); but he is a very good dancer in a style intentionally athletic.

Curious, I thought, the effect the dancing as a whole gives of being built as a continuity rather than as a rhythm; it flows and flows with a slow pulse under its rubato and it never suggests an edge or an end. I missed in it the sharpness, the brilliance of edge and the daring, the risk and commitment. I didn't enjoy the blunted effect, the sense of a generalized blur in contact, in the mutual contact of the figures of the dance too. I missed seeing a human keenness of mutual response which makes a dramatic moment on stage unique and marvelous, that instinct for beauty in the face of the very present. I felt again that homeyness of the first time, like that of a party where everybody acts nice and sweet and "good," but no one thaws out or ventures to commit himself, so that the goodness becomes stuffy and thick-skinned. There was a Wordsworth quality about it. I've seen American dancers with a similar quality, but choreographers counterbalance it by a sharpness of edge in execution and in the plastic images themselves — what the literary critics call poetic irony. All I mean to say on this subject is that on these two programs I missed seeing it. (The Chaboukiani number, at second view, seemed to have a richness of plastic imagination, in the lifts rather than the steps; but Petipa is much bolder in imagery, more decisive and keen.)

The general impression as poetic theater was far more disappointing than I expected. Obviously one doesn't draw general conclusions from a few excerpts, from seeing only two dancers, poorly programmed, badly costumed, with very uninteresting musical numbers performed between the few dances. Her I liked best in the *Sylphides*-style number on the first program, where her "slow-motion" gift and art shone at its brightest and clearest. And the exit was ravishing. That at least was a moment which I shall always remember, and remember as beautifully her own. A marvelous dancer.

Trudy Goth saw Ulanova, and said she was definitely unhappy about performing excerpts. Also she loved the baskets one can buy in Florence; very sweet and mild.

I had such a good time reading about your Danish holiday, being back in Copenhagen and watching them again, and was so happy seeing those dancers have a big success. I would adore seeing all of *Napoli,* which I agree with you is a work of genius, of the happy kind. I saw the first act in rehearsal, and what a pleasure it was, and how very Neapolitan-inspired! I loved the ensemble dance saying "A storm is rising," which ended by all the men (or was it everyone?) holding up one finger the way one does to see which way the wind is coming. And I loved the hero's return from sea: exhaustion, then realization he was safe, gratitude, and only then — so Italian, so un-Anglo-Saxon — did he realize that his beloved was lost in the waves? And then he was furious. He didn't rush to save her; he first cursed his destiny. Adorable! I thought the Lander *Etudes* very effective, but heavy and with little grace of spirit. The Galeotti piece on the other hand I was all enchanted by; and admired how neatly placed, how agreeably varied and clearly timed it was. I don't agree about *Coppélia,* though; I think the U.S. Monte Carlo version the best by far I know, and one of the great ballets — especially when Balanchine cleaned it up in '45. (He said then that the pas de huit in Act One — the girls' number after the Ear of Wheat — was the inspiration for all his choreography.) But if you have my book you'll find something about this version, also explaining why the Hours, Prayer, etc., are important to the poetic story; just folk dances at the end don't make the transfiguration necessary to a real ballet story.

But I agree with you entirely about the mime marvels at Copenhagen. I liked Gerda Karstens very much, but didn't see *Sylphide:* I only saw her giving a class in mime to the eighteen-year-olds of the scene where James is rude to the Witch; and deliciously they did it. I remember an excellent boy and excellent girl, but not their names. I remember Larsen's Coppélius as *very* fine, also everything else he did. (Didn't see the Greenland number.) In fact he was my favorite of all. I thought the company didn't have much training in continuity of movement or in large-scale line; their small, that is parlor-size, line is very good; its timid hint of line has a charm with the general Copenhagen sweetness. That is, the girls'. Margot Lander had a bigger style and much more projection. I wasn't entranced; thought she was doing it a bit too hard, a bit too star "effectiveness"; a bit too tired and without that dear sincerity of the others, whose ineffectiveness obviously bored her. (Ineffectiveness in the sense of lack of projection and theater accent where it counts.) The *Giselle* version I saw her in was a poor one, too. She was best in the *Napoli* rehearsal. I thought the company didn't turn well, or balance or land from jumps well. They have extraordinary second positions, and probably, though I don't remember, fine passés; fine batterie, charming though small arm poses, a delicious parlor propriety, excellent stage manners (all except that dear hot Icelander of theirs), and, of course, above all, a perfectly serious and poetic mime tradition.

It's the real pre-Russian style: I have an idea everybody but the Taglioni-Grisi-Elssler geniuses used to dance with small steps. However, the Blasis figures show big steps, so I'm wrong.

Ballet, October 1951

A Letter on New York City's Ballet

I hadn't expected so intense a pleasure, looking at New York again,* in the high white February sunlight, the childishly euphoric climate; looking down Second Avenue, where herds of vehicles go charging one way all day long disappearing into the sky at the end like on a prairie; looking up a side of a skyscraper, a flat and flat and a long and long, and the air drops down on your head like a solid. Like a solid too the air that slices down between two neighbor skyscrapers. Up in the winter sunlight the edge of such a building far up is miraculously intense, a feeling like looking at Egyptian sculpture. Down in the streets the color, the painted colors are like medieval color, like

*In February 1952, Denby returned to the United States after four years abroad.

the green dress of the Van Eyck double portrait in the National Gallery, intently local and intently lurid. And New York clothes — not a trace of charm, dressing is ritualistic like in Africa (or the Middle Ages); the boys are the most costumed; dressed men and women look portentously maneuverable; one set looks more dry-cleaned than the other, and those count as rich. New York is all slum, a calm, an uncomfortable, a grand one. And the faces on the street by day: large, unhandsome, lumped with the residue of every possible human experience, and how neutral, left exposed, left out unprotected, uncommitted. I have never seen anything so marvelous. A detachment from character that reminds me of the Arhats in Chinese painting. Women as well as men in middle age look like that, not comforting but O.K. if you believe in marvels, "believe in" in the sense of live with. They have no conversation, but a slum movie put on its marquee: "Sordid" — *Times:* "Unsavory Details" — *Herald Tribune.* I never saw so civilized an advertisement in Paris. Manners are calm, everybody is calm in New York except where maybe somebody is just having a fit. No one looks dominated. But one minority looks sometimes as though it suffered acutely, the adolescents. They throw themselves about the city, now supersonic, now limp as snails, marvelously unaware of adults or children. Suddenly across their blank faces runs a flash of anguish, of huntedness, of brutal vindictiveness, of connivance — the pangs of reformatory inmates; a caged animal misery. They are known as punks and jailbait and everybody defers to them, everybody spoils them as people do to what they recognize as poetic. They are not expected to make any return. A few years later they have put on weight, whether girls or boys, and the prevalent adult calm has commenced for and closed in on them too, and others are adolescent. Another magic thing about New York is that everything you look at by day, people, buildings, views, everything is the same distance away, like in Egyptian sculpture too. When I look about me in New York I feel as if I saw with an eagle's kind of eye; lovely Italy I looked at with a dear simpatico horse's eye. But you want me to tell you about the city's ballet company, which I adore.

The day after I arrived, friends took me to see a morning run-through of a new Balanchine that was to open a few days later. The dancers were in practice clothes under the poetic work-light with a piano onstage. You can imagine how eagerly we started to watch. And the pleasure at first was so keen and so peaceable it seemed to me we might easily have been Orientals watching our local court ballet any time during the last millennium or two. As the piece lengthened measure by measure I understood that nowhere in the world could I have seen a more beautiful new one nor anywhere else seen dancers able to perform its fantastic academic ritual with such an air of ease and virtuoso calm; such pretty dancers, almost Oriental in their impersonalness. Not that they behaved in any way but natural New York. That was my first impression of the New York City Ballet and of *Caracole.*

Later in the season I saw the piece several times, and though it had lost some of its delicacy in the glare of performance, the power of it had become more active and stranger. I saw a number of the company's programs and liked a great deal of what I saw. I was interested to find it a non–Diaghilev-style company. Star composers, star painters, star dancers, star poets — the NYC doesn't try to reproduce this famous formula as every other company still does. Stern as Puritan Fathers, Kirstein and Balanchine deny themselves (and us) all but two pleasures: dancers who within the limits they are kept become unique, and choreography which is the best anywhere. Not only the Balanchine pieces. But the best of his are of course for me unmatchable beauties.

The Balanchine ballets in the repertory are of every known variety: dance ballet, drama with plot, drama of atmosphere, comedy of situation, divertissement (musical show number) sentimental or farcical, exhibition grand pas de deux. (A pas de deux I like very much is the *Sylvia* one, with a very beautiful part for the man, canonically danced by Eglevsky.) Of the entire repertory the pieces that fascinate me the most are three dance ballets, *Caracole, Four Temperaments,* and *Concerto Barocco. Four Temperaments,* overloaded with brilliance like *Caracole,* is its opposite in material. It is full of Beckmesserish dance jokes, classic steps turned inside-out and upside-down, retimed, reproportioned, rerouted, girls dancing hard and boys soft, every kind of oddity of device or accent, but never losing the connective "logic" of classicism, never dropping its impetus, and developing a ferocity of drive that seems to image the subject matter of its title: internal secretions.

Classicism is extended in these three dance ballets (as generally in Balanchine's work of the last decade) without upsetting the principle of equilibrium, or shifting the terminal points of a step or port de bras — on the contrary; and still the diversity of movement they have, the range they show in setting steps to music, and the range in lyric expression are astonishing. It is easy to see they are models of style — easy to see how each step in time is undistorted, distinct, fleet, spontaneous; how phrases, periods, and sections flow on unexhausted with a deep powerful impulse. In the earlier of his dance ballets a few pantomime images like bodily *mudras* emerge from the rushing evolutions of steps; later these pointing hands become indistinguishable portions of the constellated configurations of the dancing.

One can take such dance ballets as just fooling of a fanciful kind or one can take them to be beautiful and serious; they look like both. What they show is young people dancing onstage and how lovely the bodies look. The choreography shows them graceful in the way they dance with one another, or look alone as they move, in the way they hear the music or take a climax or present themselves to the public. It makes an image of behavior, and many momentary ones: a sense of instinctive manners and cruel innocence; unconscious images suggested by devices of structure rather than by devices of gesture. So the individual keeps all her natural ambiguity as you see her decide, and see her swept on past the moment in the stream of dancing. And the force of the image comes not from her will but from the rhythm of the company's dancing and from the physical strength of the step. Often these images of unconscious action seem to me grand and intrepid; and what I love so is the undisturbed bloom like in real life that they have as they flash past. But whether Balanchine meant this I have no idea. I naturally think in terms of a story when I get excited; for people who prefer to avoid human interest, I imagine that the fantastic ingenuity of the arrangements, the costliest of hypertrophic pleasure-domes built up on nothing, the sweep and the lift of them, is fun enough.

The dance ballets invite you not to bother with a "meaning," but the drama ballets on the contrary have explicitly the meaning that their story has. The drama of them sometimes catches me off guard. I have watched the beginning, noticing I wasn't much interested, that it was barely holding my attention; and then not noticed if I was interested till, a long time later, transported far from Fifty-fifth Street, onstage in front of me I saw Destiny striking down a child of mine — a real poet — and I realized suddenly that it was I who had been watching it done, realized it only as I saw the Fifty-fifth Street curtain come down. And I was too absorbed still in the solemnity of the vision to wonder then how Balanchine could have circumvented my tense mistrust at the beginning, and made me accept his magic; and grateful to him too, because though I knew what I had seen was real, he at least assured me it was just a trick. Balanchine's gift for seriousness in the theater is a rare one. While anything happens it looks like ballet, like a step or a joke or a grace; but when it is finished it suddenly can look serious and real. The victim has been struck square. By the time it is over, the immolation has been thorough. Look at it in *Orpheus, Prodigal Son* (where it is a conversion), or *Fairy's Kiss.*

Prodigal Son is told, since it is about good and evil, in two kinds of pantomime: the dry, insect-light, insect-quick elegance and filth of atheism, and the fleshy biblical vehemence — so Near Eastern and juicy — of sin and of forgiveness, the bitter sin and sweet forgiveness. Still bolder as an image seems to me the leisure in the pacing of the scenes, which transports the action into a spacious patriarchal world, like a lifetime of faith. Very different is the ancestral religious Greece of *Orpheus.* The overslow adagio motions at the beginning and again at the close evoke the magic passes and stalkings of ritual — Orphic and Orthodox both. The forest creatures who witness Orpheus's grief appear in this magic slowed-down time from so remote and so pristine a country, it feels like a pre-Homeric Parnassus. (And don't they form a kind of protopediment or roodscreen?) Eurydice writhes at her husband's feet like a mountain lioness in heat, like the Worm of Death, like an eternal image. A pity the Furies' dance in Hell is of no value. But on earth the Maenads shudder possessed, swallow the spurted blood. Different again is the brutal romantic Switzerland of *Fairy's Kiss.* It is a land of fairy tale, reduced from the country of myth by industrial encroachment. Here the poet is only unconsciously a poet; as long as he may he thinks of himself as an average mill-owner boy. Poignant as is the reduction of consciousness, it is in this particular "world" that the image of looking under the bridal veil in horror becomes so grandiose and takes on so many tragic dreams. And the world of the believed-in fairy story is evoked by the nineteenth-century style of *Fairy's Kiss.* It isn't straight classic, but "like a classic": you can see it in the pantomime and the timing of dance steps, though the company isn't likely to distinguish.

Images such as these familiar ones (I mean to suggest) build up an imaginary country in which the story becomes credible; we recognize it as the particular country of our imagination where people would act as they do in the story, would do the deed they do. And the largeness of the images makes it a country wide enough so that the victim could escape, if he chose — like Achilles. But it is the rhythmic power of the dancing, of the dance scenes, that turns the pantomime quality of a gesture into an emblem, into an image with all its own country all around it. Dance rhythm is a power that creates the validity of the grand style. It is not rhythm used as a wow effect; I think it begins instead by quietening the audience; but it collects the audience's magic mind, its imaginative attention; it puts one into another time sense than that of practical action. One can recognize the same use of rhythm in the nineteenth-century classics, and that is I think the reason for their enduring magic. I imagine that many ballet masters and dancers don't know what to try for in preparing the old ballets, and choreographers don't know what to try for in preparing new ones. The weakening of the rhythmic power of a ballet in respect to its story is the defect of West European ballet in general. And Balanchine's effort to restore it choreographically — and also in dance execution — is a matter of interest for balletomanes to consider and discuss. He seems to me the active choreographer who best can give in his story ballets the impact, the truth, and the scale of the grand style, the structural devices to be recognized. Or at least he gives critics an opportunity of calling attention to grand values in contemporary choreography.

As for the less-grand-style ballets of his in the repertory, I'll have to skip them this time. Except for one I want to mention because it's George doing a turn disguised as Dame Ninette: a carload of respectable ideas, props, pantomime, orchestra noises, all of it honest and none of it dancing. It's *Tyl Ulenspiegel* I mean, and I don't mean to praise it, but I enjoyed seeing within its eleven minutes how many kinds of ideas did get across to me — history, economics, sociology, psychology, morals; how changes of pace presented a gesture in its actual as well as in a symbolic meaning; how casually introduced, how cleanly concentrated, how free in untying each situation was in turn. *Tyl* is a hearty Flemish grab bag — dirt and folk and anarchism and Robin Hoodness, Bosch and I suppose Rembrandt and a Flemish philosophical novel, and the final dénouement even offers the concept of the gifted man who from the solitude of intelligence slips gratefully into ordinary human happiness, the progress from "the hero" to "a man." *Tyl* is also charmingly acted by Robbins, and it has a decor by Esteban Francés, who is the company's one discovery as a big-scale ballet painter.

There is another piece too I want to call your attention to, not for its choreography, though, but for its score: it's *Bayou*. Balanchine has made it a sort of Dunham number, gently graceful, that needs only a stage surprise near the end to be a divertissement. But he missed the originality of the score, its subtlety in candor, the sense it gives of clear repose in a secret spot. The liquid continuity of the music, the easy breathing of the melody, the transparency of the harmony, the unelliptic, unabridged, so-to-speak circular or stanzalike forward motion it has — these are peculiarities of structure that might have looked beautiful reflected in dancing. Like the Furies of *Orpheus, Bayou* is a disappointment, because one can see that with better luck it could so well have become an event. Virgil Thomson, the composer, is also the composer of the opera *Four Saints,* a heavenly opera — in score, libretto, and singing — that I hope you saw in Paris; such pretty dancers, too.

Watching Balanchine's choreographic genius pouring out its gifts in profusion in the NYC repertory is as great a pleasure as I can imagine in the theater. Many fans here enjoy watching his choreography as keenly as if it were dancing itself. They are used to the dancers and to the dance style and you know how much easier that makes seeing the choreography. But I don't think anybody really wants to separate the dancers from the dance; I like ballet best when all about it, décor and music too and the evening's special good or bad luck for that matter, are all mixed up and indistinguishably beautiful. But I am trying in this letter to isolate what I think are the two remarkable features of the NYC, the grand-style choreography and the company dance style. The company dance style is particularly different from what Europeans try for and want and so on this tour it is particularly open to question and remark.

When you see the NYC doing *Concerto Barocco* or *Symphony in C* and see the de Cuevas or the Paris Opéra doing them, you realize in how different a direction the dance style of Balanchine's company is headed. And then when you have seen a good deal of the repertory, you see too what the limits are in which the dancers are quite strictly kept at present. These limits no European company would care for or be able to keep, but they do make the Americans brilliant. American ballet is like a straight and narrow path compared to the pretty primrose fields the French tumble in so happily. The NYC style is the most particularized and the clearest defined of all the American ones; the most Puritan in its uprightness. For me an immediate attraction of the NYC's style is the handsomeness of the dancing, and another is the absence of glamour, of glamorization. To have left glamour out is only a negative virtue, but there is a freshness in it to start with.

Handsome the NYC way of dancing certainly is. Limpid, easy, large, open, bounding; calm in temper and steady in pulse; virtuoso in precision, in stamina, in rapidity. So honest, so fresh and modest the company looks in action. The company's stance, the bearing of the dancer's whole body in action is the most straightforward, the clearest I ever saw; it is the company's physical approach to the grand style — not to the noble carriage but to the grand one.

Simple and clear the look of shoulder and hip, the head, the elbow, and the instep; unnervous the bodies deploy in the step, hold its shape in the air, return to balance with no strain, and redeploy without effort. Never was there so little mannerism in a company, or extravagance. None either of the becks and nods, the spurts and lags, the breathless stops and almost-didn't-make-it starts they cultivate in Paris, and cultivate so prettily. (On the analogy of painting the French go in for texture, the Americans for drawing.) As clear as the shape of the step in the NYC style is its timing, its synchronization to the score at the start, at any powerful thrust it has, at its close. So the dancers dance unhurried, assured and ample. They achieve a continuity of line and a steadiness of impetus that is unique, and can brilliantly increase the power of it and the exhilarating speed to the point where it glitters like cut glass. The rhythmic power of the company is its real style, and its novelty of fashion. Some people complain that such dancing is mechanical. It seems quite the opposite to me, like a voluntary, a purely human attentiveness.

It is an attention turned outside rather than inside. It is turned not to sentiment and charm, but to perspicuity and action. It suggests a reality that is not personal, that outlives the dancer and the public, like a kind of faith. The company is not trying for an emotional suggestion; it seems to be trying for that much harder thing, a simple statement. A painter who is a very bright critic told me that at the opening of *Symphony in C,* during the rush and surge of the finale, tears came to her eyes because it was all so entirely objective. There the company must have showed exactly what it meant to; and it is no trivial expression. They are tears such as Fonteyn can make one feel. But for a company effect I felt them only once while I was abroad, at the rehearsal of *Napoli* by the Royal Danish Ballet, for the company's objectivity of miming.

This, I think, is the general direction the NYC style has taken, and its achievement so far. I don't mean to suggest that it is the only right one in ballet; I like having different styles to look at. I think it is an interesting one, and suited to American physical traits and habits. The limits and limitations of the NYC style were not nearly as much fun to try to identify. I tried on the ground it might be amusing to hear what an American fan finds fault with.

So the NYC dancing its best looks beautiful in the dance ballets. In the story ballets when one looks for miming, for acting too, one sees with surprise the company isn't performing at all. For instance in *Prodigal Son.* By exception this was badly rehearsed and the boys danced it so soggily they looked like a YMCA gym class. But that wasn't the trouble. Robbins was attentive, simple, modest, a touching actor; but no one else acted at all. They were as neutral as in *Concerto Barocco*. The stinging butterfly hue and desert grandeur of the choreography turned into an airless Sunday-school monotone. How I wanted to see *Prodigal* done by the Danes. And *Tyl* too. Or *La Valse:* it looked like an orphanage. Fortunate young people at a ball have a hectic, mannered, almost frivolous way which is correct for stage ballroom dancing too (it's a character style, it's not classicism). In *Valse* the steps invite this edginess, this over-quickness; it would have made the ballroom vault over us all, and evoked that more and more unbearable, more unfulfillable longing of juvenile self-consciousness and soft mortality in which the mime scene could strike like an exploding thunderclap. Le Clercq and Moncion acted the scene well, but without the company to prepare it, it looked like a timid beginning. (And such miracles of rising choreographic climaxes; what a wow this would be done by your Covent Garden dancers, after a year or two of getting accustomed.) *Serenade* is danced even more meticulously than *Valse;* but despite its constant success, I would prefer it danced, so to speak, demi-caractère, not straight academic. Done as it used to be before the war, with a slight "Russian" retard and dragging in the waltzing, that tiny overtone of acting gave the whole piece a stylistic unity and coherence in which the beautiful gesture images (from the one at the opening to the very last, the closing procession) appeared not extraneous but immanent in a single conception. *Lilac Garden* is more effective too danced here and there with a slight advance before or retard behind the beat.

In *Swan Lake* Tallchief's head positions were a sharp pleasure. The neat, on-the-note timing of several striking steps in the adagio seemed to me of theoretical interest, but not this time interesting onstage. The entire adagio was taken too fast and too soldierlike in cadence to have the beauty and power it can: a développé has no force at this speed. The quartet was bad. But after the two new beautiful Balanchine Swan dances — a delight in their musical spring, their bird-look, and perfect too in their anonymity of style — after the beautiful long finale they led into — hundreds of birds beginning to take off, swirling in the air all over the stage, a beating of wings as they rise up, these great birds at arm's length — after they had gone and the toy swans were swimming back along the drop and Eglevsky looked at them immobile, and I looked with him, then as the curtain began to drop and applause started, just then I realized with a miserable pang that she had been transformed back into a beast, and that she was lost, lost forever. Lost to me too. It was as real as

Danilova and Petrov had been in the adagio. Acting or no acting, it was the drama of the story that Balanchine saved, and I was grateful to Eglevsky too for it.

Maybe the acting in the ballets I mentioned demands some familiarity with European manners. But the NYC has a chance at character dancing without European precedent in the high school jazz style of *Pied Piper*. The Negro dynamics of the jazz style (such as an overslow follow-through, a razor-sharp finesse in the rhythmic attack, an exaggerated variety of weight in playing with the beat) are special; but the NYC dancers all have shagged from way back. So I was mortified to see them dancing still in the style of *Swan Lake*, dancing the piece wrong and looking as square as a covey of mature subur-banites down in the rumpus room. All but one dancer, Le Clercq, who does the style right, and looks witty and graceful and adolescent as they all so easily might have by nature. The piece has a Robbins-built surefire finale, and the public doesn't even guess at the groovy grace it is missing.

After concentrating awhile on muffed effects like these I got so peeved with my favorite company that I started looking for mistakes in the part of the company style I like so much — the neutral, classic part; and I found a few. The boys for instance were girlish about the knee. They were pleasing in personality and partnering but what they had for plié was indecently small. Their silhouettes in the air were weak because they didn't lift the knee enough; on the ground they relied too much on their instep in place of the knee, and so were getting to mince, even when they came out to bow. They had no élancé at all. They imitated Magallanes's unobtrusive inactive way (without its singular beauty), rather than the big-scale action of Eglevsky.

In the dancing of both girls and boys, the fault that troubled me seriously was a bluntness in the rhythm, a monotonous singsong or marching-style meter; it looked like tiredness at first, but after a while it looked as if it might grow into a habit. The sameness of attack at all times (as the military say) is the danger that the company's beautiful steadiness and continuity create. And the classic, the school kinds of variety of attack, and the steps that train variety were what I next tried to watch for and saw little of. A long-sustained adagio flow where the pulse seems to vanish in the controlled développé movement; the various changes of speed possible in a passé-développé; the sudden change from slow to fast in ballonné; the unexpected pause in demi-fouetté; the change of speed in a plié with ritardando drop and accelerando rise, or a port de bras with ritardando finish in free meter — where steps with possible variations of speed and of meter occur the NYC does them in a regularized athletic one-two one-two meter. But when these steps cease being rhythmic "variables" they lose some of their interest and color; what is more, they no longer sharpen the dancer's sense of rhythmic delicacy, her sense of variety of accentuation, her sense of the difference between the artificially prolonged and retarded follow-through of adagio and the plain swing-back of allegro. The classic overrapid meeting and separating of thighs when they pass one another in an adagio movement is never seen at all, and that is a failure; and I am sure that the classic plié with a quick rise is much better in *Symphony in C,* in the syncopated preparation passages of Reed's section — because I used to see her do them correctly and now see only a mechanical plié in even meter, and the passage has lost transparency and zip in consequence.

No company I ever saw performed such subtleties of technique reliably. A great star might, but a company indicates them often rather roughly under the stress of acting, or of a collective atmosphere, or a surge of group rhetoric; similarly in other companies the boys dance with a slight difference from the girls not through technical differentiation but by getting the habit when they began to study dancing in the character of a boy or man. The NYC, however, not only does not care for such messy uncertainties but also does not encourage any character-dance approach. (To be sure, character dancing also involves rhythmic liberties.) So we have reached the limits of the company style — the present ones.

It would be absurd to suppose that so great a dramatist as Balanchine (and so great an actor) is delighted to see dramatic implications of such scope and power as his not realized by his own dancers. If they perform every piece alike in the style of virtuoso finger exercises, it is because he made the choice. But the negative advantages are clear. The company doesn't offer the fake glamour, the vulgar rhetorical delivery, the paltry characterization that often have become the defects of a company that tries to act, to characterize and make personal everything it dances. I have seen companies act in a serious ballet so that they looked the way dressingroom gossip sounds, the same kind of expression except it wasn't even occasionally fun. Better than that is dancing a few years without any "expression," just neutral. That leaves the choreography unsoiled, and also the public. It doesn't spoil the effect of the physical aspect of the grand style the dancers neutrally dance in. And it doesn't begin them in habits of silly acting. The limitation to a neutral company style made it possible to force the bloom, if one may say so, of qualities stronger in Americans than big-scale acting is, made possible the company's large and powerful impetus, its large and candid unspecific expression.

Perhaps one can guess something of the latent powers of the company style by looking at the qualities the principals and stars show that don't look out of harmony with the ensemble. There are unnervous and unfake acting performances for instance. In *The Cage* the way Kaye throws away most of her part (throws away the detail for the sake of the large shape she so can give it) is very fine and grand. (She looked exhausted when I saw her but I thought that was because of rehearsals for *La Gloire.*) She and Robbins long ago learned to do without the insistent projection that so often spoils American ballet acting, because it gives everything the same tough edge and so turns every move into a comic gesture. Moncion I saw act too little to speak of any change. Hayden and Laing, formerly very fine in a tense and even over-wrought style of acting, now seemed feeling their way toward a calmer and larger kind, such as Kaye and Robbins use. Together with the acting that Tallchief and Le Clercq show, it looks as if the NYC would welcome a simple and steady kind of acting whenever it begins to show.

Tallchief, though weak in adagio, strikes me as the most audacious and the most correctly brilliant of allegro classicists. She can lift a ballet by an entrance, and she has flashes of a grand decision that are on ballerina scale. What I missed seeing was that expressive radiance which makes beautiful not only the ballerina herself, but the whole company with her, and the whole drab area of stage space and bright imaginary world of the ballet that visibly and invisibly surrounds her — a gently indomitable radiance that is a classical ballerina's job, and that several times in my life I have seen a dancer accomplish. Le Clercq has a heavenly radiance and a lovely adagio, but neither has been trained to spread indomitably. Her New York elegance of person, her intelligence in every movement, the delicacy of her rhythmic attack we all adore. Adams has a perfect action, the best adagio, a ravishing figure, and a sweet manner that is our equivalent of your "county." Wilde has a beautiful Veronese grandeur and plasticity of shape in her dancing, a glorious jump; and Hayden has a Lautrec edge and vehement stab and a strange softness in her she seems to hate: a great actress, I would guess, if she learns calm. They are all in *Caracole,* each with a line as pure as a great ballerina's, and as characteristic as a great horse's in a horse show. And intent little Reed with the heart of gold — but individuals aren't what this letter is about, as I said to begin with. I love them all. I went by the air station when the NYC was off for Spain and when your Juniors were off to London, and how ravishing they looked, the station full of dancers both times; such an elegant and rich habitual way of moving, the little faces green from the farewell parties the night before, but the bodies delicious to watch in their unconscious young feline assurance. So they flew up into the sky.

About some of the other choreographies. Ashton's two [*Picnic at Tintagel* and *Illuminations*] are sound workmanship and each has first-rate passages. I find the subject matter of each too magnificent to suit their official-style scores, to suit, either, Ashton's own wonderfully intimate and ironic poetic eye. The more trivial the subject, the deeper and more beautiful is Ashton's poetic view of it. *Picnic at Tintagel* has a fine mystery-story opening and very pretty indecent lifts in the pas de deux. To me it seemed that Ashton's Isolde behaved like a Potiphar's Wife with a willing young Joe. She appeared in the lobby of her Central Park apartment building in her slip, found a big schoolboy there, seduced him instantly, and then again. A couple of bellhops peeked. And King Mark and some flags murdered the poor punk. Whether young Tristan ever noticed what it was he was doing with the lady — that is left in doubt; and that is the little private poignancy of the piece. It has nothing to do with the legend and very little with love; but it is a fact of life, it is true to life in its way. Tudor's *La Gloire* I was disappointed in; it didn't look like a piece to me in any direction, and Beethoven kept trampling madly on the bits of it. I saw Tudor was interested in "aplomb." The people around me, however, applauded earnestly as if they had seen something interesting; so I leave it at that. The Dollar and Bolender pieces I missed, and Boris's I'm sorry I didn't enjoy.

The Robbins ones — altogether exceptional of course in their gift for form and their ambition for sincerity — are exceptional too in the way they are unrepetitive, disciplined, driving, sharp-sighted. The dramatic pressure of *The Cage* is extraordinary. It devours the notes, it die-casts the gesture; when the curtain comes down, as Thomson said to me, there isn't a scrap left over. I was fascinated by the gesture — so literally that of the important Broadway people at parties and in offices. Bothered to be caged in with them, I looked around unhappily. No exit. But the murderous power that led to the climax and beyond — I couldn't really sense it in the force, the propulsive force, of the gesture; I felt it outside the characters. In *Tintagel* a discrepancy between what the story forces the dancers to seem to do and what it is I see them really doing onstage strikes me as harmless and fun; faced by the much greater dramatic force of *Cage,* if what is gobbling up my attention seems to be a discrepancy somehow, I get confused. No one else was bothered, as far as I could see. But I liked *Ballade* better because it didn't get started in that fascinatingly literal gesture of his that is wonderfully contemporary but so resistant to development, to the spontaneous growth kind of development. I liked it better too because at the end one girl at least discovers a way out of the trap that Robbins evidently intended to catch all of them in; she wasn't sure she wanted to get out, but it was clear she could if she chose. I liked the musicality of *Ballade* very much. And the Aronson décor too, so Debussy and real peculiar.

Something in the development of the subject matter seems to put me on the defensive. I'll blow up the impression and analyze it in terms of criticism and see where I get. Robbins's method is that of pantomime. The composition draws attention to descriptive gesture, incidental gesture made by peripheral movements; it does not draw attention to the central impulses of the body that dances. The gesture sequence is accentuated in spastic counterrhythm (an insistent device common to modern or Central European dancing, but used too, though ever so gently, by the Paris ballet dancers in inventing mannerisms for themselves). Robbins's dramatic line, the dramatic power of a piece, is developed not from the central impulses to dance — in ballet characters normal as breathing — but it is developed by applying an obsessive rhythm to what for the characters is incidental gesture. It is like seeing somebody punished very heavily for a small fault, and the main drama never coming to light. It is as if the characters were not free agents — they act under a compulsion. The effect is that of a kind of prehypnotic vortex. It destroys the reality of facts — sex, war, the South, money — and some facts one doesn't want to see destroyed; that is its danger. American writers to be sure very often use this device, but the honest and beautiful one among them is Poe. He is very careful. I think that Robbins's present technique would perfectly suit a "Fall of the House of Usher."

Robbins makes delightful and perfect ballets for musical shows, but at the NYC he wants to do something more. *Cage* as drama is as good as the best Hollywood or Broadway successes. I would say that ballet when it is more is something quite different, something freer. What bothers Robbins is that vast size, that space all around offstage of an imaginary world. But I think he takes serious ballet so seriously he is willing to get lost trying to find it; and I like that, I feel that way myself. Balanchine, Kirstein told me, believes in him entirely. So does the public, and the company's first all-Robbins night brought out a crowd of bright people who wanted to express their confidence and appreciation. I liked that too.

I think there are perhaps a few "background" notions about our ballet that we accept unconsciously but that you wouldn't know about.

First, something yours and ours have in common, a pallor, a whiteness of spirit, a thinness and meagerness of temperament that the French say they are so bored by, in our ballet, and in yours too; I think we had better not stop to sigh over it. Henry James describes the same characteristic in American acting of fifty years ago; he calls it an Anglo-Saxon shiny white hardness, as the French still do. Fonteyn has now for four years been leading a revolution against it in your country, and you were lucky she undertook it; after her ten years of the correctest rule she was the only person with the authority to try a change. I love the decisiveness of her action, and perhaps her new lovely warmth will influence our "Anglo-Saxonism" too, our own much more pronounced athleticism and shamefacedness. But actually the NYC is hardly more than 10 percent Anglo-Saxon, and it is as likely to be as Negro as white in another decade or so. Actually you English are West Europeans and can still enjoy your different classes and you can still have the pleasant characterization and glamour that come from noting the differences of manner — noting them without envy or moral disapproval. We haven't that tradition anymore. But what a ballet company needs first is an instinctively homogeneous style, an unconscious character. The NYC is less "theatrical" than Ballet Theatre was at its best; but it seems to me to be more natural in its dance behavior, to be better founded on unconscious local manners.

It may seem odd to you that we over here put up with an absence of glamour in our best ballet company in a way that Europeans never would. The normal American attitude (I recognize it in myself too) is the one expressed recently by a local anthropologist in a book about our character (*The Lonely Crowd*): "Wherever we see glamor in the object of our attention we must suspect a basic indifference on the part of the spectator." Can you imagine a European speaking so slightingly of his own local glamour? It's a Puritan point of view. But considering what a mess American dancers have so often made of glamour and of acting, it's quite as well not to force the issue of inventing them both. The balletomanes are tactfully quiet about that aspect of our ballet, and express instead their approval of the simplicity, the openness and honesty of the NYC style. They feel that the company is developing in classic action a larger scale than any other American company so far, and it is a scale they like. They remember the mistake of Ballet Theatre in glamorizing and characterizing our ballet dancing on the European plan.

Massine whipped up Ballet Theatre once and gave it (with Tudor's help) a brief glory. But he couldn't solve the two main troubles: he couldn't unite the ballerinas to the company and he couldn't get the American dancers to open their hearts instinctively to dancing as the Russian ones had done. Massine proposed success as the magic formula to solve these problems. That sounded American. He had success. He had a triumph. But not a thing was solved. Instead everybody just got nervous. So now Balanchine proposes a different magic. He begins with attention on everyone's part to carriage, to correctness, to the score. This makes a kind of objective, nonegotistic focus, and it gives a kind of disinterestedness of expression. Do you see how this might make a basis for collaboration between chorus and principal other than individual applause, and a basis too for pride in one's work and for giving one's best imagination to it? It makes one moral law for all. You may find this attention to the craft of dancing not enough to hold your interest, you luxurious Europeans; but it's not ugly.

Europeans keep forgetting what a poor country America is. We can't afford those enormous, secure, pensioned, resident, officially respected companies you all do. We have no such luxuries as your wonderful Elvin, Nerina, and Grant dancing a young life away under the ancestral Petipas, and growing more and more beautiful through the deep decades of peace that prepare their triumphant accessions. The NYC never knows if it will last another season. It is either underpaid or overworked or both. With so small a company and so large a repertory — about a dozen novelties a year — there is no time for more than a memorizing of parts. How could they work so hard and act too? You can see for yourself how impecunious the company is — so poor it can't even afford to dress all its repertory, and has to run out every now and then in little whatyoucall'ems. Under the circumstances Balanchine and Kirstein might as well give up trying for tiny advantages as the managements of big vested interest must; they can keep in mind the biggest prize of all, the true grand style. (Fortunately in art there are as many first prizes as contestants, even if so very few ever win one.)

Ballet, August 1952

Impressions of Markova at the Met

Alicia Markova has become that legendary figure, the last of the old-style ballerinas. Her second *Giselle* with Ballet Theatre this fall season broke a box-office record at the Metropolitan Opera House. Five people fainted in standing room. She did the contrary of everything the new generation of ballerinas has accustomed us to. With almost no dazzle left, Markova held the house spellbound with a pianissimo, with a rest. A musician next to me was in tears, a critic smiled, a lady behind me exclaimed "Beautiful!" in an ecstatic, booming voice. Her dancing was queerer than anyone had remembered it. A few days later, meeting a balletomane usually far stricter than I on the street, I asked him what he thought of her this season. "More wonderful than ever," he cried aggressively. When I asked if he thought she had shown this defect or that, he admitted each in turn, but his admiration was as pure as before. This is the sort of wonder a real ballerina awakens, one our young dancers are too modest to conceive of, and that Markova's dancing used to do for me, too. Though I wasn't carried away this time, I found watching her so-different method intensely interesting.

Details were extraordinary — the beautiful slender feet in flight in the soubresauts of *Giselle* Act Two, how she softly and slowly stretches the long instep like the softest of talons as she sails through the air; or in the échappés just after, how they flash quick as knives; or in the "broken steps" of the mad scene of Act One, when, missing a beat, she extends one foot high up, rigidly forced, and seems to leave it there as if it were not hers. I was happy seeing again those wonderful light endings she makes, with the low drooping "keepsake" shoulders, a complete quiet, sometimes long only as an eighth note, but perfectly still. I recognized, too, the lovely free phrasing of the *Sylphides* Prelude, so large, though not so easy as once. Best of all, better than before, I thought her acting in *Giselle* Act One. Surer than I remembered is the dance-like continuity she gives her gestures and mime scenes — all the actions of the stage business embedded in phrases of movement, but each action so lightly started it seemed when it happened a perfectly spontaneous one. In this continuity, the slow rise of dramatic tension never broke or grew confused. It was the technique of mime in the large classic style.

In classic miming, a sense of grandeur is given by stillness that is "inside" a phrase of movement the way a musical rest is "inside" a musical phrase. Markova's strong continuity of phrasing, the clarity of shape that mime gestures have when they are made not like daily-life gestures but like dance movements from deep down the back, and her special virtuosity in "rests" — these give her miming grandeur. But for dancing, her strength is too small for the grand work of climaxes. She cannot keep a brilliant speed, sustain extensions, or lift them slow and high; leaps from one foot begin to blur in the air; her balance is unreliable. In ballet it is the grand power of the thighs that gives magnanimity to the action; there is no substitute and a ballet heroine cannot do without it. Once one accepts this disappointment, one can watch with interest how skillfully she disguises the absence: by cuts, by elisions, by brilliant accents, by brio, by long skirts, by scaling down a whole passage so that it will still rise to a relative climax.

A second disappointment for me was that her powerful stage presence (or projection) no longer calmly draws the audience to herself and into her story on the stage. Markova used particularly to practice that art of great legitimate-theater personalities of drawing the public to her into her own imaginary world; she used to be fascinatingly absorbed in that world. But now she often seems like a nervous hostess performing to amuse, eager to be liked; she pushes herself out on the public. It is a musical-comedy winsomeness and looks poor in classic ballet. It was, I thought, a serious mistake for a ballerina of such wide experience to make. Another error, a more trivial one, was the absurd way she danced the *Nutcracker* pas de deux — more like a provincial *Merry Widow* number than the *Nutcracker* — with a shrunken, slovenly action, bad knees, affectations of wrists and face; and for a Sugar Plum Fairy to be carelessly dressed was unfortunate.

But despite even bad mistakes, there remains her phenomenal old-fashioned style of delicate nuances in dancing. The methods she uses showed here and there and it was fun to look. For instance the divine lightness of attack: Merce Cunningham, with whom I was discussing her technique, spoke of the illusion she gives of moving without a preparation so you see her only already fully launched, as if she had no weight to get off the ground (the stretch from plié is so quick). He remarked very vividly that in a leap she seemed at once "on top of her jump, like an animal." He also pointed out how she uses this illusion to disguise the weakness of a développé — she throws the leg up in a flash with knee half extended, but all you become aware of is the adagio motion immediately after that — a slow dreamy extension of the beautiful instep.

Markova achieves her illusion of lightness not by strength — for strength she has only the instep, shoulder, and elbow left. But she draws on other virtuoso resources — the art of sharply changing the speed without breaking the flow of a movement; the art, too, of timing the lightninglike preparation so that the stress of the music will underline only the *following* motion, done at the speed of the music, which is meant to be displayed. As in her phrase beginnings and leaps up, so the same transformation of speed from presto to adagio is used for her weightless descents and her phrase endings — though for the latter, it takes her a beat or two more to subside into stillness than it used to. For the full effect of being stilled and immobile, she often brings forward her low shoulders into a droop, a gesture like a folding-in of petals, like a return into herself. This motion softens the precise stop of the feet, because it carries over for an unaccented count like a feminine ending, like the diminuendo effect of a port de bras which is finished a count later than the feet finish the step. Her softening forward droop in the shoulders also alters the look of the next new start, since the dancer takes an upbeat of straightening her shoulders, and so seems to lift and unfold into the new phrase. Such nuances of color or breathing or dynamics give to the old-fashioned style its fullness; but they easily become fulsome. One can watch Markova, however, use them to carve more clearly the contour of a phrase, to make it more visible and more poignant. Our current fashion in classicism is to avoid these nuances to make sure that they will not be used to conceal a cardinal weakness.

In contrast to the solid, sharp, professional, rather impatient brilliance of our grand and powerful young ballerinas, the kind of effect Markova makes seems more than ever airy and mild, transparent and still. The dancer seems to begin on a sudden impulse, and to end in an inner stillness. She seems less to execute a dance than to be spontaneously inventing. She seems to respond to the music not like a professional, but more surprisingly, more communicatively. It is an "expressive" style, as peculiar looking in New York as any Parisian one. It is one our dancers look quite clumsy at, and not only our own, who hardly ever try for it, but many Europeans too, who constantly do.

I have wanted to focus attention on the difference, but I don't mean to judge between these two styles. For my part, I enjoy our own new one because the neutral look of it, a sort of pleasant guardedness, seems to suit our dancers better. Someday they will find out how to open up, but in terms of a technique that suits them. Markova happened to learn a style that suited her physique, her temperament, her environment; and a born ballerina, she made the most of it. The public responds to her now, not because of her style, not because it is the right one, but because she is a wonderfully compelling theater artist. For me she was, this fall, exhibiting her highly elaborated style rather than dancing a dance or a role, and that limited my enjoyment. But for fans who love classic dancing, and because they love it are happy to see as much as they can of its possibilities, of its richness and scope, it is well worth seeing her perform effects no one in our generation is likely to make so lightly and so lucidly.

Dance Magazine, December 1952

Some Thoughts About Classicism and George Balanchine

The beautiful way the New York City company has been dancing this season in the magnificent pieces of its repertory — in *Serenade, Four Temperaments, Symphonie Concertante, Swan Lake, Caracole, Concerto Barocco, Orpheus, Symphony in C,* and the new *Metamorphoses* — not to mention such delicious small ones as *Pas de Trois, Harlequinade,* or *Valse Fantaisie* — made me want to write about the effect Balanchine's work has had in developing a largeness of expression in his dancers, and in showing all of us the kind of beauty classic ballet is by nature about. Thinking it over, I saw questions arise on tradition, purity of style, the future of classicism, and Balanchine's intentions in choreography; and I wondered what his own answers to them would be, or what he would say on such an array of large subjects. So one evening after watching an excellent performance of *Four Temperaments,* I found him backstage and we went across Fifty-sixth Street together to the luncheonette for a cup of coffee.

He began by mentioning the strain on the dancers of the current three-month season, dancing eight times a week and rehearsing novelties and replacements all day. After it was over, he said, smiling, the real job of cleaning up their style could begin; for the present it was like a hospital, all they could do was to keep patching themselves up just to continue. I assured him they had just danced very well indeed, and then told him about my general questions. He paused a moment. Then, taking up the issue of style, he answered that there were of course several styles of classic dancing; that he was interested in one particular one, the one he had learned as a boy from his great teachers in Petersburg — classic mime and character as well as academic style. He spoke as a quiet man does of something he knows entirely and knows he loves. He sketched the history of the Petersburg style. Then he took up aspects of other styles he did not care for — a certain sanctimonious decentness in that of Sadler's Wells, a note of expensively meretricious tastiness in that of the Paris Opéra — these are not his words, but I thought it was his meaning. He was not denying the right of others to a different taste than his own; nor did he mean to minimize the achievements of these two great bodies, but only to specify points of divergence. He said he believed in an energetic style, even a soldierly one, if one chose to put it that way.

Passing from the subject of style to tradition, he mentioned as an example the dance we know as the Prince's variation in *Swan Lake*. He told me that it used to be done all in brisés and small leaps, but that one time when Vladimiroff was dancing it in Petersburg this great dancer changed it to big jetés; and now the big leaps are everywhere revered as tradition. I gathered he thought of tradition rather as a treasured experience of style than as a question of steps; it was a thought I only gradually came to understand.

At this point he noticed that Steve wanted to close his luncheonette, and so we went back to the theater and continued to speak standing in the backstage corridor. We got on the subject of notation. He emphasized the continuity of movement it could reproduce. I asked if *Four Temperaments* had been notated, adding that I felt sure the public in forty years' time would enjoy seeing it as much as we do, and would want to see it danced in the form it has now. "Oh, in forty years," he said, "ballet will be all different." After a momentary pause, he said firmly, as if returning to facts, that he believed ballet was entertainment. I realized he meant the word in its large sense of both a social and an attractive public occasion. But he looked at me and added, in a more personal tone, that when one makes a ballet, there is of course something or other one wants to say — one says what one says. He looked away, as if shrugging his shoulders, as one does after mentioning something one can't help but that one doesn't make an issue of in public.

At the far end of the corridor the dancers were now assembling for *Symphony in C,* the final ballet, and he returned to the subject of style and spoke of two ways of rising on toe — one he didn't like, of jumping up on point from the floor, the other rising from half-toe, which he wanted. Similarly in coming down in a step, he wanted his dancers to touch the floor not with the tip of the foot, but a trifle to one side, as if with the third toe, because this gives a smoother flexion. He spoke too of different ways of stretching the knee in relation to flexing the ankle as the dancer lands from a leap, and of stiff or flexible wrist motions in a port de bras. Details like these, he said, were not consciously noticed by the audience, nor meant to be. But to him they were important, and a dancer who had lived all his life in ballet noticed them at once. They corresponded, he suggested, to what in speaking one's native tongue is purity of vocabulary and cleanness of accent, qualities that belong to good manners and handsome behavior in a language one is born to and which one recognizes in it with pleasure. At that point I felt that he had, in his own way, replied to the large questions I had put at the beginning, though he had avoided all the large words and rubbery formulas such themes are likely to lead to. So I thanked him and went back to my seat and to the first bars of *Symphony in C.*

Balanchine had offered no rhetorical message. He had made his points distinctly and without insistence. It was several days before I realized more fully the larger ideas on the subject of style that his points had implied. He had suggested, for one, that style demands a constant attention to detail which the public is not meant to notice, which only professionals spot, so unemphatic do they remain in performance. The idea, too, of style as something a man who has spent many years of his life working in an art loves with attentive pertinacity. A classic dancer or choreographer recognizes style as a bond of friendship with the great artists he remembers from his childhood and with others more remote he knows only by name. For in spirit classic artists of the past are present at a serious performance and watch it with attention. And as I see Tallchief dance now in *Concerto Barocco,* I feel that they invisibly smile at her, they encourage her, they blow her little Italian kisses. They danced steps that were different but they understand what she means to do; her courage night after night is like theirs. And I think that they find a similar pleasure in the work of the company as a whole. For dancers have two sets of judges: the public and its journalists, who can give them celebrity, and the great artists of their own calling, who can give them a feeling of dignity and of proud modesty.

The bond between classic dancers is that of good style. But Balanchine in his conversation did not say that style in itself made a ballet, or that the entertainment he believed in was an exhibition of style. On the contrary he said that when he made a piece there was something or other he wanted to say. He was affirming the inner force that is called self-expression. And no doubt he would recognize it as well as an inner force in dancing. But for him there was no contradiction between creative force and the impersonal objective limitations of classic style. He knew in his own life as an artist — and what a wide, rich, and extraordinary life it has already been — that his love of style and his force of expression could not be divided, as they could not have been for others before him, and I am sure will not be for classic dancers of the future either.

That Balanchine expresses a meaning in a ballet is clear enough in those that tell a story. And he has made several striking story ballets even in the last decade. Among them are his recent vivid version of *Swan Lake; Night Shadow,* a savage account of the artist among society people; *Orpheus,* a large ritualistic myth of poetic destiny; and *Tyl,* a realist and antifascist farce. It took our bright-eyed young matinee audience to discover how good the jokes are in *Tyl;* and now the children have made it clear, the grown-ups see how touching are its sentiments.

The subject matter, however, of the so-called abstract dance ballets is not so easy to specify. On the point of the most recent, *Metamorphoses,* it happened that while it was being rehearsed, I met him and asked if what I had heard was true, that he was making a ballet on the Kafka short story "The Metamorphosis." He laughed in surprise, and said no. But he added that as a matter of fact, about a month before, going down from his apartment one night to buy a paper, there on the sidewalk in the glare of the stand and right in the middle of New York he saw a huge cockroach going earnestly on its way. As for me, Olympic athletes, Balinese dancers, Byzantine seraphs seem all to have contributed images for this ballet, besides that Upper East Side cockroach. But onstage these elements do not appear with the expression they have in life. In the athlete section the explosive force of stops and speed makes a dazzle like winter Broadway in its dress of lights; hints from Bali are wildly transformed into a whirring insect orgy; the joyous big-scale nonsense of it and then the evanescent intensity of an insect pas de deux are as simple and childlike in their vitality as a Silly Symphony cartoon; and the end is a big sky swept by powerful, tender, and jubilant wings. What Balanchine has expressed is something else than the material he began with, something subjective; and I so respond to it.

His dance ballets each express a subjective meaning. I feel it as the cumulative effect of the many momentary images they present, dramatic, lyric, or choral. And the pleasure of them is seeing these images as they happen; responding to the succession of their brilliant differences that gradually compose into a structure — an excitement rather like reading a logically disjointed but explosively magnificent ode of Pindar. One might say they are dance entertainments meant to be watched by the natives in New York rather the way the natives of other places than this watch a social village dance in West Africa or watch a Balinese kebyar or legong.

I am supposing at least that natives take their dance forms for granted and watch instead the rapid images and figures. I like that way of watching best myself; and the closer I so follow a dance ballet, the more exciting I find it, and the more different each becomes. I do not enjoy all of Balanchine's equally, or all entirely. Some, like *Firebird* or *Card Game,* have disintegrated in large sections. Others, despite brilliant dancing and passages I enjoy, do not appeal to me in their overall expression — *La Valse, Scotch Symphony, Bourrée Fantasque.* So capricious is a subjective taste. And it is unstable too.

There is a perhaps less capricious way of following a dance piece. It is that of watching its formal structure. And the excitement of doing it is a more intellectual one. I am not sure that it is a good way to watch, but I will mention some of the discoveries one so makes, since they are another approach to the meaning of a piece.

An aspect of structure, for instance, is the way Balanchine sets the score, how he meets the patterns in time, the patterns of energy from which a dancer takes his spring. When you listen closely and watch closely at the same time you discover how witty, how imaginative, how keen his response at every moment is to the fixed architecture of the music. *Pas de Trois* and *Symphony in C* are not hard to follow in this double way, and their limpid musical interest helps to give them their light and friendly objective expression. More complex are the staccato phrasings of *Card Game;* or the interweaving of melodic lines and rhythmic accents in *Concerto Barocco;* or the light play — as of counterpoint — in the airy multiplicity of *Symphonie Concertante.* In this piece the so-called imitations of the music by the dancers, far from being literal, have a grace at once sophisticated and ingenuous. The musical play and the play of dance figures, between them, create bit by bit a subtle strength — the delicate girlish flower-freshness of the piece as a whole. But in relation to the score, the structural quality his ballets all show is their power of sustained rhythm. This power may express itself climactically as in *Serenade* or keep a so-to-speak even level as in *Concertante* or *Card Game.* It makes a difference in applause but not in fascination. Taking as a springboard the force of the extended rhythms — rhythmic sentences or periods — music can construct, Balanchine invents for the dancing as long, as coherent, and as strongly pulsing rhythmic figures; whatever quality of the rhythm gives the score its particular sweep of force he responds to objectively in the sweep of the dancing. And this overall rhythm is different in each piece.

Not that one doesn't recognize rhythmic devices of accent or of climax that he repeats — such as the rhythmic turning of palms inside outside; the Balanchine "pretzels," which I particularly like; or "the gate," an opening in the whirling corps through which in dynamic crescendo other dancers leap forward. He likes bits of canonic imitation; he likes the dramatic path of a star toward a climax to be framed in a neutral countermovement by satellite dancers. And there are some devices I don't care for too, such as the star's solo supported attitude on a musical climax, which (despite its beauty in Petipa) sometimes affects me in the way a too obvious quotation does. But to notice devices in themselves apart from the flow of rhythm and of images they serve to clarify tends to keep one from seeing the meaning of a piece.

Quite another surprise in his ballets if you watch objectively is the variety of shapes of steps, the variety of kinds of movement, that he manages to make classic. "Classic" might be said, of course, to include all kinds of movement that go to make up a three-act classic ballet: academic dancing, mime, character, processions, dancers in repose. And as folk and ballroom steps have been classicized in the past in many ways, so Balanchine has been classicizing movements from our Negro and show steps, as well as from our modern recital dance. In his more recent pieces, the shapes of the steps go from the classroom academicism of *Symphony in C* and the academic virtuosity of *Caracole* through ballroom and more or less traditional character dancing to the untraditional shapes of *Four Temperaments* with its modern-style jokes and crushing impact, or of *Orpheus,* or of *Metamorphoses* and its innocent stage-show style. What an extraordinary absence of prejudice as to what is proper in classicism these odd works show.

But in what sense can all his variety of movement be classical? It is so because of the way he asks the dancer to move, because of the kind of continuity in motion he calls for. For the continuity in all these pieces is that of which the familiar classroom exercises are the key and remain a touchstone. Classic dancing centers movement in a way professionally called "placement"; it centers it for the advantage of assurance in spring, balance, and visibility. The dancer learns to move with a natural continuity in impetus, and a natural expression of his full physical strength in the thighs — thighs and waist, where the greatest strength to move outward into space naturally lies.

Balanchine's constant attention to this principle develops in his dancers a gift for coherent, vigorous, positive, unsimpering movement, and a gift too for a powerful, spontaneous rhythmic pulse in action. And a final product of it is the spaciousness which their dancing — Tallchief exemplifies it — comes to have. Clear, sure-footed dancing travels through space easy and large, either in its instantaneous collective surges or in its slow and solitary paths. So space spreads in calm power from the center of the stage and from the moving dancer and gives a sense of human grandeur and of destiny to her action. In his conversation with me he had of course only stressed the small details of motion from which the large effects eventually can grow.

The final consistency that classical style gives to a performance comes from its discipline of behavior. Handsome behavior onstage gives to an entertainment a radiance Broadway dancing knows little of. Balanchine often builds it into the dance — even when he works on Broadway — by so timing the action that if it is done cleanly and accurately the dramatic color becomes one of a spontaneous considerateness among the dancers for one another and of a graceful feeling between the girls and boys. Further subtleties of behavior, subtle alternations of contact and neutral presence, are a part of the expression his pieces have. They seem, as is natural to Americans, unemphatic and usually even like unconscious actions.

But where drama demands more conscious relationships, these require a more conscious kind of acting. What Balanchine tries for as classic acting is not an emphatic emotional stress placed on a particular gesture for expression's sake. He tries instead to have expression present as a color throughout a dance or a role, sometimes growing a trifle stronger, sometimes less. It is as if a gesture were made in its simplest form by the whole body as it dances. This is a grand style of acting not at all like the usual Broadway naturalism. In ballet a realistic gesture if it is overstressed, or if the timing of it makes the dancer dwell on it "meaningfully," gets clammy; the grand style remains acceptable at any speed or intensity; and Tallchief often exemplifies it at a high intensity — in the writhings of Eurydice, for instance, or in the quiet lightness of her last entrance in *Firebird.*

What I have tried to say is that the meaning of a Balanchine piece is to be found in its brilliance and exhilarating variety of classical style. There is nothing hidden or esoteric or even frustrated about the expression of one of his dance ballets. The meaning of it, as of classical dancing generally, is whatever one loves as one watches it without thinking why. It is no use wasting time puzzling over what one doesn't love; one had better keep looking, and sharply, to see if there isn't something one does, because it goes so fast there is always a lot one misses. Pretty people, pretty clothes, pretty lights, music, pictures, all of it in motion with surprises and feats and all those unbelievable changes of speed and place and figure and weight and a grand continuous rhythm and a tumultuous sweep of imaginary space opening up further and forever, glorious and grand. And because they are all boys and girls doing it, you see these attractive people in all kinds of moments, their unconscious grace of movement, and unconscious grace in their awareness of each other, of themselves, of the music, of the audience, all happening instantaneously and transformed again without a second's reflection. That is what one can find to love. That is the entertainment, different in each piece. All these beauties may be gathered in a sort of story, or you may see them held together only by the music. It is up to you to look and seize them as they flash by in all their brilliant poetry. And many people in the audience do.

Classic ballet is a definite kind of entertainment, based on an ideal conception of expression professionally called "style." It does not try to be the same sort of fun as some other kind of entertainment. It tries to be as wonderful as possible in its own beautiful and voluntarily limited way, just as does any other art. What correct style exists for, what it hopes for, is a singular, unforeseen, an out-of-this-world beauty of expression. In our own local and spontaneous terms this is what Balanchine intends. I wish I had found a less heavy way of treating so joyous and unoppressive a form of entertainment; for a tender irony is close to the heart of it. But I hope I have made clear at least that neither classicism nor "Balanchine style" is, as one sometimes hears people say, merely a mechanical exactness in dancing or in choreography, no personality, no warmth, no human feeling. As for his dancers, this season in particular has shown us that the more correct their style, the more their individual personality becomes distinct and attractive onstage.

The strictest fans realize that his work in creating a company is still only half done. But though still unfinished, the result is already extraordinary. London, Paris, and Copenhagen have striking stars, have companies excellent in many ways, larger, wealthier, more secure than we know how to make them. This winter the hard-worked little New York City company has shown itself, both in style and repertory, more sound, more original, more beautiful than any you can see anywhere in the Western world.

In the last five years George Balanchine has come to be recognized as the greatest choreographer of our time abroad as well as here. Such a position has its drawbacks. But for my part, though his prestige may add nothing to my pleasure in his work, I have no quarrel with it.

Dance Magazine, February 1953

Stars of the Russian Ballet: A Film Review

Stars of the Russian Ballet tries very nicely to give a front-row view of Soviet ballet. The dancers in it are members of Russia's two best companies, the stars are among the country's most brilliant. They dance *Swan Lake* (a revised version), *The Fountain of Bakhchisarai,* and *The Flames of Paris;* the latter two are Soviet productions of 1934 and 1932 and are based on character steps. At the Bolshoi each of the three would last a whole evening, but the film condenses them to eighty minutes all included.

On the screen flashes of dance and mime delighted me. It was fine to catch glimpses of many dancers, men as well as women, whose leg action was powerful and easy and whose mime was wholehearted. They created plenty of nervous excitement. But the effect as the film continued was disappointing. The dances kept disintegrating into banality, the mime into hubbub. Only in the *Swan Lake* adagio did a few film sequences suggest the grand theater power of a poetic image. The rest left me with an overdose of vitamins and virtue.

The men were thoroughly wholesome, the girls more earnest than gracious. The dancers enjoyed giving a big dynamic charge, being excited, strenuous; messiness and hamminess didn't bother them as long as there was a passionate conviction about whatever story content the piece afforded. Now and then, in a flash of mime, the storytelling was brilliant. But the dancers didn't leave it at that. They forced the emotion in blurred gestures, they tried to mime it at every step of a dance. The overall theater effect was repetitious, thick, and airless. They showed only one side of ballet, the side without wonder. They never created as a company the stillness in which wonder begins.

According to this film the Soviet choreographies are ineffectual and meager, the dancers are inelegant. That they are at their weakest in the court scenes of *Swan Lake* is only incidental. Elegance in ballet is not a mime effect or an imitation of court life. It is a sustained visual harmony of movement out of which ballet builds its theater effect of continuity and sweep. Without elegance the dancers can show no wit, no joyous freedom in absurdity; without it the choreographers cannot orchestrate a dance. Elegance is like the clean pitch in a musical instrument. Without it a choreographer cannot sustain a clean development; he cannot give his themes the larger powers of grace, of freshness, and of grandeur which sustained choreography can — nor the brilliant caress of a larger meaning, like that of poetry. In classic theatre, Western or Oriental, elegance is the medium for the communication of serious feeling. The film showed Soviet ballet attempting serious feeling without elegance, and wasting the power of its dancers. The theater excitement they created was what we call corny.

But film all over the world is poor at catching the beauty and very good at catching the silliness of any ballet. Film is like a scatterbrain with a beady swivel eye. Its field of vision is totally unlike that of a theater seat. This film showed the best intentions. But one could observe that the director had not stopped for retakes of a few dance errors, and that he had passed a few musical errors in synchronizing some *Swan Lake* sequences when the sound didn't fit the steps. Maybe he liked a bit of extra messiness as "more real," maybe he asked for an extra violence of attack in dance and mime (that a choreographer would not have permitted).

One cannot be certain how far this film falsifies the overall theater effect which the three ballets create on stage in Moscow or Leningrad. But it does photograph details of action that fans who are curious about Soviet ballet will enjoy being able to look at. A number are interesting. Beautiful are the two novel lifts in attitude (Ulanova carried by Sergeyev) in the *Swan Lake* adagio, which replace the Ivanov lifts with a développé and lead into the arabesque penchée promenade. The promenade itself did not eclipse the same passage as shown in the film *Russian Ballerina* (whenever the two films showed the same passage the older one made it look better). But the penchée of farewell in the last act was very fine. To see Ulanova's iron force clinch the leg at its extreme height, holding it against a backward arch in the spine tense as a bow, is like hearing a soprano hold a fortissimo high D without a tremor. The weightless look her body has in the air in lifts is extraordinary, and admirable the assurance with which her foot reaches the ground as she is lowered. And in the pas d'action, when she first meets the Prince, she descends beautifully from a piqué to full foot. Her shoes, and those of the chorus too, had no apparent blocking; though they gave her little support and spread easily, they gave an unusual delicacy to a number of toe steps. I admired less a mannerism she had of hopping up on toe, and another of bending back the hand emphatically from the wrist. In one renversé moment, when first one leg circled way back, then one arm with the wrist, then another arm with another wrist, she looked like a parody of herself, like an uneasy octopus.

In the girls of the swan chorus, too, one saw the handsome extreme sweep of a port de bras to a backward arm extension typical of the Maryinsky school, and which our good teachers also teach. The Soviet dancers add to such a movement a strong arch backward with both shoulders pulled back too; it gives the dancer the so-called "pouter pigeon" silhouette, and when the neck bends back as well, and one leg is stretched or lifted at the back, it makes a very grand deformation. But the Soviet dancers use it so much it turns into a mannerism. Sometimes they force the head forward despite the backbend; this gives the head a kind of clandestine look, as if it peeked out from behind a decapitated girl. Kind of creepy.

The swan chorus did the little it had to do perfectly. The Cygnets danced the steps ours do, but we should have judged their performance as average and a little slow.

Dudinskaya, who danced the Black Swan, often showed, like Ulanova, a poor neck. Her speed and sharpness were of virtuoso strength, but the violent way in which she danced her variation seemed to me very close to parody. It would be absurd to judge so celebrated an artist on the faults of one variation, especially as the passage seemed the worst-photographed spot in the film.

Sergeyev's classic action was large and harmonious. His leaps were fine in the air, but did not end cleanly. In his variation he presented the buoyancy of the dramatic moment very well, and neglected technical refinements we are used to seeing. Foot positions merely sketched, no turnout, no clear stretch in the ankles or groin, or at the base of the neck. He did not have the force of a hero or the polish of a prince, but he had a manly mildness, an uncompetitive projection, that were attractive.

In *The Fountain of Bakhchisarai,* Plisetskaya, a strikingly handsome woman, filled the part of Zarema, the harem queen. Her waist was a trifle square and the costume did not flatter her. But she had a big-scale dramatic temperament and proved to be a very strong dancer, somewhat acrobatic in style. It was noticeable that she spoiled several fine leaps by after-motions in the arms or by putting the accent of the leap not on the leg that reaches out, but on that which follows after. All through the film, in one way or another, one noticed similar deficiencies. Many striking dancers looked unevenly trained. Physically, men and women tended to look stocky in the waist. And the film sets and costumes were not at all imaginative.

In *The Flames of Paris* the great Chaboukiani appeared, whirling with a grandiosely volcanic temperament, an extraordinary whipping brilliance; but the miserable staging and direction of this ballet wasted the impact he made and blurred several other attractive moments.

The film showed as much mime as dancing. There was one interesting invention, that of Ulanova's death in the harem. She drooped against the wall on both pointes and slid, turning the feet so they sank with the arch against the floor. This moment of extinction and the brief last look of consciousness before it were wonderfully acted. As an actress she sustained the character of each of her two quite different major roles with an extraordinary wealth of nuance and no interruption. But her intensity of projection became in the film almost formidable. The shape of her gestures was often poorly invented and overcomplicated, and she delivered many of them in a half-crouch that made the feeling look ungenerous. None of these defects were apparent when she appeared onstage a few years ago in Florence in several concert numbers; her mime moments then were subtly and delicately poignant.

The mime of everyone in the film was completely sincere, and several of the male stars had flashes of grandeur. But as movement a great many of the gestures were foolish, confused, and poorly timed. Some of the chorus mime consisted of taking a very deep breath and coming up with a distorted face or a wildly flung arm. The general effect was what we call chewing the scenery. The part of acting that an actor feels seemed highly trained in these dancers; the part an audience sees, neglected.

In the last two ballets the choreography was based on national steps suitable to the story and often danced in heeled shoes. The folk steps appeared in simple forms, they were quoted and repeated. One did not see the elements of them return in more striking shapes, varied in accent and rhythm, building to a visual dramatic climax. Neither were the mime gestures clarified, ordered, and timed for a theatrical emphasis. Constantly throughout the film the absence of invention, the want of composing power were unmistakable and depressing. The new music too was hackneyed, uninventive; it was dance-able, but commonplace.

Western Symphony and Ivesiana

The two new pieces presented by the New York City Ballet during its fall season — *Western Symphony* and *Ivesiana,* both by George Balanchine — are as far apart as possible from one another in the kind of theater appeal they offer. *Western* is likable and lively, with good-natured jokes and fireworks, and it develops a dance momentum that for stamina, speed, and climax is irresistible. *Ivesiana* develops no speed of momentum at all, no beat; it is carried onward as if way below the surface by a force more like that of a tide, and the sharp and quickly shifting rhythms that appear have no firm ground to hold against an uncanny, supernatural drift. *Ivesiana* is a somber suite, not of dances, but of dense and curious theater images. Its expression is as subjective as that of *Western* is objective. But both ballets take as their subject matter familiar aspects of American life. And both are set to scores by native composers.

Ivesiana is set to six orchestral pieces by Charles Ives. They represent themselves as impressionist music, and the six titles specify what each is about. The material is noises of nature and scraps of everyday music treated as of equal musical value. The stream and pulse of the sonority, the extraordinary harmony, the eddies of conflicting rhythms sound unlike European music and fantastically apt to their local subject matter. The dimensions are compressed rather than intimate. The wonder of the score lies in the nobility of expression in relation to its subject matter that it achieves. It does so with the utmost succinctness but with no meagerness — quite on the contrary, with a kind of eerie grandeur as true and sure as that of an Emily Dickinson lyric.

This queerly magnificent music is not in our regular concert repertory, and it is worth going to the ballet just to hear it. Watching the ballet, however, one hears it as if with a heightened distinctness, hears its characteristic nuances and its grand expressive coherence as the theater images on stage shockingly confront one.

Such a theater image is the action onstage to the music entitled "The

Unanswered Question." Out of the darkness a beautiful young girl in white appears aloft, carried by a team of four men, and a shadowy fifth precedes the cluster, turning, crawling, reaching toward her. Carefully, as in a ritual or a circus act, the girl is lowered and lifted, revolved in fantastic and horrifying fashions. In all the shapes her body takes, she is never any less beautiful or less placid. At moments her hair brushes the questioner's face. There is no awareness of his question or of his humiliation on anyone's part but his own. And the cortege moves forward again and disappears — like a great ponderous knot floating about in a shoreless obscurity. This scene, with its casual ghastly incident when the girl falls backward headfirst into space, is the central one of the ballet.

The ballet begins with "Central Park in the Dark." A close wedge of girls appears way upstage in the dark and oozes forward spreading, covering the stage, kneeling, swaying. A girl runs in searching among them, a boy enters, they meet, and the stage looks like an agitated wood that surges around them — oddly bushy like the park itself — as they struggle together, lose, and catch one another in the monstrous dark. She drops; instantly with a frantic gesture he rushes off. Slowly the wood shrinks to the faraway clump it first was; much more slowly the girl feels her way with her hands across the deserted forestage. Next comes "Hallowe'en." It is a rushing whirl and whirr, a flurry as brittle and spooky as that of leaves at the end of New England October; and leaves too, or with the leaves, a boy and girl whirl and leap forward and away together and are struck down.

After the hymnlike "Unanswered Question" comes a noisy city scene, "Over the Pavements." Five boys and a girl jump, crawl, intertwine, innocently brutal, while several bands blare at once — a sightless massive energy like that of city streets — then the girl drops her head on a boy's shoulder, he runs off after the others, she skips unpreoccupied in another direction. Next, to a jazz that is small, sour, meticulously insane, comes "At the Inn." It is the elegant summer "inn" of New England, and a young couple side by side — with an intoxicated abandon and a miraculous rhythmic edge — invent a dizzy fluctuation of tango, maxixe, Charleston, and mambo steps, wander into a horrid combination and out of it, and approach a rough climax, but stop, shake hands, leave each other. After that comes a brief concluding section called "In the Night," in which, in a phosphorescent dark light never seen before, a great number of erect figures move on their knees very slowly onward in unconnected directions; and over the nocturnal murmur of the orchestra, as if across invisible meadows, float the smallest and purest notes of bells. As one listens for them, it is as if the stage, as if the whole company, had sunk half out of sight into another and slower world.

It all happens in twenty minutes, and it makes a great deal to see as it piles up. Painful situations, strokes of wit, local allusions, kinds of movement, shifts of impulse, intertwined rhythms, hallucinating contradictions — there is nothing comfortable to rest on. Details are as cozy as gravel. Events happen unexpectedly quick or distressingly slow, very odd or very obvious. The point of view contracts and expands: at one moment a part of a body grows overvisible, at another the sides of the stage overempty. The scale telescopes and so does the rhetoric: suddenness of expositions, brevity of climaxes, conclusions that open instead of shutting down. One can find it very irritating.

But the piece in its appalling shifts is steadily expressive. The theatricality is sanguine and decisive. It doesn't waste a note or a motion. There is no vagueness for ear or for eye. *Ivesiana* juxtaposes anguish with innocent fact. It compresses a conflict and drops it into a reach of eternity. The tone is keen and positive. The ballet as one listens and watches moves very rapidly through an enormous range of fancy without a disproportion or a discontinuity. The speed kind of turns your stomach, but no harm.

There are many jokes at lightning speed. For instance, the innocence with which the boy and girl separate at the end of "Pavements" comes as a quick joke. But it makes the characters much more actual. The unexpected handshake in "At the Inn" looks like a gag. But the way it fits the musical conclusion that immediately follows gives it a second expression, a scary realness. At the climax of "Central Park," when the boy tosses and grabs the drooping girl in an awkward position, the flash is comic; but the shock of the humor is that it suits the tragic situation so realistically. In "The Unanswered Question" the views of the revolving girl which are ludicrous only make her body the more personal and the poignancy of heartbreak the weirder, the more intimate. Jokes such as these show you a concise flash of fact at the moment you expect a flow of sentiment. They take the place of a tragic pathos, which would need a great deal more time and repetition to develop. Such queer fun is typical of New England. Both Ives and Balanchine theatricalize in it a large-scale tragic glee.

And so for the general audience, the meaning of the piece is not elusive. The meaning is the same in the music and onstage. It offers a view of our local life, not from the point of view whether it is good or bad, whether it is pleasant or unpleasant, but seen as a vivid fact wide open to tragedy. The view is Ives's. Balanchine has inserted no different meaning of his own. He has taken that of the score, its condensed amplitude, the characteristic structural devices, the particular evocations of feeling, and has found steps, qualities of movement, situations, theater effects that correspond.

For the more special dance fan, Balanchine has found fresh developments, fresh values in familiar steps and in figurations he himself has already used. The startling weights, reversals, sequences in multiple rhythm flow with a miraculous easy vigor. To experienced classicists "Hallo-we'en" and "Over the Pavements" will be a delight; a pity they were blurred on opening night by an unsteadiness in the pit. Classicists will find that the surprises (of action as of sound) are created by an imaginative tension of classic syntax. Onstage the surprises develop by a tightening of the gesture value of classic elements. The tenseness of continuity gives to such a surprise the appearance of a normal event — the look not of a stop but of a flowering. I want to see it all again. "It's a dictionary of movement," a painter exclaimed after the opening; and a teenager kept repeating, "It's fantastic movement, that's what he does, it's fantastic movement." Intermission talk had a look of concentration I remember seeing last at the premiere of *Deaths and Entrances*. The gallery had booed and cheered the ballet loudly. And one young man up there, just as the boy onstage rushed off at the climax of the first section, had cried out as if at pistol point, "Svengali!"

Ivesiana for a critic is as remarkable a novelty as *Four Temperaments* was. At first sight it is more phenomenal, less appealing. The older piece fuses weighty dance contrasts in the driving sweep of a strong beat; the newer one, with nearly no beat, condenses contrasting elements of gesture into solid theater images and floats their weight fantastically on a sustained acuity of harmony. In ballet theory this cannot be done successfully. But neither could the other. Ballets such as both of these are an active part of intellectual life in the United States; they are, it seems to me, among its triumphs. In any case, they are a fight. That is why the spirit, the vitality of the New York City company depend on dancing them. The way the company undertakes the incredible difficulties of *Ivesiana* — no other company in the world would be equal to them — shows it enjoys the battle. It danced *Four Temperaments* several years before it won that one. *Ivesiana* is still a draw.

The ballet is wonderfully lit by Jean Rosenthal. It is performed in practice clothes as an economy: the score was so difficult to play that extra orchestra rehearsals were expensive. I wish there were costumes, but the money could not have been spent better. And the New York City Ballet orchestra won a musical distinction our symphony orchestras can envy.

The other new ballet of the season, *Western Symphony,* was also danced in practice clothes. Costumes had been designed and are promised next season. I heard by chance what they were like: cowboy clothes for the boys, and for the girls dance-hall dresses of the Golden Eighties. There is a subtle and pervasive something in the dances of *Western,* a situation between the girls and boys, that these costumes would make charming and clear. Without them, one may unconsciously question what sort of American girls these dancing partners are, and why the score by Hershey Kay so insistently evokes a honky-tonk or dance-hall glamour.

Actually no one questions anything, the piece is so much fun to watch. Clear in any case is the healthy, normal Western American quality of movement it has. And Walter Terry in a brilliant first-night review in the *Herald Tribune* stated at once the historic aspect of the ballet: that the Americanness of the boys and girls is expressed in terms of strictly classic steps. He pointed out that the expression they have does not come from "Westernizing" a familiar step. The step is left intact but the sequence gives it a novel speed, metric accent, and visual emphasis which create an overall Western look — a Western strength in physical impulse and rhythm, in playfulness or sentiment. He showed how different this procedure is from that used in other Western ballets — *Rodeo* or *Billy the Kid* — and other Americana. It is like the difference between writing in dialect and in straight English, one might say. Mr. Terry's point will become more and more interesting and will be long remembered.

In *Western* — the action is like a big dance party, nothing but dancing — the dancers do everything possible with a four-bar and an eight-bar phrase. In the first section they fill it neatly full; in the second, they brush away a bar or two as if with a sigh; in the third, they leap over the bar marks in a long rolling motion like an easy canter; in the fourth — I get so excited by the syncopation I can't tell you what they did, but it was wonderful. The fourth section is all climax and goes on and on getting more so — at least it does if the orchestra keeps to tempo. I liked especially the manly mixture of false dreams and true in the sentimental second part — a part that is like a cowboy's vision of a pure ballerina. At a rehearsal I saw Balanchine miming this cowboy; it was so real, one would have thought he had never been anything else.

Something about the dancing gives an illusion of the clear desert air. "It clears your eyes," a young poet remarked to me as we came out after the performance. The company never looked so easy and fresh, though the piece isn't easy at all to dance. Tanaquil Le Clercq and Jacques d'Amboise were the special heroes of the first night. But Patricia Wilde and Herbert Bliss had danced beautifully, and Janet Reed and Nicholas Magallanes couldn't have been more touching and true in their delicate comedy. Miss Le Clercq and Miss Reed were brilliant too — quite differently brilliant — at the opening of *Ivesiana,* together that time with Allegra Kent, Todd Bolender, and Francisco Moncion.

The two ballets, one sociable, the other singular, are Balanchine's first direct treatment of American subject matter. He seems to know all about it, and have a great deal more to show us.

Center, October 1954

Dancers, Buildings, and People in the Streets

On the subject of dance criticism, I should like to make clear a distinction that I believe is very valuable, to keep the question from getting confused. And that is that there are two quite different aspects to it. One part of dance criticism is seeing what is happening onstage. The other is describing clearly what it is you saw. Seeing something happen is always fun for everybody, until they get exhausted. It is very exhausting to keep looking, of course, just as it is to keep doing anything else; and from an instinct of self-preservation many people look only a little. One can get along in life perfectly well without looking much. You all know how very little one is likely to see happening on the street — a familiar street at a familiar time of day while one is using the street to get somewhere. So much is happening inside one, one's private excitements and responsibilities, one can't find the energy to watch the strangers passing by, or the architecture, or the weather around; one feels there is a use in getting to the place one is headed for and doing something or other there, getting a book or succeeding in a job or discussing a situation with a friend, all

This essay was prepared as a lecture to dance students at the Juilliard School but was never delivered. Denby was notoriously shy about public speaking.

that has a use, but what use is there in looking at the momentary look of the street, of One-hundred-and-sixth and Broadway. No use at all. Looking at a dance performance has some use, presumably. And certainly it is a great deal less exhausting than looking at the disjointed fragments of impression that one can see in traffic. Not only that the performance is arranged so that it is convenient to look at, easy to pay continuous attention to, and attractive, but also that the excitement in it seems to have points of contact with the excitement of one's own personal life, with the curiosity that makes one want to go get a special book, or the exciting self-importance that makes one want to succeed, or even the absorbing drama of talking and listening to someone of one's own age with whom one is on the verge of being in love. When you feel that the emotion that is coming toward you from the performance is like a part of your own at some moment when you were very excited, it is easy to be interested. And of course if you feel the audience thrilled all around you just when you are thrilled too, that is very peculiar and agreeable. Instead of those people and houses on the street that are only vaguely related to you in the sense that they are Americans and contemporary, here in the theater you are almost like in some imaginary family, where everybody is talking about something that concerns you intimately and everybody is interested and to a certain extent understands your own viewpoint and the irrational convictions you have that are even more urgent than your viewpoint. The amplitude that you feel you see with at your most intelligent moments, this amplitude seems in the theater to be naturally understood onstage and in the audience, in a way it isn't often appreciated while you are with the people you know outside the theater. At a show you can tell perfectly well when it is happening to you, this experience of an enlarged view of what is really so and true, or when it isn't happening to you. When you talk to your friends about it after the curtain goes down, they sometimes agree, and sometimes they don't. And it is strange how whether they do or don't, it is very hard usually to specify what the excitement was about, or the precise point at which it gave you the feeling of being really beautiful. Brilliant, magnificent, stupendous, no doubt all these things are true of the performance, but even if you and your friends agree that it was all those things, it is likely that there was some particular moment that made a special impression which you are not talking about. Maybe you are afraid that that particular moment wasn't really the most important, that it didn't express the idea or that it didn't get special applause or wasn't the climax. You were really excited by the performance and now you are afraid you can't show you understand it. Meanwhile, while you hesitate to talk about it, a friend in the crowd who talks more readily is delivering a brilliant criticism specifying technical dance details, moral implications, musico-logical or iconographic finesses; or else maybe he is sailing off into a wild nonsensical camp that has nothing to do with the piece but which is fun to listen to, even though it's a familiar trick of his. So the evening slips out of your awareness like many others. Did you really see anything? Did you see any more than you saw in the morning on the street? Was it a real excitement you felt? What is left over of the wonderful moment you had, or didn't you really have any wonderful moment at all, where you actually saw onstage a real person moving and you felt the relation to your real private life with a sudden poignancy as if for that second you were drunk? Dance criticism has two different aspects: one is being made drunk for a second by seeing something happen; the other is expressing lucidly what you saw when you were drunk. I suppose I should add quite stuffily that it is the performance you should get drunk on, not anything else. But I am sure you have understood me anyway.

Now the second part of criticism, that of expressing lucidly what happened, is of course what makes criticism criticism. If you are going in for criticism you must have the gift in the first place, and in the second place you must cultivate it, you must practice and try. Writing criticism is a subject of interest to those who do it, but it is a separate process from that of seeing what happens. And seeing what happens is of course of much more general interest. This is what you presumably have a gift for, since you have chosen dancing as a subject of special study, and no doubt you have already cultivated this gift. I am sure you would all of you have something interesting and personal to say about what one can see and perhaps too about what one can't see.

Seeing is at any rate the subject I would like to talk about today. I can well imagine that for some of you this is not a subject of prime interest. Some of you are much more occupied with creating or inventing dances than with seeing them; when you look at them you look at them from the point of view of an artist who is concerned with his own, with her own, creating. Creating, of course, is very exciting, and it is very exciting whether you are good at it or not; you must have noticed that already in watching other people create, whose work looks silly to you, but whose excitement, even if you think it ought not to be, is just as serious to them as that of a creator whose creating isn't silly. But creating dancing and seeing dancing are not the same excitement. And it is not about creating that I mean to speak; I am telling you this so you won't sit here unless you can spare the time for considering in a disinterested way what seeing is like; please don't feel embarrassed about leaving now, though I agree it would be rude of you to leave later. And it is not very likely either that I shall tell you any facts that you had better write down. I rather think you know all the same facts I do about dancing, and certainly you know some I don't; I have forgotten some I used to know. About facts, too, what interests me just now is how different they can look, one sees them one way and one sees them another way another time, and yet one is still seeing the same fact. Facts have a way of dancing about, now performing a solo, then reappearing in the chorus, linking themselves now with facts of one kind, now with facts of another, and quite changing their style as they do. Of course you have to know the facts so you can recognize them, or you can't appreciate how they move, how they keep dancing. We are supposed to discuss dance history sometime in this seminar and I hope we will. But not today.

At the beginning of what I said today I talked about one sort of seeing, namely a kind that leads to recognizing onstage and inside yourself an echo of some personal, original excitement you already know. I call it an echo because I am supposing that the event which originally caused the excitement in oneself is not literally the same as the event you see happen onstage. I myself, for instance, have never been a Prince or fallen in love with a creature that was half girl and half swan, nor have I myself been an enchanted Swan Princess, but I have been really moved and transported by some performances of *Swan Lake,* and by both sides of that story. In fact, it is much more exciting if I can feel both sides happening to me, and not just one. But I am sure you have already jumped ahead of me to the next step of the argument, and you can see not only that I have never been such people or been in their situation, but besides that I don't look like either of them; nor could I, even if I were inspired, dance the steps the way they do. Nor even the steps of the other dancers, the soloists, or the chorus.

You don't seem to have taken these remarks of mine as a joke. But I hope you realized that I was pointing out that the kind of identification one feels at a dance performance with the performers is not a literal kind. On the other hand, it is very probable that you yourselves watch a dance performance with a certain professional awareness of what is going on.

A professional sees quite clearly "I could do that better, I couldn't do that nearly so well." A professional sees the finesse or the awkwardness of a performer very distinctly, at least in a field of dance execution he or she is accustomed to working in; and a choreographer sees similarly how a piece is put together, or, as the phrase is, how the material has been handled. But this is evidently a very special way of looking at a performance. One may go further and say that a theater performance is not intended to be seen from this special viewpoint. Craftsmanship is a matter of professional ethics; a surgeon is not bound to explain to you what he is doing while he is operating on you, and similarly no art form, no theater form is meant to succeed in creating its magic with the professionals scattered in the audience. Other doctors seeing a cure may say, "Your doctor was a quack but he was lucky"; and similarly professionals may say after a performance, "Yes, the ballerina was stupendous, she didn't fake a thing" — or else say, "She may not have thrilled you, but there aren't four girls in the world who can do a something or other the way she did" — and this is all to the good, it is honorable and it is real seeing. But I am interested just now to bring to your attention or recall to your experience not that professional way of seeing, but a more general way. I am interested at the moment in recalling to you how it looks when one sees dancing as nonprofessionals do, in the way you yourselves I suppose look at pictures, at buildings, at political history or at landscapes or at strangers you pass on the street. Or as you read poetry.

In other words the way you look at daily life or at art for the mere pleasure of seeing, without trying to put yourself actively in it, without meaning to do anything about it. I am talking about seeing what happens when people are dancing, seeing how they look. Watching them and appreciating the beauty they show. Appreciating the ugliness they show if that's what you see. Saying this is beautiful, this ugly, this is nothing as far as I can see. As long as you pay attention there is always something going on, either attractive or unattractive, but nobody can always pay attention, so sometimes there is nothing as far as you can see, because you have really had enough of seeing; and quite often there is very little, but anyway you are looking at people dancing, and you are seeing them while they dance.

Speaking personally, I think there is quite a difference between seeing people dance as part of daily life, and seeing them dance in a theater performance. Seeing them dance as part of daily life is seeing people dance in a living room or a ballroom or a nightclub, or seeing them dance folk dances either naturally or artificially in a folk dance group. For that matter classroom dancing and even rehearsal dancing seem to me a part of daily life, though they are as special as seeing a surgeon operate, or hearing the boss blow up in his office. Dancing in daily life is also seeing the pretty movements and gestures people make. In the Caribbean, for instance, the walk of Negroes is often, well, miraculous — both the feminine stroll and the masculine one, each entirely different. In Italy you see another beautiful way of strolling, that of shorter muscles, more complex in their plasticity, with girls deliciously turning their breast very slightly, deliciously pointing their feet. You should see how harmoniously the young men can loll. American young men loll quite differently, resting on a peripheral point; Italians loll resting on a more central one. Italians on the street, boys and girls, both have an extraordinary sense of the space they really occupy, and of filling that space harmoniously as they rest or move. Americans occupy a much larger space than their actual bodies do; I mean, to follow the harmony of their movement or of their lolling you have to include a much larger area in space than they are actually occupying. This annoys many Europeans; it annoys their instinct of modesty. But it has a beauty of its own, which a few of them appreciate. It has so to speak an intellectual appeal; it has because it refers to an imaginary space, an imaginary volume, not to a real and visible one. Europeans sense the intellectual volume but they fail to see how it is filled by intellectual concepts — so they suppose that the American they see lolling and assuming to himself too much space, more space than he actually needs, is a kind of a conqueror, is a kind of nonintellectual or merely material occupying power. In Italy I have watched American sailors, soldiers, and tourists, all with the same expansive instinct in their movements and their repose, looking like people from another planet among Italians, with their self-contained and traditionally centered movements. To me these Americans looked quite uncomfortable, and embarrassed, quite willing to look smaller if they only knew how. Here in New York, where everybody expects them to look the way they do, Americans look unself-conscious and modest despite their traditional expansivity of movement. There is room enough. Not because there is actually more — there isn't in New York — but because people expect it, they like it if people move that way. Europeans who arrive here look peculiarly circumspect and tight to us. Foreign sailors in Times Square look completely swamped in the big imaginary masses surging around and over them.

Well, this is what I mean by dancing in daily life. For myself I think the walk of New Yorkers is amazingly beautiful, so large and clear. But when I go inland, or out West, it is much sweeter. On the other hand, it has very little either of Caribbean lusciousness or of Italian contrapposto. It hasn't much to savor, to roll on your tongue; that it hasn't. Or at least you have to be quite subtle, or very much in love, to distinguish so delicate a perfume.

That, of course, is supposed to be another joke, but naturally you would rather travel yourself than hear about it. I can't expect you to see my point without having been to countries where the way of walking is quite different from what ours is here. However, if you were observant, and you ought to be as dance majors, you would have long ago enjoyed the many kinds of walking you can see right in this city, boys and girls, Negro and white, Puerto Rican and Western American and Eastern, foreigners, professors, and dancers, mechanics and businessmen, ladies entering a theater with half a drink too much, and shoppers at Macy's. You can see everything in the world here in isolated examples at least, peculiar characters or people who are for the moment you see them peculiar. And everybody is quite peculiar now and then. Not to mention how peculiar anybody can be at home.

Daily life is wonderfully full of things to see. Not only people's movements, but the objects around them, the shape of the rooms they live in, the ornaments architects make around windows and doors, the peculiar ways buildings end in the air, the water tanks, the fantastic differences in their street facades on the first floor. A French composer who was here said to me, "I had expected the streets of New York to be monotonous, after looking at a map of all those rectangles; but now that I see the differences in height between buildings, I find I have never seen streets so diverse one from another." But if you start looking at New York architecture, you will notice not only the sometimes extraordinary delicacy of the window framings, but also the standpipes, the grandiose plaques of granite and marble on ground floors of office buildings, the windowless side walls, the careful, though senseless, marble ornaments. And then the masses, the way the office and factory buildings pile up together in perspective. And under them the drive of traffic, those brilliantly colored trucks with their fanciful lettering, the violent paint on cars, signs, houses as well as lips. Sunsets turn the red-painted houses in the cross streets to the flush of live rose petals. And the summer sky of New York for that matter is as magnificent as the sky of Venice. Do you see all this? Do you see what a forty- or sixty-story building looks like from straight below? And do you see how it comes up from the sidewalk as if it intended to go up no more than five stories? Do you see the bluish haze on the city as if you were in a forest? As for myself, I wouldn't have seen such things if I hadn't seen them first in the photographs of Rudolph Burckhardt. But after seeing them in his photographs, I went out to look if it were true. And it was. There is no excuse for you as dance majors not to discover them for yourselves. Go and see them. There is no point in living here if you don't see the city you are living in. And after you have seen Manhattan, you can discover other grandeurs out in Queens, in Brooklyn, and in those stinking marshes of Jersey.

All that is here. And it is worth seeing. When you get to Rome, or to Fez in Morocco, or to Paris, or to Constantinople, or to Peking — I hope you will get there. I have always wanted to — you will see other things beautiful in another way; but meanwhile, since you are dance majors and are interested and gifted in seeing, look around here. If you cut my talks and bring me instead a report of what you saw in the city, I will certainly mark you present, and if you can report something interesting I will give you a good mark. It is absurd to sit here in four walls while all that extraordinary interest is going on around us. But then education is a lazy, a dull way of learning, and you seem to have chosen it; forget it.

However, if you will insist on listening to me instead of going out and looking for yourselves, I will have to go on with this nonsense. Since you are here I have to go on talking and you listening, instead of you and me walking around and seeing things. And I have to go on logically, which we both realize is nonsense. Logically having talked about what you can see in daily life, I have to go on to that very different way of seeing, which you use in seeing art.

For myself, I make a distinction between seeing daily life and seeing art. Not that seeing is different. Seeing is the same. But seeing art is seeing an ordered and imaginary world, subjective and concentrated. Seeing in the theater is seeing what you don't see quite that way in life. In fact, it's nothing like that way. You sit all evening in one place and look at an illuminated stage, and music is going on, and people are performing who have been trained in some peculiar way for years, and since we are talking about a dance performance, nobody is expected to say a word, either onstage or in the house. It is all very peculiar. But there are quite a lot of people, ordinary enough citizens watching the stage along with you. All these people in the audience are used to having information conveyed to them by words spoken or written, but here they are just looking at young people dancing to music. And they expect to have something interesting conveyed to them. It is certainly peculiar.

But then, art is peculiar. I won't speak of concert music, which is obviously peculiar, and which thousands every evening listen to, and evidently get satisfaction out of. But even painting is a strange thing. That people will look at some dirt on a canvas, just a little rectangle on a wall, and get all sorts of exalted feelings and ideas from it is not at all natural, it is not at all obvious. Why do they prefer one picture so much to another one? They will tell you and get very eloquent, but it does seem unreasonable. It seems unreasonable if you don't see it. And for all the other arts it's the same. The difference between the "Ode on a Grecian Urn" and a letter on the editorial page of the *Daily News* isn't so great if you look at both of them without reading them. Art is certainly even more mysterious and nonsensical than daily life. But what a pleasure it can be. A pleasure much more extraordinary than a hydrogen bomb is extraordinary.

There is nothing everyday about art. There is nothing everyday about dancing as an art. And that is the extraordinary pleasure of seeing it. I think that is enough for today.

Center, December 1954

Romeo and Juliet: A Film Review

The Russian feature-length ballet film *Romeo and Juliet* is more fun to watch if you don't like classic dancing than if you do. The whole cast keeps behaving like the operatic boyars and muzhiks one is acquainted with from Russian historical films. They rush up and down stairways, they fence by hundreds, they stare, feast, dance, and mourn with an unquenchable agility and vehemence. Seen close up, they ham an emotion with a capital letter. They do a little classic dancing too, and tie it in by heavy character acting. They are completely convinced, if not completely convincing. You can't miss any point they make, but you do miss a delicacy of implication. The action hasn't that aura, or overtone, of grace and human sweetness that in Shakespeare or in classic ballet lets the wonderful side of a meaning appear as if of its own accord. Instead, the film has a great deal of energetic obviousness, the enthusiastic conventionality we are used to in the ballets of our screen musicals. On that level *Romeo* does very well.

But one expected another level. This *Romeo* intended to show Russian ballet at its best. It has been adapted from one of the best postwar stage productions, the *Romeo and Juliet* of the Bolshoi of Moscow. It has been choreographed and co-directed by Leonid Lavrovsky, the choreographer of the theater version. The original ballet score by Prokofiev is the film score. It is danced by the Bolshoi Ballet, headed by the most celebrated of Soviet ballerinas, Galina Ulanova, who created the same Juliet in Moscow. Very likely the film keeps the style, the general plan, and many of the best moments of the stage version; certainly it shows every sign of care and devotion in its realization. And on this level one looks for a general effect much more interesting, and for a show with more sparkle.

But a local ballet fan is too curious about Soviet ballet to leave it at that. He comes to the film delighted with the chance to see the differences in style between these dancers and ours. He watches the detail for moments when what they do will show the kind of force the style has.

And he does see effects that communicate. Juliet, with the Friar's potion in her bodice, as she begins to dance with County Paris has a moment when she thinks she is dancing with Romeo; the insane flash of it is real, though the style is melodramatic. Romeo has a strange rushing entrance in the tomb scene, and he lifts high what he believes is Juliet's corpse with a gesture that brings back the grandeur of the verse. Mercutio in the midst of the sword fight in which he is to die has a rush of darting and twisting leaps that makes one see his spirit all quickness and no venom. Two acrobats leap through the carnival crowd with a vivid gusto. And when the whole population of Verona is dancing its stamped and Slavic step in the carnival square, in the general enthusiasm the remoter groups can't bear the beat and gradually shift to a later one of their own; this shift is so real it pulls you right into the crush of the crowd. These moments are not effects of classic dancing, they are effects of acting, of mime. And I was delighted as by a sort of virtuoso mime specialty, when Tybalt made his face look the absolute peak of fury, and then slowly altered it to look twice as furious.

But the local fan keeps thinking, what about showing us some choreography? There are groups strolling, crowds milling, pretty girls in tears, people running very fast or standing still, cutting capers, feasting, brawling, and constantly making faces and violent gestures. At the ball there is lots of genial ogling and drunken lurching, and with this motivation, slices of four or five dance numbers. But as far as their choreography goes, that turns out to be surprisingly commonplace, uninteresting in its material or in its development to the score. The big folk dance in the square, choreographically speaking, is nothing at all. But the unimaginative choreography of the two decisive pas de deux is what astonishes the fan most. The situations are the greatest — those of the balcony and of the bedroom scenes; the dancers are the best. And here at the poetic climax Juliet's dances have no brilliance of choreographic invention, no power of choreographic expression at all — they are elementary; while Romeo's part consists of giving his partner support with now and then the crumb of a leap thrown in. The dancers carry the situation by mime, like fine actors putting across a decisive scene in which they have only a banal text to work with.

The choreographic text is consistently elementary so as not to distract from the mime expression. Very likely the point of our best ballets would be lost on them if they saw them. They would take them for exercises in virtuosity. How could they know that they were meaningful when all the dancers looked so pleasant and so civil?

One comes to see that these Russians don't try for the same lucidity of dance action and of dance rhythm that we are used to, and that an interesting choreographic text calls for. They like to be off the measure. They prefer to fling out a whole step sequence to the general rush of a musical phrase or two, as if they heard in the music only its rhetoric or drive. They prefer to let the mime element — the acted emotion — blur the shape of the step and the classic carriage of the body. There is an exception in the classic-style group dance with mandolins, but the discipline here is meant to register as nice party manners. Only Ulanova shows a consistent powerful exactness of line in feet and legs, but even with her the mime emphasis makes the shoulders rise, the wrists tense, the floor contact thicken. And the habitually lifted rib cage breaks the line of her back and shortens her neck.

Once a local fan gives up looking for what we call choreography and classic style, he can see that the whole of this *Romeo* — dancing and mime — is keyed to a dominant mime image, a melodramatically violent one intended to characterize the environment of the brawling Capulets and Montagues. That the violence is a Slavic one, and not an Italian, is natural enough. But Shakespeare uses the brutal families as a foil for the marvelously civilized lovers — whose strength and delicacy suddenly become a wonderful and growing power that gives to the tragedy its joyous radiance. The kind of point Shakespeare makes can be and has been made by classic ballet when the piece (as in Petipa) takes its key from its lucidly dazzling grand pas de deux, just as the English play takes its key from its most dazzling sweet moments of verse.

But the Russian choreographer has turned the foil into the protagonist, and has taken his key from the rude and heavy mime motions that signify brutality. Everything in the ballet is oppressed by some reflection of the key. And the insistent intentionalness of the mime key has a depressing effect in another way. The effect is that the only human relations left in the piece are intentional ones.

Anyway the heavy mime style bores you. So when Lady Capulet, with an awesome gesture, rends her bodice in grief over Tybalt, you find yourself peeking at her underwear to see if that too is in period. When Juliet in the bedroom scene keeps falling agonized to her knees, you notice that it isn't in front of the Madonna that she drops but in front of a full-length mirror — and you see Ulanova-Juliet with a ballerina's practice mirror in her bedroom.

But after an irreverent breather, the fan can watch again. Not the acting, but the movement. And how beautifully Ulanova runs. How handsomely they all run. And the fan is struck by how the men sail through the air, all of them, with a fine sustained stretch that few of our boys achieve. They sustain the extension through the powerful middle of the body, they don't hold it as well in the ankles, knees, and nape, classic style. So they increase the effect of a weight that sails. The weight the dancers suggest in their action becomes the men better than it does the women. And the men's strong stance is a pleasure. And as the fan watches, he gets to see that the expressive vigor of their action comes from the dynamic sforzando attack they give to a stretching motion, a sforzando that comes from the midriff, and that has been trained in many gradations. Ulanova is a virtuoso of both the attack and the development that follows.

And one can well imagine — when a stage is full of heavy men and women dancing with this kind of powerful sforzando thrust and leaping up with a powerfully sustained extension in the air, so that a continuous pulse of ferocious energy pours out over the audience while the orchestra blares full strength — that the theater effect becomes so overwhelming one doesn't so much watch the dance as abandon one's self to the orgiastic discharge of it. One can well imagine the mass scenes of *Romeo* or any other piece creating such an effect, so that when Ulanova appears, so slight and small compared to the rest of the cast but so rapid and decisive and so occupied with a particular inner life, the shock of seeing an individual again is shattering. One doesn't ask for more, one sees her through tears of gratitude. One can well imagine it, but the film doesn't show anything like it.

Nor could it. A large stationary stage accumulates energy (or else lucidity) in a way that the swiveling narrow field of a camera can't. A camera can't keep its mind on dancing. In a mass scene its eye catches a hardness of strain in a movement and reminds you that the dancers have been repeating this take so often they are past their best form. The camera eye looks at a few steps of Ulanova's and observes that her waist is not a pretty one. It also observes her worn face, but after a few moments that turns out to be in its own way quite pretty. Of all her many dance qualities, it is her lovely airiness in lifts and supported leaps that best keeps a trace of its stage magic in this film.

It has been a long film but it is over now. The fan has caught the copious visceral vitality of these dancers, which would make them a stage success anywhere. Their style has less visual and musical continuity than it has visceral. Conventional ideas when they take this expression become what some of us call vital, human, and earthy. What a wow this company would make of *Schéhérazade.* The expression of their style is strongest just where that of our ballet is weakest, and vice versa. When they come to New York, what fun it will be to see the contrast. As for myself, as I went down into the subway on my way home, I began to wonder what Rubens would have done if he had been a Russian choreographer.

The Nation, May 12, 1956

Three Sides of *Agon*

One

Agon, a ballet composed by Igor Stravinsky in his personal twelve-tone style, choreographed by George Balanchine, and danced by the New York City Ballet, was given an enormous ovation last winter by the opening-night audience. The balcony stood up shouting and whistling when the choreographer took his bow. Downstairs, people came out into the lobby, their eyes bright as if the piece had been champagne. Marcel Duchamp, the painter, said he felt the way he had after the opening of *Le Sacre*. At later performances, *Agon* continued to be vehemently applauded. Some people found the ballet set their teeth on edge. The dancers show nothing but coolness and brilliantly high spirits.

Agon is a suite of dances. The score lasts twenty minutes, and never becomes louder than chamber music. Onstage the dancers are twelve at most, generally fewer. The ballet has the form of a small entertainment, and its subject — first, an assembling of contestants, then the contest itself, then a dispersal — corresponds to the three parts into which the score is divided.

The subject is shown in terms of a series of dances, not in terms of a mimed drama. It is shown by an amusing identity in the action, which is classic dancing shifted into a "character" style by a shift of accentuation. The shift appears, for example, in the timing of transitions between steps or within steps, the sweep of arm position, in the walk, in the funniness of feats of prowess. The general effect is an amusing deformation of classic shapes due to an unclassic drive or attack; and the drive itself looks like a basic way of moving one recognizes. The "basic gesture" of *Agon* has a frank, fast thrust like the action of Olympic athletes, and it also has a loose-fingered goofy reach like the grace of our local teenagers.

The first part of the ballet shows the young champions warming up. The long middle part — a series of virtuoso numbers — shows them rivalizing in feats of wit and courage. There is nothing about winning or losing. The little athletic meet is festive — you watch young people competing for fun at the brief height of their power and form. And the flavor of time and place is tenderly here and now.

Two

Agon shows that. Nobody notices because it shows so much else. While the ballet happens, the continuity one is delighted by is the free-association kind. The audience sees the sequence of action as screwball or abstract, and so do I.

The curtain rises on a stage bare and silent. Upstage four boys are seen with their backs to the public and motionless. They wear the company's dance uniform. Lightly they stand in an intent stillness. They whirl, four at once, to face you. The soundless whirl is a downbeat that starts the action.

On the upbeat, a fanfare begins, like cars honking a block away; the sound drops lower, changed into a pulse. Against it, and against a squiggle like a bit of wallpaper, you hear — as if by free association — a snatch of "Chinatown, My Chinatown" misremembered on an electric mandolin. The music sounds confident. Meanwhile the boys' steps have been exploding like pistol shots. The steps seem to come in tough, brief bursts. Dancing in canon, in unison, in and out of symmetry, the boys might be trying out their speed of waist, their strength of ankle; no lack of aggressiveness. But already two — no, eight — girls have replaced them. Rapidly they test toe power, stops on oblique lines, jetlike extensions. They hang in the air like a swarm of girl-size bees, while the music darts and eddies beneath them. It has become complex and abstract. But already the boys have re-entered, and the first crowding thrust of marching boys and leaping girls has a secret of scale that is frightening. The energy of it is like that of fifty dancers.

By now you have caught the pressure of the action. The phrases are compact and contrasted; they are lucid and short. Each phrase, as if with a burst, finds its new shape in a few steps, stops, and at once a different phrase explodes unexpectedly at a tangent. They fit like the stones of a mosaic, the many-colored stones of a mosaic seen close-by. Each is distinct, you see the cut between; and you see that the cut between them does not interrupt the dance impetus. The novel shapes before you change as buoyantly as the images of a dream. They tease. But like that of a brilliant dream, the power of scale is in earnest. No appeal from it.

While you have been dreaming, the same dance of the twelve dancers has been going on and on, very fast and very boring, like travel in outer space. Suddenly the music makes a two-beat cadence and stops. The dispersed dancers have unexpectedly turned toward you, stopped as in a posed photograph of athletes; they face you in silence, vanish, and instantly three of them stand in position to start a "number" like dancers in a ballet divertissement.

The music starts with a small circusy fanfare, as if it were tossing them a purple and red bouquet. They present themselves to the public as a dance team (Barbara Milberg, Barbara Walczak, Todd Bolender). Then the boy, left alone, begins to walk a Sarabande, elaborately coiled and circumspect. It recalls court dance as much as a cubist still life recalls a pipe or guitar. The boy's timing looks like that of a New York Latin in a leather jacket. And the cool lift of his wrong-way-round steps and rhythms gives the nonsense so apt a turn people begin to giggle. A moment later one is watching a girls' duet in the air, like flying twins (*haute danse*). A trio begins. In triple canon the dancers do idiotic slenderizing exercises, theoretically derived from court gesture, while the music foghorns in the fashion of musique concrète. Zanily pedantic, the dance has the bounce and exuberant solemnity of a clown act. The audience laughs, applauds, and a different threesome appears (Melissa Hayden, Roy Tobias, Jonathan Watts).

For the new team the orchestra begins as it did for the previous one — first, the pushy, go-ahead fanfare, then the other phrase of harmonies that keep sliding without advancing, like seaweed underwater. (The two motifs keep returning in the score.)

The new team begins a little differently and develops an obvious difference. The boys present the girl in feats of balance, on the ground and in the air, dangerous feats of lucid nonsense. Their courage is perfect. Miss Hayden's deadpan humor and her distinctness are perfect too. At one point a quite unexpected flounce of little-girl primness as in silence she walks away from the boys endears her to the house. But her solo is a marvel of dancing at its most transparent. She seems merely to walk forward, to step back and skip, with now and then one arm held high, Spanish style, a gesture that draws attention to the sound of a castanet in the score. As she dances, she keeps calmly "on top of" two conflicting rhythms (or beats) that coincide once or twice and join on the last note. She stops and the house breaks into a roar of applause. In her calm, the audience has caught the acute edge of risk, the graceful freshness, the brilliance of buoyancy.

The New York audience may have been prepared for *Agon*'s special brilliance of rhythm by that of *Opus 34* and *Ivesiana,* two ballets never shown on tour. All three have shown an acuteness of rhythmic risk never seen and never imagined outside the city limits. The dangerousness of *Agon* is as tense as the danger of a tightrope act on the high wire. That is why the dancers look as possessed as acrobats. Not a split second leeway. The thrill is, they move with an innocent dignity.

At this point of *Agon* about thirteen minutes of dancing have passed. A third specialty team is standing onstage ready to begin (Diana Adams, Arthur Mitchell). The orchestra begins a third time with the two phrases one recognizes, and once again the dancers find in the same music a quite different rhythm and expression. As the introduction ends, the girl drops her head with an irrational gesture more caressing than anything one has seen so far.

They begin an acrobatic adagio. The sweetness is athletic. The absurdity of what they do startles by a grandeur of scale and of sensuousness. Turning pas de deux conventions upside down, the boy with a bold grace supports the girl and pivots her on pointe, lying on his back on the floor. At one moment classic movements turned inside out become intimate gestures. At another a pose forced way beyond its classic ending reveals a novel harmony. At still another, the mutual first tremor of an uncertain supported balance is so isolated musically it becomes a dance movement. So does the dangerous scoop out of balance and back into balance of the girl supported on pointe. The dance flows through stops, through scooping changes of pace, through differences of pace between the partners while they hold each other by the hand. They dance magnificently. From the start, both have shown a crescendo and decrescendo within the thrust of a move, an illusion of "breath" — though at the scary speed they move such a lovely modulation is inconceivable. The fact that Miss Adams is white and Mr. Mitchell Negro is neither stressed nor hidden; it adds to the interest.

The music for the pas de deux is in an expressive Viennese twelve-tone manner, much of it for strings. Earlier in the ballet, the sparse orchestration has made one aware of a faint echo, as if silence were pressing in at the edge of music and dancing. Now the silence interpenetrates the sound itself, as in a Beethoven quartet. During the climactic pas de deux of other ballets, you have watched the dancer stop still in the air, while the music surges ahead underneath; now, the other way around, you hear the music gasp and fail, while the two dancers move ahead confidently across the open void. After so many complex images, when the boy makes a simple joke, the effect is happy. Delighted by the dancers, the audience realizes it "understands" everything, and it is more and more eager to give them an ovation.

There isn't time. The two dancers have become one of four couples who make fast, close variations on a figure from the pas de deux. The action has reverted to the anonymous energy you saw in the first part. Now all twelve dancers are onstage and everything is very condensed and goes very fast. Now only the four boys are left, you begin to recognize a return to the start of the ballet, you begin to be anxious, and on the same wrestler's gesture of "on guard" that closed their initial dance — a gesture now differently directed — the music stops, the boys freeze, and the silence of the beginning returns. Nothing moves.

During the stillness, the accumulated momentum of the piece leaps forward in one's imagination, suddenly enormous. The drive of it now seems not to have let up for a moment since the curtain rose. To the realization of its power, as the curtain drops, people respond with vehement applause in a large emotion that includes the brilliant dancers and the goofiness of the fun.

The dancers have been "cool" in the jazz sense — no buildup, inventions that did not try to get anywhere, right after a climax an inconsequence like the archness of high comedy. But the dramatic power has not been that of jokes; it has been that of unforeseeable momentum. The action has had no end in view — it did not look for security, nor did it make any pitiful appeal for that. At the end, the imaginary contestants froze, toughly confident. The company seems to have figured jointly as the offbeat hero, and the risk as the menacing antagonist. The subject of *Agon,* as the poet Frank O'Hara said, is pride. The graceful image it offers is a buoyancy that mystifies and attracts.

Three

A program note says that "the only subject" of the ballet is an interpretation of some French seventeenth-century society dances. The note tells you to disregard the classic Greek title (*Agon*) in favor of the French subtitles. It is a pity to. The title and the subtitles are words that refer to civilized rituals, the former to athletics, the latter to dancing. Athletic dancing is what *Agon* does. On the other hand, you won't catch anyone onstage looking either French or Greek. Or hear musically any reason they should. French baroque manners and sentiments are not being interpreted; elements or energies of forms are.

The sleight-of-hand kind of wit in the dancing is a part of that "interpretation." You see a dancer, rushing at top speed, stop sharp in a pose. The pose continues the sense of her rush. But the equilibrium of it is a trap, a dead end. To move ahead, she will have to retract and scrounge out. She doesn't, she holds the pose. And out of it, effortlessly, with a grace like Houdini's, she darts away. The trap has opened in an unforeseen direction, as music might by a surprising modulation. At times in *Agon* you see the dancer buoyantly spring such traps at almost every step. Or take the canonic imitations. At times a dancer begins a complex phrase bristling with accents and a second dancer leaping up and twisting back an eighth note later repeats it, then suddenly passes a quarter note ahead. The dissonance between them doesn't blur; if you follow it, you feel the contradictory lift of the double image put in doubt where the floor is. Or else you see a phrase of dance rhythm include a brief representational gesture, and the gesture's alien impetus and weight — the "false note" of it — make the momentum of the rhythm more vividly exact. These classic dissonances (and others you see) *Agon* fantastically extends. The wit isn't the device, it is the surprise of the quick lift you feel at that point. It relates to the atonal harmonies of the score — atonal harmonies that make the rhythmic momentum of the music more vividly exact.

At times you catch a kind of dissonant harmony in the image of a step. The explosive thrust of a big classic step has been deepened, speeded up, forced out farther, but the mollifying motions of the same step have been pared down. In a big step in which the aggressive leg action is normally cushioned by mildly rounded elbows, the cushioning has been pared down to mildly rounded palms. The conciliatory transitions have been dropped. So have the transitional small steps. Small steps do not lead up to and down from big ones. They act in opposition to big ones, and often stress their opposition by a contrariness.

The patterns appear and vanish with an unpredictable suddenness. Like the steps, their forms would be traditional except for the odd shift of stress and compactness of energy. The steps and the patterns recall those of baroque dancing much as the music recalls its baroque antecedents — that is, as absurdly as a current Harvard student recalls a baroque one. Of course, one recognizes the relation.

Agon shifts traditional actions to an off-balance balance on which they swiftly veer. But each move, large or small, is extended at top pitch. Nothing is retracted. The ardent exposure is that of a grace way out on a limb.

The first move the dancers make is a counteraccent to the score. Phrase by phrase, the dancers make a counterrhythm to the rhythm of the music. Each rhythm is equally decisive and surprising, equally spontaneous. The unusualness of their resources is sumptuous, like a magnificent imaginative weight. One follows the sweep of both by a fantastic lift one feels. The Balanchinian buoyancy of impetus keeps one open to the vividly changeable Stravinskyan pressure of pulse and to its momentum. The emotion is that of scale. Against an enormous background one sees detached for an instant the hidden grace of the dancer's individual move, a chance event that passes with a small smile and a musical sound forever into nowhere.

The Bolshoi at the Met

In the spring of 1959, The Great Moscow Bolshoi Ballet disappointed some balletgoers. "We'd all expected so much, and they aren't superhuman after all," a bright young lady exclaimed as we met at the door after a performance of *Swan Lake;* she quickly added the warmest praise for Ulanova in *Romeo and Juliet.*

About Ulanova I quite agreed. At first sight her vividness of motion, unique among the dancers around her, reminded me of Martha Graham's. As for the company, the first half hour shows it is a great one — highly skilled, convinced, attentive, lively. In *Romeo* everybody did a great deal of pantomime. They didn't all prove striking actors — nor would that be possible. But the company doesn't make hasty or shrunk-up or "unpurposeful" gestures. The movement of a gesture has that amplitude of strength, that full support from the waist, traditional among Russians, but which the Bolshoi has excellently trained. The large-scale easy power of movement, whether of mime or dance, I found a remarkable pleasure.

But let me describe the Bolshoi *Romeo and Juliet.* The score is Prokofiev's; the story, Shakespeare's. Costumes and sets look like stock nineteenth-century stage properties — Renaissance style. The action shows you, one after another, the familiar "big" scenes of Italian grand opera — the morning market, the street affray with drawn swords, the ballroom festivity, the carnival, the duel with a slow death followed by another with a quick one, the clan oath of vengeance, the family row, the burial by night with torches and tapers. Regulation opera-house humor is offered; the regulation populace of Italian opera turns up, wenches, pedlars, down to the ragged urchins played by girls en travesti. Every bit of it done in earnest, with complete conviction, and, of course, total laryngitis. It goes on for nearly four hours. At first you wonder that despite the Italian opera model nobody onstage behaves with an Italian irony or elegance; then you realize that everybody is behaving like the brutal boyars and dimwitted serfs in a conventional movie about Ivan the Terrible.

The pantomime points of the crowd scenes are made obvious and then made obvious again. Succinctness, surprise, leaps in logic — the fun of pantomime — are avoided. The crowd slowly prepares a mass climax, then it slowly milks it, then comes a lull in interest, a cover scene, carefully protracted. The pace is that of an army's indoctrination lecture.

When the crowd dances, the dancing is more stage business. Briefly the love scenes — the balcony, bedroom, and tomb duets — hint at a kind of dance that isn't stage business: on the balcony, a few classic steps; in the bedroom, a few lifts; in the tomb, a single lift, a very fine one. But even alone together the lovers keep pantomiming: the ballet doesn't venture into the other world of metaphor a dance can develop. In Shakespeare the love scenes develop an expression wonderfully alien to the Verona scenes, and that radiant difference makes the drama. Pasternak says of the play, "And to the din of butchery and cooking, as to the brassy beat of a noisy band, the quiet tragedy of feeling develops, spoken for the most part in the soundless whispers of conspirators."

The company's opening bill in New York was *Romeo*. Balletgoers here had seen many a pantomime piece more brilliant and beautiful. But what they had looked forward to seeing was the Bolshoi's fabulous dance power, and *Romeo* kept that under cover all evening.

Ulanova's vividness saved the first night. When she bent her neck toward her partner in a lift of the bedroom scene, the gesture had the tragic quiet Pasternak speaks of. Or take the opposite kind of moment. Faced with marriage to County Paris, Juliet, her mantle flung round her, desperately rushes along the apron to Friar Lawrence; armed by him with the sleeping potion, she flings the mantle round her again, and rushes desperately along the apron back home. The fling, the rush, the exact repeat are pure *Perils of Pauline*. But Ulanova's art at that moment is so brilliant the audience breaks into delighted applause.

You can find out something about Bolshoi style by trying the gymnastics of Ulanova's fling and rush yourself. Standing in the middle of the room, fling an arm across your chest, and at the same time raise the breastbone as high as it will go, bending it over at the top so it pushes the neck back. Don't let go, keep forcing the breastbone further, but in addition push the neck forward as hard as you can, and lift your head until you feel "desperately resolved." (It may make you cough.) And now, keeping the stance you are in unchanged, rush about the room with an incredible lightness and rapidity. If your family is watching, they will pick you off the floor, and urge you to try harder.

The special stance of fling and rush you just tried (it involves a backbend between the shoulder blades) is not classical. It has been called the pouterpigeon silhouette by Walter Terry, and that is just how it looks. But when Ulanova does it, you feel it means "Here is my heart."

But if you notice that, you also notice her feet. In light runs on toe (bourrée steps) they seem to touch the floor sensitively. You see how keen the pointed foot looks in the air, during attitudes, arabesques, and passés, how clearly the leg defines and differentiates the different classic shapes. Below the waist Ulanova is a strict classicist; above the waist she alters the shape of classic motions, now slightly, now quite a lot, to specify a nuance of drama (for example, the pouter-pigeon silhouette). Neither element — the lightness below or the weight above — is weakened for the sake of the other; the combined motion keeps fluid. And often while one movement is ebbing to its end, another seems already welling up in the midriff.

The Bolshoi women share Ulanova's method, but not her vividness. The pacing — the pulse — of their movement is less varied, more predictable. Ulanova shows the unguarded timing of a spontaneous gesture. And she keeps that "motivation" throughout a role. You watch the rhythm of a specific character, the irremediable individuality. The imaginary creature onstage is much more unforeseeing than anyone around her. That holds your eye and your sympathy. Ulanova uses no other charm. She does not take the audience into her confidence; she attends to the literal mimic meaning at every moment. Her manner is that of a heroic postmistress. And yet in the pas de deux from *Sylphides,* where the meaning lies in a particular buoyancy of dancing to music, she was also at her most poignant.

At the age of nearly fifty, Ulanova does not have the luscious ease of a young ballerina. Other women of the company are stronger, more acrobatically striking, or fresh and sweet. None of them can give to a stage heroine a convincing heroism.

Though not as vivid actresses as I had expected, the principal women of the Bolshoi are dancers with authority, handsome feet, and charming figures. The impression of heaviness they give is due to effects of Bolshoi style. The pouter-pigeon stance, for instance. The first time you see the *Swan Lake* Swans hit it full strength, stepping in slow straddles and uncoiling their arms Hindu style, they look like women of great weight specially trained to move; they looked prepared for immolation. When several women go into the stance with men on stage, you wonder that the men pay little attention. Later you see why. The Bolshoi women go into pouter-pigeon in all kinds of situations, at several angles, with different steps and gestures, and out again. The stance is a regulation formula. For a formula, it is rather unattractive. It shortens the woman's neck, it makes the head look helpless, the figure dumpy. Other formulas are no less hard on the women. You keep seeing open mouths, hunched shoulders, jutted chins, arms turned inside out at the socket and avidly reaching; you keep seeing elbows bent stiff or stretched stiff, hands crooked at the wrist, impatient arms, agitated hands, bobbing heads. When the women go into this formula they look fidgety. Another formula has them look so preoccupied with an inner trouble they can't be gracious to each other or to the men. The general idea seems to be that when a woman feels deeply, she looks a bit countrified.

The men of the Bolshoi haven't the women's light feet, or their heavy emotion. They are pleasant to each other and to the women, and four-square in their bearing. They don't try for a classic distinctness in low shoulders, upright neck, and level head; they don't much turn out at the thigh, or clearly stretch their feet, or define their descent from a leap. They are self-effacing, and reliable lifters; but given the chance, several become striking dramatic dancers and mimes.

The difference between the style for men and the style for women throws the sexes into relief. On the other hand, relations between the sexes keep to a Victorian propriety. This isn't so easy in some of the big lifts, where the mutual holds and tosses are far from Victorian.

But in two folk-hero parts, Vasiliev, a very young man of nineteen, showed what the Bolshoi style for men is capable of. One or two other men leapt as high as he, but none as they leapt and danced had his power of sculptural contour in motion or his power of upbeat in rhythm. None as actors had his lion-hearted magnanimity toward the heroine, the entire company, and the whole world. In dance or mime Vasiliev's instinct for generosity and delight couldn't be bigger and truer. His style is plain; his poetic gift — no simple one — is as radiant as that of the fabulous Russian dancers of the past.

Three of the youngest women principals, Timofeyeva, Maximova, Kondratieva, are ravishingly pretty and only the least bit stuffy. A fourth, Bogomolova, according to the local experts, can meet both Bolshoi and Western standards of ballerina technique. Samokhvalova could too, very likely. Bolshoi technique stresses big jumps more than quick toes; it stresses mobility of shoulder and upper spine, and acrobatics like those of a vaudeville adagio team. Western ballerina technique requires a sharply versatile, high-speed exactitude of step and of ear and a high-tension stamina — which are not Bolshoi characteristics.

But as one grows used to Bolshoi style, the gifts of a score or more of principals, men and women, become evident. The "Highlights" programs showed their dance power best, and on those, in good-natured acrobatic audacity, the ballerina Plisetskaya outdid anybody in the world. I grew to like the individual dancers better and better.

The productions however did not gain by being seen twice. *Swan Lake,* a revised version, developed less momentum than the traditional one in London, and no poignancy. *Giselle* began well, but, becoming longer and longer, lost its drive in each act. *Stone Flower,* a Moscow novelty, tried for dance momentum and fun, but like the other Bolshoi choreography, it kept losing the upbeat of the rhythm.

The Bolshoi's dance rhythm — choreographically speaking — is neither big like Fokine's nor clear like Moiseyev's. The dances are apt to go on without gathering momentum, without getting anywhere. They come down heavy on the downbeat and slur the upbeat. At a climax they pound the downbeat. They haven't the lilt of lifting off it, or the fun of matching a counter-rhythm to the musical rhythm. They miss the upbeat buoyancy of a musical momentum, the exhilaration of a rising sweep of impetus. The rhythm is weak on resilience.

The dancers are expected to perform it with rubato, ahead or behind the music. They "shape" each phrase, treating the time values of the rhythm more elastically than the orchestra does. Each phrase has urgency, each phrase lacks repose.

You see the dancers do with devotion what they are asked to. During climaxes of emotion they are not asked for the calm and completely erect carriage of the classic ballerina and of her partner. They are not asked for the climactic suspense, the extreme responsibility of the lightest finish, the lightest musical phrasing. Since Diaghilev's time great Russian dancers have been showing us these extreme traditional resources of their art. At tragic and at happy climaxes they have shown us the power of radiance ballet can achieve. The lovely young Bolshoi ballerinas do not spread that radiance. The young Soviet violinists and pianists who visit us are in command of all the traditional musical resources, not only of amplitude of strength but also of edge and elegance and quiet. No reason the dancers should not have them too.

The Bolshoi has formalized its style and it does what it does on principle. It covers up with care the brilliantly unreasonable resources of expression which are the glory of ballet dancing. It does so to stress instead an acted mime meaning. Four or five in the company can do this convincingly; the rest, though sincere and convinced, haven't a gift for vivid acting. Nor has the choreography a gift for narration. At a three-hour stretch the company's mime of deep feeling and psychological motivation isn't absorbing. Where the Bolshoi convinces all evening is in the ample strength of a movement, and in the weight of one. And for these dance qualities, too rare in the West, it will always be welcome.

The Bolshoi means to uncover its dance power in the next few years. When it does, it will add to the literal meaning of pantomime the metaphorical meaning of dancing. As of now, Western ballet — and even our own part of it — offers more fun, a fiercer luster, more grace of irony, and much more imaginative excitement and poetic courage, though it isn't stronger and is ever so much less secure.

Hudson Review, Winter 1959–60

Martha at Sixty-Eight

Martha is sixty-eight. The moves she makes are sketched. At crucial moments the timing is extremely vivid. She holds her audience by imagination. She does it all evening long in *Clytemnestra,* several seasons old now, a masterpiece as weird as Melville. But her public wants to see her every year, and that keeps her troupe going. The news is what the troupe has done to itself. It has blossomed.

It hadn't found out how to until the end of last season; it had been a strong severe bud for about twenty years. It had been bold about being in earnest, but timid about being lively. (Remember the then Sadler's Wells on its first postwar night in Paris? — like that.) Now it dances with "go," taking headlong risks, a nervy, vivid, big-time performance style. This year's new pieces were on the daft side, but that didn't stop the ensemble performance style. The troupe caught its fever from the amazing dancer in it, Paul Taylor; but the point is, the Graham style doesn't blur when the troupe gives it a whirl — it gets clearer. That is Martha's latest victory.

Twenty years ago I used to watch her get herself into an amazing full-force move or stance that left her no way out; then she found an astonishing way to get out and go on. That was how I began watching her technique. When the drama got stuck tight, she would pick up a prop and find a way to go on. I watched her drive her role so far into tragedy, she was stuck with it; she shook it, got it loose, and went on with it.

What has got her ensemble style unstuck has been ballet — not the steps, but the balance and spring. On its own account and in its own terms ballet has reinvented several of her inventions — the starfish- or octopus-type mobility, the angular accents, hip or shoulder thrusts, asymmetrical stances and moves, the sudden changes of pace. There are more. To be sure, somebody or other in daily life keeps inventing all these kinds of moving and stopping, if only a child.

Not that the Graham style and ballet are fusing. Music parts them. Ballet moves inside it, modern dance outside. A Graham piece makes a free-verse-type rhythm different from the musical rhythm of the score it is timed to. Its form is unlike the form of the score. That makes me "read" it as a kind of mime.

As I look back on twenty years of Graham choreography as on some ritualized kind of mime, the vivid decision of its action, the rapidity and range of its gesture meanings jumping by free association from close at hand to remote, the turbulence and vehemence of the dramatic powers invoked have been extraordinary. It has been unique. I know ballet fans who feel passionately that the work is wrong in principle. As for me, its principles make those of ballet the clearer. A life of such enormous energies that keeps pouring itself according to its fate into the imaginative world of dance is a godsend.

Unpublished, Spring 1961

Balanchine Choreographing

When George Balanchine was about to choreograph *Variants,* to a new score by Gunther Schuller, I was asked to report the process as clearly as I should be able to; Rudolph Burckhardt was to take photographs. Mr. Balanchine very generously gave us permission to attend rehearsals.

The wall clock in a large classroom at the School of American Ballet marked five minutes before the hour. Two dancers, Melissa Hayden and Arthur Mitchell, were doing a few final stretches at the barre; they paused and began to wipe their faces and necks. Balanchine stood beside the piano intently reading his copy of the score. He turned to the pianist and asked a question; the pianist played several dissonances and they discussed the point for a moment. Balanchine went back to reading. The dancers had come to the center of the room, where they stood gossiping in subdued voices, glancing toward the piano and then into the mirror which faced them the whole length of the wall. Still absorbed, the choreographer put down his score, looked pleasantly at the dancers, and went over to join them. He signaled to the pianist. The music began with a single note, then a pause, then a chromatic tinkle of rapid notes; the tinkle stopped, started off willfully in another direction; dissonant chords accompanied unpredictably. Balanchine clapped his hands and the pianist broke off. The pianist then repeated from the beginning and broke off at the same point.

Balanchine took his dancers to a far corner of the room — equivalent to the upstage wings, stage left. He placed the boy in front of the girl. At the single first note, they were to run to the center of the room and stop at the beginning of the tinkle. They did this to music. Then without music he showed the boy how to step aside, turn toward the girl, take a step sideways upstage, and offer her his right hand. Taking the girl's part, he showed her how to take the boy's right hand in her left, at the same time turning to face him and stepping boldly back, so that she ended clasping his hand at arm's length, standing with bent knee on one foot, leaning toward him, her other leg extended horizontally behind her in a ballet pose called arabesque. The moves for both dancers were very fast, the final pose was held for a moment. All this the dancers did at once with no difficulty, and repeated it to music. Then Balanchine, substituting for the boy, showed him how to step back, raising the hand by which he held the girl; the action pulled her forward; she caught her balance on both feet, her knees bent a bit like the boy's. Still clasping each other's hand, but with rounded backs pulling away from one another, the two bodies seen in profile made a kind of O figure, which held them poised. The dancers did this at once and repeated everything from the beginning, to music. "Tha-at's right," said Balanchine in an absorbed way, looking at the final pose. "Then maybe we do this."

Taking the girl's part, he showed her how to raise the hand which joined her to the boy, bending her arm at the elbow, and at the same time turning away, so she pulled him after her in profile for a few rapid steps on toe toward the side of the room. That they did easily. Next, as she stood, one foot before the other on toe (in fourth position), the boy, pulling back from the waist, and bracing himself one foot against the other, stopped her. At this stop their bodies made a second and different O figure. But the dancers could barely manage it. The boy couldn't, in this fast move, brace himself very firmly. Balanchine, who had first done it, now did it again. He showed the boy the foot position — the left on the ground, the right turned out, pressed on the instep of the left and pointed down. The dancer tried again, the choreographer showed once more. When Balanchine did it, the pull back from the waist looked quicker and sharper; when he braced his feet, the toe of the raised one seemed to cling to the floor. But when at the third try the dancers did this figure no differently from at first, he said, "Tha-at's right," and went on. Taking the girl's part, he showed her how to turn the wrist of the hand by which she held the boy, then turn that arm at the shoulder, and extend it, so without letting go she now had room to step ahead. She took two steps, swung out in a deep lunge, and ended poised on one foot, with bent knee; her free arm had swung ahead, the free leg back in arabesque again. She had pulled the boy a step or two after her. With this move the dancers had no trouble.

Now Balanchine asked them to go back to the beginning and set the whole sequence to counts. They went back to the far corner; but as they stood ready, he stopped them. He now put the boy behind the girl instead of in front of her. This required a change at the end of the first run to center, because now when they stopped, the boy had to step aside and downstage to give her his hand, instead of aside and upstage. No difficulty. They were about to start when he stopped them again. He told them not to run in on the first note as before, but to wait a moment and run in on the silence; he explained that the single first note would be played on the vibraphone, and would reverberate; there wouldn't be a silence onstage as there was now with the piano. They now began again.

The run looked different. Before, the boy running ahead seemed to be blocking the girl's escape. Now she stopped of her own free will and gave him the opportunity to invite her to dance. It was less tense; but with less time, the run became faster and fresher.

At the first note of the tinkle they started to count. They counted aloud by eighth notes to a bar or half-bar, doing the motions and rests at the same speed, or within a hair's breadth, as they had been doing them before, but with more edge. They were delighted to find when they reached the last lunge that everything fitted. "Tha-at's right," the choreographer said. The second O figure, the bothersome one, had lost a half-count's rest in the process, but he went ahead. Taking the girl's final lunging pose, he found after a few tries that she could easily step back erect, and then whirl toward the boy, still holding his hand. Whirling around twice, she wrapped herself first in her arm and then in his. As she whirled, her unattached arm was wrapped in with her. She now stood facing front, close to the boy, imprisoned so to speak, and he could step closer yet, and put his free arm lightly around her waist. But no further initiative was left her. Balanchine took the imprisoned girl's part; then he took the boy's part; he seemed to consider various directions but he found none he liked. The dance had run itself into a blind alley. He asked the dancers to repeat the last moves, and watched them twice. They looked as if their hearts were bravely sinking. Then as they stood in the final pose, he went up to the girl, took her by the shoulders, and started pushing her toward the floor. After a moment, she understood and tried sinking out of the arms wrapped around her. Balanchine took her place and did it easily. She tried again, and struggled hard, but something or other was in her way. It couldn't be done. Watching her closely as she struggled, he went up to her and started pulling on the unattached arm that was wrapped in front of her, her right arm. With a happy smile, she caught on; she went back to the previous lunge, and the whirl that followed; wrapping herself up, then extricating the extra arm, she found room easily to sink down out of her imprisonment, duck under the arm she held the boy's hand by, and come up outside, free to move anywhere, but still holding his hand. For the dancers this move was a Houdini-style joke, and they were delighted. Setting the move to counts was easy.

The girl now stood facing center stage, and in a few steps she led the boy there; now they both stood center, facing front; they let go of each other's hand and began to a ⅜ count a stylized lindy kick figure, in counterrhythm to each other, just as the music burst into a ⅜ bar of jitterbug derivation.

By that time three-quarters of an hour had passed since the rehearsal began; everybody had worked cheerfully and fast. But beginning with the ⅜ lindy-type figure everybody's concentration seemed to double. Balanchine invented one novel figure after another. They began and ended within what seemed to be a bar or two. The figures kept the dancers within hand's reach of each other, and now more, now less, kept the flavor of a lindy-type couple dance. Very rapid, unexpectedly complex, quite confined, the figures, sharply contrasted, kept changing direction. But in sequence the momentum carried through. When the entire ballet was finished, this turned out to be a general characteristic it had.

At that first rehearsal, the choreographer did not mention that he intended it, or what he intended. Nor did the dancers ask. They concentrated on the moves he was making. They hurried to learn each figure as it was invented, to repeat it by counts, and to memorize the sequence by counts to the score. At the end of two and a half hours about one minute of the ballet had been made. Onstage this turned out to be the first half of the fourth of the ballet's seven sections — a section for solo vibraphone and a chamber-sized orchestral group.

As for the part described in detail — the ten-second introduction — onstage it turned out that the composer wanted for it a tempo radically different from the one it had been choreographed at; the steps were changed, and passed unnoticed.

Making a ballet takes an unbounded patience from everybody concerned. An outsider is fascinated to be let in on the minuteness of the workmanship. But then he finds no way out of that minuteness. Listening to the same few bars pounded again and again on the piano, watching the same movements started at top speed and broken off, again and again, the fascinated outsider after two hours and a half of that finds himself going stir crazy. Seeing a ballet in the theater one is carried into a world of zest and grandeur by the momentum of action and music. In performance the dancers look ravishing. In rehearsal they look like exhausted champions attempting Mount Everest, knowing how limited the time is, step by step, hold by hold, roped together by the music, with the peak nowhere in sight.

In the second half of the Hayden-Mitchell pas de deux, Balanchine invented a figure in which the girl, facing front, poised with bent knee on one toe, performed a little "turned-in" adagio exercise, as she reached back for support to her partner, who was doing a sideways shuffle behind her in $\frac{5}{8}$. The dancers caught on after a few tries. Even after they had, the choreographer, pher, calling the counts sharply, made them repeat it — quite unlike his usual procedure. He did it again at a much later rehearsal after — though he wasn't aware of it — Miss Hayden had pulled a calf muscle the night before onstage. As she repeated the figure again and again — so she told me — the injury became painful. But as she kept repeating it, angry though she was, and trying to give the rhythm a keener edge, she found the key she had been looking for — the key to the character of her role.

At the third rehearsal, Balanchine began a pas de deux for Diana Adams and John Jones. From the start it was a violently explosive dance. Within a few minutes, Miss Adams stopped with a slightly pained look and turned away, but a moment later she was back at work. She didn't mention that her right arm had been badly wrenched. For the rest of the rehearsal, many of the very fast moves she memorized required her partner to give her sudden pulls to her arm, now to one, now to the other, often while the arm was suddenly being turned inside out. Rehearsal the next day was even more strenuous. After two hours of it, at a move the unsteady execution of which puzzled the choreographer, she apologized, saying she was sure she could do it right at a later rehearsal when her arm was better. He at once changed the next move to her good arm, saying, "We need that arm tonight." And work went on. That evening she was to dance the ballerina part in the full-length *Nutcracker,* the season's first performance, and all the reviewers would be watching her. She danced it beautifully.

Variants was rehearsed during the ballet season, when the dancers in addition to performance and class have repertory rehearsals as well; union rules specified the hours available. Besides inventing his ballet at such hours, Balanchine also had every morning and evening decisive responsibilities in running the company and planning its future.

Between September and November, he had made four new pieces. The first, to the most recent Stravinsky score, was followed by a ballet to Donizetti music; then he presented an hour-long ballet set to two song cycles by Brahms and called *Liebeslieder Walzer. Liebeslieder Walzer* — with a cast of eight — turned out to be a masterpiece, glorious and magical. No other choreographer, no other company could have done it; but one isn't aware of that, the poetry of it — the secret image — is so absorbing. Two weeks after *Liebeslieder* he presented *Ragtime,* a duet witty and deceptively elementary in the way the Stravinsky score is. Six days after *Ragtime,* he began *Variants.*

Balanchine usually prepares a ballet far in advance. He has said that he prepares for a long time by playing and studying the score — "I listen, listen, listen, listen." On the other hand, he does not look for steps until the actual performers are with him in the rehearsal studio.

Variants had been commissioned at his request. Like some of Schuller's previous music, it was to be in third-stream style, scored for the Modern Jazz Quartet and symphonic orchestra. The choice implied a third-stream-type ballet, a nonexistent species. Balanchine prepared for it by listening to jazz albums. He didn't study the score during the summer layoff while he was growing roses, because until September Schuller was too busy to begin writing it. The last installment of the piano version was delivered in November.

The composer's plan — a suite — featured the Jazz Quartet artists singly and jointly accompanied by small orchestral groups; the introduction was for full orchestra, the conclusion for full orchestra plus the Quartet. The choreographer's plan was a dance suite. He wanted half the cast — two solo boys and eight ensemble girls — to be Negroes; but the girls weren't found. He picked his dancers, cast each of the dance numbers, decided which numbers to make first. At that point the first rehearsal sheet was posted, the date for opening night confirmed.

At the start of the first rehearsal he chose a way of working which he kept until the whole piece had been created. At every point he took each role. The process looked like this. Standing near the dancer, he signaled the pianist to play ahead, and clapped his hands when he wanted him to break off. The pianist repeated the fragment once or twice while Balanchine listened intently. Then without music he took the position in which the dancer would have to start, and stood absorbed, sometimes turning his head very slightly in this direction or that, sometimes slightly moving on his feet. He was inventing the next figure. He seemed to test the feel of it, and decide. That done, he glanced at the dancer, stressed the starting position, and without music showed the move. The first time he showed it, he did it from start to finish at full performance force and speed.

The dancers reproduced it, adding to it at once — in ballet style — the full extension of the body, the turnout of legs and feet, the toe step or leap he had merely implied. A nondancer might have wondered how they could guess so much; but they seemed to guess right almost always. As expert dancers they were following out the logical balletic consequences of the main move he had shown. Sometimes they asked about a detail left in doubt, and he specified the answer in ballet terminology.

Moving at the speed and force he had shown, the fully extended bodies of the dancers sometimes developed a sudden momentum that was scary. But the jet of it took the dancer to the right spot at the right instant. The impetus came from eccentric swings from the shoulder or waist, the support from handholds. When the choreographer first showed such a move, he literally threw himself into it, and let his feet take care of themselves. When the dancers couldn't manage the move, he repeated it. Between them they tracked down the trouble to a change of hand, a specific angle or stance, or an extra step which he had taken instinctively and which the dancers had overlooked.

Soon, when he made such a move the first time, he repeated it at once, stressing how the feet stepped and the hands reached for support. At the second rehearsal, he spent more than a half hour on a fantastic sequence lasting a few bars that wouldn't work to counts: after that whatever took too long to learn he discarded before it was set by counts to the music. (Had he been making a piece in regulation ballet steps to music easy to remember by ear, the process would have been far less cumbersome.)

Balanchine's care was for the mechanics of momentum. He did not mention expression. Watching him do a move full force, an outsider might often have been struck by his expression in it — a quality of gesture which was directly to the point. It was beautiful. The dancers did not imitate that. Their expression when it appeared was their own, and he did not criticize it. Expression seemed to be treated as a Jeffersonian inalienable right. And perhaps it is.

Later rehearsals were moved to the theater building, to a gloomy echoing room upstairs modeled on a chapter room in a castle of the Knights Templar. Here Balanchine took the dancers by shifts and choreographed from ten-thirty to six. "I work like a dentist," he remarked. He sometimes looked exhausted, but a joke revived him. When dancers lost the count, he did not nag or look depressed. The phrases he made for the chorus were easy motions, but their peculiar timing required exact counts. He kept checking the counts in the score. During ten-minute or half-hour breaks, he stayed alone in the rehearsal room, rereading the score, playing it, checking on the metronome speed. The composer, who was to conduct the ballet, watched a rehearsal, and Balanchine brought up the metronome speed; he referred to the metronome speed given in the score; Schuller, experienced with orchestras but not with Balanchine choreography, evaded his insistence. Solo rehearsals, chorus rehearsals, stage rehearsals, orchestra rehearsals, dress rehearsals, lighting rehearsals.

The first orchestra rehearsal for the dancers came the day before opening. The dancers had become used to recognizing landmarks or cues in the piano score. The colorful orchestration obliterated these. But they had expected as much. Since they had memorized the score by counts, they could perform to the measure whatever unforeseen noises the orchestra made. Disaster threatened nevertheless. Finding the music difficult, the instrumentalists slowed down; but the dancers, rushing headlong, couldn't slow down without toppling. The momentum of their off-balance rushes worked at a specific speed that had been agreed on between composer and choreographer and fixed by metronome. The dancers had to rely on it and now it turned unreliable. The choreographer's well-known coolness adjusted what was possible. And suddenly the first night's performance was over. There was polite applause.

Having seen as I had how the ballet grew and the adorably unselfish work that went into it, my view of the first night was not that of a theatergoer or of a critic. But the first night flop did not deter later audiences. They came at least to hear the Modern Jazz Quartet and the new Schuller score. The concentration of the dancers, the virtuosity of the ballerinas were watched by these music fans with close attention; they appreciated the range of resource by which the dancing matched the twelve-tone logic of the score.

The dance fans agreed about all the virtuosity, but they found the twelve-tone "third-stream" angle more strain than fun. In addition, the piece had been announced as "new jazz," and it wasn't contemporary jazz in its dancing. They objected to the thirties-type jive steps, to the show biz-type gesture, to the sour nightclub look of the staging. As for the dancing, the partners couldn't let each other alone for a moment, the dances couldn't leave out a beat, nobody could dance except on top of the beat. Current jazz dancing separates partners, omits beats, lets the beat pull away, anticipates it; and that elasticity of attack characterizes the gesture, and varies it. The source of style isn't professional, but year by year emerges in the private dancing of a few high school students; the measure of style is its "go." The dance fans had seen the athletic overtones of *Agon,* which in some unliteral way came closer to the image of jazz than any jazz ballet yet has. They hoped that *Variants* would do for jazz what *Liebeslieder* does for the waltz.

In performance onstage, *Variants* keeps reminding one of conventional Broadway — that sort of jazz plus modern plus ballet. The numbers suggest corny types of stage jazz — the hot number, the ritual-magic one, the snake-hips, the arty, the pert one; the long finale quotes from the show, and ends with a decorative modernistic collapse for the entire cast, capped by a Brigitte Bardot "beat" pose for the two leading ladies. The dancers suggest that hard-shell type of dance very handsomely. But the rhythm they dance to isn't show-dance rhythm; it isn't quite jazz either. One recognizes jazzlike steps but one doesn't feel at home. The action of a step keeps being pointed up differently, retimed, rerouted, tightened, enlarged by ballet logic. At a retard several short numbers end with, one seems to watch a powerful momentum sink quickly from the dancers into the floor (like water into sand), leaving their last moves massive. The emotion is one of grandeur, the gesture is showbiz. Becoming interested, one sees a massive dance momentum started, developed, ended within two minutes, a drive different from one number to the next. By the time one has found out how to "see" the piece, the finale comes and ruins it. The finale, four times as long as the previous numbers, and crowded, has no momentum; nor has it any in the score.

Schuller's score features the shy, extremely musical sonorities of Lewis's Modern Jazz Quartet surrounded by orchestral sonorities, original in color or jazz implication. Such a texture takes more rehearsal than a ballet company can afford. The Quartet, progressive style, implies a jazz beat while playing a variable nuance behind. Not the orchestra. It plays by measure.

The progressive-style "delayed" beat, when featured, troubled the dancers who were dancing to the measure. But the jazz beat does not take over the score. The structural drive of the score is twelve-tone, not by beat but by phrase. To the specific twelve-tone phrase, to its momentum and shape, Balanchine had set the dance — first by ear, then checking and rechecking the count of the measure by the written notes.

Unlike Balanchine's twelve-tone part of *Episodes* — particularly the section danced by Paul Taylor, in which the shape of a "step" became equivalent to the shape of a musical phrase — *Variants* did not keep surprising the onlooker by the dramatic fantasy of its gesture. But it did have extraordinary moments — during the Adams-Jones duet, for instance, when, at the speed of fury, the complexity and the force of momentum disassociate the gesture from its Broadway connotations, and burst open its hard shell. At such moments *Variants* became a jazz ballet more powerful and grandly integrated than any yet.

Between two rehearsals Balanchine, after answering a question of mine about jazz, added, "In any case, we don't do jazz here, we do ballet; we try to make it as interesting as possible." Before rehearsals began, Schuller brought up the matter of jazz nuances of rhythm; the choreographer listened and then said that the way he made dances, the dancers were "inside the nuance."

Watching Balanchine at work, one could see he was thinking in terms of ballet action flavored by jazz action. One did not see him worry where the flavor might take him, or worry about the overall shape of a dance before he had made it. He seemed to be eating his way through the score, finding his way move by move. After he had found a move, one could see that it took its point from the pressure of drama and, if one may say so, the pressure of visibility which at that moment of the dance were at stake. (The previous move might be topped by a contradiction or an unexpected evasion, as in dramatic dialogue.) But looking for a new move, he seemed to find it by following an instinctive dance impulse of his body. Nearly always he trusted to his body's first response, while he was concentrating on the exact force of momentum the music offered for the next move.

The force of dance momentum derived from the score is a resource of ballet that he has developed further than anyone anywhere. He keeps enlarging its powers of speed, agility, intelligence, and fun. With twelve dancers he finds a momentum that feels like forty dancers; with forty, it feels like a hundred. His company dances three times as much per minute as any other.

Momentum and gesture are the dramatic resources of dancing, which ballet combines in several ways. One way is that of the nineteenth-century prolonged dance climax, a grand pas de deux with related choral and soloist numbers. The climax may be a tragic or a festive event but — like in opera — the scale of it is expressed by lyric meditations on it. In principle the shining virtuoso dance feat is also a gesture-metaphor derived from the dramatic situation, and an echo of the feat reverberates in the other numbers before and after, which prolongs the momentum.

Balanchine's so-called abstract ballets extend this traditional merging of gesture and dance momentum. The specific gesture is implicit in the actions of the step. It appears in the formal momentum in shape and rhythm so organically fused that one responds to both of these poles of dramatic meaning jointly, and follows the highly active meditation with delighted astonishment. The individual's absorbed gesture, carried by a powerfully developed momentum which reverberates its secret, reveals a grander and more innocent meaning than one expects to see. Remembered, it grows on the scale of the momentum. This power of poetry has long been the glory of ballet, and Balanchine's is that he succeeds in it so often. But the question of how he does it is not answered by watching him at work.

Kulchur, 1962

Forms in Motion and in Thought

In dancing one keeps taking a step and recovering one's balance. The risk is a part of the rhythm. One steps out of and into balance; one keeps on doing it, and step by step the mass of the body moves about. But the action is more fun and the risk increases when the dancers step to a rhythmic beat of music. Then the pulse of the downbeat can lift the dancer as he takes a step, it can carry him through the air for a moment; and the next downbeat can do it again. Such a steady beat to dance on is what a dancer dreams of and lives for. The lightness that music gives is an imaginary or an imaginative lightness. You know it is an illusion, but you see it happen; you feel it happen, you enjoy believing it. There is a bit of insanity in dancing that does everybody a great deal of good.

It has been doing people good for a long time. Looking at Paleolithic cave paintings, one can recognize the powerfully developed dance sense our ancestors had fifteen thousand years ago. What are all those bison of theirs floating on, if not on a steady beat? A Brooklyn teenager would feel at home among the Magdalenian cave painters once the dancing started and he heard that beat. And a late-Paleolithic youth who dropped in on a gym or a ballroom going wild at two in the morning to the blasts of a name band would see right away that it was a bison ritual. And if he broke into a bison step, the kids near enough to see him would only say, "Wow," or "Dig that rustic shag."

And an educated late-Paleolithic magician, if he dropped in on a performance of classic ballet in an air-conditioned theater, would find a good deal he was familiar with — the immense, awesome, drafty cavern, the watching tribe huddled in the dark, and in a special enclosure the powerful rhythmic spectacle which it is taboo to join in. As a magic man he would find it proper that the dancers are not allowed to speak, not allowed to make any everyday movements, to show any signs of effort, or even of natural breathing; and equally correct that the musicians are kept hidden in a ritual pit. The orchestra conductor would strike him as a first-class wizard. This singular character stands up in the pit waving a wand and is respectfully treated by the audience as invisible. Though it is hard for him, he does his best not to look at the dancers; when his eyes stray to the stage, he pulls them down at once, visibly

This essay had its genesis in a lecture, prepared in 1954, for dance students at the Juilliard School. Denby revised it extensively for book publication a decade later.

upset. He keeps in constant agitation, without ever doing a dance step or touching an instrument, and his costume consists of a pair of long black tails. The Magdalenian visitor, familiar with demented clowns who represent pre-male types of fertilization, would recognize the ironic function of this indispensable figure. And as the curtain fell, he would clap with the rest, delighted by a ceremony so clever in its nonsense and so sweeping in its faith.

If a New Yorker were to tell him, "But you're missing the point, ballet is an art, it isn't a ritual," he might answer, "You no like that word 'ritual'? You say it about our ballet, so I think maybe a nice word." And his Paleolithic girlfriend might add, "Please, are you a critic? We hear critics will roast fat dancer tonight, just like we do at home. Yum, yum."

Students of culture have suggested that an art of dance preceded that of Paleolithic painting. One can see it might well be so. One can see hints of dance at stages of living one thinks of as extremely remote. The stage of culture at which our species showed the first hints of dancing need not have been beyond that of several species of contemporary wild animals. Some of them that can be greedy and fierce have sexual maneuvers that are harmless and take time. On the one hand such a ceremony can be interrupted, it doesn't necessarily lead into the sexual act; on the other hand the act may occur with a minimum of ceremony. The animals seem to be aware of a ritual that is imaginative and that is fairly impractical. Their ceremonies aren't all sexual ones either. Wolves and fishes have special fighting ones. And the birds that swoop low and soar up sharply at dusk over a town square or in a clearing of the woods are very likely catching an insect in their open bills, but they seem to be ritualizing the action in a way they don't ritualize their feeding during the day. It is a special bedtime one. Standing among the ruins of the Palatine toward sunset late in October, I saw a flock of migrant birds keeping close like a swarm, beating their small wings almost in unison, forming — the swarm of them — a single revolving vibrating shape which kept changing in the air — a shape that distended, that divided like an hourglass, that streamed out like a spiral nebula and then condensed again into a close sphere, a series of choreographic figures which rose and fell above the city as the flock drifted upstream and out of sight. A social celebration and a prehistoric pleasure.

Birds seem to have made a number of dance inventions that strikingly resemble our own. They have sociable group numbers, intimate duets and perhaps trios, and private solos. You see the performers assume a submissively graceful or a show-off air. They seem to be enjoying a formal limitation as they move in relation to a center, and even as they move in relation to a lapse of time. Much as we do, they compose their piece out of contrasted energetic and gliding motions, out of reiterated gestures, out of circular paths and straight lines. Bees even use path patterns for a sign language. A returned honeybee performs for her hive-mates a varying number of circles which she keeps cutting with a straight line always in one direction, and her audience understands from her choreography in what direction and how far off are the flowers she has newly discovered. After that she passes around samples of the honey, as if she were giving her dance a title. Such an action does not seem like a ritual to us, but the bees find it very practical.

A formal path involves electing a base from which to move, it involves giving a spot an arbitrary imaginative value. It is a feat of imagination essential to dancing. Birds understand the feat. Cats are very good at it when they play games. One can see their cat eyes brightening with an imaginative light as they establish their base. Kittens begin to play with no sense of a base and gradually learn to imagine. It would be fun to see lions playing from a base the same way, pretending to hunt a bright rag on the end of a rope, pouncing, prancing, darting, tumbling head over heels. I imagine they do it in a wild state and would enjoy doing it in the circus if a lion tamer could be found to play with them.

Animals tame or wild do not seem to mimic anybody but themselves. One notices that their dancelike inventions are formal in principle. One may infer from it how far back in our history or how deep in our nature the formal aspect of dancing is.

But one notices too that the wild animals don't enjoy watching our performances as much as we do theirs. Rattlesnakes are glad to escape from a bunch of fertility-celebrating Indians. Hungry wolves and lions have never been known to venture on a group of enthusiastically stepping Russians or Africans. Our primitive social celebrations intimidate them. It may be they find the energy of them overpowering, or else that they are appalled by the excessive regularity of them, which is foreign to their habits. None of them time their movements to a regular beat of artificial noise as we do. Dancing to a beat is as peculiarly human a habit as is the habit of artificially making a fire.

Stepping to a manmade beat is a dance invention of a formal nature that we alone have made. Presumably we first danced without a beat, the way animals and small children do. Even trained animals don't catch the formality of a

beat. Seals and monkeys like to clap, they can learn to play
can't keep time either way. Riders can direct horses to keep
remember a circus orchestra taking its beat from an old she-ele
danced the conga, but it was her rhythm, not the orchestra's. How c
species ever have been bright enough to invent the beat? Nowadays we
even bright enough to explain it.

There used to be an opinion that the beat was invented by externalizing o
objectifying our heartbeat, that it was first beaten and then stepped to. The
prevalent opinion now seems to be that both the regular acoustic beat and
the regularly timed step were invented simultaneously, as a single invention.
One tries to imagine unknown races of men — tens of thousands of years
before the elegant Magdalenians — as they hopped in the glacial snow for
fun, laughing and yelling, and first heard a kind of count, an oscillating one-
two in their ritual action. They may have heard it in the grunt of their own
shout, broken as they landed full weight from a leap, over and over. Or else
heard it when an older woman, out of pleasure at the tumultuous stepping of
the young men, clapped sedately, and one of the boys found himself keeping
time with her, and both she and he got more and more excited by the mutual
communication. Or else they might have heard a beat when a word shouted
over and over as they were stepping turned into a unison metric chant that
they stepped to. Perhaps as they stepped and exaggerated a hoarse panting
noise of breathing, they heard each other's breath and their own coming
simultaneously and were thrilled by the simultaneous step action.

However people began to keep time, one imagines the eerie thrill they felt
as they found themselves aware of hearing a beat from the outside and of
taking a step from the inside, both of them at once. One can still feel a far
echo of that thrill as one first finds oneself hitting the beat; or later in life, as
one finds oneself stepping securely to a complex rhythm one isn't able to
follow consciously. It is a glorious sensation inside and outside of one. For
our ancestors the experience, subjective and objective at the same instant,
must have been a wonderful intensification of identity. So peculiar a thrill
could have been discovered and then forgotten and rediscovered by exceptional geniuses among successive races and successive climatic epochs. The
invention ended by becoming an immensely popular one. But we cannot say
that it has been entirely successful. Even now, after fifty or a hundred thousand years of practice, a number of us still can't keep time, and shuffle about a
ballroom floor missing the measure.

thing as grace of movement. Animals, small
without a beat but with the grace of dancing
...utiful to people who like to watch them. But
...nuch for those who watch as for those who do
...ment and an extra power. The extra power is like
People are so to speak their better selves. They fly

...dance till dawn in a ballroom or who are performers onstage
...ly pour out as much extra energy as they otherwise would be able
...y grimly in a matter of life or death. The wild animals cannot waste
...ich energy on fun. To our species the invention of stepping to a regular
...at of manmade noise offers an occasion for the extravagant expense of
powers which is the special achievement of our human civilization. And
when there is grace in the extravagance and beauty in the excess, we are
delighted with ourselves.

Looking back, then, one can see that animals invented for their ceremonies
a formal limitation of movement. They do not move in every possible way,
they move in a few particular ways. For us the added formal invention of the
beat increased the artificiality much further. What had once been only instinctive animal patterns became human objective rhythms as well. They
gained an objective measure. The subjective-objective or double awareness
of stepping which the beat awakened gave an extra exuberance of power to
the dancers. It also sharpened a sense of representation, the sense that a step
action can also be a magic emblem. So dancing became exhilarating not only
to do, but also to watch, to remember, and to think about. From being an
instinctively formal pleasure, it became the kind of beautiful communication
we call an art. In this way our ancestors invented an art — and perhaps all of
art — when they regularized their dancing to a timed beat and a timed step.

The rhythmic stress of stepping is a habit of communication or expression
which reaches into the present from unrecognizable races, from epochs and
festivals when individuals of genius first made fires, first spoke in sentences.
They grin and glare at us, and sit down beside us, these astonishing geniuses,
and we feel their powerful wonder as they watch our young people dance, as
they watch the bright ballet danced onstage at the same time as we do. They
wonder at it, but they know how to watch it, they can see that it is some
special kind of dancing.

I seem to be prowling about the subject like a nature photographer prowling about the countryside. The subject is expression in ballet. And I think you see what I am concerned with. I am bringing up some very general features of expression, and am trying to catch the expression of ballet from various points of view. Unless you can catch it in motion, you don't catch it at all. What I have caught of it seems to be as unspecific as a blur on the edge of the camera field. But you will notice something or other about it, I believe, and recognize something about the expression, and see it independently of what I say, as a fact of nature — I mean as a fact of human nature. That is what I am concerned with.

We were discussing the beat of the step in general terms. As you step to a beat, you feel the rhythmic pressure of your foot against the floor. You have the rhythm in your feet, so people say, and your feet start to dance. The rhythm of steps is beaten by the floor contact. It is stamped, or tapped or heel-struck, or shuffled. The onlookers catch the rhythm and they instinctively participate in the dancing as long as they stay with the step rhythm.

As the dancer steps he can hear the beat elsewhere than in the feet. And he often makes gestures that are visible rhythmic accents. In the Sahara there is a beautiful solo dance in which the girl moves only on her knees and beats the rhythm with sharp elbow, wrist, and finger positions. But in any dance the shape of the body is just as evident when it isn't hitting the beat as when it is. Between beats it keeps moving rhythmically, it keeps making contrasting motions. And as it does, it makes visual shapes the rhythm of which is a sculptural one. Watching the dancers, one sees this other rhythm of shape that their bodies make. Sometimes the dancers and onlookers are so obsessed with the acoustic beat of the step rhythm that they take very little interest in the visual shape rhythm; on the other hand, they sometimes take a great deal of interest in the action of the shapes.

Watching the shape of a movement is something we all do a great deal of in everyday life. You may recognize your friends at a distance by the shape of their walk, even unconsciously. One can often recognize foreigners in America or Americans abroad by a characteristic national shape of walking that one has never particularly thought about. As for average citizens passing down a city street, plenty of them have oddities in the shape of walking one notices right away — a turned-out forearm that dangles across the back, or a head that pecks, a torso that jiggles up and down, a chest that heaves from side to side. Men and women walking on the street keep making personal shapes with their legs — they snap their heels at the sidewalk, they drawl one thigh past the other, they bounce at each step or trip or stalk or lope, or they waddle, they shuffle or bombinate. Sometimes an oddity looks adorable, but one recognizes it perfectly well as an oddity.

Battalions of parading soldiers manage to avoid the oddities of civilian walking. They show very clearly the basic shape of a walking step — the swinging arm following the opposite leg, the twist at the waist, the dip in the figure's height and the roll. Marching West Pointers can give it a massive containment, and marching parachutists can give it an undulant grace. Young women marching don't seem to give it anything pleasantly collective. They don't seem to take an innocent pride in the achievement of a step the way young men do — a pride as innocent as that of a trained dog. A collective step becomes depersonalized or homogenized only after considerable training. And then it is a monotonous shape, of interest only in multiplication.

In a parade the body looks more two-footed than usual. Two feet traveling from place to place haven't mathematically much choice in the order they can go in. Soldiers at Forward March go from two feet to one foot, then they keep going from one foot to the other foot, and they go from one foot to both feet at Halt. That makes three kinds of step, and two more exist: a hop on the same foot, and a broad jump from both feet to both feet. These five kinds are all there are. Soldiers could be trained to do all five instead of only three, and you can see right away that once they were trained, the five would look hardly less monotonous than the three.

Dancers have no more feet than other people, and so they live with the same limitation. One could try to watch a ballet from the point of view of the five kinds of step, and see how it keeps scurrying about from one kind to another inside the narrow limits of a two-footed fate. One could try, but one doesn't. As you watch a ballet, the dancers do plenty of different steps and often some new ones you hadn't seen before. One doesn't keep watching the feet to see the sequence in which they are contacting the floor. You keep watching the whole shape of the body before and after the floor contact.

Between a ballet and a parade, take watching a ballroom dance, especially one where the partners break, like a lindy or a mambo or a Virginia reel. You see the steps exhibiting the dancer's figure, the boy's or the girl's, in a series of contrasting shapes. You see it advancing toward a partner, or turning on itself; it lightly bends and stretches; the thighs close and separate, the knees open and shut, the arms swing guardedly in counteraction to the legs, or they lift both at once. The feet, the hands, the head may refuse a direction the body inclines to or they may accept it. When the waist undulates Cuban-style, the extremities delay following it with an air of detachment. As you watch a good dancer, it all looks very cute, the figure and its movable parts, and you get to know them very pleasantly.

The contrasting shapes you see the figure making are as depersonalized as those of a military step — they are sometimes close to a marching step, and the difference is no more than a slight containment, a slight glide of the foot. But the next moment they are quite unmilitary. The dancers move backward and sideways as much as forward, they kick and spin, they interweave and sway and clap, and the boys and girls keep making mutual shapes. One can see that the dance shapes add particular motions to the basic kind of step they relate to. But one also sees that if you take basic steps to be walking steps, then dance steps don't originate in them. Dance steps belong to a different species, so to speak. They don't give the body that useful patient look that walking does. They were invented for mutual fun and for the lively display of sculptural shapes. In Basque folk dancing and in ballet it is normal for a dancer to leap up and make a rapid quivering back-and-forth shape with his feet that is as far from common sense as a bird's brief trill. An entrechat suits the kind of common sense dancing has, but not any other kind.

The action of ballet exhibits the dancer's figure much further and more distinctly than that of a ballroom dance. The shapes are more exact and more extreme. The large reach of all the limbs, the easy erectness of the body regardless, the sharpness of pointed feet, the length of neck, the mildness of wrists, the keen angle of knee bends, the swiftness of sweeping arms, the full visibility of stretched legs turned out from thigh to toe, spreading and shutting; the figure in leaps, spins, stops in balance, slow-motion deployments, the feet fluttering and rushing and completely still. As it passes through such a dazzling series of transformations, you see the powerfully erect figure, effortless and friendly. It appears larger than life, like in an illusion of intimacy. And you are astonished when a performer who onstage looked so big, at a party turns out to be a wisp of a girl or a quite slender-looking boy.

A ballet dancer has been carefully trained to make the shapes of classic dancing, and one can readily see that they have specific limits. Classic steps limit the action of the joints to a few readily visible differences, so the trajectory of the body as it makes the shape is defined. A classic dancer has a habit of many years' standing of rotating, bending, and stretching the several joints of legs and arms, of the neck and spine in movements of which the start, the trajectory, and the finish have become second nature. How such a movement draws after it the rest of the body, or how it joins a movement before it or one after it, have become for him instinctive. The whole of the shape is second nature to him, and so are its component parts. He can alter a specific detail without becoming confused in the main shape. He is familiar with the impetus he must give that will mold it very clearly in each of its dimensions. And in all these shapes, whether large or small, the dancer has come to judge his momentum and his balance at varying speeds by instinct. So they appear effortless and unconfused and in harmony.

A classic dancer's legs seem to move not from the hip joint but from further up, from the waist and the small of the back; and the arms not from the shoulder, but from lower down, from the same part of the back as the legs; it lengthens both extremities and harmonizes them. The head moves at the end of a neck like a giraffe's that seems to begin below the shoulder blades. The head can also move without the neck, just from the joint where head and spine meet, tilting against a motionless neck. Then you see its small motion enlarged by the unexpected contrast to so very long and separate a neck. In the same way a flick of ankle or of wrist can be magnified by the long-looking immobile leg or arm it is at the far end of. So aspects of scale appear.

Classic action exhibits the dancer's body very clearly, but it steadily exhibits aspects of it that everyday life shows only at rare moments. Classic arms, for instance, keep to a few large trajectories and positions, they keep distinct from the torso, and the quality they exhibit in arms is the long lightness of them. They minimize the activity of elbow and wrists. In everyday life arms and hands do all the chattering, and the legs growl now and then. On the contrary in classic dancing the legs seem to carry the tune, and the arms add to it a milder second voice.

Classic legs, turned out from the hip joint down, look unusually exposed. One sees the inside surface of them, though the dancer is facing you. One sees the modeling of their parts, the differentiated action of the joints flexing or rotating — the lively bend of the knee especially. One watches the torque and powerful spread of the thighs at their base. The ballerina holds the bone turned in its socket rigid, and the leg extends itself to its complete stretch in the air, sideways, to the back, or to the front. The visually exposed action of the legs, fully turned out, fully bending and stretching, can look wonderfully generous.

No matter how large the action of legs and of arms, the classic back does not have to yield, and its stretched erectness is extremely long. It bends in or out when it chooses. The low-held shoulders open the breast or chest. But classicism doesn't feature the chest as a separate attraction the way advertising does; a slight, momentary, and beautiful lift of the rib cage is a movement of the upper back. At the back of the torso or at the front, it is the waist that one keeps looking at. Looking at it you see the figure's changing silhouette at a glance. The waist is the center of the dance shape, or the implied center. You seem to sense in its quickness a lightning anticipation of the next motion. The power of the waist is that of an athlete's, but the quickness of it is a child's.

Among the ways classicism exhibits the body that are different from those of everyday life, the most different is that of toe steps, which look like tiny stilts the girl is treading on. She can step onto them, or she can rise onto them, rising with a soft flick of both feet. She can step about on them with a fanatic delicacy and a penetrating precision. She can spin on them like a bat out of hell. When she jumps or runs on them one hears a muffled tapping that sometimes sounds fleshy. From the side you see the sole curving like a bending knife blade with at the back the queer handle of the heel. From the front they over-elongate the leg and alter the body's proportions; and the extreme erectness of the foot seems in keeping with the extremely pulled-up waist and the stretched lightness of the slender ballerina. Sometimes a figure on a single toe pointe, as its shape deploys from so narrow a balance, looks intently alone by itself, and, even if a partner supports it, intently individual. At other times one feels the contrast between the large pliancy of the knees, the lesser one of the ankles, and the scarcely perceptible give of the bones of the arch.

Toe steps sharpen one's eye to the figure's contact with the floor. The action of rhythm and the action of shape meet and keep meeting at the moment of floor contact. Classic dancing can make that moment keen to the eye so the rhythm it sees has an edge. Take for instance the moment on the ground between two leaps. You see the feet arriving stretched through the air, the ankles flex in a flash, you see the feet on the floor, motionless in their small position, catch the flying body's momentum, and instantly the ankles flash again as the legs stretch off into the air in the new leap. The feet have tossed the dancer's momentum forward, without a wobble or a blur. The eye has caught their moment of stillness the more sharply because the position they held is a familiar one that keeps returning. And that almost imperceptible stillness of theirs cuts the first shape from the second, and makes the rhythm of motion carry.

In these peculiar appearances and the recurrent complete stillness of the classic body, the eye recognizes or the imagination recognizes the sensual meaning of the exhibited parts, and the dramatic implication of their motions. It sees these implications and meanings appear and disappear. They are exhibited without the continuity or the stress that could present them as if in states of greed or of anxiety. Their moment-by-moment sensual innocence allows the imagination the more unembarrassed play.

The steps keep unfolding the body in large or small ways, and reassembling it in vertical balance like a butterfly. The peculiarity of its grace in motion is consistent and is shared by all the figures onstage. The expressive meaning is divided between recognizable details and the visual grace, the very light alternation of weight of an overall unrecognizable consistency. The consistency is as if the most usual and easy of ballet steps set a pitch for the eye — a pitch of carriage and balance in action — to which everything that is done onstage keeps a clear relation by its quality of impulse and of carriage. The overall effect is that of a spontaneous harmony of action. But its common sense remains that of a dance.

The peculiar values of classic style we have been considering are an invention extending from nowadays back into a collective past. They are in that sense traditional values. Ballet began as the kind of dancing current at village festivals around the Mediterranean from the times of King Minos and Daedalus to those of da Vinci. Young Boccaccio and young Dante before him danced these local steps; and Homer had danced them locally as a boy. The village dances changed so slowly that they were always traditional. At the edge of the holiday crowd, when the piper played, the tots tried to do the steps before they could keep time. Everyone had grown up knowing the sequences and the tunes that went with them, and knowing from having watched it the harmony that the dance could show. People always liked to watch the boys and girls do it, and liked giving a prize to the sweetest dancer. The steps were a part of the brightness of the recurrent holiday, and they brought back other bright faces and festivals that the little region had known in the past. The sense of such holidays was strong at the center of civilization for a long time, and one finds echoes of it reaching back from verses of *The Divine Comedy* to a carved Minoan cylinder three thousand years earlier depicting harvesters marching home with a band, singing and joking. In classic Greek representations of a dance step the harmony is sometimes so rich it implies contrary steps and extended phrases. Scholars have traced a number of ballet movements to classic Greek prototypes. No reason to suppose that the ancient dances were simple.

When, around the middle of the millennium before Christ, urban prosperity spread to Europe from the East, the country steps were theatricalized, first for Greek theaters, and later for the elaborate and ornate theaters of the Roman Empire. Then prosperity retreated eastward again, and for another thousand years dancing was again that of lively young people doing their local steps at balls or church festivals, with here and there some hired mimes or an anxious acrobat passing the hat. These hard-bitten comics were tramps and outsiders.

When prosperity and a pleasure in grace of behavior spread again — this time from Renaissance Italy — the country dances were theatricalized once more. Like the earlier Greek professionals, the new Italian ones rearranged the steps to new tunes, they turned them out a bit to face the public, and gave them a thread of story. They saw that the pleasure of the dances was their harmony. The pantomime they took over was that of the original holiday occasion, that of pleasant social behavior. Professionals developed indoors a sense of lyric expression in dancing. But the outdoor mimes, thanks to the same prosperity, had developed their capers and their insistent explosive pantomime into a rowdy Italian buffoonery. These two opposite kinds of expression had existed in the ancient theaters as well, and existed time out of mind, sometimes blending, sometimes not. By the seventeenth century, when theater dancing became organized, the ballet dancers were likely to sustain the sentiment, but the comics were likely to steal the show.

And here we are watching ballet in the prosperous mid-twentieth century. In a number of professional terms and steps dancers can recognize three hundred years of continuity behind them. Balletgoers can recognize two hundred years in a number of documents that evoke an artistic excitement related to their own. Though the comics still steal the show, the element which holds a ballet together and which creates the big climaxes is the one we call classic dancing. Classicism has stretched the ancient country steps and all the others it has added to them — it has stretched them vertically and horizontally to heighten the drama of dance momentum. But in its extended range of large-scale theater steps and their spectacular momentum, ballet has kept the gift of harmony it began with. Today's professionals of ballet are artists, they are virtuosos, craftsmen specialized for life. But as one watches them, just when they are at their best, history seems to vanish. The quality of character that makes a dancer seems the same as three or four thousand years ago. The nature of the pleasure they give by their genius as dancers does not seem to have changed much since Minoan times.

One July noon, in an Aegean village on the Greek island of Mykonos, two friends and I, after visiting a monastery, were waiting in the sun for the single daily bus. The torrent of heat and light was so intense that we went into a café for shelter. Inside the radio was playing folk tunes and a young farmer was dancing solo to it, while two stood around watching him and waiting for their turn. But when the second young man began, the miracle happened. The traditional steps produced an effect entirely different. The rapidity of decision, the brilliance of impetus, the grace were unforeseeable, as if on another scale. He was a dancer in the class of the classic stars one sees onstage. It was an extraordinary delight to watch him. He finished his turn. But while the next young farmer was dancing the bus honked outside, and we foreigners ran out to catch it.

An extraordinary delight such as this is the standard of theater performance. It is the standard that nature sets. A genius for dancing keeps turning up in a particular boy or girl who is doing the regulation steps he or she grew up with. Outside the theater or inside it, the gift creates an immediate communication. For some people watching such great moments at a ballet performance, the steps themselves disappear in a blaze of glory. For others the steps remain distinctly visible, but they make as much sense as if one could do them oneself. One understands them. It is like the sensation of understanding a foreign language because a girl has looked so ravishing speaking it.

But for professionals as they watched ballet dancers of genius at such great moments, and knew each step they were doing from long experience, it was the revelation of the large-scale effect possible in the familiar steps that fascinated them. Being professionals, they tried to catch the technical method. And what they caught of it during several hundred years has become classic style.

Style in its professional aspect is a question of good habits in the way steps are done. And so ballet has gradually settled on several habits it prefers. It has decided on the turned-out thighs, on the pulled-up waist that joins them to the erect spine, on the low-held shoulder line. It has decided on a few main movements of the head, of the arms, of the torso, of the several leg joints. And on fifty or so main steps. These main steps and the main movements that can modify them are the habitual exercises with which good habits of balance and carriage, with which habits of harmony and rhythm can be trained in apprentices to reach a large-scale theater effect. They form a common basis of action for professionals. And the history of them is that they have always been specifically dance steps or elements of dance steps, enlarged in scale by constant use in the theater.

In ancient Italian towns the narrow main street at dusk becomes a kind of theater. The community strolls affably and looks itself over. The girls and the young men, from fifteen to twenty-two, display their charm to one another with a lively sociability. The more grace they show, the better the community likes them. In Florence or in Naples, in the ancient city slums the young people are virtuoso performers, and they do a bit of promenading any time they are not busy. A foreigner in Rome who loses his way among the fifteenth- and sixteenth-century alleys and squares, hunting in those neighborhoods for the sibyls of Raphael or the birthplace of Metastasio, discovers how bright about their grace the local young Romans can be. They appreciate it in themselves and in each other equally. Their stroll is as responsive as if it were a physical conversation. Chunkily built though they are, they place their feet; they articulate the arms and legs; the boys stress the opening, and the girls the closing, of the limbs. Their necks and waists have an insinuating harmony. They move from the waist turning to look, or stepping back in effacé to let a girl pass, or advancing a sheltering arm (like in croisé). They present their person and they put an arm around each other's waist or shoulder with a graceful intimacy. Their liveliness makes these courteous formalities — which recall ballet — a mutual game of skill. The foreign ballet fan as he goes home through the purple Roman dusk, charmed by the physical caress of it, confuses the shapes of Raphael with those of the performance. But he realizes that it means that ballet was originally an Italian dance, and he becomes aware of the lively sociability of its spirit and of its forms.

The general question I have been considering is harmony in classic dancing. But I hope the reference to Italy has not been misleading. Classic dancing doesn't look Italian when Americans do it, or when English dancers do it, or Russian, or French, or Danish dancers; it doesn't, and can't, and needn't. But it has harmony when any of them do it. It has a visual harmony of shapes due to the specific action of the body that we were considering earlier. Let us go back to the single step, and make sure where we are, close enough to the Atlantic seaboard.

As one lies with closed eyes in bed or on a beach far from town trying to recall what a single step looks like, one sees several steps and dancers combined in a phrase, and sees the shape of a phrase as if it were an extended step, many-legged and many-armed, with a particular departure, trajectory, and arrival. And as phrases succeed one another, one sees them take direction onstage, and one sees the visual momentum their paths can have with relation to a center of action, or to several centers, coming downstage, retiring back, escaping to the sides, appearing from the wings. The momentum of phrases accentuates the angle at which a figure is presented, or at which it acts, the directions it takes or only aspires to take. The momentum disengages a leading quality of motion, hopping, fluttering, soaring, stopping dead. It carries along a single figure, or several mutually, or a group. It draws the figures deeper into dramatic situations, serious or comic ones.

But the action of a step determines the ramifications, the rise and fall of the continuous momentum. You begin to see the active impetus of the dancers creating the impetus moment by moment. They step out of one shape and into another, they change direction or speed, they erect and dissolve a configuration, and their secure and steady impetus keeps coming. The situations that dissolve as one watches are created and swept along by the ease and the fun and the positive lightness of it. They dance and, as they do, create in their wake an architectural momentum of imaginary weights and transported presences. Their activity does not leave behind any material object, only an imaginary one.

The stage by its stationary center and its fixed proportions accumulates the imaginative reality. Stage area and stage height appear to be permanent actualities. Within them the brief shape that a dancer's body makes can look small and lost, or it can spread securely and for an instant appear on their scale. One can respond to the visual significance — the visual spaciousness — of such a moment of dance motion without being able to explain it reasonably in other terms.

The shape the dancer makes at such a moment has no specific representational aspect. You have seen the same shape before with different feelings. And yet often the whole house responds to such a moment of classic climax. It seems not to insist on being understood rationally. It presents no problem, it presents a climax of dancing. One can leave the ambiguity of it at that and enjoy at once both the climactic beauty of it and the nonsense.

Or else as one responds in the moment to the effortless sense of completion and of freedom that its spaciousness gives one, one may feel that the expression of the motion one is watching has been seen throughout the piece without being fulfilled until now. It is the expression the piece is about. One feels the cumulative drama it rises on. Then its visual spaciousness offers to one's imagination a large or a tragic image to recognize. It is not frightening; the lucidity of the moment is as sweet as happiness. Like a word you have often heard, that spoken without pressure at a certain moment is a final one, as large as your life, so the classic shape is an effortless motion that replies. To the symbolist poet Mallarmé, it appeared as an emblematic reply — as of blossom or dagger or cup — a climactic perception of mutual identity. As in a lucidity of perception there is in the motion no sense of intention or pressure. The significance of it appears in the present moment, as the climactic significance of a savage ritual appeared at the moment it occurred in our racial past.

As you lie on the hot deserted beach far from town and with closed eyes recall the visual moment of climax, and scarcely hear the hoarse breathing of the small surf, a memory of the music it rose on returns, and you remember the prolonged melodious momentum of the score as if the musical phrase the step rose on had arrived from so far, so deep in the piece it appears to have been.

The power of projection that music has strikes me as mysterious but it is a fact of nature. I have heard people who considered themselves unmusical modestly make acute remarks on the music of a ballet; and I once sat next to a deaf mute who followed the performance with delight and enrolled in a ballet school afterward. However one is conscious of it, without music classic dancing is no more real than swimming is real without water around it. The more ballet turns to pantomime, the less intimate its relation to the music becomes; but the more it turns to dancing, the more it enjoys the music's presence, bar by bar. Even when the steps stand aside and let the music alone, they are intimately aware of it.

We spoke of the beat at the beginning and here we are back to it. Take a specific ballet step. An assemblé looks different if it lands on one of the measure or if it lands on four; an entrechat looks different if the push from the floor comes on the downbeat, or if on the downbeat the legs beat in the air. A promenade en arabesque done at the same speed looks different if it is done in three-four time or in four-four. The stress of the measure supports a different phase of the step; it gives the motion a different lift and visual accent and expression. And as the stress of the beat can give a different look to the step, so can the stresses of the other kinds of musical emphasis — the stresses of dynamics, of melody, of harmony, of timbre, of pathos.

All these stresses offer their various support to the steps. They are like a floor with various degrees of resilience to dance on. The steps step in some places and not in others. They make a choice of stresses.

But as you hear the piece the stresses merge into a musical momentum that varies and into a musical expression that changes; and they build into large coherent sections and finally into a completed structure of musical sound with a coherent identity. We are used to sensing the coherence of music sometimes in one way, sometimes in another. And while we sense a coherence it has, we can believe in the coherence of long sequences of dancing we are watching. We see their coherence from the point of reference of the musical meaning. A long dance gathers power by coherence.

But the relation of eye and ear is a mutual one. The visual action also makes particular stresses in the music more perceptible, and continuities more clearly coherent. Watching the sweep of the dance momentum, you feel more keenly the musical one, and the visual drama can give you an insight into the force of character of the score. A dance happily married to its score likes to make jokes without raising its small voice, and the thundering score likes it too.

But the steps of classic dancing have always enjoyed being timed to the notes of music, and their rhythm has always responded to musical rhythm. Inside the labyrinth of complex musical structures, you see ballet following the clue of the rhythm, you see it hearing the other musical forces as they affect the current of the rhythm, as they leave or don't leave the rhythm a danceable one. You see the dance listening and choosing its own rhythmic response. A dance ballet gets its power of projection by the choice of its response to the larger structures of musical rhythm. So its power of character reveals itself in a more complexly happy marriage. Timed as classic dancing is to strict measures of time, confined to a limited range of motion, lighter in the stress it communicates than everyday motion, the power of character, the power of insight it develops and sustains in reference to its chosen score, is a power of its own creation. Mutually to the music, you watch the dance take shape and make sense and show the dazzling grace of an imaginative freedom. It is worth watching for.

What we have been considering is what is usually called the form of classic dancing. I am not suggesting that a ballet has no content, and I am not suggesting either that its form is its content. I have heard these statements but they make no sense to me. I think the meaning of the two words is approximately clear, and that they describe different ways of approaching an event, or of discussing it. I have been avoiding the distinction because I have been discussing what classic dancing looks like regardless of the subject matter of the ballet, what one is aware of at the moment one sees the dancer move, what one is aware of before one makes the distinction between content and form. It is a fairly confused awareness, but it is real enough. One doesn't, as far as I can see, make any sharp distinction between content and form in the case of pleasant events while one is enjoying them, or of people one is in love with; one instinctively doesn't.

The forms of classic dancing are one may say no less instinctive for being formal. The way a cat comes up to you at night in a deserted city street to be patted, and when you crouch to pat her, the way she will enjoy a stroke or two and then pass out of reach, stop there facing away into the night, and return for another stroke or two, and then pass behind you and return on your other side — all this has a form that you meet again onstage when the ballerina is doing a Petipa adagio. And while cats one meets on different nights all like to follow the same adagio form, one cat will vary it by hunching her back or rolling seductively just out of reach, another, another night, by standing high on her toes as you pat her, and making little sous-sous on her front paws; a third by grand Petersburg-style tail wavings; a fourth, if you are down close enough, by rising on her hind paws, resting her front ones weightlessly on you, raising her wide ballerina eyes to yours, and then — delicate as a single finger pirouette — giving the tip of your nose a tender nip. When a cat has had enough adagio, she sits down apart; or else, changing to mime, she scampers artificially away, pretending to be scared by the passing of a solitary nocturnal truck. Dogs — dogs that you take on daytime country walks are virtuosos of allegro. They invent heroic dashes, sharp zigzags running low ending in grand jetés that slow down; or else in the midst of a demi-manège at cannonball speed they stop dead. They mean you to get the joke, and they make it deadpan like troupers. Then they come up to you at an untheatrical dog-trot, smiling, breathing hard, with shining eyes; they enjoy your applause, but they distinguish between the performance when they were pretending and the bow they take after it is finished when they are honest dogs again.

One watches ballet just as one would the animals, but since there is more to be seen, there is more to watch. More to be seen and also more to recognize: not only the formal shapes but also the pantomime shapes with their specific allusions. And everybody likes to see pantomime in the course of a ballet evening. It gives the feeling of being back in a more familiar rational world, back safe from the flight through the intuitive rhythmic world of irrational symbols and of the charming animals.

We have been considering ballet from its aspect as dancing. Its aspect as pantomime is equally interesting; so is its aspect as an art of the choreographer and as an art of the dancer. They are all part of ballet just as much as what I have been discussing — and I love them just as much, and they don't lose any of their beauty merely by being unmentioned.

Dancers, Buildings and People in the Streets, 1965

Dance Magazine Award Acceptance Speech

I remember that Doris Hering told me that you should thank your teachers on this occasion, that it was customary, and I'm only too glad to. But there are so many of them that I can't even name them all. Of course there's one man who has taught me to see and hear more than anyone else, and you can guess who I mean — Mr. Balanchine. And he goes right on teaching me. I am very much interested in not only all the variety in which he sets the music and the different kinds of events that happen to the musical events, but also the fact that all his great ballets are very different from each other in a way that has to do with subject matter — but that subject matter is never directly expressed. You go home and can feel the subject matter, and perhaps you can think it through, but he hasn't actually told you. And that keeps you interested because the subject matter is so much larger than if someone had just said "This is what happens." It's so much more like the real subject in life and the things that you feel which are always much too big to be put into words and to be classified because they go off in all directions.

April 1966

BIBLIOGRAPHY OF DENBY'S WRITINGS

Die Neue Galathea. Mainz, Germany: B. Schott's Sons, 1929.

Ballet. New York: J. J. Augustin, 1945.

In Public, in Private. Prairie City, Ill.: Press of James A. Decker, 1948. [two editions]

Looking at the Dance. New York: Pellegrini and Cudahy, 1949. [reprints: New York: Horizon, 1968; New York: Curtis Books, 1973; New York: Popular Library, 1978.]

Mediterranean Cities. New York: Wittenborn, 1956.

The Second Hurricane. New York: Boosey and Hawkes, 1957.

"C" Magazine 1, no. 4 (September 1963). Special Denby Issue.

Dancers, Buildings, and People in the Streets. New York: Horizon, 1965. [reprints: New York: Curtis Books, 1973; New York; Popular Library, 1979.]

Mrs. W's Last Sandwich: A Romance. New York: Horizon, 1972. [reprinted as *Scream in a Cave.* New York: Curtis Books, 1973.]

Miltie Is a Hackie. Calais, Ver.: Z Press, 1973.

Snoring in New York. New York: Angel Hair/Adventures in Poetry, 1974.

Two Conversations with Edwin Denby. New York: Byrd Hoffman Foundation, 1974.

Collected Poems. New York: Full Court Press, 1975.

Aerial. New York: Eyelight Press, 1981.

Mag City 14 (1983). Special Denby Issue. *New York.*

The Complete Poems. New York: Random House, 1986.

Dance Writings. New York: Knopf, 1986.

Edwin's Tao: Being a Rough Translation of Selections from Lao Tze's Tao Teh Ching. New York: Crumbling Empire Press, 1993.

INDEX